INTELLECTUAL PROPERTY
AND PUBLIC HEALTH
IN THE DEVELOPING WORLD

Intellectual Property and Public Health in the Developing World

Monirul Azam

OpenBook Publishers

https://www.openbookpublishers.com

This study is based on the author's doctoral thesis, 'The Impact of TRIPS on the Pharmaceutical Regulation and Pricing of Drugs in Bangladesh: A Case Study on the Globalising Standard of Patent Protection in WTO Law', which has been approved for the award of PhD Degree by the Faculty of Law, University of Bern, examined by Professor Thomas Cottier (University of Bern) and Professor Frederick Abbott (Florida State University College of Law) on 22/5/2014.

Digital material and resources associated with this volume can be found at http://www.openbookpublishers.com/9781783742288#resources

Every effort has been made to identify and contact copyright holders and any omission or error will be corrected if notification is made to the publisher.

ISBN Paperback: 978-1-78374-228-8
ISBN Hardback: 978-1-78374-229-5
ISBN Digital (PDF): 978-1-78374-230-1
ISBN Digital ebook (epub version): 978-1-78374-231-8
ISBN Digital ebook (mobi version): 978-1-78374-232-5
DOI: 10.11647/OBP.0093

Cover image: Pranjal Mahna (2010), CC BY-NC-ND 2.0. https://www.flickr.com/photos/charlie_brown_in/4813687658

All paper used by Open Book Publishers is SFI (Sustainable Forestry Initiative), PEFC (Programme for the Endorsement of Forest Certification Schemes) and Forest Stewardship Council(r)(FSC(r) certified.

Printed in the United Kingdom, United States, and Australia
by Lightning Source for Open Book Publishers (Cambridge, UK).

Contents

This study is dedicated to my parents,
Ishaque and Sanowara, whose inspiration
and sacrifice made me what I am today.

Preface

This study could not have been completed without the profound encouragement, persistent support and forbearance of my loving family members. I would like to express my deep gratitude to Prof. Thomas Cottier, who has been an excellent source of support, inspiration and advice throughout this difficult writing process. I think if I had listened to him properly, this study would have been completed earlier. I am also grateful to Rosemarie, Secretary of the World Trade Institute (WTI) in Bern for her kind cooperation throughout the process of my work at the WTI. My sincere thanks to colleagues and friends at the WTI, who provided useful comments during annual workshops in February 2010 and March 2012 and also at the brown bag presentation on 27 July 2011.

I am very grateful to Prof. Shah Alam, former dean in the Faculty of Law (presently chairman-in-charge, Law Commission of Bangladesh), for encouragement and advice as a student and colleague which shaped a global vision of legal education in my mind; and also to Professor Morshed Mahmud Khan who, as a supervisor of my LLM thesis at the Department of Law, University of Chittagong, initially encouraged me to conduct my research on intellectual property law. I gratefully acknowledge the inspiration and motivation I received from Prof. Mpasi Sinjella, former director of the WIPO Academy, and Prof. Marco Ricolfi, director of the WIPO-Turin IP Programme, to do further higher study and research in the field of intellectual property. I am also grateful to officials at the Department of Patents, Designs and Trademarks, and at the Directorate of Drug Administration in Bangladesh for their cooperation during my field studies. I am also thankful to the pharmaceutical industries in Bangladesh and all other participants for their cooperation during the survey and interviews in Bangladesh. However, as per requests from the participants of surveys and interviews, this study maintains the anonymity and confidentiality of the participants throughout.

I would like to acknowledge the kind cooperation of Sheikh Rafiqul Islam Raju (former consultant of English for Law, Bar Council of Bangladesh) and his team in Dhaka throughout the process of field research in Bangladesh. I am also grateful to my colleagues and former teachers at the Department of Law, University of Chittagong – particularly to the late Prof. Khabir Uddin Ahmed, Prof. Zakir Hossain, Prof. Mohiuddin Khaled, Prof. Abdullah-al-Faruque and Dr. Jafar Ullah Talukder – for their kind support and encouragement.

The revision of this study as a book was to some extent also influenced and complemented by my previous and ongoing research work in the field of intellectual property at the University of Chittagong; the University of Turin, Italy; the WIPO Academy, Geneva; Central Queensland University, Australia; Stockholm University, Sweden; the Tokyo Institute of Technology and the United Nations University, Japan. This study has also addressed comments of two anonymous reviewers suggested by Open Book Publishers. I also received valuable comments and inputs during my visits to and presentations at several conferences and workshops at the WIPO and WTO headquarters in Geneva, and also at the University of Oxford and Yale Law School. I hereby express deep gratitude to each of these institutions for their generous fellowship and library support. I am grateful to Prof. Marianne Levin (Department of Law, Stockholm University) for being so kind and supportive, and for her critical comments on some chapters of this book.

I am also grateful to the *Chicago-Kent Intellectual Property Journal* and the *Akron Intellectual Property Journal* for kind permission to re-publish Chapter Three and Chapter Four of this book, which were published earlier as follows:

M. Monirul Azam, 'The Experiences of TRIPS-compliant Patent Law Reforms in Brazil, India, and South Africa and Lessons from Bangladesh', *Akron Intellectual Property Journal* 7.2 (2014): 61–100;

M. Monirul Azam, 'Globalizing Standard of Patent Protection in WTO Law and Policy Options for the LDCs: The Context of Bangladesh', *Chicago-Kent Journal of Intellectual Property* 13.2 (2014): 402–88.

This book contains some repetitions across different chapters. I intentionally maintained these repetitions so that chapters could be read both as part of a book and alone, online or as study material. As a guest speaker at the Swedish Patent Office over the last five years, taking part in training programs for the Least Developed Countries (LDCs) on industrial property in the global economy, I realized that government officials, academics and industry experts in the LDCs need to have an appropriate understanding of legal flexibilities and how to address them in their national legislation. For this reason, I revised some chapters to be used as ready reference texts, free from ambiguous jargon and complex structures and case laws.

Finally, I am indebted to my loving family members for putting up with me during these difficult years of writing and travelling, particularly my wife, Tanya, my son, Anas, and my daughter, Ilyana. I would like to thank my parents, brothers, sister and in-laws for their support and inspiration. Special thanks to Dr. Alessandra Tosi from Open Book Publishers for her continuous support and cooperation to publish this as a book. A research grant from the Japan Society for the Promotion of Science suppported the revision of this book. I would also like to thank Professors Hideto Nakajima and Norichika Kanie for their support during my time at the Tokyo Institute of Technology and the United Nations University, respectively.

The cut-off research date for this book was 31 December 2015. Therefore, further updates after December 2015 are not reflected here.

Tokyo, Japan
Tokyo Institute of Technology/United Nations University
3 February 2016

List of Tables

List of Figures

Abbreviations

ACTA	Anti-counterfeiting Trade Agreement
AMTC	Affordable Medicines and Treatment Campaign
ANVISA	National Health Surveillance Agency (Brazil)
API	Active Pharmaceutical Ingredient
ARV	Anti-retroviral
BAPI	Bangladesh Association of Pharmaceutical Industries
BIISS	Bangladesh Institute of International and Strategic Studies
BIT	Bilateral Investment Treaties
CEO	Chief Executive Officer
CEWG	Consultative Expert Working Group
CIPIH	Commission on Intellectual Property Rights, Innovation and Public Health
CMH	Commission on Macroeconomics and Health
DCC	Drug Control Committee
DCO	*Drugs (Control) Ordinance, 1982*
DDA	Directorate of Drug Administration
DGDA	Directorate General of Drug Administration
DPDT	Department of Patents, Designs and Trademarks
DRA	Drug Regulatory Authority
DRR	*Drugs Registration Regulations*
EU	European Union
EVI	Economic Vulnerability Index
FDA	Food and Drug Administration
FDI	Foreign Direct Investment
FTA	Free Trade Agreement

GATT	General Agreement on Tariffs and Trades
GDP	Gross Domestic Product
GMP	Good Manufacturing Practice
GNI	Gross National Income
GSK	GlaxoSmithKline
HAI	Human Assets Index
HDI	Human Development Index
HFA	Hydro–Fluoro–Alkaline
INPI	National Institute for Industrial Property
IP	Intellectual Property
IPC	Intellectual Property Rights Committee
IPR	Intellectual Property Rights
KEI	Knowledge Ecology International
LDC	Least Developed Countries
MCC	Medicines Control Council
MNC	Multinational Corporation
MNPC	Multinational Pharmaceutical Company
MPP	Medicines Patent Pool
MRDT	Medical Research and Development Treaty
MRP	Maximum Retail Price
MRSCA	*Medicines and Related Substances Control Act, 1997* (South Africa)
NCE	New Chemical Entity
NDP	*National Drug Policy, 1982* (Bangladesh)
NGO	Non-governmental Organisation
NHS	National Health Strategy
NME	New Molecular Entity
NRA	National Regulatory Authority
OSDD	*Open Source Drug Discovery* Project
PCT	*Patent Cooperation Treaty*
PDA	*Patents and Designs Act, 1911* (Bangladesh)
PMPRB	Patented Medicine Prices Review Board
R&D	Research and Development
REPS	Regulatory Enforcement Pyramid of Sanctions

RRT   Responsive Regulations Theory

SDGs   Sustainable Development Goals

SFDA   State Food and Drug Administration

SIAPS Systems for Improved Access to Pharmaceuticals and Services

SIPO   State Intellectual Property Office

SME   Small and Medium-sized Enterprise

TAC   Treatment Access Campaign

TB   Tuberculosis

TIFA   Trade and Investment Framework Agreement

TPP   Trans-Pacific Partnership

TRIPS Trade-related Aspects of Intellectual Property

UN   United Nations

UNAIDS Joint United Nations Programme on HIV/AIDS

UNCTAD United Nations Conference on Trade and Development

UNICEF United Nations Children's Fund

US   United States of America

VAT   Value-added Tax

WHA   World Health Assembly

WHO   World Health Organization

WIPO   World Intellectual Property Organization

WTO   World Trade Organization

Abstract

This study explored how to design national patent laws and undertake the required institutional and infrastructural reforms that are optimal in terms of enabling developing countries and Least Developed Countries to promote innovation in their domestic pharmaceutical sectors and ensure access to medicines. Individual countries were free to determine their own patent laws prior to the establishment of the World Trade Organization. However, the Agreement on Trade-related Aspects of Intellectual Property Rights (the TRIPS Agreement), which is binding on all WTO members, aims at establishing strong minimum standards for intellectual property rights. Such minimum standards include the implementation of patent protection for pharmaceuticals. Bangladesh is a member of the WTO and, as an LDC, has been granted transitional periods until 1 July 2021 to protect IPRs under the TRIPS Agreement. Further, being an LDC, Bangladesh can also exploit the waiver for pharmaceutical patents until 1 January 2033. This study analyses experiences of implementing TRIPS-compliant patent laws in Brazil, China, India and South Africa, and explores potential policy options for the LDCs with a case study on the pharmaceutical sector in Bangladesh.

Bangladesh has attained a degree of self-sufficiency with respect to the manufacture of pharmaceuticals: local industry now caters for 97% of local needs via the production of generic medicines that are free from the patent regime. However, this policy has both disadvantages and advantages. One advantage is the availability of lower-priced pharmaceuticals, and one disadvantage is that Bangladesh missed out on the opportunity to develop an innovative research and development (R&D)-based pharmaceutical industry. Further, the lack of a pharmaceutical patent regime over the years has created a vacuum in terms of the existence of relevant regulatory bodies (Patent Offices and the Directorate General of Drug Administration) and has also led to the local pharmaceutical industry being unprepared for the post-TRIPS situation. Brazil, China, India and South Africa were in a similar position prior to becoming TRIPS compliant, so those countries' experiences are an important basis for the analysis of the transition to TRIPS compliance in pre-compliant countries. This study combines doctrinal analysis, comparative reviews and a case study, using a survey and interviews to answer specific research questions.

The study examines three underlying research questions:

1) What are the policy options used by Brazil, China, India and South Africa for the implementation of the TRIPS Agreement and preservation of the local pharmaceutical sector?

2) What are the (potential) policies for the LDCs (such as Bangladesh) to promote their local pharmaceutical industry and access to medicines?

3) What are the infrastructural and institutional issues that need to be addressed by the LDCs to deal with a post-TRIPS patent regime?

To answer research question 1, the study used doctrinal analysis and comparative reviews, whereas to answer research question 2 it conducted a case study in selected LDCs (Bangladesh) using a survey instrument and interviews to examine the views of identified stakeholders such as the pharmaceutical industry, regulatory bodies in Bangladesh, public health groups and academics. Then, considering the findings in relation to research questions 1 and 2, and the perceptions of different stakeholders, this study further identified infrastructural and institutional issues that need to be addressed by the LDCs (such as Bangladesh) to deal with a post-TRIPS patent regime.

This research makes a contribution to the body of knowledge on TRIPS and intellectual property in four ways, as this study:

- analyses the contemporary literature examining TRIPS and its effect on access to medicines in developing countries and the LDCs, particularly India, Brazil, China, South Africa and Bangladesh;

- presents a case study using a survey and interviews to evaluate the status of the pharmaceutical industry and perceptions of other stakeholders regarding TRIPS and its implementation in Bangladesh;

- produces recommendations that may facilitate the utilisation of TRIPS flexibilities in the LDCs, such as Bangladesh, and

- identifies the infrastructural and institutional issues that need to be addressed by Bangladesh in a post-TRIPS patent regime, efforts which may also be replicated by other developing countries and the LDCs.

1. Setting the Scene

1.1 Background

Prior to the creation of the World Trade Organization in 1995, individual countries were free to determine their own patent laws. This position has now changed. All members of the WTO are required to adopt patent laws that comply with the Agreement on Trade-related Aspects of Intellectual Property Rights,[1] including the implementation of patent protection for pharmaceuticals. The developed members of the WTO negotiated mandatory protection for pharmaceutical products and processes in the TRIPS Agreement on the basis that such mandatory protection will provide the necessary incentives for continued pharmaceutical innovation. In contrast, the developing countries and the Least Developed Countries argued that enacting patent laws that comply with TRIPS may restrict production and supply of low-cost generic medicines by their local pharmaceutical industries or by the pharmaceutical industries in other developing countries, and hence could increase the price of pharmaceuticals to the point that pharmaceuticals become inaccessible to their populations.

The LDCs need to reorganise and restructure national IP legislation and related institutional and infrastructural set-ups for the implementation of the TRIPS Agreement. Given the extent of

---

1   Agreement on Trade-related Aspects of Intellectual Property Rights, 15 April 1994, Marrakesh Agreement Establishing the World Trade Organization, Annex 1C, U.N.T.S. 299, 33 I.L.M. 1197, art. 65 (1994) [hereinafter TRIPS Agreement], http://www.wto.org/english/docs_e/legal_e/27-trips.pdf

     http://dx.doi.org/10.11647/OBP.0093.01

the reorganisation and the restructuring required, LDCs[2] (of which Bangladesh is one) were granted several transition periods.[3] The initial transition period ended on 31 December 2005. Later, by a decision of the Council for TRIPS on 29 November 2005, LDC members as a group were granted an extension of the transitional period for 7.5 years to apply the provisions of the TRIPS Agreement "until 1 July 2013, or until such a date on which they cease to be an LDC member, whichever date is earlier". The Council for TRIPS took the decision following the request by the LDCs as a group, pursuant to Article 66.1 of the TRIPS Agreement, for a 15-year extension of the transition period in order for those LDCs to be able to apply the provisions of the agreement. The group had cited socioeconomic, administrative and financial constraints, as well as the need to create a viable technological base, as reasons duly motivating the request. The decision was negotiated between the LDCs and some key developed countries during informal consultations and was adopted by the formal Council for TRIPS meeting on 29 November 2005. However, during the consultations, several developed country members, particularly the United States of America (the US), insisted that each LDC member should request an extension on an individual basis and that extensions would be granted on a case-by-case basis.

---

2   There are no World Trade Organisation definitions of 'developed' or 'developing' countries. *Least-developed Countries*, 'Understanding the WTO: The Organization', World Trade Organization, http://www.wto.org/english/thewto_e/whatis_e/tif_e/ org7_e.htm. "The WTO recognizes as [LDCs] those countries which have been designated as such by the United Nations. There are currently 48 [LDCs] on the UN list, 34 of which to date have become WTO members" (ibid.). According to the United Nations, LDCs are countries that exhibit the lowest indicators of socioeconomic development, with the lowest human development index (HDI) ratings of all the countries in the world. A country is classified as an LDC if it meets three criteria: low income (three-year average GNI per capita of less than $992, which must exceed $1,190 to leave the list), human resources weakness (based on indicators of nutrition, health, *education* and adult *literacy*) and economic vulnerability (based on instability of agricultural production, instability of exports of goods and services, economic importance of non-traditional activities, merchandise export concentration, handicap of economic smallness and the percentage of population displaced by natural disasters). However, countries "graduate" from the LDC classification when indicators exceed these criteria (ibid.). See for details, *Criteria for Identification and Graduation of LDCs*, UN-OHRLLS, http://unohrlls.org/about-ldcs/ criteria-for-ldcs

3   See for details, WTO, 'Responding to Least Developed Countries' Special Needs in Intellectual Property', http://www.wto.org/english/tratop_e/trips_e/ldc_e.htm

Nevertheless, given the recognition of the extent of the restructuring required and the vulnerability of the LDCs, the transition period did not prove to be long enough to introduce protection for pharmaceutical patents and to take adequate measures to ensure access to medicines. Therefore, the Doha Declaration on the TRIPS Agreement and Public Health (known as the Doha Declaration) was adopted by the WTO Ministerial Conference of 2001 in Doha on 14 November 2001, extending the transitional period for LDCs to introduce pharmaceutical patent protection until 1 January 2016.[4]

On the other hand, WTO members agreed on 11 June 2013 to further extend the deadline for LDCs until 1 July 2021 to protect IP under the TRIPS Agreement.[5] It was noted that the decision could not prejudice the extension of pharmaceutical patents granted under the Doha declaration and that LDCs could seek further extensions to this period. Accordingly, on behalf of the LDC group, Bangladesh submitted a document requesting extension of the waiver for the LDCs with respect to pharmaceutical patents as long as the WTO Member remains a Least Developed Country pursuant to Article 66.1 of the TRIPS Agreement.[6] The LDC group stated that LDCs are "struggling to provide their population with prevention, treatment and care. Patent protection contributes to high costs, placing many critical treatments outside the reach of LDCs".[7] Justifying the request for extension, the LDCs further pled "special needs and requirements of least developed country Members, their economic, financial and administrative constraints and their need for flexibility to create a viable technological base".[8]

The Council for TRIPS approved the waiver for pharmaceutical patents until 1 January 2033 or until such a date on which the least developed countries cease to be LDC Members, whichever date comes first.[9] Granting the extension is seen as being in line with both the

---

4   See WTO, 'Decision of the Council for TRIPS on the Extension of the Transition Period under Article 66.1 of the TRIPS Agreement for Least-developed Country Members for Certain Obligations with Respect to Pharmaceutical Products', 27 June 2002 (Document IP/C/25).

5   WTO, 'Decision of the Council for TRIPS of 11 June 2013' (Document IP/C/64).

6   WTO, 'Communication from Bangladesh on behalf of the LDC Group', 23 February 2015 (Document IP/C/W/605).

7   Ibid.

8   Ibid.

9   WTO, 'Decision of the Council for TRIPS of 6 November 2015' (Document IP/C/73).

Doha Declaration and the Sustainable Development Goals. The SDGs were adopted by the United Nations General Assembly in September 2015, approving seventeen goals to be pursued by all countries to end poverty and to fight inequality and injustice. They represent an important milestone in envisioning what the world could look like in 2030, if global development is put on an inclusive and sustainable path. Among the seventeen goals, the third set targets to ensure healthy lives and promote wellbeing for all ages and also to achieve universal health coverage, including access to safe, effective, quality and affordable essential medicines and vaccines for all.[10] It (SDG 3) further affirmed the right of developing countries to utilise TRIPS Agreement flexibilities to ensure access to medicines for all.[11] With the deadlines of 2033 (the extension) and 2030 (the SDGs) in mind, it is important for the LDCS to take concrete and coherent steps to improve intellectual property and health-related infrastructure to ensure healthy lives and access to medicines for their citizens.

Therefore, it is vital for the LDCs to utilise the transitional period properly to initiate infrastructural and institutional capacity building, so that after the expiration of the transitional period, they will be able to balance pharmaceutical innovation and access to medicines.

Among the 48 countries classified as LDCs (of which 34 are WTO members),[12] Bangladesh is one of the few with an adequate pharmaceutical manufacturing capability, and it is nearly self-sufficient in pharmaceuticals.[13] Bangladesh's pharmaceutical industry now accounts for 97% of the country's pharmaceutical needs (the remaining 3% includes insulin, vaccines and high-end, anti-cancer drugs, the production of which are very capital intensive and hence not economically feasible for Bangladesh), which amounts to around

---

10 M. Monirul Azam and Mahesti Okitasari, 'Environmental Governance and National Preparedness towards 2030 Agenda for Sustainable Development: A Tale of Two Countries', *Global Environmental Research Japan* 19.2 (2015): 217.

11 UN, *Report of the Open Working Group of the General Assembly on Sustainable Development Goals*, Resolution 68/970, 2014.

12 For details of the 34 LDCs that are WTO members, see WTO, 'WTO and the Least Developed Countries', http://www.wto.org/english/thewto_e/whatis_e/tif_e/org 7_e.htm

13 Mohammad Abu Yusuf and Qamrul Alam, 'WTO TRIPS Agreement: Current State of Pharmaceutical Industry and Policy Options for Bangladesh', *International Business Research* 1.1 (2008): 135–45.

US$ 1.7 billion.[14] Pharmaceuticals from Bangladesh are exported to 107 countries in Asia, Africa and Europe.[15]

Being an LDC, Bangladesh can still produce generic versions of patented pharmaceuticals, so the country can serve the pharmaceutical needs of poorer countries with no or low manufacturing capacity by supplying cheap generic versions of patented drugs.[16] Bangladesh is in a unique situation, as it is the one of the few LDCs with sufficient capacity to produce and export generic medicines where this is legally possible, at least until January 2033. Considering this unique feature of the Bangladeshi pharmaceutical industry, one industry expert in Bangladesh stated that "Medicine price in Bangladesh is among the lowest in the world and that has been possible because the country has much competitive generic drug skills, and it doesn't have to pay royalty to innovators for producing patented medicines. For example, cholesterol lowering drug Crestor 10mg (rosuvastatin) tablet costs around $7.25 in the US versus a comparable Bangladeshi generic price of $0.25 while diabetes drug Januvia 50mg (sitagliptin) is priced at $11.25 against the local generic price of $0.25. Bangladesh has [also] introduced the generic version of revolutionary hepatitis C drugs Sovaldi (sofosbuvir) and Harvoni (sofosbuvir+ledipasvir) which are available locally at $6.5 and $13 per tablet compared to the originator brands at $1,000 and $1,125 respectively".[17]

Therefore, it has become an important research area to investigate whether Bangladesh's pharmaceutical sector can gradually evolve to provide low-cost substitutes for important patented drugs to other developing countries and LDCs, and whether it can contribute to global access to cheap medicines. Given its position, it is important to explore how Bangladesh can exploit the opportunities available to it, while also considering how Bangladesh may initiate capacity-building processes

14 Mohammad Monirul Azam and Kristy Richardson, 'Trips Compliant Patent Law and the Pharmaceutical Industry in Bangladesh: Challenges and Opportunities', *LAWASIA Journal* (2010b): 141–54.

15 See for details, 'Reports and Statistics from Directorate of Drug Administration in Bangladesh', http://www.dgda.gov.bd/index.php

16 Anne St Martin, 'The Impact of Trade Related Aspects of Intellectual Property Rights (TRIPS) on Access to Essential Medicines in the Developing World' (a research report submitted to Worcester Polytechnic Institute, 1 May 2006), p.2.

17 Shawkat Haider, 'Access to Medicines for All', *Dhaka Tribune*, 20 November 2015, http://www.dhakatribune.com/op-ed/2015/nov/20/access-medicine-all

to implement a TRIPS-compliant patent law that balances the interests of pharmaceutical producers with the need to ensure access to drugs for local populations (in anticipation of the introduction of pharmaceutical patents not only for process, but also for product and future TRIPS-compliant patent law in Bangladesh). Apart from pro-development TRIPS-compliant national patent law, it is necessary to investigate how Bangladesh can achieve institutional and infrastructural capacity building to progress from being simply a generic producer to having an innovative pharmaceutical industry, and thus graduating from the LDCs.

This study makes a contribution to knowledge because it focuses on the pharmaceutical industry in Bangladesh and also analyses policy options required for an LDC such as Bangladesh to become TRIPS compliant on the basis of experiences of developing countries such as India, China, Brazil and South Africa, who all played vital roles as producers and exporters of generic copies of brand-name patented products.

This study uses a research method that involves legal doctrinal analysis and a comparative review to analyse the patent laws of India, Brazil, China, South Africa and Bangladesh. The aim is to understand the nature, scope, effectiveness and weaknesses, if any, of ensuring access to medicines and preserving the local pharmaceutical industry while making progress towards TRIPS compliance.

This study also investigates stakeholders in the pharmaceutical industry in Bangladesh by way of a case study using a survey instrument, in addition to interviews with relevant stakeholders to gain an understanding of their strategies for TRIPS compliance. As participants in the research presented in this book, the stakeholders represented different categories of companies within the pharmaceutical industry operating in Bangladesh: multinationals and national pharmaceutical producers (small, medium and large). The study also investigates the perceptions of other stakeholders such as public health groups, IP and pharmaceutical academics, researchers and the national regulatory bodies: the Patent Office and Directorate of Drug Administration (DDA).

This study makes a contribution to the literature in the field of global and comparative IP law as follows:

- First, it evaluates implications of the pharmaceutical patent regime, as an integral part of the globalising standard of patent protection in WTO law, for the relevant laws, regulatory bodies and pharmaceutical industry in Bangladesh.

- Second, it analyses both the contemporary literature examining TRIPS and its effect on access to medicines in developing countries and the LDCs and the policy options for public health-oriented patent law reforms in developing countries (particularly, India, Brazil, China, South Africa and Bangladesh).

- Third, it identifies future research directions to provide an ongoing consideration of the policy options needed to reach the right balance between pharmaceutical innovation, access to affordable pharmaceuticals and TRIPS compliance.

Although human rights perspectives are becoming increasingly important in reforms of IP policies and laws, and could be useful in exploring the balance between the rights of inventors and creators and the public interest, this study has not examined human rights-based approaches as potential policy options within the TRIPS Agreement.[18] Further, this study does not deal with issues relating to medicine arising out of traditional knowledge and how that may be affected by TRIPS. Finally, this study does not explore in detail effects of enforcement mechanisms under the TRIPS Agreement; rather, it focuses on the patent law reforms, in particular on the context of pharmaceutical patents.

1.2 The Advent of TRIPS and Pharmaceutical Patents

The establishment of the WTO has been an important exercise in a number of ways. First, it represents an entirely new chapter in the jurisprudence of post-World War II international organisations through the establishment of a multilateral trading system that provides a

---

18   For human rights perspectives on intellectual property (IP), see R.D. Anderson and H. Wager, 'Human Rights, Development and The WTO: The Cases of Intellectual Property and Competition Policy', *Journal of International Economic Law* 9.3 (2006): 707–47; L.R. Helfer, 'Towards a Human Rights Framework for Intellectual Property, *UC Davis Law Review* 40.3 (2007): 971–1020; D.B. Barbosa, M. Chon and A. M. von Hase, 'Slouching towards Development in International Intellectual Property', *Michigan State Law Review* 1 (2007): 114–23.

binding dispute settlement mechanism for its members.[19] Second, the WTO has also undertaken the onerous task of evolving a binding law of international trade among the member countries.[20] Third, the WTO has in many ways replaced the internal sovereignty of the member countries.[21] This is because every member is required to adjust its domestic laws to conform to the WTO agreements.[22] Indeed, as a founding member, Bangladesh's legal system has been subject to reorganisation to satisfy the requirements of the WTO.[23]

The TRIPS Agreement is one of the most controversial agreements of the Uruguay Round in terms of its objectives and consequences, which established global minimum standards of IPR protection. It represents a major departure from previous international IPR treaties and agreements, which aimed not to standardise IPR legislation between countries, but to guarantee non-discrimination under national IP

---

19 See Mohammad Monirul Azam and Morshed Mamud Khan, 'WTO TRIPS Agreement: Implications for the Developing Countries', *Journal of the Institute of Bangladesh Studies* 27 (2004): 23; see also, for background study, John H. Jackson, *The Jurisprudence of GATT and the WTO* (Cambridge University Press, 2000).

20 Member countries have agreed to be bound by the commitments under various WTO agreements. These include the principles of national treatment and the "Most Favoured Nation" clause to ensure non-discrimination between nationals and foreign nationals, as well as goods and services. Similarly, members have to introduce patent protection for pharmaceuticals under the WTO TRIPS Agreement.

21 This has been the most important argument for the opponents of the WTO, as decision making on important issues of national interest has been encompassed within the WTO framework. See *WTO and Implications for South Asia*, ed. by K.C. Reddy (Serials Publications, 2006), p.1.

22 Membership of the WTO is conditional on the full acceptance—without reservation—of almost all WTO agreements; see *General Agreement on Tariffs and Trade: Multilateral Trade Negotiations (The Uruguay Round): Final Act Embodying the Results of the Uruguay Round of Trade Negotiations*, 15 December 1993 (1994), 33 I.L.M. 1 [referred to as WTO agreements]. The WTO Agreement has four annexures, the first three of which are integral parts of the agreement. Annexure 1 deals with agreements on trade in goods, trade in services and trade-related aspects of IPRs. Annexure 2 deals with dispute resolution, with Annexure 3 providing for a process of multilateral surveillance of national trade policies. Only Annexure 4 deals with agreements that are not necessarily binding on member states. Article XVI(4) of the WTO Agreement provides that "each Member shall ensure the conformity of its laws, regulations and administrative procedures with its obligations as provided in the annexed Agreements". See Michael J. Trebilcock and Robert Howse, *The Regulation of International Trade*, 2nd edn (Routledge, 1999).

23 Mohammad Monirul Azam, 'Establishment of the WTO and Challenges for the Legal System of Bangladesh', *Macquarie Journal of Business Law* 3 (2006): 23.

systems.[24] The TRIPS Agreement is particularly distinctive with respect to earlier international IPR agreements in three important ways. First, TRIPS makes it mandatory for WTO members to provide existing types of IPR protection that include patents, copyright, trademarks, trade secrets, industrial designs, layout designs for integrated circuits, and geographical indications, which removed the flexibilities in previous IPR agreements regarding the granting of IPRs based on the stage of development of a particular country.[25] Second, it specifies the minimum standards for national IPR legislation, such as the extent of coverage, the terms of protection and the mechanisms for enforcement. Third, it brings national IPR legislation under the coverage of the WTO's dispute settlement procedures, which include the option of cross-retaliation in cases of non-compliance.[26]

The TRIPS Agreement was the brainchild of an industry coalition of developed nations including the US, the European Union (EU) and Japan. The main impetus for the agreement came from the pharmaceutical, software and entertainment industries, with the chief executive officer (CEO) of Pfizer playing a lead role as chair of the Intellectual Property Rights Committee (IPC).[27] The IPC was created during the Uruguay Round of negotiations with the goal of putting IPRs firmly on the agenda.[28] The pharmaceutical industry was primarily interested in eliminating what it felt was unfair discrimination against the patenting of medicines, but it was also motivated to try to gain control over uses of its clinical and regulatory data to delay registration of generic equivalents—in essence seeking another form of exclusive rights. One of the arguments advanced by the developed countries for

---

24 Earlier IPR conventions such as the Berne Convention of 1886 and the Paris Convention of 1883 under the auspices of the World Intellectual Property Organization (WIPO) provided some general principles regarding copyright, related rights and industrial property, but they lacked effective enforcement mechanisms, and there were no binding guidelines for making national intellectual property laws; see Mohammad Monirul Azam, *WTO, Intellectual Property and Bangladesh* (New Warsi Book Corporation, 2008).

25 The exceptions are utility models and plant breeders' rights, although TRIPS members are obliged to provide some kind of effective plant variety protection.

26 J.J. Simons, 'Cooperation and Coercion: The Protection of Intellectual Property in Developing Countries', *Bond Law Review* 11.1 (1999): 1.

27 Sylvia Ostry, *Intellectual Property Protection in the WTO: Misuses in the Millennium Round* (Fraser Institute Conference, Santiago, 19 April 1999), p.3.

28 John Madely, *Hungry for Trade* (Zed Books, 2000), pp.96–97.

including IPRs in the negotiations was that stronger IPRs would create an incentive for innovation and would stimulate the development of new technologies, such as patent protection for pharmaceuticals.[29] This incentive for innovation would consequently encourage greater domestic and foreign investment in research into new pharmaceuticals and tropical diseases.[30] The argument propounded was that foreign investment and technology transfer would, in turn, benefit developing countries and LDCs.[31] In contrast, developing countries argued that the

---

29   A text codifying the Intellectual Property Rights Commission's (IPC's) consensus position was released on 14 June 1988 in Washington, Brussels and Tokyo, with the title *Basic Framework of GATT Provisions on Intellectual Property: Statement of Views of the European, Japanese and United States Business Communities*. For a more complete history of the TRIPS negotiations and pharmaceutical patents, see P. Drahos, *Who Owns the Knowledge Economy: Political Organizing behind TRIPS* (2004), http://www. thecornerhouse.org.uk/resource/who-owns-knowledge-economy

30   Mansfield claimed that 65% of pharmaceuticals and 30% of chemical inventions would not have taken place without patent protection; see E. Mansfield, 'Intellectual Property Protection, Direct Investment and Technology Transfer: Germany, Japan and the United States' (Discussion Paper No. 27, World Bank and International Finance Corporation, 1995); E. Mansfield, 'Patents and Innovation: An Empirical Study', *Management Science* 32.2 (1986): 173–81; Other studies reaching similar conclusions include Scherer et al. (1959), Taylor and Silberston (1973), Arundel and van de Paal (1995) and Cohen et al. (1997); see W.M. Cohen, R.R. Nelson and J. Walsh, 'Appropriability Conditions and Why Firms Patent and Why They Do Not in the U.S. Manufacturing Sector' (Working Paper, Carnegie Mellon University, 1997); A. Arundel and G. van de Paal, *Innovation Strategies of Europe's Largest Industrial Firms* (unpublished manuscript, Maastricht Economic and Social Research and Training Centre [MERIT], 1995); C.T. Taylor and Z.A. Silberston, *The Economic Impact of the Patent System* (Cambridge University Press, 1973); F.M. Scherer, S.E. Herzstein, A.W. Dreyfoos, W.G. Whitney, O.J. Bachman, C.P. Pesek, C.J. Scott, T.G. Kelly and J.J. Galvin, *Patents and the Corporation: A Report on Industrial Technology under Changing Public Policy* (Harvard University Press, 1959).

31   However, the evidence linking intellectual property rights (IPRs) to foreign direct investment (FDI) and technology transfer is mixed. Stronger IPR protection has been found to encourage FDI and technology transfer in certain industries, most notably in chemicals and pharmaceuticals. As with trade, IPRs may play less of a role in high-tech industries due to the difficulty in imitating these industries' products, while in low-tech industries other factors such as market size, cheap labour and political stability may be more important in determining FDI flows than IPRs. Smarzynska (2004) finds that weak IPR regimes deter FDI in high-tech sectors (i.e. drugs, cosmetics and healthcare products, chemicals, machinery and equipment, and electrical equipment), with some evidence suggesting that FDI is deterred in other industries also. She also finds evidence to suggest that stronger IPR protection encourages firms to set up local production facilities rather than focusing solely on distribution networks. Branstetter et al. (2004) suggest that technology transfer is higher following IPR reforms, with an increase in technology transfer, as measured by intra-firm royalty payments from parent firms

introduction and strengthening of patents for pharmaceutical products would not lead to an increase in research and development (R&D) investment by enterprises in developing countries because of the non-existence of technical infrastructure and financial and human resources. That is why "the non-patentability of pharmaceutical products existing prior to the TRIPS Agreement gave developing countries the opportunity to progress and to acquire basic technology through reverse engineering before being able to invest in R&D".[32] Consequently, almost 50 developing countries, which were not granted patent protection for pharmaceuticals during the Uruguay Round, fiercely resisted including pharmaceuticals under the patent regime, claiming that vastly higher drug prices would be associated with such patents.[33]

Therefore, developing countries and the LDCs are apprehensive of strong patent protection as it may be harmful to their pharmaceutical industries and may have severe negative consequences for their citizens in terms of access to affordable medicines.[34] A potential consequence of the introduction of pharmaceutical patents is that prices of pharmaceuticals

---

to affiliates located in IPR-reforming countries. See for details, B. Smarzynska, 'The Composition of Foreign Direct Investment and Protection of Intellectual Property Rights: Evidence from Transition Economies', *European Economic Review* 48 (2004), 39–62; L.G. Branstetter, R. Fisman and C.F. Foley, 'Do Stronger Intellectual Property Rights Increase International Technology Transfer? Empirical Evidence from U.S. Firm-level Panel Data' (Working Paper No. 3305, World Bank Policy Research, 2004). However, Primo-Braga and Fink (1998) found no evidence of a relationship between FDI flows and IPR protection, and Maskus et al. (2005) argued that strong IPR protection is not a necessary condition for firms to invest in particular countries. If it were, then large countries with high growth rates but weak IPR regimes, such as Brazil and China, would not have received the large foreign investment inflows that they have. See for details, C.A. Primo-Braga and C. Fink, 'The Relationship between Intellectual Property Rights and Foreign Direct Investment', *Duke Journal of Comparative and International Law* 9 (1998): 163–88, and K.E. Maskus, S.M. Dougherty and A. Mertha, 'Intellectual Property Rights and Economic Development in China' in *Intellectual Property and Development: Lessons from Recent Economic Research*, ed. by C. Fink and K.E. Maskus (World Bank/Oxford University Press, 2005).

32 See for details, WHO, *Globalization and Access to Drugs: Implications of the WTO/ TRIPS Agreement*, Health Economic and Drugs Series, No. 007 (1998), p.46, http:// apps.who.int/medicinedocs/en/d/Jwhozip35e/3.5.html

33 Jane O. Lanjouw, 'The Introduction of Pharmaceutical Product Patents in India: "Heartless Exploitation of the Poor and Suffering"?' (Working Paper No. 6366, Yale University and the NBER, 26 August 1997), p.2.

34 Martin Khor, 'Rethinking Intellectual Property Rights and TRIPS', in *Global Intellectual Property Rights—Knowledge, Access and Development*, ed. by Peter Drahos and Ruth Mayne (Palgrave Macmillan, 2002), pp.201–13.

will increase and the availability of cheap pharmaceuticals for poorer citizens will diminish.[35] Here the apprehension of the negative consequences of patent protection for pharmaceuticals is not only applicable to the LDCs that are WTO members, but may also place non-WTO member LDCs at a disadvantage, given such countries' dependence on imports of cheap generic medicines.[36]

Historically, product patent protection was excluded in most developed countries as well.[37] For example, in France, product patent protection was prohibited under the law of 5 July 1844 and limited patent protection was only permitted on 2 January 1966.[38] In Germany, product patents were explicitly excluded under the law of 25 May 1877, but were then introduced from 4 September 1967.[39] In Switzerland, product patents for pharmaceuticals were prohibited by the constitution and were only introduced in 1977.[40] In Italy, pharmaceutical patents were prohibited until 1978.[41] In Spain, product patents were introduced in 1986 just after its accession to the European Economic Community, and the relevant laws came into effect from 1992.[42] The rationale behind the non-granting of product patent protection for pharmaceuticals in each of these example countries was to allow local pharmaceutical companies to imitate and produce patented medicines by using new processes.[43] Over the years, these developed countries gained self-sufficiency in

---

35   Ma El Farag Balat and M.H. Loutifi, 'The TRIPS Agreement and Developing Countries: A Legal Analysis of the Impacts of the New IPR's Law on the Pharmaceutical Industry in Egypt', *Web JCILI* 2 (2004): 3.

36   For example, after the introduction of patent protection for pharmaceuticals in India in line with the TRIPS Agreement, Bhutan (a non-WTO member and LDC) is now facing problems of cheap availability of drugs; see Tandi Dorji, 'Effects of TRIPS on Pricing, Affordability and Access to Essential Medicines in Bhutan', *Journal of Bhutan Studies* 16 (Summer 2007), 128–41.

37   Xuan Li, 'The Impact of Higher Standards in Patent Protection for Pharmaceutical Industries under the TRIPS Agreement—A Comparative Study of China and India', *The World Economy* 31.10 (2008): 14.

38   Ibid.

39   Ibid.

40   Ibid.

41   Ibid.

42   M. Boldrin and D.K. Levine, *Against Intellectual Monopoly* (Cambridge University Press, 2008), pp.212–42.

43   Edwin Cameron and Jonathan Berger, 'Patents and Public Health: Principle, Politics and Paradox', *SCRIPT-ed* 1.4 (2004): 532. http://www2.law.ed.ac.uk/ahrc/script-ed/docs/cameron.asp

pharmaceutical manufacturing and invested in R&D,[44] which enabled and facilitated the transformation of their pharmaceutical industries into innovative and research-based industries by using imitated technology.[45] Now, given the advent of TRIPS, the argument being mounted is that these countries are acting in a hypocritical way: they are supporting the implementation of IP protection for pharmaceuticals only after experiencing maturity for their own pharmaceutical industries.[46]

For LDCs, the freedom to rely on imitated technology until such time as pharmaceutical production is at a similar stage of development—before the implementation of pharmaceutical patent protection—is no longer an option,[47] given the *immediate* obligation of WTO member countries to implement the TRIPS Agreement. In that context, the transitional period to implement the TRIPS Agreement or to implement the pharmaceutical patent provisions is quite meaningless for those countries that do not have the technological capabilities to produce generic pharmaceuticals.[48] Although Bangladesh is an LDC, it is in a somewhat unique position.

Bangladesh has a considerable number of generic producers who can reduce the price of pharmaceuticals by utilising the freedom of imitation. Bangladesh also exports to the less regulated markets of Asia and Africa and to some countries in Europe. However, the apprehension is that after the introduction of pharmaceutical patents, as required by TRIPS, the local pharmaceutical industry will face the issue of survival. If the industry fails, there will be an effect on access to pharmaceuticals. Thus, multinationals and other large pharmaceutical companies in Bangladesh

---

44 Sanjaya Lall, 'Indicators of the Relative Importance of IPRs in Developing Countries' (UNCTAD-ICTSD Project on IPRs and Sustainable Development, 1 June 2003), p.1.

45 'The Introduction of Pharmaceutical Product Patents in India', p.2.

46 S. Srinivasan, 'How TRIPS Benefits Indian Industry and How It May Not Benefit the Indian People', *Indian Journal of Medical Ethics* 5.2 (2008): 68.

47 In a case study of the United Nations Conference on Trade and Development (UNCTAD) in Bangladesh (2007), it was revealed that without imitation, learning would be made extremely difficult for countries with low technological capabilities. See for details, Padmashree Gehl Sampath, 'Intellectual Property in Least Developed Countries: Pharmaceutical, Agro-processing, and Textiles and RMG in Bangladesh' (study prepared for UNCTAD as a background Paper for *The Least Developed Countries Report*, Geneva: UNCTAD, 2007a).

48 Padmashree Gehl Sampath, 'Innovation and Competitive Capacity in Bangladesh's Pharmaceutical Sector' (Working Paper Series, Paper No. 2007–031, United Nations University, Maastricht Economic and Social Research and Training Centre [UNU-MERIT], September 2007b), p.2.

believe that by lowering protection for pharmaceuticals, Bangladesh has missed out on the opportunity to encourage an innovative and R&D-based pharmaceutical industry.

Thus, the debate centres on how to reach a balance between meeting the high costs of pharmaceutical R&D and creating incentives to stimulate access to those pharmaceuticals in developing countries and LDCs. By focusing on Bangladesh, this study contributes to the debate by providing a better understanding of the implications of a TRIPS-compliant patent regime on pharmaceutical patents for an LDC.

1.3 The Requirements of TRIPS

The existing patent law of Bangladesh needs to be amended and updated to conform to the TRIPS Agreement's requirements, as in its current form it can neither promote access to medicines, nor facilitate innovation in the local pharmaceutical sector, nor encourage investment in R&D and technology transfer. The *Patents and Designs Act, 1911* (PDA) of Bangladesh is a century-old colonial law inherited from the then British Government in the Indian subcontinent without any major modification.[49] That is why, in the context of pharmaceutical patents, Bangladesh will have to consider the following provisions of the TRIPS Agreement when amending its patent law:

1) to ensure that the patent is available and enjoyed without discrimination as to the place of invention, the field of technology and whether products are imported or locally produced[50]

2) patents for both products and processes[51]

---

49 The law relating to patents in Bangladesh is the *Patents and Designs Act, 1911* (PDA) with some minor amendments to date.

50 Article 27.1 of the TRIPS Agreement.

51 Although patents were always issued to protect the production process, without patent restrictions on products, pharmaceutical companies were still able to use reverse engineering techniques on essential medicines to understand their molecular structure and develop new ways to recreate those drugs. Compounds produced through these alternate processes were then sold as "generic" versions of the original drug, which drove down the price of the original product through market competition. However, if product patent is granted, for the duration of patent protection, even if they are using an alternative process, other companies cannot introduce generic products to the market; hence, the monopolised price of the patent holder is protected.

3) to incorporate patentability requirements such as novelty, inventive steps and industrial application considering national developmental goals and provisions of the TRIPS Agreement

4) the status/exclusion of pharmaceutical patents during the waiver period until 1 January 2033 and the likely provision for a "mailbox" during the transitional period

5) utilisation of flexibilities such as exceptions for government use, compulsory licenses, parallel imports, experimental use and public interest[52]

6) provisions for the use of patents without the authorisation of patent holders, but with a number of conditions and limitations

7) a minimum 20-year term for patent protection.[53]

While the necessary reforms are being implemented for TRIPS compliance, the wider issue that needs to be given due consideration is how Bangladesh can strike a balance between the competing interests of a variety of stakeholders, including domestic generic-medicine producers, the domestic R&D community, multinational pharmaceutical companies (MNPCs) and the citizens of Bangladesh.

1.4 TRIPS Flexibilities and the Doha Declaration

The TRIPS Agreement provides "flexibility" for members to determine their own approach regarding the relationship between IPRs and access to pharmaceuticals in a number of ways. The World Intellectual Property Organization (WIPO) Committee on Development and Intellectual Property (CDIP) defines "flexibilities" as "legal tools that countries can use as they see fit in their national developmental plans and within the framework of the mandatory standards of international obligations".[54] In the context of the TRIPS Agreement, it further states, "the term flexibilities means that there are different options through which TRIPS obligations can be transposed into national law so that

---

52   Articles 6, 7, 30 and 31 of the TRIPS Agreement.
53   See Article 33 of the TRIPS Agreement.
54   See WIPO, *Study on Patent Related Flexibilities in the Multilateral Legal Framework and Their Legislative Implementation at the National and Regional Levels* (WIPO Committee on Development and Intellectual Property [CDIP], Fifth Session, WIPO Secretariat, Geneva, 26–30 April 2010), p.8.

national interests are accommodated and yet TRIPS provisions and principles are complied with".[55] The TRIPS Agreement permits the following flexibilities to:

- Define the nature of invention and to regulate the criteria of patentability within the broad framework of TRIPS Agreement rules.

- Establish exceptions to patent rights.

- Grant government use and compulsory licenses.

- Have recourse to a range of options with respect to the protection of data submitted for regulatory purposes.

- Determine country-based policies with respect to exhaustion of rights and to allow parallel importation of medicines.

- Restrict the "unfair commercial use" option of "protection of undisclosed test data" to promote generic competition and reduce prices.[56]

However, these flexibilities are ambiguous and therefore need to be operationalised and implemented at the national level while adjusting to national developmental goals, the public interest and the stage of development of a particular country.[57]

Therefore, the countries had difficulties in exploiting the flexibilities contained in the TRIPS Agreement, particularly in the context of dealing with public health emergencies and ensuring better access to medicines. In particular, three conflicting situations urgently raised the need to address ambiguity and inconsistency in the TRIPS agreement in the context of public health. First, in 1997 the South African government introduced the *Medicines and Related Substances Control Act* to ensure the

---

55 Ibid, para. 34.

56 Article 39.3 of the TRIPS Agreement requires member countries to establish protection for submitted test data. However, this requirement is in fact narrowly drawn, and countries maintain substantial flexibility in its implementation. The public interest in limiting protection for data is to promote competition and to ensure that data protection does not become the means to block the timely entrance of generic competitors to off-patent drugs, because generic competitors drive down price, thereby promoting greater accessibility to medicines. See Carlos Correa, *Protection of Data Submitted for the Registration of Pharmaceuticals: Implementing the Standards of the TRIPS Agreement* (South Centre, 2002).

57 Carlos Correa, *Intellectual Property Rights, The WTO and Developing Countries: The TRIPS Agreement and Policy Options* (Zed Books, 2000); Christopher May and Susan K. Sell, *Intellectual Property Rights: A Critical History* (Lynne Rienner Pub., 2005).

availability and affordability of HIV/AIDS-related medicines. This law employed parallel imports and compulsory license, which triggered a legal battle between South Africa and 39 pharmaceutical companies, and involved strong pressure from the US government and trade bodies.[58] Second, in 2001 disputes erupted between the U.S. and Brazil regarding the compatibility of the working requirements in the national patent law, in which the US government argued that the provision for granting compulsory licenses in case of the patent's non-working in Brazil within 3 years of its issuance was tantamount to a protective measure and hence inconsistent with the TRIPS Agreement.[59] Third, the anthrax scare after the September 11th, 2001 terrorist attack in New York had created a potential health threat, which caused developed countries like the U.S. and Canada to threaten to use compulsory licenses to stockpile an adequate supply of Cipro (an antibiotic used in the treatment of anthrax).[60] These measures by the US and Canada revealed "a hypocritical behavior [by them] in its eagerness to use the threat of a compulsory license for what it perceived as a health emergency while on the other hand forcing developing countries to stick to restrictive patent laws in the face of increasingly dire health crises".[61]

Considering the inconsistency and ambiguity of how to define a national public health emergency, and on what grounds it might be permissible for a national government to grant compulsory licenses pursuant to the TRIPS Agreement, the anthrax scare created an impetus to clarify TRIPS flexibilities. The African countries had a strong conviction that the TRIPS Agreement should not prevent them from using measures vital to ensure access to medicines and to fulfil public health needs.[62] That

---

58 Case No 4138/98 in the High Court of South Africa; see, M. Monirul Azam, 'The Experiences of Patent Law Reforms in Brazil, India and South Africa and Lessons for Bangladesh', *Akron Intellectual Property Journal* 7.2 (2014): 61–100.

59 WTO, 'Measures Affecting Patent Production—Request for Consultation by the United States' (WT/DS199/1); WTO, 'Brazil—Measures Affecting Patent Protection—Request for the Establishment of a Panel by the United States' (WT/DS199/3); see also, Azam (2014).

60 See Sharifah Rahma Sekalala, 'Beyond Doha: Seeking Access to Essential Medicines for HIV/AIDS through the World Trade Organisation', p.5, http://siteresources.worldbank.org/INTRAD/Resources/SSekalala.pdf

61 Ibid., p.5.

62 WTO, 'Submission by the African Group to the TRIPS Council for Special Discussion on Intellectuel Property and Access to Medicines', 20 June 2001 (Document IP/C/W/296) https://www.wto.org/english/tratop_e/trips_e/paper_develop_w296_e.htm

is why the African group requested the TRIPS Council to arrange a special discussion on intellectual property and access to medicines.[63]

During the discussion, the developing countries not only sought clarity through a declaration but support for their efforts to use the flexibilities in the TRIPS Agreement to deal with national public health needs.[64] But the meeting triggered strong protest from the U.S., which argued, along with Japan, Switzerland, Australia and Canada, that strict patent protection for pharmaceuticals was an important incentive for pharmaceutical innovation and hence vital for public health.[65] However, on 14 November 2001, the WTO Doha Ministerial Conference adopted a declaration on TRIPS and Public Health which offered a much needed clarification, confirming that "the TRIPS Agreement does not and should not prevent members from taking measures to protect public health. Accordingly … the Agreement can and should be interpreted and implemented in a manner supportive of WTO members' right to protect public health and, in particular, to promote access to medicines for all".[66] The Doha declaration in particular confirmed the public health-oriented use of the TRIPS Agreement.

First, Para. 5a of the Doha Declaration indicates that the pressures to obstruct the use of available flexibilities run counter to the objectives and purpose of the TRIPS Agreement (as mentioned in Articles 7 and 8 of the TRIPS Agreement). Carlos Correa argued that "in legal terms, it means that panels and the Appellate Body must interpret the Agreement and the laws and regulations adopted to implement it in light of the public health needs of individual Members".[67]

Second, Para. 5b confirms that "each member has the right to grant compulsory licences and the freedom to determine the grounds upon which such licences are granted".[68] Carlos Correa stated that "the use of this terminology [compulsory licences] may help to create awareness,

---

63   Ibid.
64   Sekalala, p.6.
65   See, 'US Statement at TRIPS Council Meeting', 20 June 2001, https://www.wto.org/english/news_e/news01_e/trips_drugs_010620_e.htm
66   WTO, 'Declaration on the TRIPS Agreement and Public Health (Doha Declaration)', 14 November 2001 (WT/MIN(01)/DEC/2), para. 4, https://www.wto.org/english/the wto_e/minist_e/min01_e/mindecl_trips_e.htm
67   Carlos Correa, 'Implications of the Doha Declaration on the TRIPS Agreement and Public Health' (WHO, 2002).
68   Para. 5b, Doha Declaration.

particularly among health ministries in developing countries and LDCs, about the possible utilization of compulsory licences to meet public health and other objectives".[69]

Third, Para. 5c states that "each member has the right to determine what constitutes a national emergency or other circumstances of extreme urgency, it being understood that public health crises, including those relating to HIV/AIDS, tuberculosis, malaria and other epidemics, can represent a national emergency or other circumstances of extreme urgency". The Declaration further places "the burden on a complaining Member to prove that an emergency or urgency does *not* exist".[70] This recognition is considered an important achievement for developing countries in the Doha Declaration, as it implies that specific measures to deal with an emergency may be adopted based on the national situation and be preserved until the underlying situation ceases, without temporal restrictions.

Fourth, Para. 5d clarifies Members' right to adopt the principle of exhaustion of rights and determine by which parallel imports may be determined. The Declaration states that "the effect of the provisions in the TRIPS Agreement ... is to leave each Member free to establish its own regime for such exhaustion without challenge".[71] This provision approved the Members' freedom to apply an international exhaustion principle, confirming that it would be legitimate and fully consistent with the Agreement to do so.

Fifth, Para. 6 identifies the problem inherent in Article 31(f) of the TRIPS Agreement, which stipulates that a compulsory license can only be issued to serve the domestic market. This had caused grave concerns to many developing countries, since they did not have enough manufacturing capability or infrastructure to take advantage of the compulsory licensing provisions. Although the declaration instructed the TRIPS Council to find an expeditious solution by 2002, it took nearly two years of negotiations to reach a solution. On 30 August 2003, the General Council of the WTO adopted the Decision on Implementation of Paragraph 6 of the Doha Declaration on the TRIPS Agreement and Public Health (the August 30th Decision). It granted rights to developing

---

69   Correa (WHO, 2002).
70   Ibid.
71   Para. 5d, Doha Declaration.

countries to waive the provisions under Article 31(f) and also allowed member countries to export generic pharmaceutical products made under compulsory licenses to meet the needs of importing countries subject to certain conditions.[72] The provisions of the August 30th Decision were formally approved as an amendment to the TRIPS Agreement on 6 December 2005, and it will formally be inserted into TRIPS once it has been ratified by two-thirds of WTO members.[73] Nevertheless, delays in the ratification procedure have no material implications. The waivers of the Decision became operational on 30 August 2003 and will remain so until the amendment is in effect.[74]

Despite having endorsement for the public health-oriented measures for implementing the TRIPS agreement, most of the developing countries and the LDCs have not properly implemented the Doha Declaration and the flexibilities in the TRIPS Agreement. The reasons behind this are the complexity of patent-related legal provisions, lack of institutional support, fear of trade retaliation, and limited skills in the negotiations and diplomacy necessary to exploit the technical and financial cooperation of the developed countries.[75] In this context, the experiences of India, Brazil, China and South Africa could lead to a better understanding of different approaches to dealing with public health-oriented patent law reforms and to implementing TRIPS-compliant patent laws by utilising the TRIPS flexibilities and other governmental interventions in ways that do not conflict with the TRIPS obligations. The policy options used by Brazil, China, India and South Africa generate important lessons for the LDCs in determining which legislative and other policy options they use.

---

72 See for details, WTO, 'Implementation of Paragraph 6 of the Doha Declaration on the TRIPS Agreement and Public Health, Decision of the General Council of 30 August 2003' (WT/L/540 and Corr.1), https://www.wto.org/english/tratop_e/trips_e/implem_para6_e.htm

73 Although it was originally to be adopted by 1 December 2007, the General Council decision of 30 November 2015 (Document WT/L/965) extended the deadline to 31 December 2017, as the August 30th Decision is yet to be ratified by two-thirds of the members.

74 For details on the operational procedure of the August 30th Decision, see chapter 3 of this study.

75 Mohammad Monirul Azam, 'Establishment of the WTO and Challenges for the Legal System of Bangladesh', *Journal of Business Law* 3 (2006): 23–45.

1.5 The Experiences of Brazil, China, India and South Africa

Brazil's experience regarding TRIPS-compliant patent law for pharmaceuticals, and enforcing societal and national obligations to ensure access to medicines, represents a situation in which exploitation by MNPCs was not only largely thwarted, but gave way to significant reforms in public health policy and the reinstating of local drug companies as viable contenders in the domestic market.[76]

In Brazil, the government decided to take measures to facilitate access to pharmaceuticals in the context of the HIV/AIDS crisis while making TRIPS-compliant patent law. This included, for instance, a strong compulsory licensing regime.[77] As part of the compulsory licensing regime, inventors had the duty to manufacture the product in Brazil. The US Government objected to this requirement and initiated a WTO dispute. However, the dispute was later withdrawn due to pressure imposed upon the US by public health organisations and human rights groups.[78] Brazil has also adopted a decree that establishes certain rules concerning the granting of compulsory licenses in cases of national emergency and public interest.[79] The definition of "public interest" is broad and includes such matters as public health, nutrition, the protection of the environment and elements of primordial importance for technological, social or economic development. The possibility of being able to issue compulsory licenses in each of these cases implies that the country's most basic health needs would be fulfilled. In contrast, China

---

76 Mathew Flynn, 'Corporate Power and State Resistance: Brazil's Use of TRIPS Flexibilities for Its National AIDS Program', in *Intellectual Property, Pharmaceuticals and Public Health*, ed. by Kenneth C. Shadlen, Samira Guennif, Alenka Guzman, and N. Lalitha (2011).

77 Brazil, *Industrial Property Law, No 9.279, 14 May 1996*.

78 Médecins Sans Frontières (MSF) and other public health groups, along with 120 Brazilian non-governmental organisations (NGOs) requested that the United States government withdraw its request for a WTO dispute settlement procedure on the Brazilian patent law. The US brought a complaint before the WTO Dispute Settlement Body (DSB) in Geneva, requesting measures that might handicap the successful Brazilian AIDS programme, which is largely based on Brazil's ability to manufacture affordable treatment. See WT/DS199/1 (8 June 2000), *Brazil: Measures Affecting Patent Protection*, 30 December 2009, http://www.wto.org/english/tratop_e/dispu_e/cases_e/ds199_e.htm

79 Brazil, 'Presidential Decree on Compulsory Licensing', Decree No. 3, 201, 6 October 1999.

initially tried to attract more foreign investment in the pharmaceutical sector rather than adopt an explicitly public health-oriented approach while introducing TRIPS-compliant patent law.

China has experienced the transformation from a communist economy to a socialist market economy. Accordingly, its patent legislation has undergone several changes since 1978, due first to constant pressure from US foreign trade policy and then to maintain the availability and affordability of medicines while also adjusting to TRIPS obligations. China was primarily concentrated on the low-cost source of pharmaceutical ingredients and generics, and continued to revise its patent law to attract more investment in the pharmaceutical sector. It had raised the bar for entering the pharmaceutical business by passing laws since 1998, including the *Drug Management Law and Regulations on Pharmaceutical Manufacturing*.

Subsequent to its accession to the WTO, Chinese regulations in 2002 extended pharmaceutical patents to 20 years and data exclusivity for six years. But considering the potential threat to the availability and affordability of patented medicines, in 2012 China amended its patent law further to allow eligible companies compulsory licenses for producing generic versions of patented drugs during state emergencies or unusual circumstances, or in the interests of the public. Again, for "reasons of public health", eligible drug makers can also ask to export these medicines to other countries, including members of the WTO. It is interesting to note that since the change in China's patent law, Gilead has offered certain concessions, including giving China a substantial donation of HIV drugs (Tenofovir) if it continues to buy the same amount.[80] It was further stated that "this is all a negotiation game; this offer from Gilead came about once the news that the Chinese was considering issuing a CL [Compulsory License] came out. The end game is okay, you get a better deal or you use the CL, it's a strategy that many countries use".[81] Therefore, the Chinese experience of transformation towards a market economy, and its ability to improve innovation and

---

80   Statement by Paul Cawthorne, coordinator for MSF's Access Campaign in Asia; see for more details, http://www.aljazeera.com/news/asia-pacific/2012/06/2012694923 223634.html

81   Said by Paul Cawthorne, coordinator for MSF's Access Campaign in Asia; quoted in Tan Ee Lin, 'China Changes Patent Law in Fight for Cheaper Drugs', 8 June 2012, http://www.reuters.com/article/us-china-medicines-patents-idUSBRE8570TY20120608

maintain the availability and affordability of medicines, will have important lessons for other developing countries and the LDCs.

India's experience is different from those of Brazil and China. It tried to promote the availability and affordability of pharmaceuticals by changing its patent laws in such a way as to promote generics and the innovative capabilities of local industries.[82] India entered into the WTO in 1995 and went through a long process of amendments to create a TRIPS-compliant patent regime, effective from beginning of 1 January 2005. The effect of stronger intellectual patent rights created problems for the larger Indian drug firms and greatly damaged smaller local firms' abilities to meet the rising costs of remuneration for experienced and efficient pharmacists and other technical people.[83]

The Indian TRIPS-compliant patent law was criticised by public health organisations such as Oxfam as being "likely to bring about a legal regime that is less favourable from the point of view of access to drugs for the people of this country".[84] Public health organisations such as the Affordable Medicines and Treatment Campaign (AMTC), an Indian advocacy group, also argued that the new patent law in India generally provided stronger protection to patent holders, which implied that the balance of interests between inventors and the general public was being shifted in favour of the former.[85]

However, like Brazil, India also incorporated options concerning compulsory licenses for use in cases of public interest. Now India is also using compulsory licensing options to encourage local production in cases of inadequate supply or excessive price of particular medicines. This is based on the earlier experiences of Brazil, which has both effectively and consistently managed to control the costs of several patented drugs by constantly threatening the use of the "national emergency" clause provided for under the TRIPS Agreement with regard to compulsory licensing.[86] Another important provision in the Indian *Patent Act, 2005,*

---

82 Katia Gomez, 'Inside the TRIPS Agreement', *Journal of International Affairs at UCSD* 8 (2009).

83 Ibid, p.9.

84 Philippe Cullet, 'Patent Bill, TRIPS and Right to Health', *Economic and Political Weekly* 36.43, 27 October 2001, http://www.ielrc.org/content/a0108.pdf

85 Ibid.

86 Dipika Jain, 'Access to Drugs in India: Exploration of Compulsory Licensing as an Effective Tool' (unpublished LLM Paper, Harvard Law School, 2009), p.8.

which Bangladesh may replicate, is that generic drugs that were already on the market at the time the Act was passed (i.e. before 2005) were exempted and thus could remain on the market.[87]

Compared to India, China and Brazil, South Africa has a larger health crisis to deal with, including a large number of HIV/AIDS patients and enormous problems of medicine access. Thus, the case of South Africa (economically the strongest African country) is particularly illustrative of a public health crisis and showcases the role that domestic and international patent laws and policies may play in this context.[88]

Despite its problems, South Africa has never used compulsory licenses. Prior to the revision of drug policy undertaken by its post-apartheid government, approximately 20% of the population, mostly white, was covered by private healthcare, while the black majority relied on public sector care, which was blighted by "irrational use of resources, poor working conditions and inadequate infrastructure".[89]

Therefore, the vast majority of South Africans did not have access to healthcare at all, making healthcare reform one of the most important items on the agenda of the post-apartheid government. The post-apartheid constitution also mandated the state to take reasonable measures to provide access to healthcare services for everyone,[90] which is why the then government appointed a National Drug Policy Committee to revamp South Africa's healthcare system.

After a series of investigations and consultations with stakeholders, including representatives of the pharmaceutical industry and the World Health Organization (WHO), the National Drug Policy Committee found that among the most notable deficiencies were the lack of equity in access to essential drugs, the comparatively high prices for pharmaceuticals in the private sector and the losses of drugs through poor security in the public sector.[91]

---

87   Ibid., pp.6–7.
88   William W. Fisher III and Cyrill P. Rigamonti, 'The South Africa AIDS Controversy: A Case Study in Patent Law and Policy, Harvard Law School', 10 February 2005, http://cyber.law.harvard.edu/people/tfisher/South Africa.pdf
89   South African Department of Health, 'National Drug Policy for South Africa', 3 (1996), p.3.
90   Articles 27(1)(a) and 27(2) of the Constitution of the Republic of South Africa, Act. 108 of 1996.
91   South African Department of Health, 'National Drug Policy for South Africa', 4 (1996), pp.10–11.

The pharmaceutical companies in South Africa argued that simply lowering drug prices could not solve the access problem, because South Africa did not have adequate infrastructure for the distribution of drugs. They cited the example of India where, despite the availability of generic versions of AIDS drugs, accessibility to medicines remained a problem.[92]

However, considering excessive pricing of medicines by multinational corporations (MNCs) in South Africa, the government inserted the new section 15C into the South African *Medicines and Related Substances Control Act, 1997* (MRSCA).[93] The primary purpose of this amendment was to enable South Africa to benefit from lower prices abroad for the same drugs.

The MNCs, mostly led by the US pharmaceutical industry, vigorously opposed the enactment of section 15C, arguing that it was tantamount to a complete abrogation of patent rights and that it violated South Africa's obligations under the TRIPS Agreement.[94] As a representative of Bristol-Myers Squibb put it, "Patents are the lifeblood of our industry. Compulsory licensing and parallel imports expropriate our patent rights"; the spokesman added that the only beneficiary of the erosion of patents would be the generic drug industry.[95] Nevertheless, the planned modifications, including section 15C, were signed into law by President Nelson Mandela on 12 December 1997. In an attempt to block the implementation of the amendments, the pharmaceutical companies took the matter to court and challenged the constitutionality of the amended MRSCA before the High Court of South Africa in February 1998.[96] The position taken by South Africa was the reflection of a struggle between excessive pricing of patented medicines by

---

92 Sabin Russell, 'New Crusade to Lower AIDS Drug Costs', *The San Francisco Chronicle* (24 May 1999), A1.

93 *Medicines and Related Substances Control Amendment Act No. 90 of 1997*, South African Government Gazette No. 18, 505 of 12 December 1997 (amending the *Medicines and Related Substances Control Act No. 101 of 1965*, as amended by Act Nos. 65/1974, 17/1979, 20/1981 and 94/1991).

94 US subsidiaries accounted for 27% of the pharmaceutical market in South Africa, which was greater than the share of the South African local pharmaceutical industry; for details, see Lynne Duke, 'Nkosazana Zuma — Activist Health Minister Draws Foes in S. Africa', *Washington Post*, 11 December 1998, A41.

95 Quoted in 'The South Africa AIDS Controversy', p.13.

96 For details, see also 'Notice of Motion in the High Court of South Africa' (Transvaal Provincial Division), Case No. 4183/98.

the pharmaceutical companies and the societal and constitutional obligation to ensure access to medicines and right to health. Again, it was also fairly representative of the broader international struggle over the meaning of TRIP, especially over the scope of and exceptions to internationally recognised IPRs.[97] However, due to numerous legal and political challenges such as settlement of court cases, delays in the formation of a pricing committee and effective implementation of MRSCA only began in 2007.

While the experience of India, China, Brazil and South Africa offer important lessons for the LDCs like Bangladesh, relevant policies and recommendations of the World Health Organisation (WHO) can also help the LDCs gain wider international support and access to relevant financial and technical support to deal with the public health consequences of the TRIPS Agreement.

1.6 The Role of the WHO

The WHO is a specialised agency of the UN system of agencies and has a membership of 193 countries, making it one of the biggest organisations in terms of country membership in the world.[98] After the introduction of the TRIPS Agreement under the WTO, the role of the WHO and its involvement in the area of IP and public health have grown immensely during the past decade. Sell stated rightly that "[*since TRIPS, the*] WHO increasingly has been drawn into trade issues [*including IP issues*], and NGOs have had considerable access to the institution" (emphasis added).[99]

Considering the influence of the WHO in the field of global public health and relevant policymaking, Volansky remarked that the "WHO

---

97 Heinz Klug, 'Pharmaceutical Production and Access to Essential Medicines in South Africa', in *Intellectual Property, Pharmaceuticals and Public Health—Access to Drugs in Developing Countries*, ed. by Kenneth C. Shalen, Samira Guennif, Alenka Guzman and N. Lalitha (Cheltenham: Edward Elgar, 2011), pp.29–56.

98 The UN adopted the WHO under Article 57 of the UN Charter. For details, see the agreement between the UN and the WHO, 12 November 1948.

99 S. Sell, 'TRIPS-plus Free Trade Agreements and Access to Medicines', *Liverpool Law Review* 28.1 (2007): 41–75.

remains the predominant figure that guides, monitors, teaches, and even regulates Member States on global health".[100]

The WHO has issued several resolutions of vital importance in the area of IP and public health through its General Assembly.[101] The World Health Assembly (WHA) in May 2003 was particularly important as it dealt with improving access to essential medicines. During the discussions, the US presented an industry-friendly resolution that ignored the Doha Declaration on the TRIPS Agreement and Public Health. Further, the US's proposal recommended that the WHO should refrain from becoming involved in issues related to the implementation of TRIPS and should rather direct any such issues raised by member states to the WTO and WIPO for assistance.[102]

After a prolonged and contentious discussion, a compromise was worked out by the US and the developing countries, which culminated in the establishment of a time-limited independent commission: the Commission on Intellectual Property Rights, Innovation and Public Health (CIPIH).[103] The CIPIH was set up by the director general of the WHO in February 2004. Its main focus was on reviewing existing R&D efforts, examining the role of IP in stimulating innovation and making concrete proposals for action by national and international stakeholders to encourage research on diseases prevalent in developing countries and LDCs.

In April 2006, CIPIH issued its final report (the CIPIH Report), making numerous recommendations for improving public health in developing countries and LDCs.[104] These recommendations cover many areas related to institutional, legislative, health and negotiation

---

100 M. Volansky, 'Achieving Global Health: A Review of the World Health Organization's Response', *Tulsa Journal of Comparative International Law* 10 (2002): 223–24.

101 The World Health Assembly (WHA) is the supreme decision making body for the WHO. It generally meets in Geneva in May each year, and is attended by delegations from all 193 member states.

102 See for details, Mohammed K. El Said, *Public Health Related TRIPS-Plus Provisions in Bilateral Trade Agreements: A Policy Guide for Negotiators and Implementers in the Eastern Mediterranean Region* (WHO and ICTSD, 2010), p.1.

103 WHO, *Resolution of the World Health Assembly: Intellectual Property Rights, Innovation and Public Health, WHA56.27* (Geneva: WHO, 2003), http://www.who.int/intellectualproperty/documents/en/

104 For details, see WHO, 'Commission on Intellectual Property Rights, Innovation and Public Health', http://www.who.int/intellectualproperty

policies.[105] Following the issuance of the CIPIH Report at the WHA in May 2006, member states adopted a resolution entitled "Public health, innovation, essential health research and intellectual property rights: towards a global strategy and plan of action".[106] The global strategy underscores that the "WHO shall play a strategic and central role in the relationship between public health and innovation and intellectual property within its mandates".[107]

Again, the WHA adopted resolution WHA61.21 and resolution WHA62.16 in May 2008, which approved a global strategy and plan of action on public health, innovation and IP (hereafter "the global strategy") to foster innovation and improve access to medicines for people in developing countries.[108] The eight elements of the global strategy are designed to promote innovation, build capacity, improve access and mobilise resources. The global strategy includes prioritising R&D needs, promoting R&D, building and improving innovative capacity, the transfer of technology, and the application and management of IP to contribute to innovation and promote public health, among other measures.[109]

The CIPIH Report and global strategy, along with relevant recommendations and discussion at the WHA, should be of great importance for the developing countries and the LDCs when formulating policy options for making TRIPS-compliant patent law and also promoting public health.

However, the individual cases of Brazil, China, India and South Africa provide both optimistic and multifaceted perspectives on how leading developing countries can operate within the confines of TRIPS standards. The experiences of Brazil, China, India and South Africa

---

105 Ibid.

106 See WHO, *Public Health, Innovation, Essential Health Research and Intellectual Property Rights: Towards a Global Strategy and Plan of Action*, A59/A/Conf. Paper No. 8 (Geneva: WHO, 2006), http://www.who.int

107 See Third World Network Brief on *WHO: WHA strengthens WHO's Mandate on IP and Health* (27 May 2008), http://www.twn.my/title2/health.info/2008/ twnhealthinfo20080602.htm

108 See for details, 'The Global Strategy and Plan of Action on Public Health, Innovation and Intellectual Property', http://www.who.int/phi/implementation/ phi_globstat_action/en/

109 Ibid.

indicate that the provisions they have adopted are now considered as justified under the TRIPS Agreement, although these were challenged in their initial stages by the US and other developed country members of the WTO, and by a number of MNPCs. The limits of permissible exceptions are not known, but there is no reason to think that TRIPS cannot be further qualified to foster the realisation of basic health needs.

Bangladesh has the potential to become a substantial producer of generic medicines and could supply cheaper generic medicines to other developing countries and to the LDCs. On the other hand, there is a concern that the local pharmaceutical industry may not survive and that the price of pharmaceuticals may increase substantially after the introduction of TRIPS-compliant patent law in Bangladesh. Therefore, there may be good grounds for heeding the Indian, Brazilian and South African experiences in a way that takes into account the needs of the local population and industry. The subject of a multilateral trading system and the challenges induced in complying with the WTO system nationally and internationally has generated intense academic interest, with a consequently enormous output of literature.

1.7 Research Questions and Methodology

The aims of the research are to identify how developing countries like India, Brazil, China and South Africa created a policy space not only for preserving their local pharmaceutical sector and promoting innovation and investment in it, but also for maintaining the affordability and availability of medicines domestically. Considering the critical socioeconomic conditions, the infrastructural and institutional limitations in the LDCs, this study intends to explore how LDCs like Bangladesh can ensure the promotion of pharmaceutical innovation but still provide affordable pharmaceuticals by building on the experiences of Brazil, China, India and South Africa and also the guidelines of the WHO. The thesis examines three underlying research questions:

1) What are the policy options used by Brazil, China, India and South Africa for the implementation of the TRIPS Agreement and the preservation of the local pharmaceutical sector?

2) What (potential) policies can the LDCs (such as Bangladesh) use to promote local pharmaceutical industry and access to medicines?

3)   What are the infrastructural and institutional issues that need to be addressed by the LDCs to deal with a post-TRIPS patent regime?

This study combines doctrinal analysis, a comparative review and a case study using field research and employing a survey instrument and interviews to explore the identified research questions. This kind of combined research method has been applied in several legal research studies. For example, in the IP law field (the subject area within which this book lies) a study on copyright and access to knowledge in eight African countries applied the research method of combining doctrinal analysis, qualitative impact assessments and a comparative review.[110] Moreover, Lorenzo Cotula, in his PhD thesis on property rights, negotiating power and foreign investment in Africa, applied doctrinal and comparative legal analysis along with a further component of field studies for data collection.[111]

The doctrinal analysis here uses interpretive methods to examine relevant sources of patent law and to construct the protection of pharmaceutical patents in India, Brazil, South Africa and China from the perspective of both the local pharmaceutical industry and in terms of access to medicines. As the core research question involves options to be adopted in Bangladesh to promote the local pharmaceutical industry and access to medicines, the doctrinal analysis assesses those options adopted by India, Brazil, China and South Africa while adopting TRIPS-compliant patent law based on flexibilities available within the TRIPS Agreement. Therefore, the doctrinal analysis explores whether options adopted by these countries are compatible with TRIPS obligations, and to what extent these options are viable for an LDC such as Bangladesh.

The legal analysis relies on both primary and secondary sources (patent law, government reports, regulations, orders and judicial decisions, and academic literature). As the research questions cut across different bodies of law (from the TRIPS Agreement to various branches of national law, patent law and pharmaceutical regulations), the spectrum of primary sources used is quite broad.

---

110 Chris Armstrong, Jeremy de Beer, Dick Kawooya, Achal Prabhala and Tobias Schonwetter, *Copyright and Access to Knowledge in Eight African Countries* (2010).

111 Lorenzo Cotula, 'Property Rights, Negotiating Power and Foreign Investment: An International and Comparative law Study on Africa' (unpublished PhD thesis, University of Edinburgh School of Law, 2009).

The advantage of doctrinal research is that it is a systematic formulation of the law in particular contexts, it clarifies ambiguities within rules, and it places them in a logical and coherent structure to describe their relationship to other rules.[112] Doctrinal research is therefore concerned with the discovery and development of legal doctrines, and it clarifies the nature of a law. The validity of doctrinal research findings is unaffected by the empirical world. Doctrinal research makes no attempt to explain, predict or even to understand human behaviour, which is considered one of its major disadvantages. In asking "what is the law?", doctrinal research takes an internal, participant-oriented epistemological approach to its object of study and, for this reason, is sometimes described as research *in* law.[113] This is the source of the criticism that doctrinal research is not research *about* law at all.[114]

There have been many other criticisms made of doctrinal methodology; for example, that it is too theoretical, too technical, uncritical and narrow in its choice and range of subjects, and that it does not take full account of the social and economic significance of the legal process. In response to these criticisms, doctrinal research is defended on the grounds that it provides the foundations for further socio-legal research and may be combined with other non-doctrinal research.[115]

Therefore, it is important to understand that doctrinal research is not simply a single isolated category of scholarship. Some element of doctrinal analysis will be found in all but the most radical forms of legal research. For example, although legal reform-oriented research and socio-legal research appear as separate categories, their practitioners emphasise the importance of doctrinal legal analysis within their socio-legal work.[116] This particular study uses doctrinal analysis to understand "what the patent law is" in Bangladesh, Brazil, India and South Africa. However, it also analyses the historical, political and local pharmaceutical industry motivations behind the patent law reforms in

---

112 H.L.A. Hart, *The Concept of Law* (Clarendon Press, 1961).

113 H.W. Arthurs, *Law and Learning: Report to the Social Sciences and Humanities Research Council of Canada by the Consultative Group on Research and Education in Law* (Information Division, Social Sciences and Humanities Research Council of Canada, 1983).

114 Terry Hutchinson, *Researching and Writing in Law*, 3rd edn (Law Book Co, 2010), p.22.

115 Ibid., p.23.

116 F. Cownie, *Legal Academics: Culture and Identities* (Hart Publishing, 2004), pp.55–56.

these countries. To better formulate policy options for Bangladesh, it also uses a comparative review.

Comparative legal research methods have long been used in cross-national studies to identify, analyse and explain similarities and differences among countries' legal systems and practices. The benefit of this kind of comparative review is to gain a deeper understanding of other countries and their legal process so as to identify best practices and draw important lessons that may be replicated in other countries. Comparative legal research is very beneficial in a legal development process where modification, compliance, amendment and changes to the law are required.[117] It is typical for those who undertake this kind of research to examine the law as it is, while providing ideas and views for future legal development. For example, Olu Fasan investigated implementation of the TRIPS Agreement with a comparative study of Nigeria and South Africa.[118] Jakkrit Kuanpoth undertook a comparative analysis between the patent laws of India and Thailand and identified some lessons for developing countries in general.[119] Daya Shanker analysed the TRIPS Agreement with reference to some specific TRIPS flexibility categories, including compulsory licenses and parallel imports, as used in Argentina, Brazil and India, and thus suggested possible options for developing countries.[120]

The current study employs a comparative review to compare and contrast the perspectives of India and Brazil and to some extent South Africa and China, to identify all possible options used by them in the context of the implementation of the TRIPS Agreement and to draw lessons for LDCs such as Bangladesh.

To answer the selected research questions on Bangladesh, this study further adopts field research in Bangladesh, which is conducted as a case study using a survey instrument and undertaking interviews of some selected stakeholders in the relevant area of research. This

---

117 V.V. Palmer, 'From Lerotholi to Lando: Some Examples of Comparative Law Methodology', *American Journal of Comparative Law* 53 (2005): 261–2.

118 Olu Fasan, 'Commitment and Compliance in International Law: A Study of the Implementation of the WTO TRIPS Agreement in Nigeria and South Africa', *African Journal of International and Comparative Law* 20.2 (2012): 191–228.

119 Jakkrit Kuanpoth, *Patent Rights in Pharmaceuticals in Developing Countries: Major Challenges for the Future* (Edward Elgar, 2010).

120 See 'Fault Lines in the World Trade Organization'.

component mainly draws on the data from field studies conducted in Bangladesh. The purpose of this component is to complement the doctrinal analysis and comparative review by addressing the research questions in a way that better reflects the perceptions of the relevant stakeholders. A case study is conducted in a selected geographical area or with a very limited number of individuals as subjects of study; the aim is to collect factual background on a problem and draw inferences for possible strategies.[121] Case studies, in their true essence, explore and investigate contemporary, real-life phenomena through detailed contextual analysis of a limited number of events or conditions, and their relationships. There are several categories of case study: exploratory, descriptive, explanatory, interpretive and evaluative.[122] For example, Robert Lewis-Lettington and Peter Munyi conducted a case study in Kenya regarding willingness and ability to use TRIPS flexibilities, using doctrinal analysis and a descriptive and explanatory case study approach. Amy Kapczynski conducted a case study on TRIPS implementation in India's pharmaceutical sector based on field research and interviews.[123] In the current case study, I follow interpretive and evaluative case study methods.

Through interpretive case studies, I aim to interpret the data by developing conceptual categories, supporting or challenging the assumptions made regarding them and, in terms of evaluative case studies, going further to add my own judgment on the phenomena found in the data. Gaining both qualitative and quantitative data enables the researcher to examine the views of all stakeholders regarding the introduction of pharmaceutical patents, including their conflicting positions, so as to provide policy options for the smoother implementation of a TRIPS-compliant patent law.

The survey instrument is designed to gain an understanding of the perceptions of different stakeholders regarding TRIPS-compliant patent law and pharmaceutical patent protection. It was also useful to collect some qualitative data about the pharmaceutical companies,

---

121 Zaidah Zainal, *Case Study as a Research Method*, http://psyking.net/htmlobj-3837/case_study_as_a_research_method.pdf

122 Ibid.

123 Amy Kapczynski, 'Harmonisation and Its Discontents: A Case Study of TRIPS Implementation in India's Pharmaceutical Sector', *California Law Review* 97 (2009): 1571–650.

their strategies and innovation capacities. Obtaining qualitative and quantitative data was also useful in answering the research questions by pinpointing major concerns and motivations for the transition from a pre-TRIPS to a TRIPS-compliant patent regime. Obtaining qualitative and quantitative data via interviews was also helpful in understanding institutional details about the pharmaceutical industry, the DDA, the Patent Office, research and educational institutions, and public health groups. Interviews, in particular, were very valuable in understanding the required policy directions needed for the reform of patent law from the participants' perspectives, showing how they weighed the costs and benefits for themselves, and the extent to which they trusted in the change to a TRIPS-compliant pharmaceutical patent system.

1.8 Chapter Summary

This book is structured in five chapters. Chapter 1 offers an overall summary. It also includes a statement of the importance of this research regarding its contribution to the existing body of research, background information about the TRIPS Agreement, an introduction to pharmaceutical patents and a description the research method adopted.

Chapter 2 focuses on the situation in Bangladesh and contains an overview of the current patent law and the pharmaceutical industry of Bangladesh. In focusing on Bangladesh, the opportunities and challenges for the pharmaceutical industry are presented in the context of the requirement for TRIPS-compliant patent law. The chapter also examines the effect of TRIPS on the pharmaceutical regulation and pricing of drugs, considering the situation before TRIPS and possible implications of the introduction of TRIPS and pharmaceutical patents.

Chapter 3 examines the situations in Brazil, China, India and South Africa with reference to the options these countries have used in their progress to TRIPS compliance. This forms the basis of the analysis of possible options for Bangladesh to proceed to TRIPS compliance.

Chapter 4 presents the policy options identified in the research as an outcome of the globalising standard of patent protection in WTO law. There are two categories of policy options. The first involves a focus on various legislative changes that will be required to the existing patent law of Bangladesh; the second focuses on potential governmental/

policy interventions and discusses changes in policy direction that may be needed.

Chapter 5 discusses the infrastructure and institutional issues that are needed for LDCs such as Bangladesh—while implementing TRIPS successfully—to progress towards innovation and graduate from the LDC category. The chapter concludes by summarising this work's contributions to knowledge and the options for further research in relevant fields.

2. Case Study on Bangladesh's Pharmaceutical Industry, Legislative and Institutional Framework and Pricing of Pharmaceuticals

2.1 Introduction

This chapter discusses the legislative framework for patents and the pharmaceutical sector, including the role of regulatory bodies, and the nature and strength of the pharmaceutical industry in Bangladesh. Developing countries and LDCs are apprehensive[1] about strong patent protection, considering that patent protection may be harmful to the nascent stage of their pharmaceutical industries and may have negative implications for access to medicines by their populations. However, Bangladesh and other LDCs could continue production of the generic versions of patented medicines until 1 January 2033. Based on the data gathered by way of case study, this chapter explores the situation in Bangladesh along with the challenges and opportunities for the pharmaceutical industry during the waiver period. This chapter suggests that in the case of Bangladesh, the main health bottleneck is neither patents nor drugs, but rather the lack of proper health care services, health infrastructure and efficient health care personnel. Again, most of the necessary drugs for the local market are off-patent, but patented drugs and the related issues of price, availability and affordability could become a concern for Bangladesh in situations of

---

1   See generally, Vandana Shiva, *Protect or Plunder* (Zed Books, 2001) and Edwin Mansfield, 'Patents and Innovation: An Empirical Study', *Management Science* 32.2 (1986): 173–81.

          http://dx.doi.org/10.11647/OBP.0093.02

multi-drug resistance and in relation to diseases like HIV-AIDS, cancer and cardio-vascular problems. This is why it is vital that Bangladesh should adopt intellectual property policies for pharmaceuticals that not only meet societal goals for accessibility and affordability, but also promote innovation and the capability of local industries.

2.2 Legislative Framework: Pharmaceutical Patents and Pharmaceutical Regulation

Considering that Bangladesh may need to devise a proper plan of action during the transition period to initiate proper institutional and infrastructural capacity building, it is important to understand existing legal and institutional mechanisms for dealing with pharmaceutical patents, and to identify their limitations and weaknesses.

2.2.1 Patent Regime: Patent Law and the Patent Office

Bangladesh inherited its patent law from the British Government during its rule in India, which was subsequently divided into the three countries of India, Pakistan and Bangladesh.[2] Bangladesh essentially

---

2   Patent law in the Indian subcontinent, including Bangladesh, has its origin in the 19th century, when it was under the rule of the British East India Company. The first legislation relating to patents was enacted in 1856 as *Act VI of 1856* and was based on the *British Patent Law of 1852*. Subsequently the power to rule the Indian subcontinent was transferred from the East India Company to the British Crown via the *Government of India Act, 1858*. New legislation for granting "exclusive privileges" for invention was introduced in 1859 as *Act XV of 1859*. This legislation contained certain modifications of the earlier legislation, namely the grant of exclusive privileges solely to useful inventions and the extension of the priority period from 6 months to 12 months. However, this Act excluded importers from the definition of inventor, and was also substantially based on the *British Patent Act of 1852* with certain departures, which included allowing assignees to make applications in India and also taking prior public use or publication in India or the UK for the purpose of ascertaining novelty. Later the British Government enacted the *Patents and Designs Protection Act of 1872* and the *Protection of Inventions Act of 1883*. These two Acts were consolidated into the *Inventions and Designs Act of 1888*. Finally abolishing the earlier patent laws, the Indian *Patents and Designs Act, 1911* (PDA) was enacted, consolidating all the patent and design issues, including the establishment of the Office of Controller of Patents and Designs. Bangladesh adopted the same law as established by the *Patents and Designs Act of 1911*, and Bangladesh's law remains unchanged today. See Mohammad Monirul Azam, 'Globalising Standard of Patent Protection in WTO and Policy Options for the

retains the colonial law; only a few minor amendments have been made since the enactment of the legislation. Although Bangladesh's IP laws are often considered outdated and their enforcement is viewed as weak,[3] Bangladesh has never been on the US Trade Representatives' *Special 301 watch list*. Either it is not considered a feasible threat for economic loss or there is an understanding with the trade bodies in Bangladesh for future compliance with the TRIPS Agreement.[4]

The present legislative regime relating to patents and the pharmaceutical industry comprises the *Drugs Act, 1940*, the *Patent and Designs Act, 1911* (PDA) and the *Patent and Design Rules, 1933*. In 2003, amendments were made to the PDA to establish the Department of Patents, Designs and Trademarks (DPDT). The DPDT is controlled by the Ministry of Industries and has the jurisdiction to issue patents and designs.[5] The current patent law in Bangladesh is largely the same as it was in India, prior to changes in 1970.[6]

In common with other countries, Bangladesh follows a process for granting patents and has certain criteria for "something" to be patented: novelty, an inventive step and industrial application.[7] When an application is made by the first and true inventor or an assignee/legal representative, an examination of the specification commences. An examination of the specification can trigger one of three outcomes: (i) the specification is correct and the invention is patent-worthy, (ii)

LDCs', *Chicago-Kent Journal of Intellectual Property* 13.2 (2014): 402–88. See also, Controller General of Patents, Designs and Trademarks (CGPDT), India, *History of Indian Patent System*, http://ipindia.nic.in/ipr/patent/patents.htm

3   Mohammad Monirul Azam, 'Journey Towards WTO Legal System and the Experience of Bangladesh: The Context of Intellectual Property' (Paper accepted for presentation at the Society of International Economic Law 2010 Conference, International Economic Law and Policy [IELPO], University of Barcelona, 2010).

4   This list identifies countries that deny what the US Trade Representatives consider adequate and effective protection for intellectual property rights. For details, see USTR, *Special 301 Report, 2009*, 10 July 2010, https://ustr.gov/about-us/policy-offices/press-office/reports-and-publications/2009/2009-special-301-report

5   See 'Innovation and Competitive Capacity'.

6   Ibid.; Sampath pointed out that current patent law in Bangladesh is similar to Indian patent law post-1970, which was followed until the introduction of TRIPS-compliant patent law in 2005. In fact, India introduced process patenting and other restrictive measures and prohibited product patents in 1970. However, Bangladesh has never introduced these changes in its patent law; rather, it has tried to encourage local industry by way of separate pharmaceutical regulation under its *Drugs Control Ordinance, 1982* (DCO).

7   WTO, *Intellectual Property and Bangladesh*, p.270.

the specification does not reflect any new invention and is therefore rejected, or (iii) the specification is accepted subject to modification or amendment. There are provisions for appeal to the registrar and further to the High Court Division of the Supreme Court. Any amendments or modifications may be made to the original patent under an application for patents of addition.[8] If such an application is successful without objection, or if an objection is found to be unjustified, the DPDT will issue a certificate of patent registration. Once granted, a patent is valid for 16 years from the date of application.[9]

There have been disputes among scholars in Bangladesh about the patentability of pharmaceutical products under the PDA.[10] Some consider that the patenting of pharmaceutical processes, but not of pharmaceutical products, should be adopted in Bangladesh.[11] Other scholars argue that in the absence of a clear legislative provision or any court ruling on the distinction between processes and products, both pharmaceutical products and processes are patentable under the PDA.[12] To some extent this is a purely academic debate, as in 2008 the DPDT suspended the patenting of pharmaceuticals in Bangladesh until 1 January 2016 or until the end of the TRIPS waiver periods in accordance with the Doha Declaration.[13] The DPDT's notification stipulates that applications relating to patents for medicines and agricultural chemicals will be preserved in a "mailbox" to be considered after the expiration of the waiver periods for the pharmaceutical patent.

Prior to the suspension, the available information indicates that from 1998 to 2007, patent applications and patents granted in Bangladesh

---

8   PDA (Bangladesh), section 15A.

9   PDA (Bangladesh), section 14.

10   Section 2(10) of the PDA provides that the term "manufacture" includes any art, process or manner of producing, preparing or making an article, and also any article prepared or produced by manufacture. See also Md Mahboob Murshed, 'Trips Agreement and Patenting of Pharmaceutical Products', *The Daily Star* (Dhaka), 3 August 2006, http://archive.thedailystar.net/law/2006/08/03/index.htm (accessed by searching the Internet Archive index).

11   Ulrike Pokorski da Cunha, *Study on the Viability of High Quality Drugs Manufacturing in Bangladesh* (commissioned by Deutsche Gesellschaft für Technische Zusammenarbeit [GTZ] GmbH, 2007), https://www.unido.org/fileadmin/user_media/Services/PSD/BEP/en-high-quality-drugs-bangladesh-2007.pdf

12   Murshed (2006).

13   Jashim Uddin Khan, 'New Patent Rights of Drug Suspended', *The Daily Star* (Dhaka), 14 March 2008, http://www.thedailystar.net/news-detail-27621

increased two times more than in previous periods and that 90% of those patents were owned by MNCs.[14] In 2007, the DPDT registered 269 foreign patent applications, of which 50% related to multinational pharmaceutical formulas.[15] Table 2.1 shows the numbers and types of patents granted in Bangladesh from 1995 to 2012, highlighting that patent applications in Bangladesh increased significantly from 1998. This trend continued until the 2008 suspension in granting pharmaceutical patents. Most of the applications filed belong to foreigners and multinational corporations (MNCs).[16] It is suggested that nearly 50% of the patents during this period (until 2007) refer to pharmaceutical patents.[17]

The number of granted patents decreased after 2007 because of the suspension of pharmaceutical and agrochemical patents by the DPDT, but overall patent applications increased between 2007 and 2012. It was confirmed by one official at the DPDT that most applications still relate to pharmaceutical and agrochemical products.[18] Although the DPDT formally suspended pharmaceutical and agrochemical patents from 2008, available records at the DPDT show that since 2006, DPDT has transferred a good number of pharmaceutical and agrochemical products to the mailbox due to the lack of clear legal provisions for pharmaceutical products in Bangladesh. Table 2.2 includes a number of mailbox applications for pharmaceutical and agrochemical products between 2006 and June 2013.

---

14   Nazmul Hasan, 'General Secretary, Bangladesh Association of Pharmaceuticals Industries General Secretary', *The Daily Star* (Dhaka), 14 March 2008, http://www. thedailystar.net/story.php?nid=27621

15   Ibid.

16   Md Farhad Hossain Khan and Yoshitoshi Tanaka, 'IP Administration and Enforcement System Towards Modernization of IP Protection in Bangladesh and a Comparison of the IP Situation between Japan and Bangladesh', *IP Management Review* 2 (2004): 1–11.

17   See 'New Patent Rights of Drug Suspended'; Mohammad Monirul Azam and Yacouba Sabere Mounkoro, 'Intellectual Property Protection for the Pharmaceuticals: An Economic and Legal Impacts Study with Special Reference to Bangladesh and Mali: A Course' (a course Paper submitted as a partial requirement for the Legal and Economic Foundations of Capitalism, MS in Law, Economics and Finance, IUC, December 2008), http://legriotdudeveloppement.blogspot. se/2012/06/intellectual-property-protection-for.html

18   Interview with an official of the Department of Patents, Designs and Trademarks (DPDT), Dhaka, Bangladesh, 24 January 2013.

Table 2.1: Patent applications and granted patents in
Bangladesh (1995–2012)

	Patent applied for			Patent granted		
Year	Local	Foreign	Total	Local	Foreign	Total
1995	70	156	226	6	74	80
1996	22	131	153	18	52	70
1997	46	119	165	15	61	76
1998	32	184	216	14	126	140
1999	49	200	249	26	122	148
2000	70	248	318	4	138	142
2001	59	236	295	21	185	206
2002	43	246	289	24	233	257
2003	58	260	318	14	208	222
2004	48	268	316	28	202	230
2005	50	294	344	21	161	182
2006	22	288	310	16	146	162
2007	29	270	299	27	269	296
2008	60	278	338	01	36	37
2009	55	275	330	28	103	131
2010	55	287	342	20	71	91
2011	32	274	306	06	79	85
2012	65	289	354	14	139	153

Source: Department of Patents, Designs and Trademarks, Dhaka, Bangladesh, 2013.

Of the mailbox applications (see Table 2.2), more than 90% related to pharmaceuticals. The great majority of applications were submitted by MNPCs.[19]

---

19   Email interview with a deputy registrar of the DPDT, Dhaka, Bangladesh, 19 July 2013.

Table 2.2: Mailbox applications (pharmaceutical and agrochemical products)

Year	Number of applications
2006	111
2007	221
2008	183
2009	143
2010	123
2011	118
2012	94
2013 (June)	26

Source: Department of Patents, Designs and Trademarks, Dhaka, Bangladesh, 2013.

The reason for the smaller number of patent applications from local (i.e. Bangladeshi) researchers and research institutions is directly related to the low level of research conducted in Bangladesh; the lack of technical and financial resources to do innovative research; the low priority given to research and patenting by both research institutions and the government; and a low level of awareness about the benefits of patents among researchers, research institutions and industry.[20] In terms of capacity to effect any change, the DPDT cannot yet accept online applications (relying on paper copies and the manual processing of applications), and its (single) office is located in the capital city of Bangladesh—Dhaka. Consequently, researchers or research institutions working outside of Dhaka have limited or no access to the DPDT.[21] In addition to the role of the Patent Office and the PDA, the legislative and

---

20 Mohammad Monirul Azam and Kristy Richardson, 'Pharmaceutical Patent Protection and TRIPS Challenges for Bangladesh: An Appraisal of Bangladesh's Patent Office and Department of Drug Administration', *Bond Law Review* 22.2 (2010a): 1–15.

21 Mohammad Monirul Azam, *Status of Intellectual Property Teaching in Bangladesh* (report submitted to WIPO) (2013).

institutional framework with respect to pharmaceuticals also requires consideration.

2.2.2 Pharmaceutical Regulations: Relevant Laws and the Regulatory Body

In Bangladesh, key legislation relating to pharmaceuticals includes (1) the *Drugs Act, 1940* and its amendments (the *Drug Rules, 1945* and the *Drug Rules, 1946*); and (2) the *Drugs (Control) Ordinance, 1982* (DCO 1982) and its amendments [*Drug (Control) (Amendment) Ordinance, 1984* and *Drugs (Control) (Amendment) Act, 2006*].

The DDA, the national regulatory authority (NRA) in Bangladesh, was established in 1976 under the Ministry of Health and Family Welfare. The DDA was empowered to regulate Bangladesh's 838 manufacturers of allopathic, Unani, Ayurvedic, herbal and homeopathic, and biochemical products.[22] It was upgraded in January 2010 and became the Directorate General of Drug Administration (DGDA).[23] The DGDA is responsible for dealing with the production, quality, registration, safety, efficacy, import, export and distribution of pharmaceuticals based on the power delegated to it by the different pharmaceutical regulations. Figure 2.1 lists the milestones that marked the gradual development of the pharmaceutical regulatory framework in Bangladesh.

The *Drugs Act, 1940* regulates the import, export, manufacture, distribution and sale of pharmaceuticals in Bangladesh. The Act was originally enacted by the Government of India in 1940, was adopted by the Government of Pakistan in 1957 and then subsequently adopted in Bangladesh in 1974.

---

22   See for details, Jude Nwokike and H.L. Choi, *Assessment of the Regulatory Systems and Capacity of the Directorate General for Drug Administration in Bangladesh* (submitted to the US Agency for International Development by the Systems for Improved Access to Pharmaceuticals and Services [SIAPS] Program) (Arlington, VA: Management Sciences for Health, 2012).

23   Although the Directorate of Drug Administration (DDA) was upgraded to the Directorate General of Drug Administration (DGDA) in 2010, most government documents are yet to be replaced with the new name; thus, DGDA and DDA are used interchangeably throughout the study, which does not signify any major differences between the activities of the former DDA and the current DGDA.

Figure 2.1: Milestones in the gradual development of pharmaceutical regulation in Bangladesh

1940	*Drugs Act* (XXIII of 1940)
1945	*Drug Rules, 1945* (under the *Drugs Act, 1940*)
1946	*Bengal Drugs Rules, 1946*
1966	Gazette of Pakistan: Office of the Chief Controller of Imports and Exports. Public Notice, 1966
1970	Dacca Gazette, Part I: Government of East Pakistan, Health Department Notification, 1970
1976	Directorate of Drug Administration (DDA), the national regulatory authority for drugs, is created
1982	*Drugs (Control) Ordinance, 1982, Drugs (Control) (Amendment) Ordinance, 1982,* and *National Drug Policy, 1982*
1984	*Drugs (Control) (Amendment) Ordinance, 1984*
1992	Institute of Public Health produces tetanus vaccines First edition of the National Formulary published
2001	WHO approves oral cholera vaccine tested at the International Centre for Diarrhoeal Disease Research, Bangladesh (ICDDR-B)
2002	ICDDR-B studies establish that zinc treatment of diarrhoea reduces under-5 mortality by 50%
2003	Second edition of the National Formulary published
2005	*National Drug Policy, 2005*
2006	*Drug (Control) Ordinance Amendment Act, 2006* Third edition of the National Formulary published
2009	South-East Asia Regional Office/Department of Family and Community Health/Immunization and Vaccine Development mission to discuss institutional development plan to build DDA capacity
2010	DDA upgraded to the Directorate General of Drug Administration (DGDA) WHO mission to assess pharmaceuticals in healthcare delivery in Bangladesh
2012	*Revised New Drug Policy, 2012* drafted and submitted for approval
2016	DGDA has sent their recommendations for the proposed *Drug Act 2016* and *Drug Policy, 2016* to the Ministry of Health and Family Welfare.

Source: Nwokike and Choi, p.21 (2012).

The *Drugs Act, 1940* permits the import of certain classes of pharmaceuticals only under licenses or permits issued by the relevant authority appointed by government.[24] All classes of pharmaceuticals imported into the country are required to comply with the prescribed standards and must be labelled and packed in the prescribed manner.[25] Similarly, licenses are required for the manufacture, sale or distribution of pharmaceuticals.[26] Further control over manufacturing and sales is exercised by periodic inspection of licensed premises.[27] Surveillance of the standard of pharmaceuticals is maintained by taking samples from pharmaceuticals that are manufactured or offered for sale, for testing in the Central Drugs Laboratory.[28] The Act also establishes a Drugs Technical Advisory Board and a Drugs Consultative Committee. The Drugs Technical Advisory Board advises the government on technical matters arising from the enforcement and administration of the Act, whereas the Drugs Consultative Committee was established to advise the government and the board to ensure the proper application and functioning of the Act throughout the country. Both the Drug Technical Advisory Board and Drug Consultative Committee work as complements to the DGDA, which is the only responsible regulatory body in Bangladesh for licensing the production of medicines, controlling ongoing production and, if necessary, withdrawing licenses.

As the DGDA is responsible for the registration of pharmaceuticals, it needs to conduct inspections of pharmaceutical plants to ensure

---

24 *Drugs Act, 1940* (Bangladesh), Chapter III.

25 Section 8(1) of the *Drugs Act, 1940* provides that the expression "standard quality", when applied to a drug, means that the drug complies with the standard set out in the schedules of the Act. Section 10 of the Act prohibits the import of certain drugs, such as (a) any drug not of standard quality, (b) any misbranded drug, and (c) any drug, for the import of which a licence is prescribed, otherwise under, and in accordance with, such licence etc.

26 *Drugs Act, 1940* (Bangladesh), Chapter IV.

27 *Drugs Act, 1940* (Bangladesh), §§ 21–22.

28 Section 35 of the *Drugs Act, 1940* provides that "no patent or proprietary medicine or pharmaceutical specialty or any other medicine, whether allopathic, Unani, and Ayurvedic (forms of traditional medicines), homoeopathic or biochemic, for the time being not recognised by the accepted pharmacopoeias shall be offered for sale to the public or advertised for such sale, unless two samples thereof shall have been sent to the Director Central Drug Laboratory, and the latter shall have determined that the medicine or specialty is suitable or proper for use by the public".

quality and efficacy of medicines licensed for distribution in the local market and also for exporting overseas. It also issues licenses for the import of raw materials for different pharmaceuticals and packed pharmaceuticals. The DGDA monitors quality control parameters of marketed pharmaceuticals through the Drug Testing Laboratory, which is located within the Institute of Public Health at Mohakhali, Dhaka, and is equipped with standard testing facilities.

There are 33 district (regional) offices of the DGDA situated in different district headquarters (regions) in Bangladesh. All officers of the DGDA function as "drug inspectors" pursuant to drug legislation, and they assist the licensing authority in properly discharging their responsibilities.[29] In addition, "a number of committees, such as the Drug Control Committee (DCC), a standing committee for procurement and import of raw materials and finished drugs, a pricing committee and a number of other relevant expert committees are there to advise the licensing authority and to advise on matters related to pharmaceuticals".[30]

However, the DGDA needs qualified technical staff to monitor quality, safety and efficacy of pharmaceuticals produced by pharmaceutical companies in Bangladesh, as well as pharmaceuticals imported, registered and sold in pharmacies across Bangladesh. The DGDA itself has acknowledged that it does not have sufficient staff to monitor all domestic manufacturers.[31] During the surveys for this study, most of the local pharmaceutical companies either strongly agree (50%) or agree (27%) that the DGDA maintains the quality of medicines produced in Bangladesh. However, one large and another medium-sized local pharmaceutical company and also three large multinational pharmaceutical company operating in Bangladesh disagree about the role of the DGDA in maintaining the quality of medicines. Table 2.3 reflects the position of different sized pharmaceutical companies regarding the role of the DGDA.

---

29   See DGDA for details, http://www.dgda.gov.bd/index.php/downloads/background
30   Ibid.
31   Bangladesh Pharmaceutical Market, Q 2, 2010 (Espicom Business Intelligence, 2010).

Table 2.3: Survey results relating to whether the DGDA adequately controls the quality of medicines produced in Bangladesh

Scale	Pharmaceutical industry (large, medium and small local industry) or multinational (*n*)				Total	%
	Large	Medium	Small	Multinational		
Strongly agree	3	3	5	0	11	50
Agree	1	5	0	0	6	27
Unsure	0	0	0	0	0	0
Disagree	1	1	0	3	5	23
Strongly disagree	0	0	0	0	0	0

Although survey data indicate that the majority of participants agreed regarding the role of the DGDA for maintaining the quality of medicines in Bangladesh, the actual situation of quality control by the DGDA is not satisfactory. One top executive of a leading pharmaceutical company in Bangladesh said that most of the leading pharmaceutical companies and the Bangladesh Association of Pharmaceutical Industries (BAPI) rarely raise the issue of inadequacy of the quality control by the DGDA as there is an apprehension that this claim could have a negative effect on their pharmaceutical exports.[32] However, he further added that most of the export-intensive pharmaceutical companies in Bangladesh maintain strict internal quality control with respect to the guidelines of the WHO and of the importing countries.[33] The overall situation of the DGDA with respect to quality control is well reflected by the following remarks of an expert in another study:

> if we say that DDA is not maintaining and monitoring quality of medicine in Bangladesh that will have negative impact on our exports whereas if we say it is working properly that is also not the reflection of true

---

32   Interview with the Chief Executive Officer (CEO) of a leading pharmaceutical industry in Bangladesh.

33   Ibid.

scenario as they don't have sufficient institutional and technical facilities to monitor huge number of pharmaceutical companies operating in Bangladesh therefore most of consumers in the local market rely on the reputation of the company to determine good quality or less quality of a particular medicine.[34]

In 2009, the Government of Bangladesh reorganised the DGDA to provide it with more financial and technical resources and more administrative power so that it could work more efficiently. To some, these promised developments have yet to materialise.[35] Apart from the weak role played by the DGDA, the *Drugs Act, 1940* has been criticised as grossly inadequate for the control of prices of pharmaceutical raw materials and processed pharmaceuticals. It also largely failed to prevent the appearance of substandard and spurious pharmaceuticals on the market, unethical promotion, and the proliferation of harmful and useless pharmaceuticals.[36] To address these weaknesses, the Government of Bangladesh introduced amendments to the *Drugs Act, 1940* and the *Drug Rules* of 1945 and 1946 to provide further regulation relating to labelling and packing, biologicals, and other special products. Also in 1982, Bangladesh formulated its first *National Drug Policy, 1982* (NDP 1982) and enacted the *Drug Control Ordinance* (DCO 1982), which broadened the power of the DDA beyond the operation of the *Drugs Act, 1940*.

The prime objective of the NDP 1982 was to ensure that procurement, local production, quality control, distribution and utilisation of all drugs came under unified legislative and administrative control.[37] The NDP was intended to be the uniform policy for both the private and public sector, and for both the traditional and modern medical systems.[38] It was framed to work as an integral part of national health policy to

---

34   Quoted in Mohammad Monirul Azam, 'The Impact of TRIPS on the Pharmaceutical Regulation and Pricing of Drugs in Bangladesh: A Case Study on the Globalising Standard of Patent Protection in WTO Law' (unpublished PhD thesis, University of Bern, 2014), p.182.

35   Interview with a staff member of the DDA, Dhaka, Bangladesh, 23 December 2009.

36   Zafarullah Chowdhury, *The Politics of Essential Drugs: The Makings of a Successful Health Strategy: Lessons from Bangladesh* (Zed Books Ltd., 1995), p.49.

37   Ibid., p.59.

38   Ibid.

promote access to affordable medicine and healthcare for all. The major recommendations of the NDP 1982 were as follows:

- There should be a basic list of 150 essential drugs and a supplementary list of 100 specialised drugs to be prescribed by specialists and consultants.

- The 45 most essential drugs among the list of 150 drugs that are used by government healthcare centres at the rural level were to be manufactured and/or sold under their generic names only.

- A National Formulary incorporating all formulations of essential and supplementary drugs was to be prepared and published not later than 1983. This was one of the most important initiatives to promote the use of generic drugs, because at that time most physicians relied on the drug promotion literature supplied by pharmaceutical companies to prescribe medicines; most of the time patients were prescribed costly branded medicines despite the availability of cheaper generic versions on the local market.[39]

- Product patents in respect to pharmaceutical substances should not be allowed. Process patents could be allowed for a limited period, if only the basic substance was manufactured within the country. However, this was not formally adopted in national patent law in Bangladesh until 2008. In 2008, due to pressure from local pharmaceutical companies and public health non-governmental organisations (NGOs), a notification in the *Official Gazette* of the DPDT prohibited pharmaceutical patents until 1 January 2016, utilising the Doha waiver for pharmaceutical patents for LDCs.

- To ensure good manufacturing practice (GMP), each manufacturing company should employ qualified pharmacists. No manufacturer should be allowed to produce drugs without adequate quality control practice. However, small national drug manufacturers might be allowed to do this on a collective basis.

- A properly staffed and equipped National Drug Control Laboratory with proper facilities was to be set up as early as possible as and no later than 1985.

- The government was to control the prices of finished drugs as well as raw materials, packaging materials and intermediates. The maximum retail price (MRP) of finished drugs was to be determined

---

39   Ibid., pp.117–19.

on the basis of cost of production and reasonable profit. The DDA
was to be responsible for the control of pricing and its enforcement.

- Multinational companies would not be allowed to manufacture
  simple products such as common analgesics, vitamins, antacids, etc.
  These were to be manufactured exclusively by local pharmaceutical
  firms.

- The *Drugs Act, 1940* was to be revised and replaced by new drug
  legislation with provision for a system of drug registration and
  control: control over prices of finished products and raw materials,
  and over the manufacture and sale of drugs.

The DCO 1982 was enacted to meet the objectives of the NDP 1982.
The DCO 1982 regulates the manufacture, import, distribution and sale
of pharmaceuticals in Bangladesh; promotes the local pharmaceutical
industry; and discourages imports of medicines.[40] According to the
DCO 1982, (i) no medicine of any kind can be manufactured for sale or
be imported, distributed or sold unless it is registered with the licensing
authority; (ii) no drug or pharmaceutical raw material can be imported
into the country except with the prior approval of the licensing authority;
(iii) the licensing authority cannot register a medicine unless such
registration is recommended by the DCC; (iv) the licensing authority
may cancel the registration of any medicine if such cancellation is
recommended by the DCC on finding that such a medicine is not safe,
efficacious or useful; (v) the licensing authority is also empowered to
temporarily suspend the registration of any medicine if it is satisfied
that such a medicine is substandard; (vi) the government may, by
notification in the *Official Gazette*, fix the maximum price at which any
medicine may be sold and at which any pharmaceutical raw material
may be imported or sold; (vii) no person is allowed to manufacture any
pharmaceuticals except under the personal supervision of a pharmacist
listed in Register "A" of the Pharmacy Council of Bangladesh; (viii) no
person, being a retailer, is allowed to sell any pharmaceutical without
the personal supervision of a pharmacist listed in any register of the
Pharmacy Council of Bangladesh; and (ix) the government may, by

---

40 Interview with a policy analyst from a leading public health NGO, in Dhaka,
Bangladesh, 12 February 2009.

notification in the *Official Gazette*, establish drug courts as and when it considers necessary.[41]

Further, the DCO 1982 introduced a rigorous enforcement framework for manufacturing, importing, distributing and selling unregistered products or counterfeit medicines, with penalties of imprisonment for up to 10 years and fines. It specifically introduced the following issues:

- Dealing in substandard medicines is punished with imprisonment for up to five years and fines.

- Importing raw materials without prior approval is punished with imprisonment for up to three years and fines.

- Selling or importing medicines at prices higher than the maximum price fixed by the government is punished with imprisonment for up to two years with fines.

- Illegal advertisement and claims are punished with fines.

- Drug courts and related procedures were established for enforcing penalties.

The *Drug (Control) (Amendment) Ordinance, 1984* defines the process to appeal against an order or decision made by the regulatory authority.

The NDP 1982 and DCO 1982 resulted in substantial benefits for Bangladesh: in particular, they facilitated the increase in local production of essential drugs from 30% to 90%; furthermore, they helped local companies to gain a substantial market share of 97% of local needs, and as a result reduced the prices of medicines substantially in the local market.[42] They also reduced the dependence on imports and, through prioritisation of useful products, helped Bangladesh to save approximately US$600 million.[43] The DCO 1982 has also contributed markedly to the improvement in quality of medicines and resulted in the reduction of substandard drugs from 36% to 9%.[44]

---

41   DCO 1982 (Bangladesh), § 23.
42   See for details, *The Politics of Essential Drugs*; and The World Bank, 'Public and Private Sector Approaches to Improving Pharmaceutical Quality in Bangladesh', 15 (March 2008),   http://www-wds.worldbank.org/external/default/WDSContentServer/WD SP/IB/2008/09/01/000334955_20080901071115/Rendered/PDF/451900NWP0Box31u ality0no2301PUBLIC1.pdf
43   *Assessment of the Regulatory Systems*, p.11.
44   *The Politics of Essential Drugs*, p.50.

In a 1992 study by the DDA, based on the nominal retail prices of 30 important drugs in Bangladesh, 10 years after the introduction of the NDP and DCO in 1982, it was revealed that the retail prices of most drugs produced locally showed a downward trend from 1982 to 1992, or at worst were static.[45] During that time, the minimum price decrease was 23.1% and the maximum decrease was 96.8 %.[46] However, among the 30 most important drugs reviewed in the DDA study, the prices of a small number of drugs including aspirin, paracetamol, ampicillin, amoxicillin, cloxacillin, antacids and chloroquine increased.[47] Therefore, the NDP and DCO of 1982 were successful in partially meeting the objectives of reducing prices of medicines and promoting the local production of essential medicines and the local pharmaceutical industry.

While evaluating the role of the NDP and DCO of 1982, a foreign health expert who advised on Bangladeshi policy remarked that "it was pro-people and anti-poverty, an attempt to give people access to essential drugs. The policy had flaws but it was strong and it was enforced and mobilised throughout the country. The government took on the big drug companies and won".[48] It is also worth noting that the Association of Pharmaceutical Industries in Bangladesh initially opposed the adoption of the NDP and related ordinance in 1982, but later appreciated the policy, which is rightly reflected by Zafarullah Chowdhury, the prime mover and shaker behind the NDP in 1982:

> the pharmaceutical association of Bangladesh which had fought tooth and nail against the NDP since 1982 suddenly printed a full page newspaper advertisement in several dailies declaring that '... the ordinance [the DCO 1982] represents a philosophy whose scope extends beyond the need of today into the realms of the future ... it has been applied, tested and has to its credit today many examples of beneficial aspects' ... in the

---

45 Ibid, p.51.

46 Ibid.

47 The first four of these drugs are manufactured from locally produced raw materials. Local pharmaceutical companies believe this was due to the introduction of a 15% value-added tax on locally produced raw and packaging materials.

48 Quoted in Oxfam, *Make Vital Medicine Available for People—Bangladesh* (25 July 2010), http://policy-practice.oxfam.org.uk/publications/make-vital-medicines-available-for-poor-people-bangladesh-112437

advertisement association showed by means of graphs the substantial drop in imports but dramatic growth in local production.[49]

However, since the introduction of pharmaceutical patents under the TRIPS Agreement, and due to substantial progress in pharmaceutical production in the meantime, the NDP and DCO need to be updated to mediate between the country's obligation to become TRIPS compliant and the local need to preserve the pharmaceutical industry and public health goals. Notably, combination pharmaceuticals are not considered therapeutically useful and are therefore not allowed in Bangladesh.[50] This was a useful simplification when the DCO was drafted; however, nowadays it is obsolete and hampers the manufacturing of useful (often patented) combination therapies.[51]

The Government of Bangladesh formulated the NDP 2005 to wipe out the limitations of the earlier regulations. The NDP 2005 was formulated to take advantage of the opportunities available to Bangladesh during the transition period leading to the implementation of TRIPS. The NDP was again revised and reformulated in 2012. In particular, and relevantly, the policy was formulated with the following objectives:

1) to guide the drug sector of the country to perform better in the competitive world market;

2) to make it more applicable, effective and adaptive to the remarkable technological advancements that have been made in the medicine world;

3) to ensure that the common people have easy access to useful, effective, safe and good-quality essential and other drugs at affordable prices;

4) to make the country a producer and exporter of good-quality drugs in the world;

5) to strengthen the DGDA with more efficient manpower and infrastructure facilities, making it more effective as a drug regulatory authority (DRA);

---

49   *The Politics of Essential Drugs*, pp.185–89.
50   Ibid.
51   Ibid.

6) to provide, on a priority basis, required services and facilities to local drug manufacturing industries of all the recognised systems of drugs so that self-sufficiency is attained in the manufacture of both drugs and pharmaceutical raw materials;

7) to update, from time to time, the criteria for registration of import of all systems of medicines in line with the quality guidelines followed in developed countries to ensure the safety, efficacy and usefulness of such medicines;

8) to encourage all local and foreign companies to manufacture good-quality essential drugs in adequate quantities in the country;

9) to continue the current system of controlling prices of the commonly used essential drugs as listed and updated from time to time by the government;

10) to encourage foreign companies to invest, manufacture and sell drugs in Bangladesh with the corresponding assurance of the transfer of new technology and technical knowledge to the country;

11) to ensure that no discrimination occurs between local and multinational companies with manufacturing plants in Bangladesh, while applying the principles of this policy;

12) to encourage both local and multinational manufacturers to establish full-fledged R&D facilities in the country.[52]

The implementation of the above policy measures in anticipation of future TRIPS-compliant patent law is crucial for Bangladesh, considering the present situation and future challenges for its pharmaceutical industry. Unfortunately, apart from policy revision, there is little policy action on the part of the government to encourage investment, public-private partnership, joint research, institutional support and modernisation in the pharmaceutical sector. These are very important components to ensure that the interests of Bangladesh's pharmaceutical producers and investors are balanced, and that there is progression of local innovation against the need to ensure access to pharmaceuticals for the local population in a post-TRIPS-compliant regulatory environment.

---

52   *National Drug Policy, 2005* (Bangladesh), 14 July 2010, http://apps.who.int/medicine docs/documents/s17825en/s17825en.pdf

2.2.3 Changes Required in Patent Law and Pharmaceutical Regulation in Bangladesh

Existing patent law and pharmaceutical regulation in Bangladesh does not utilise exceptions and limitations available under the TRIPS Agreement to protect public health. Therefore, the laws need to be revised to ensure the right balance between pharmaceutical innovation and access to medicines after the introduction of pharmaceutical patents. In addition, some existing limitations need to be removed from domestic patent law and pharmaceutical regulations to maintain the principle of non-discrimination and compliance with the TRIPS Agreement.

In Bangladesh, existing pharmaceutical regulations and patent law impose certain limitations on pharmaceuticals. For instance, pharmaceutical patents (both product and process) are prohibited in Bangladesh until expiration of the pharmaceutical patent waivers under the TRIPS Agreement.[53] There are also other limitations, such as restrictions on the manufacture of certain medicines;[54] import of certain drugs manufactured in Bangladesh and of pharmaceutical raw materials;[55] marketing approval and licensing;[56] local production

---

53 During interviews, officials at the DPDT and DGDA confirmed the prohibition of pharmaceutical patents in Bangladesh until the country graduates as an LDC or the TRIPS waiver period elapses, whichever is earlier.

54 Section 8 of the DCO 1982 (Bangladesh) prohibits the manufacture, import, distribution and sale of certain medicines as follows: "8. Prohibition of Manufacture, etc, of certain medicines.—(1) On the commencement of this Ordinance, the registration or licence in respect of all medicines mentioned in the Schedules shall stand cancelled, and no such medicine shall, subject to the provisions of sub-section (2), be manufactured, imported, distributed or sold after such commencement".

55 Import restrictions are laid down in section 8 for certain pharmaceuticals, mostly those manufactured in Bangladesh. Section 9 of the DCO 1982 (Bangladesh) lays down import restrictions for pharmaceutical raw materials as follows: "9. Restriction on import of certain pharmaceutical raw material—(1) No pharmaceutical raw material necessary for the manufacture of any medicine specified in any of the Schedules shall be imported. (2) No drug or pharmaceutical raw material shall be imported except with the prior approval of the licencing authority. (3) The licencing authority may award an approval under sub-section (2) on such conditions as it deems fit to specify".

56 Section 10 of the DCO 1982 (Bangladesh) stated that with the approval of the licensing authority (DGDA) a foreign manufacturer may be allowed to manufacturer any drug only under licensing agreement with any manufacturer

facilities;[57] ingredients;[58] advertising;[59] and test data.[60] These limitations either need to be removed or revised to meet the requirements of the TRIPS Agreement. Table 2.4 demonstrates that a number of changes need to be in place as part of moves towards TRIPS compliancy.

Bangladesh has made substantial progress in promoting local production of essential drugs by way of prohibiting pharmaceutical patents and putting restrictions on the import and production of drugs by MNCs that are produced locally. One participant who was interviewed appreciated the positive effects of these restrictions: "during (the) 1980s, 80% of local pharmaceutical market was controlled by MNCs, but now more than 80% of local market is controlled by the local generic producers".[61]

Therefore, there is serious apprehension that Bangladesh's withdrawal of these restrictions may have negative effects on the local market. One participant during an interview mentioned that "in principle if there is any patent on a particular product, it cannot be produced by the local generic producer without permission from the patent holder and without paying royalties, which will increase the price of pharmaceuticals".[62]

However, the "National Formulary", which contains brief descriptions of all the pharmaceutical products produced in Bangladesh, shows that almost 90% of the pharmaceuticals produced in Bangladesh are off-patent; therefore, introduction of pharmaceutical patents may not create any problems for the generic production of these pharmaceuticals.

---

in Bangladesh if the drug is its research product and is registered under the same brand name in any of the countries specified in the DCO.

57　See sections 8, 9 and 10 of the DCO 1982 (Bangladesh).

58　Only single ingredient products are allowed for production and distribution in Bangladesh.

59　Without the prior approval of the DDA, it is not possible to publish any advertisements relating to the use of any drug or any claim with respect to therapies or treatment. See section 14 of the DCO 1982 (Bangladesh).

60　There is no test data protection in Bangladesh.

61　Interview with an expert from an international public health NGO, Dhaka, Bangladesh, 15 January 2012.

62　Interview with a deputy registrar from the DPDT, Dhaka, Bangladesh, 16 January 2012.

Table 2.4: Changes required for TRIPS-compliant pharmaceutical regulation in Bangladesh

Issues	Existing pharmaceutical regulation in Bangladesh	Changes needed for TRIPS compliance
Product patent for pharmaceuticals	Currently, pharmaceutical patents are prohibited	Both process and product patents for pharmaceuticals need to be introduced
Duration of patent protection	Currently, patent law provides protection for only 16 years	Protection should be extended to 20 years
Local production facilities and local working	Certain pharmaceutical products are excluded from licensing unless made in local production facilities by MNCs	It is not mandatory to have a local production facility but there is debate regarding local working provisions as a grounds for issuing compulsory licenses
Import restrictions	Import restrictions on pharmaceuticals and pharmaceutical raw materials that are locally produced: if an item is not on the DDA's essential drug list but is produced by at least three local companies, it may not be imported	No import restrictions whether locally produced or not as this would be discriminatory and hence a violation of WTO and TRIPS principles
Marketing approval restrictions	Marketing approval is not granted to MNCs if a particular pharmaceutical product is locally produced	No restrictions on the marketing based on products made locally or imported
Production restrictions	MNCs are not allowed to produce some drugs, such as vitamins and antacids	There must not be any restriction as this would be discriminatory
Single ingredient	Only single-ingredient products are allowed for production and distribution in the local market	Combination drugs need to be allowed
Advertising restrictions	No advertising is allowed on pharmaceutical products	Although unethical advertising may be restricted, advertising must be allowed
Test data protection	There is no test data protection for pharmaceuticals	There may be pressure from the MNCs and developed countries like the US and the EU for the introduction of test data protection

Another participant mentioned that Bangladesh has tried to promote local pharmaceutical production by imposing restrictions under the pharmaceutical regulations rather than by prohibiting pharmaceutical patents expressly under the national patent law; therefore, the removal of these restrictions will have a severe effect on the pharmaceutical business in Bangladesh.[63] He provided the example that in the absence of import restrictions, "if any importer can offer lower price for any particular product then the local producer will be under pressure to reduce price; otherwise they will have to lose the market, as being a low income country, price is the most important factor to choose a particular product".[64]

From the perspective of consumers, the removal of restrictions may increase competition in the market and may even reduce the price of some pharmaceutical products. One participant during an interview also mentioned that a "TRIPS-compliant regime will lead to an increase in the flow of technology transfer and FDI [foreign direct investment] in Bangladesh and will result in the development of new drugs more suited to the needs of Bangladesh. It will also help Bangladesh to transform from 'copycats' to innovative companies".[65]

However, one participant argued that "in Bangladesh people have distrust regarding MNCs as they charged very high prices for medicines prior to 1982 (before the introduction of DCO 1982), taking advantage of low-level technological and manufacturing capacities of local pharmaceutical companies".[66]

As Bangladesh needs to introduce pharmaceutical patents and the above-mentioned changes need to be made to existing pharmaceutical regulations and patent law, there is fear among stakeholders in Bangladesh that these changes will have a serious negative effect on the pricing of medicines in the country. Considering this great apprehension regarding the viability of the pharmaceutical industry and the negative consequences for drug prices, it is important to examine the status of

---

63 Interview with the CEO of a medium-size local pharmaceutical company, in Dhaka, Bangladesh, 17 January 2012.

64 Ibid.

65 Interview with a marketing manager from a multinational pharmaceutical company (MNPC) operating in Dhaka, Bangladesh, 21 January 2012.

66 Interview with a policy analyst from a leading public health NGO in Bangladesh, 24 January 2012.

the pharmaceutical industry in Bangladesh, and the likely effect of patenting pharmaceuticals on the pricing of drugs.

2.3 The Pharmaceutical Industry in Bangladesh

The pharmaceutical industry of Bangladesh began in the 1950s when a few multinationals and local entrepreneurs set up manufacturing facilities in what was then East Pakistan. Now 265 companies are listed with the DGDA as producing medicines in Bangladesh.[67] The pharmaceutical industry is currently the second largest taxpayer and meets 97% of local pharmaceutical requirements.[68]

2.3.1 The Nature and Size of Firms

The pharmaceutical industry in Bangladesh is represented by all three sectors: private enterprises, the state-owned Essential Drug Company Limited and *Ganashastha Kendra* (as a civil society based public health research and policy center and also essential medicine producer).[69] Among the 265 pharmaceutical entities registered for the production of various types of formulations under the DGDA of Bangladesh, some 154 are regular in operation according to the DGDA. On the other hand, BAPI (or *Bangladesh Aushad Shilpa Samity* in Bengali), established in 1972 with just 33 members, has also been playing a vital role in the development of this sector. Today, BAPI is a very strong organisation with as many as 144 companies as members. However, only 20–30 companies have large manufacturing units, including five MNCs that have their own manufacturing plants in Bangladesh. There are two joint venture companies: Roche Healthcare and Sun Pharma. Sun Pharma, an Indian company, began its operation in partnership with

---

67   See DGDA, Bangladesh, 13 June 2013, http://www.dgda.gov.bd/index.php/ 2013-03-31-05-16-29/drug-manufacturers/allopathic

68   The remaining 3% consists of imported hi-tech products such as insulin, other hormonal products, anti-cancer products and blood components/derivatives infusions. See Sayedul Islam, *Bangladesh Zooms in Pharma as Priority Sector* (27 July 2006), http://saffron.pharmabiz.com/article/detnews.asp?articleid=34473&sectio nid=50

69   *Study on the Viability of High Quality Drugs Manufacturing.*

one local company. Although 265 companies have a valid license from the government, around 25 local companies dominate 86% of the total market. MNCs account for roughly 5% of the market.

Table 2.5: Allopathic pharmaceutical companies in Bangladesh

Nature/type of company	Number	Quality control practice
World class, large scale	5	Maintain international standards
Multinationals	5	Maintain international standards
Export oriented, medium scale	15	High standard in quality control
Local market oriented, medium scale	40	Satisfactory standard in quality
Small scale	80	Substandard quality
Licensed-oriented pharmaceutical company	120	Incomplete production unit

Source: Information collected from the Bangladesh Association of Pharmaceutical Companies, the Directorate General of Drug Administration, the Export Promotion Bureau of Bangladesh and the Board of Investment Bangladesh, 2012.

In addition to the 265 allopathic companies mentioned in Table 2.5, 201 Ayurvedic, 268 Unani, 25 herbal and 79 homeopathic drug manufacturing companies operate in Bangladesh. The DGDA monitors and regulates the activities of all 838 companies.

2.3.2 Competitive Scenario

It is notable that the pharmaceutical market in Bangladesh is now mostly dominated by local players. The top 10 selling companies are Bangladeshi, so competition mostly occurs among these companies. Table 2.6 provides a brief summary of the top 10 pharmaceutical companies in Bangladesh in 2014. Among the local companies, Square Pharmaceuticals is the largest firm in the market, followed closely by

Incepta, Beximco, Opsonin, Renata and Eskayef.[70] Other firms in the top 10 list include Aristopharma, ACI, ACME and Healthcare.[71] The market is extremely concentrated: the top 10 firms cater to about 68.1 % of the market, and two companies, Square and Incepta, hold more than 28% of the entire market. The top 20 companies represent around 85%, and the next 11 firms 8.60%, of the total market.[72]

Table 2.6: The top 10 pharmaceutical companies in Bangladesh (2014)

Position	Company	Sales (billion taka)	Market share (%)	Growth (%)
1st	Square	21.15	18.7	7.3
2nd	Incepta Pharma	11.78	10.4	15.6
3rd	Beximco	9.56	8.5	7.6
4th	Opsonin Pharma	6.35	5.6	19.8
5th	Renata	5.74	5.1	13.5
6th	Eskayef	5.09	4.5	12.0
7th	Aristopharma	5.07	4.5	15.7
8th	ACI	4.69	4.1	9.9
9th	ACME	4.51	4.0	14.1
10th	Healthcare	3.09	2.7	35.4

Some of the world's leading MNCs have also worked in Bangladesh for a long time, but due to the high value of products, limited product lines and strong local competition, they have not climbed to leading positions in Bangladesh. These include some of the world's pharmaceutical giants, such as GlaxoSmithKline (GSK) (UK), Sanofi Aventis (Spain), Novartis (Switzerland), Novo Nordisk (Denmark)

---

70   IMS Health data, 2014.
71   Ibid.
72   IMS Health data, 2014 and statistics from DGDA, 2014.

and Eli Lilly (US). Table 2.7 provides a comparison of the performance of these top five MNCs in Bangladesh.

Table 2.7: Top five Multinational pharmaceutical companies operating in Bangladesh (2014)

Company	Sales (billion taka)	Market share (%)	Growth (%)	Industry position (2014)
Sanofi Bangladesh	2.19	1.94	7.66	12
Novo Nordisk	2.04	1.81	–1.99	14
GlaxoSmithKline	1.79	1.59	5.93	17
Novartis	1.76	1.56	28.45	18
Sandoz	1.45	1.28	21.09	20

2.3.3 Local Sales, Export and Import

The pharmaceutical market in Bangladesh was worth US$1.5 billion in 2011 and it is still expanding.[73] Pharmaceuticals are estimated to be the third largest industry in the country, and account for 1.3% of the country's Gross Domestic Product (GDP) and 40.9 % of its total healthcare expenditure. According to Business Monitor International, the pharmaceutical market size will reach US$2.27 billion by 2016.[74]

The Bangladeshi pharmaceutical marketplace is predominantly a branded generic marketplace. Pharmaceutical companies in Bangladesh can sell to private sector pharmacies, the government and its public healthcare facilities, and to international organisations operating in Bangladesh (e.g. the United Nations Children's Fund [UNICEF]). Government sales are less profitable than private sector sales, since

---

73   See for details, K. Saad and Safwan, 'An Overview of the Pharmaceutical Sector in Bangladesh' (Brac EPL Study, Dhaka, Bangladesh, May 2012).

74   See *Business Monitor International*, Bangladesh Pharmaceuticals and Healthcare Report Q4, 2012.

the government pays less and only on consignment. However, pharmaceutical firms still target public facilities as those doctors then become familiar with the drugs and prescribe them in their private practices. As drugs are not readily available at public facilities, patients receiving treatment in any public or private hospital may need to go to the private pharmacy to procure the required drugs.

In addition to meeting local needs, Bangladesh exports a wide range of pharmaceutical products (therapeutic class and dosage forms) to 92 countries[75] in Asia, Africa and Europe. In 2006–07 total exports were US$28.12 million with a growth rate of around 47%.[76] Bangladesh also exports specialised products like HFA (hydro-fluoro-alkaline) inhalers, suppositories, hormones, steroids, oncology and immunosuppressant products, nasal sprays, injectable and IV (intra-venous) infusions.[77] Many of the larger manufacturers in Bangladesh are now venturing into the production of anti-cancer drugs, anti-retroviral (ARV) drugs for the treatment of HIV/AIDS[78] and anti-bird flu drugs. Some of the most stringent regulatory authorities in the world have approved Bangladeshi pharmaceutical products for export.[79] Table 2.8 shows that pharmaceutical exports from Bangladesh rapidly increased between 1975 and 2006.

Other statistics also reflect that pharmaceutical exports from Bangladesh are rapidly increasing every year. The statistics for drug exports from Bangladesh between 2006 and 2011 are as follows: 2006, 2663.39 million taka; 2007, 2477.41 million taka; 2008, 3277.19 million taka; 2009, 3471.69 million taka; 2010, 3813.50 million taka; and 2011, 4212.25 million taka.

---

75 Directorate of Drug Administration, Bangladesh, 10 June 2014, http://www.lightcastlebd.com/blog/2015/12/market-insight-how-the-bangladesh-pharmaceutical-sector-is-performing-in-2015
76 See, Azam and Richardson (2010a): 6.
77 Ibid.
78 Ibid.
79 For example, the Gulf Central Committee for Drug Registration, the Therapeutic Goods Administration of Australia, the medicines and healthcare products regulatory agencies of the UK and United States (US) food and drug administrations. These bodies have already issued good manufacturing practice clearance to many local pharmaceutical companies in Bangladesh.

Table 2.8: Pharmaceutical exports from Bangladesh (1975–2006) in US$ (millions)

	1975	1980	1985	1990	1995	2000	2002	2003	2004	2005	2006
Pharmaceutical exports	0.37	0.15	0.04	0.12	2.74	5.61	6.60	9.05	12.69	21.26	27.54
Total exports	382.6	749.3	934.4	1523.7	3427.5	5752.2	5986.1	6548.4	7603.0	8651.5	10,514.0
Pharmaceutical exports as a percentage of total exports	0.097%	0.020%	0.004%	0.008%	0.080%	0.098%	0.110%	0.138%	0.167%	0.246%	0.262%
Pharmaceutical export growth rate		−59%	−73%	200%	2183%	105%	18%	37%	40%	68%	30%

Source: World Bank Study on the pharmaceutical industry in Bangladesh, 2008.

Although the Government of Bangladesh declared the pharmaceutical industry to be a "thrust sector" and actively promotes pharmaceutical exports, the exporters of pharmaceuticals from Bangladesh need to cope with the following constraints and impediments:

- reliability of drugs produced in Bangladesh and bad image of substandard drugs[80]

- absence of a "bio-equivalence test facility" in the country[81]

- delay in issuing a "Free Sale Certificate" by the NRA[82]

- export registration procedures for drugs in highly regulated importing markets like Europe and the US are very complex[83]

- lack of information on registration and other regulatory formalities in importing countries[84]

- inordinate delays and bureaucratic hassles during Customs procedures for shipment of samples[85]

- inadequate funds for overseas sales and market promotion[86]

- absence of adequate export incentives[87]

- lack of support and cooperation by the foreign missions and offices of the Government of Bangladesh[88]

- difficulty in finding reliable distributors/agents in importing countries[89]

Although pharmaceutical companies in Bangladesh provide finished pharmaceutical products for the local market and for export to so many countries, local companies still rely mostly on imported raw materials. More than 750 basic raw materials, including packing materials, are imported into Bangladesh for use by local pharmaceutical companies.

---

80 *Bangladesh: World Pharmaceutical Market,* Q2 2010, Espicom Business Intelligence Report 2010.

81 Interview with a Bangladesh Association of Pharmaceutical Industries (BAPI) official, 15 March 2009.

82 Interview with a BAPI official, Dhaka, Bangladesh, 16 March 2009.

83 United Nations Conference on Trade and Development (UNCTAD)/World Trade Organization (WTO), *Bangladesh: Supply and Demand Survey on Pharmaceuticals and Natural Products, International Trade Centre* (September 2005).

84 Ibid.

85 Interview with a BAPI official, Dhaka, Bangladesh, 16 March 2009.

86 Ibid.

87 Ibid.

88 Ibid.

89 *Bangladesh: Supply and Demand Survey.*

Two categories of raw materials imported into Bangladesh are active ingredients/basic materials and excipients.

In Bangladesh, pharmaceutical products (including raw materials) are imported mostly from India, China, Italy, Germany, Switzerland and France. Other important sources of imports are Japan, Korea, Singapore, Austria, Belgium, Cyprus, Denmark, Greece, Hungary, Netherlands, Ireland, Spain, the UK and the US. It is argued that almost 85% of the required raw materials are imported, whereas the percentage of imported finished products is negligible—around 3% of total consumption in the local market.

However, a number of packing materials used by local companies are now produced locally, and these include cartons, product literature, white bottles, empty syringe/injectable, strips, cork, plastic containers and droppers, among others. Imported packing materials include aluminium foil, coloured bottles, foil (blister and strip), alu alu, rubber stoppers, flip-off seals, tear-off seals, tubes, PVC, PVDC, and so on.

2.3.4 Production Capacity and Range

Pharmaceutical companies in Bangladesh manufacture around 450 generic drugs for 5300 registered brands with 8300 different strengths and dosages. These include a wide range of products such as anti-ulcerants, fluoroquinolones, anti-rheumatic non-steroid drugs, non-narcotic analgesics, antihistamines and oral anti-diabetic drugs. Some larger firms are also starting to produce anti-cancer and ARV drugs.[90]

Among the registered companies, 35–40 local companies— including five MNCs—are in regular operation and produce products as recommended by the national DCC and the DGDA. Among the MNCs, Aventis, GSK, Organon and Novartis have manufacturing plants in Bangladesh, while Sun Pharmaceutical and Roche Healthcare are operating as a joint venture in Bangladesh. 20 of these companies, including MNCs, are experiencing tough competition in the local market.

---

90   Board of Investment, Bangladesh, *Market Overview: Bangladesh is Poised for Major Growth in its Pharmaceutical Industry*, http://www.boi.gov.bd/site/page/7b31 d826-368c-4ed9-8077-d16310433060/Life-Science

Among the available 450 generic products, 117 are essential and controlled drugs, and 333 are decontrolled products.[91] Although most of the active pharmaceutical ingredient (API) is imported, 21 local companies are now producing API at a "limited range and mostly intermediate in nature".[92] The main customers for this limited production are other local companies producing various types of formulations. Square, Beximco, Opsonin, Jayson, Remo Chemicals, Drug International, Gonoshastha, Globe, Pharmatek, Seftchem, Syripsn and Global Capsules are prominent suppliers of limited API in the local market.

More than 40 different types of active ingredients are produced by local companies. These include oral rehydration solution, paracetamol BP, amoxicillin trihydrate/powder, ampicillin compacted/powder, cloxacillin sodium BP, cefalexin trihydrate compacted, EG shell, diclofenac sodium, empty hard gelatine, sodium chloride, potassium chloride, parasulphate and zinc sulphate, among others. Another 4–5 companies have begun new projects to produce active ingredients in groups such as cephalosporin, macrolide antibiotic, anti-ulcerative and anti-inflammatory. One company has set up a plant to produce anti-cancer and hormonal products.

Any pharmaceutical product produced locally by at least three local pharmaceutical companies is not allowed to be imported. Private importers, agents and distributors directly import necessary goods, and market and distribute them through their own distribution channels. The end users are unable to import directly any product for their own use, as product registration is mandatory before import, except under certain conditions.[93]

Any prospective manufacturer/importer has to apply in prescribed form for product registration and certifications, and must provide the following information:

- name and address of the manufacturer
- manufacturing license number

---

91 *Bangladesh: Supply and Demand Survey.*
92 Interview with a BAPI official, Dhaka, Bangladesh, 15 March 2009.
93 Government departments are not importing formulations other than basic materials. International humanitarian agencies and organisations are importing formulations occasionally for direct supply to end users. No NGO imports formulations, but they do import raw materials (Ganashastha Pharmaceuticals).

- list of drugs
- proposed MRP
- estimated treatment cost (daily and full course)
- product data sheet
- technical data sheet
- pharmaceutical data sheet
- toxicological data sheet
- clinical data sheet
- report on environmental impact assessment/analysis
- names of the existing manufacturers and market size
- bio-data on the production, factory and quality control manager

Another important issue for the pharmaceutical industry is the technology used for pharmaceutical research and production.

2.3.5 Use of Technology

The leading pharmaceutical companies have been able to adopt advanced technology from developed countries. Pharmaceutical companies in Bangladesh have product development teams that continuously undertake R&D activities, mostly related to reverse engineering activities rather than basic research to make new inventions. Common R&D activities undertaken by the local pharmaceutical industry are:[94]

- bibliographic searches aided by resource libraries
- design and selection of process-maximising efficiency
- environmental impact assessment reduction
- accelerated and longer stability testing
- product quality optimisation
- translation of new scientific insights into products

However, several companies have been conducting studies on vaccines for critical diseases, such as cancer and diabetes, in collaboration with foreign experts. Many studies are also being carried out to produce

---

94 *Bangladesh: Supply and Demand Survey.*

herbal medicines. Formulations development is ongoing in many companies irrespective of their size.

There has been good progress in raw materials development in collaboration with Western countries. Test methods are developed and validation is done according to the British Pharmacopoeia and the United States Pharmacopeia. Stability studies and validation of processes are also undertaken for new formulations.

As packing materials and packaging are very important for export marketing, companies with considerable exports take extra care to use modern and standard packaging systems with attractive printing materials and convenient storage and handling options. However, as per the existing price control system, no company can claim an extra cost for attractive packaging.

So far, there are no research findings on the "new molecule" in Bangladesh, which may become a great drawback after the introduction of pharmaceutical patents. As pharmaceutical companies are not improving their innovative capacity, it will become difficult for them simply to rely on producing generic medicines in the long term.

2.3.6 Innovation Capacity and Research and Development

During the survey, most pharmaceutical companies in Bangladesh agreed that local pharmaceutical companies do not invest enough in R&D to make new medicines. The findings of the survey on patenting and innovative capacity among pharmaceutical companies in Bangladesh are briefly described below.

Large, medium and small pharmaceutical companies in Bangladesh all suggested that they do not have any new inventions or patents.[95] Some large-scale companies mentioned that they had begun basic research, with a view to preparation for the post-TRIPS product patent regime.[96] Some medium-sized and small companies mentioned that they are considering utilising traditional knowledge to make country-specific

---

95   This was agreed by all the large, medium and small pharmaceutical companies that
       were surveyed in Bangladesh.
96   This was mentioned by two large local pharmaceutical companies during surveys.

traditional medicines as an alternative in a post-TRIPS regime.[97] On the other hand, multinationals operating in Bangladesh stated that they have new inventions and patented pharmaceuticals elsewhere, some of which were also patented in Bangladesh prior to 2008. However, none of them were interested in disclosing details or discussing any possible effects of those patented pharmaceuticals in Bangladesh.[98]

Table 2.9 reflects that 50% of the participants in the survey strongly agreed that Bangladesh has no capacity to produce new medicines; 36% also agreed with this statement, whereas 14% disagreed.

Table 2.9: Survey results regarding whether Bangladesh has the capacity to produce new medicines

Scale	Pharmaceutical industry (large, medium and small local industry) or multinational				Total	%
	Large	Medium	Small	Multinational		
Strongly agree	2	2	4	3	11	50
Agree	2	5	1	0	8	36
Unsure	0	0	0	0	0	0
Disagree	1	2	0	0	3	14
Strongly disagree	0	0	0	0	0	0

During the interviews, an official from a multinational pharmaceutical company operating in Bangladesh stated that they have no innovative capacity in the local manufacturing unit, although they have many patents that are mostly based on their R&D in developed countries.[99]

---

97   This was mentioned by four medium and two small local pharmaceutical companies during surveys.
98   During interviews, representative from three MNCs discussed their innovation outside of Bangladesh and some patent applications in Bangladesh. However, none of them disclosed any further information during surveys or interviews.
99   Interview with an official from an MNPC operating in Dhaka, Bangladesh, 12 March 2009.

Although pharmaceutical researchers in Bangladesh consider it possible to improve innovative capacity in Bangladesh, most of the local pharmaceutical companies think only about quick cash profit rather than long-term investment for R&D.[100] Therefore, researchers suggest that the government should provide the necessary funds for some basic research in the pharmaceutical sector.[101]

At present, applying for new pharmaceutical patents is also impossible in Bangladesh, as patent protection for pharmaceuticals is not allowed until 1 January 2016. This in itself creates a barrier for the local pharmaceutical industry in Bangladesh and will become a huge impediment in a post-TRIPS environment. Tension is evident between the current capacity of the industry (pre-TRIPS position) and its potential to develop and change. Samson H Choudhary, the then CEO of Square Pharmaceuticals, commented in 2009 that the NDP, while encouraging local industry, removed the incentive for technological advancements.[102]

Unfortunately, there appears to be no incentive to increase and encourage investment in R&D. No government initiatives are in place to support or promote R&D. The failure to support and promote R&D is potentially a major barrier to the post-TRIPS survival of the pharmaceutical industry in Bangladesh.

2.3.7 Government Incentives for Supply of Raw Materials and Exports

The Government of Bangladesh introduced a flat rate of duty of 7.5% on the import of raw materials in 1997. Pharmaceutical products produced from imported raw materials for ultimate export enjoy "duty draw back facilities". Locally procured raw materials enjoy the "value-added tax refund" benefit if the products are exported. To date, there is no special incentive for export production.

---

100 This was mentioned by two pharmaceutical researchers from the Department of Pharmacy, University of Dhaka, interviewed 12 March 2009.

101 Ibid.

102 As stated during the Bangladesh Pharmaceutical Expo, 22 January 2009.

There exists no provision for cash incentives for pharmaceutical export, such as tax reduction or low interest rates for investment loans from governmental financial institutions. However, this issue has been repeatedly discussed within the government and among stakeholders. Exporters are actively pursuing this cash incentive to remain competitive in the export market. For finished goods, the expected rate of cash incentive is 20%, and for raw materials to be used for export it is 30%. However, existing export policy in Bangladesh offers incentives that are applicable to all exporters, including pharmaceutical companies, such as exemptions from value-added tax (VAT) of 15% on products produced for export, tax exemptions for corporate export income, export credit guarantees for pre-shipment and post-shipment.

To further develop the pharmaceutical export sector, skilled human resources will be a crucial element.

2.3.8 Human Resources

In Bangladesh, there exists a pool of qualified professionals and experts engaged in the pharmaceutical industry sector. Leading local pharmaceutical companies have their own ongoing "product development research", although this is mostly limited to reverse engineering rather than basic research for new innovation. Every company hires a number of pharmacists, sonologists and chemists who obtained their higher education from local universities and then undertook advanced degrees in developed countries. Technologies adopted in Bangladesh were introduced by multinationals and have been steadily replicated by local professionals. This sector now employs the highest number of science graduates in Bangladesh. There is also a strong pool of business graduates and management professionals working in the pharmaceutical industry who are expert in sales and marketing at both local and international levels.

Moreover, the suppliers of pharmaceutical items regularly provide demonstrations of technology and technical know-how to local staff for their professional development. However, local universities in Bangladesh providing instruction in pharmacology, microbiology, chemistry, biochemistry and other related subjects lack adequate clinical laboratories and practical facilities to train their graduates with modern technologies and to provide them with the necessary tools to do innovative research. There is also no practical link or collaboration between the local pharmaceutical industry and the universities, the establishment of which should be considered seriously for the future supply of skilled and innovative manpower in local industry, and for future collaborative innovative research to enable the transition of local industry from copycat to innovative practices.

2.4 (Potential) Effects of Pharmaceutical Patents on the Pricing of Drugs in Bangladesh

In Bangladesh, prior to the introduction of DCO 1982, the prices of pharmaceuticals were very high. Due to a number of limitations introduced under the DCO 1982, the prices of pharmaceuticals were substantially reduced in Bangladesh. There is concern in Bangladesh that pharmaceutical prices will increase substantially after the introduction of pharmaceutical patents and the removal of the restrictions imposed under the DCO 1982. Some pharmaceutical companies even claim that prices have already increased in Bangladesh since the introduction of TRIPS-compliant patent law in India and China, as Bangladesh depends on them for the supply of raw materials.[103]

However, a researcher working in one of the leading pharmaceutical companies remarked that patent protection for pharmaceuticals in China and India will have no effect on the price of raw materials in Bangladesh.[104] He further added that price may become a concern only if the local market becomes dependent on a particular drug patented in India, China or another country, or on a drug solely distributed by multinationals.[105] He claimed that the increase in the price of raw materials is sometimes used as a pretext to increase the price of drugs.[106]

---

103 Interviews with the CEOs of a medium-sized local pharmaceutical company and another leading pharmaceutical company, Dhaka, Bangladesh, 22 December 2008.

104 Interview with a pharmaceutical researcher from a leading local pharmaceutical company, Dhaka, Bangladesh, 23 December 2008.

105 Ibid.

106 Ibid.

However, during the survey (see Table 2.10), most participants—particularly local large, medium and small pharmaceutical companies in Bangladesh—either agreed (54%) or strongly agreed (23%) that TRIPS has influenced the rise of pharmaceutical prices. Representatives of some local pharmaceutical companies mentioned that they are still unsure about this, whereas all the multinationals either disagreed or strongly disagreed that TRIPS will have an effect on pharmaceutical prices. To date, there have been no empirical studies or field studies in Bangladesh investigating the possible effect of TRIPS on pharmaceutical prices. Survey participants here confirmed that they can provide no conclusive evidence regarding a price increase due to TRIPS and indicated that price increases were based on assumptions regarding the situation in other countries.

Table 2.10: Survey results on whether TRIPS has influenced the rise in pharmaceutical prices

Scale	Pharmaceutical Industry (large, medium and small local industry) and multinational				Total	%
	Large	Medium	Small	Multinational		
Strongly agree	1	3	1	0	5	23
Agree	3	5	4	0	12	54
Unsure	1	1	0	0	2	9
Disagree	0	0	0	2	2	9
Strongly disagree	0	0	0	1	1	5

To understand how the patenting of pharmaceuticals may have influenced prices, local drug demand and sales in Bangladesh, I identified 10 top-ranking drugs in terms of local sales along with the brand names of the drugs and the names of the supplying pharmaceutical companies in Bangladesh (see Table 2.11). Of the top 10 drugs in terms of local sales, none were supplied by multinationals (Table 2.11). Also, none of the drugs in the top 10 are patented in Bangladesh. Even after the introduction of pharmaceutical patents, therefore, there will be no increase in price for these top 10 drugs in Bangladesh. Again, among the top 20 drugs in terms of sales, only two were supplied by multinationals, and they are also not patented in Bangladesh.[107]

Table 2.11: Top 10 drugs in terms of sales in Bangladesh*

Rank	Brand	Company	Growth (%)
1	Seclo	Square	35.05
2	Losectil	Eskayef	−6.43
3	Maxpro	Renata	22.41
4	Pantonix	Incepta	13.11
5	Cef-3	Square	13.92
6	Napa	Beximco	4.34
7	Neotack	Square	3.58
8	Napa-Extra	Beximco	12.04
9	Sergel	Healthcare	28.73
10	Zimax	Square	−4.22

*Based on the information collected from the Directorate of Drug Administration, Association of Pharmaceutical Industries, 2013–14, the Pharmaceutical Market Review in Bangladesh and IMS Health data 2013–14.

I also examined the retail prices of the 10 most important drugs in Bangladesh (in terms of responses about retail pharmaceutical sales from different pharmacies in two major cities in Bangladesh: Chittagong and Dhaka). Table 2.12 shows changes in the retail prices of these 10 important drugs in Bangladesh.

After the introduction of pharmaceutical patents in India and China (the major supplier of pharmaceutical raw materials to Bangladesh), the prices of 5 of the 10 most important products increased, 4 decreased

---

107 IMS Health data, 2014.

and 1 product's price remained stable. As all 10 products are off-patent, there should be no substantial price increase after the introduction of pharmaceutical patents and the removal of restrictions in Bangladesh.

Table 2.12: Changes in retail price of 10 important drugs
(in taka, the local currency)

Pharmaceutical product	Retail price 1981 (taka)	Retail price 1991–92 (taka)	Retail price 2009–10 (taka)	Remarks increase=I decrease=D stable=S
Amitriptyline 25-mg tablet	0.80	0.45	0.80	I
Aspirin 300-mg tablet	0.10	0.44	0.90*/0.50**	I
Atenolol 100-mg tablet	6.00	3.00	1.25	D
Cloxacilin 500-mg capsule	3.60	5.65	5.10*/5.70**	D
Cotrimoxazole tablet	2.00	0.65	1.70	I
Fursemide 40-mg tablet	0.60	0.50	0.50	S
Indomethacin 25-mg capsule	1.91	0.52	0.50*/0.90**	D
Metronidazole 200-mg tablet	0.70	0.63	0.80*/1.00** (for 400-mg tablet)	I
Paracetamol 500-mg tablet	0.25	0.52	0.50	D
Rifampicin 150-mg capsule	5.18	3.50	5.90	I

*price of local generic drug; **price of similar product offered by multinational corporations (MNCs) in Bangladesh; unless indicated, prices were similar for local and MNC products.

Source: Directorate of Drug Administration, price of pharmaceuticals, 1981 and 1991–92 and retail price 2009–10, collected from retailers' sales data records and invoices.

In this respect, it may also be important to monitor disease and the major causes of death in Bangladesh, to enable the evaluation of possible effects of TRIPS on the availability and pricing of the pharmaceuticals necessary to deal with diseases that are prevalent in Bangladesh. The main causes of death in Bangladesh are identified in Table 2.13.

Table 2.13: Causes of death in Bangladesh

	Cause of death	Prevalence (%)
1	Old age complications/senility	12
2	Asthma	6
3	Stroke/paralysis	6
4	Fever	5
5	Heart disease	5
6	Pneumonia	4
7	Diarrhoea	3
8	Hypertension	3
9	Gastritis/peptic ulcer	2
10	Diabetes	2
11	Drowning	2
12	Hepatitis B	2
13	Tuberculosis	2
14	Malnutrition	2
15	Typhoid	1
16	Tetanus after delivery	1
17	Accident/injury	1
18	Cancer	1
19	Tetanus	1
20	Anaemia	1

Source: National case studies on the institutional framework and procedures regulating access to pharmaceutical products needed to address public health problems, by Nazmul Hasan, CEO of Beximco; Health and Demographics, BBS 2000.

Table 2.14 provides statistical data about the prevalence of diseases and the proportion of mortality rates.

Table 2.14: Diseases prevalent in Bangladesh

	Disease or symptom	Proportion of mortality (%)	Prevalence per 1000
1	Fever with cold or cough	24	44
2	Fever	14	26
3	Peptic ulcer	8	15
4	Diarrhoea	5	9
5	Blood dysentery	3	6
6	Asthma	3	5
7	Arthritis	3	5
8	Hypertension	3	5
9	Waste	2	5
10	Scabies	2	4
11	Influenza	2	3
12	Malaria	2	3
13	Diabetes	1	3
14	Toothache	1	3
15	Pneumonia	1	2
16	Dengue	1	2
17	Boil	1	2
18	Typhoid	1	2
19	Senility	1	2
20	Accident	1	2

Source: National case studies on the institutional framework and procedures regulating access to pharmaceutical products needed to address public health problems, by Nazmul Hasan, CEO of Beximco; Health and Demographics, BBS 2000.

Tables 2.13 and 2.14 indicate a high percentage of imprecise diagnoses or undiagnosed illnesses, evidenced by the high prevalence of fever with no identified cause, or by ascribing deaths to "old age complications".[108]

Fever is identified as one of the prime causes of death in Bangladesh: it is an infectious disease that might be successfully treated by antibiotics, anti-malarial drugs or other medications. This suggests that in the case of Bangladesh, the main health bottleneck is not patents or drugs; rather it is a lack of proper healthcare services and/or efficient healthcare personnel.[109] The high incidence of death due to tetanus after delivery also points to the need for better healthcare staff and better-equipped healthcare infrastructure. Malnutrition (which influences both the incidence and morbidity of other illnesses) and waste may also be cases of diagnosis failure, indicating that better infrastructure is required.[110] Further, during interviews, one participant agreed that pharmaceuticals necessary for the treatment of tuberculosis (TB) and malaria are cheaper in Bangladesh compared to neighbouring countries.[111] Therefore, problems with treating malaria and TB are not related to the availability of drugs, but to the lack of proper healthcare infrastructure, particularly an inadequate number of physicians and/or testing facilities.[112]

In Bangladesh, most drugs used for prevalent diseases are off-patent; therefore, there is little possibility of a price increase for these products.[113] During interviews, one participant argued that even if there is an increase, it would actually be due to a devaluation of the local currency against a strong US dollar, causing an increase in the costs of importing raw materials.[114] There are two other contributing factors that increase pharmaceutical prices in the local market. The first is the lack of a proper energy supply, which is required to maintain high quality; thus a pharmaceutical manufacturing plant must have its own power generation. Second, investment in pharmaceutical manufacturing relies

---

108 See *Study on the Viability of High Quality Drugs Manufacturing.*
109 Ibid.
110 Ibid.
111 Interview with a policy analyst from a public health NGO in Bangladesh, 27 January 2012.
112 Ibid.
113 Interview with a patent examiner at the DPDT, Dhaka, Bangladesh, 19 January 2009.
114 Interview with a marketing and business analyst from a leading MNPC in Bangladesh, 21 January 2009.

strongly on private equity because of the relatively high interest rates in Bangladesh and the legal limitations on banks with respect to the volume of lending sums.[115]

One participant argued that even if there is an increase in price, which may not affect off-patent drugs, the price may increase only for patented drugs imported from India, China and other countries.[116] Typically, developed market therapeutical groups, such as those addressing diabetes, cardiovascular disease, allergies or psychological disorders, are among the most important in Bangladesh, whereas HIV/AIDS and anti-malarial drugs are not.[117] This is because drugs substituted for those produced by local producers are not patented in Bangladesh, so there may not be an increase of price for these drugs. However, some interviewees argued that local producers would be prevented from producing new patented drugs to be used in the treatment of these diseases.[118] As there are very few AIDS and malaria patients in Bangladesh, even if there was an increase in price for these drugs, there would be only a minimal effect on the overall access to medicines in Bangladesh. In a WHO Bangladesh report, it was reiterated that there is no significant drug availability problem in Bangladesh; most of the drugs for diseases prevalent in Bangladesh are produced by the local pharmaceutical industries.[119]

In another study, it was reported that around 85% of the drugs sold in Bangladesh are generic and 15% are patented.[120] Most of the patented drugs are in the category of new or second generation drugs addressing diabetes, cardiovascular disease, allergies or psychological disorders, sexual problems, cancer, HIV/AIDS and anti-malarial diseases.[121] As some off-patent drugs are available for these diseases, patented drugs are used only in exceptional cases, such as drug resistance or extremely critical situations.[122] However, it is argued by local experts that after the introduction of pharmaceutical patents, the prices of these patented

---

115 See *Study on the Viability of High Quality Drugs Manufacturing*.
116 Interview with a patent examiner, in Dhaka, Bangladesh, 18 January 2012.
117 Ibid.
118 During interviews, an expert on patent law in Bangladesh and a patent examiner at the DPDT, Dhaka, Bangladesh shared this concern.
119 Nwokike and Choi (2012).
120 'An Overview of the Pharmaceutical Sector in Bangladesh'.
121 Ibid.
122 Ibid.

drugs will increase and create access problems in the case of drug resistance.[123]

Considering the above situation, Bangladesh may need to develop its patent laws and pharmaceutical regulations in a way that can promote innovation and access to medicines, and at the same time preserve the local pharmaceutical industry and encourage multinationals to participate in technology transfer and invest in the pharmaceutical sector of Bangladesh.

2.5 Waiver for the Least Developed Countries and the Pharmaceutical Industry in Bangladesh: Opportunities and Challenges

Of the 48 countries classified as LDCs,[124] Bangladesh is the only one that has the pharmaceutical manufacturing capability to be (nearly) self-sufficient in pharmaceuticals.[125] Considering the manufacturing capacity of local pharmaceutical companies and the waiver for pharmaceuticals until 2033, Bangladesh has the ability and opportunity to produce generic versions of patented medications to service the pharmaceutical needs of other poor countries that have no or low manufacturing capacity.[126]

Given the extension for TRIPS compliance granted to LDCs until January 2033, Bangladesh is free to continue to permit the production of generics for patented pharmaceuticals and to allow the sale and export of generic pharmaceuticals.[127] Thus, there would seem to be no impetus to comply with TRIPS before the transition period begins. However, in saying that, generic products produced and manufactured in Bangladesh cannot be exported to other national markets where patent protection exists and the Bangladesh-based company does not have market approvals with respect to the pharmaceutical product. Consequently, during the transition period, export markets are

---

123 Interview with an expert on Pharmaceutical Technology, University of Dhaka, Bangladesh, 29 January 2012.
124 Of those 49 countries, 34 are WTO members.
125 'WTO TRIPS Agreement: Current State of Pharmaceutical Industry', pp.21–23.
126 Martin (2006).
127 Having become TRIPS compliant, countries such as India and China are no longer allowed to produce generic forms of patented drugs.

limited to those in which patent protection is not available. Arguably, opportunities need to be developed and exploited during the remaining transition period, as they may be curtailed or unavailable in a TRIPS-compliant environment. Much depends on the policy direction taken by the government. In some areas, the government has taken action to support local participation in joint ventures with foreign companies and toll manufacturing for foreign companies.

In the context of the joint venture as a possible opportunity for Bangladesh during the transition period, large foreign pharmaceutical companies from highly regulated markets are actively looking for joint venture projects in developing countries and LDCs. Several contracts have reportedly been signed between Bangladesh and certain Indian and Chinese pharmaceutical companies. Bangladesh has the ability to manufacture APIs for foreign companies for export. To that extent, the Government of Bangladesh has already taken the initiative via the NDP 2005 to set up an API park to facilitate the production of raw materials and finished products.

Similarly, toll manufacturing for foreign companies is an opportunity that should be exploited during the transition period. Toll manufacturing is a contract to manufacture a finished or semi-finished product for a client company. It is also referred to as toll processing, tolling, toll conversion, contract manufacturing or custom manufacturing, and can be defined as performing a service for a fee (toll). Toll manufacturing saves the client company capital investment, since the toll manufacturer already has the plant and equipment necessary to make the product.[128] Toll manufacturing can take advantage of financial and tax incentives available in various markets.[129] It presents an option[130] for Bangladesh, which has a very strong manufacturing base in pharmaceutical products and manufacturing costs that are lower

---

128 *What is Toll Manufacturing?* (13 May 2010), http://fhsons.tripod.com/toll.htm

129 See Nazmul Hasan in a presentation on 'Future Prospects of Pharmaceutical Industry in Bangladesh', considering the opportunity for toll manufacture with the pharmaceutical companies in Bangladesh, 12 October 2009, http://documents.mx/documents/future-prospects.html

130 The global contract manufacturing market for pharmaceuticals was U$54.54 billion in 2013 and is expected to reach U$79.24 billion in 2019, increasing at an average annual rate of 7.5%. For details see *Strong Growth Ahead for Contract Manufacturing*, http://www.pharmamanufacturing.com/articles/2016/strong-growth-ahead-for-contract-manufacturing

than in other countries.[131] The further exploitation of the compulsory licensing regime is another alternative that should be pursued by the government for exporting pharmaceuticals to markets with little or no manufacturing capacity, as suggested by the chief executives of some leading pharmaceutical companies in Bangladesh.[132] However, existing patent law in Bangladesh does not support compulsory licensing for exporting pharmaceuticals.[133] In addition, there are challenges around the risk of producing substandard products, the complexities of export registration, the lack of existing testing labs, the lack of local investment in R&D and pricing anomalies.[134] These challenges need to be overcome in the long term and require a governmental strategy to be put in place. However, at this stage, for Bangladesh, the lack of investment in R&D represents a challenge that will have a substantial effect on the local pharmaceutical industry in a TRIPS-compliant patent regime.

During the surveys, most of the pharmaceutical companies in Bangladesh agreed that local pharmaceutical companies do not have enough investment in R&D to make new medicines. The findings of the survey on patenting and innovative capacity among pharmaceutical companies in Bangladesh are briefly summarised below.

Although some large-scale companies indicated that they had begun basic research,[135] none of the local pharmaceutical companies in Bangladesh have so far contributed to any new inventions, or applied for any product patents.[136] On the other hand, multinationals operating in Bangladesh agreed that they had new inventions, but that they were patented elsewhere; some were also patented in Bangladesh prior to 2008 and some were transferred to the mailbox to be considered after the introduction of pharmaceutical patents in Bangladesh. However, during surveys and interviews, none of the respondents disclosed any

---

131 Some of the larger pharmaceutical companies in Bangladesh, such as Square and Beximco, have already begun toll manufacturing.
132 This was mentioned by the CEOs of two leading pharmaceutical companies in Bangladesh during interviews, Dhaka, Bangladesh, 10–11 March 2015.
133 A compulsory licensing regime and other required patent law reform options are explained in Chapter 4 of this study.
134 These institutional and technical options are explained in Chapter 5 of this study.
135 This was mentioned by representatives from two large local pharmaceutical companies during surveys.
136 During surveys, none of the local companies provided any information on basic research or potential pharmaceutical patent applications.

details or answered queries on the possible effects of those patented pharmaceuticals in Bangladesh.[137]

Despite the impressive growth in sales in the local market and exports of pharmaceuticals from Bangladesh over the years, there is uncertainty and tension between stakeholders (pharmaceutical companies, government officials, public health experts, and IP and pharmaceutical technology academics) with respect to two issues.[138] The first is the question of what options are available for Bangladesh to serve its local industry and meet societal demands for access to medicines, while the TRIPS pharmaceutical patent regime is being developed. The second relates to what kind of technical and institutional capacity building is necessary for Bangladesh to cope with the challenges of a post-TRIPS patent regime.

2.6 Which Way for Bangladesh?

The introduction of the DCO 1982 helped Bangladesh become self-sufficient in pharmaceutical production locally and reduce prices substantially. However, unlike India and Brazil, Bangladesh failed to encourage R&D for pharmaceutical innovation as well as imitation. Therefore, it is crucial that the country now decide what will be its best mode of operation. There are at least two options for Bangladesh: to introduce pharmaceutical patenting with effective measures for the access to medicine, or to argue for continuation of the waiver for pharmaceutical patenting, thereby avoiding a patent regime until the country reaches the threshold of innovation and qualifies for graduation

---

137 Three MNCs responded to surveys but did not provide any information on medicines they had patented in Bangladesh.

138 He considers that "pharmaceuticals' manufacturing opportunities in Bangladesh are brighter than ever because of the country's LDC status until 2016, this is a win-win situation for both Bangladesh and foreign pharmaceutical or investment companies because investors/companies will get high returns on their investment and this will create high paid jobs in Bangladesh". He adds that "the cost of medicines has increased in China and India since they entered the WTO. Bangladesh has a unique opportunity to pare the costs of manufacturing medicines due to the low-cost high-qualified manpower and its LDC status". See Hasan, Nazmul, 'Post 2005: Great time ahead for exports', *Pharmabiz* (27 January 2005), http://www.pharmabiz.com/article/detnews.asp?articleid=25953&sectionid=50&z=y

to a patent regime. In this respect, it may not be out of place to examine the advantages and disadvantages of both options.

In the context of Bangladesh, without any pharmaceutical patent regime, the advantages are cheaper generics for essential medicines. Continuing to imitate pharmaceuticals patented in other countries (as patenting of pharmaceuticals is suspended in Bangladesh until 2016) may result in profits for the local pharmaceutical industry by way of exports to non-WTO members, LDCs and countries with no patents for particular medicines. This may include the creation of more employment and the generation of more foreign income through exports, and stiff competition among the locals and multinationals operating in Bangladesh—where the consumer will have better and/or cheaper options. Again, by restricting imports of drugs that are manufactured in Bangladesh, the country can prevent foreign exchange and impose prohibition on drug promotion by multinationals, restricting them from producing certain medicines like vitamins and antacids, which will remain an exclusive business opportunity for the local industry.

However, a patent-free regime for pharmaceuticals will also have major disadvantages for Bangladesh because leading local pharmaceutical companies are more interested in export than in ensuring adequate supply in the local market. Sometimes this may create an artificial crisis, resulting in shortage of supply and charging of higher prices. Again, in the absence of a patent, there may not be any technology transfer and foreign direct investment (FDI) in the pharmaceutical sector. Further, in a situation such as multi-drug resistance, patients cannot afford costly new or patented medicines as these are not produced by the generic producers in Bangladesh. Another problem related to a prohibition on pharmaceutical patents is that local pharmaceutical companies prioritise short-term cash profit and do not invest in R&D. Thus there will be no incentive for innovative researchers and "brain drain" may increase.

On the other hand, the introduction of pharmaceutical patenting will have some advantages, and it may not create obstacles for access to the essential medicines listed by the DGDA of Bangladesh. This is because essential medicines are mostly off-patent, and multinationals may be encouraged under corporate social responsibility to make drug donations by reducing the price of new patented drugs in the local market, but only if there is a pharmaceutical patent regime. It will also encourage technology transfer and FDI in the pharmaceutical sector, and create incentives for innovative research and options for commercialisation. Again, in a situation such as multi-drug resistance, patients will have access to drug donations and reduced price medicines under the National Health Service (which is currently dysfunctional).

Further, local pharmaceutical companies will be compelled to invest in R&D or perish (with no option for quick cash) and there may be an opportunity for more joint ventures and public-private partnerships.

Nonetheless, a pharmaceutical patent regime may also have some disadvantages. It may even endanger the existence of the local pharmaceutical industry. There is an apprehension regarding higher prices for patented drugs if efforts for drug donation and bargaining for reduced prices fail. Higher prices will create a situation in which multinationals have the lion's share of the local market and the local industry is marginalised. There is also concern that there may not be any real technology transfer and FDI in the pharmaceutical sector even after the introduction of pharmaceutical patents, and that MNCs may simply become sales offices rather than manufacturing units. There will be no discrimination between imported and locally produced drugs, and local pharmaceutical companies will face serious competition. The DDA may not have the capacity to ensure the quality of all medicines, resulting in lower-quality medicines on the market. Further, the DPDT does not have enough expertise to deal with large volumes of pharmaceutical patents; therefore unnecessary patenting may restrict generic competition and encourage "ever-greening" — extending the life of a patent by making small changes.

Considering the advantages and disadvantages of the introduction of pharmaceutical patenting, it is difficult to decide which course of action will most benefit Bangladesh. The next chapter will explore the extent to which the paths taken by India, China, Brazil and South Africa under the TRIPS Agreement and other options for government intervention may be used as potential policy blueprints for LDCs like Bangladesh.

The challenges and opportunities highlighted here all require action on the part of the Bangladeshi government; government intervention lies at the centre of what may help Bangladesh to develop a TRIPS-compliant patent law that balances the (economic) interests of pharmaceutical producers with the (social) need to ensure access to pharmaceuticals for the local population.

3. The Experiences of TRIPS-compliant Patent Law Reform in Brazil, China, India and South Africa—Lessons for Bangladesh

This chapter analyses the policy options adopted by Brazil, China, India and South Africa in their transition to a TRIPS-compliant patent law and the introduction of pharmaceutical patents. This comparative review identifies potential public health-oriented policy options that use the TRIPS flexibilities as well as additional possibilities for governmental intervention, options which do not conflict with the TRIPS Agreement and can therefore be employed by LDCs like Bangladesh.

3.1 Background

The debate over the consequences of patenting essential products like medicines is not new and has taken place globally.[1] Countries have thus developed divergent approaches: some[2] have chosen to

---

1 It is relevant to note that "almost 50 developing countries, which were not granted patent protection for pharmaceuticals during the Uruguay Round, fiercely resisted including pharmaceuticals under the patent regime, claiming that vastly higher drug prices would be associated with such patents"; see 'The Introduction of Pharmaceutical Product Patents in India', p.2.; also see, for the debate on the patent system, Haiyang Zhang, 'Rethinking the Patent System from the Perspective of Economies', in *Emerging Markets and the World Patent Order*, ed. by Federick M. Abbott, Carlos M. Correa and Peter Drahos (Edward Elgar, 2013), pp.61–77.

2 Countries such as Italy, Switzerland, Brazil and India prohibited pharmaceutical patent protection for a considerable period of time to encourage "learning by imitation" and promote their local pharmaceutical industries. See 'The Impact of Higher Standards in Patent Protection', pp.1367–68.

  http://dx.doi.org/10.11647/OBP.0093.03

exempt medicines from all or parts of patent law,[3] and others, such as "Canada and Australia, have patent regimes which were moderated by mechanisms to control prices or to facilitate local production under compulsory licenses".[4] Countries such as India, South Africa and Brazil have adopted other legal means to allow competitors to circumvent the negative effects of patents, by allowing the patenting of processes but not of products.[5]

In implementing a patent law that complies with the TRIPS Agreement as adopted under the WTO, countries such as India, Brazil and South Africa were confronted with two major concerns: first, the future of their local pharmaceutical industries, and second, access to affordable medicines.[6] These countries' reactions depended largely on

---

3   Historically, product patents have been excluded from protection in most developed countries. For example, in France, product patent protection was prohibited under a law effective 5 July 1844, and only limited patent protection has been permitted since 2 January 1966. In Germany, product patents were explicitly excluded under a law effective 25 May 1877, but were then introduced on 4 September 1967. In Switzerland, product patents for pharmaceuticals were explicitly prohibited by the constitution and were only introduced in 1977. In Italy, pharmaceutical patents were prohibited until 1978. In Spain, product patents were introduced in 1986, just after the country's accession to the European Economic Community, and the relevant laws came into effect in 1992. The rationale behind not granting product patent protection for pharmaceuticals in each of the example countries was to allow local pharmaceutical companies to imitate and produce patented medicines by using new processes. See Michele Boldrin and David K. Levine, *Against Intellectual Monopoly* (Cambridge University Press, 2008).

4   See Lydia Mugambe, 'The Exception to Patent Rights under the WTO-TRIPS Agreement: Where is the Right to Health Guaranteed?' (unpublished LLM thesis, University of Western Cape, South Africa, 2002): "In an affidavit filed in support of the Treatment Action Campaign, Professor Colleen Flood of the University of Toronto explained how patent law in Canada had evolved since 1923 with the 'expressly stated goal of making food and medicine affordable to the public'. To facilitate this, various legal devices, including compulsory licensing and administrative mechanisms (the Patented Medicines Prices Review Board), were established. However, as is common in developing countries, Canada has been pressured to strengthen intellectual property protection. In contrast, in Australia, the government negotiate with industry as a monopolist purchaser and is thus able to provide drugs to the community at greatly reduced prices under a Pharmaceutical Benefits Scheme".

5   'The Impact of Higher Standards in Patent Protection', pp.1368–69.

6   K.M. Gopakumar, 'Product Patents and Access to Medicines in India: A Critical Review of the Implementation of TRIPS Patent Regime', *The Law and Development Review* 3.2 (2010): 324–68.

the nature of their pharmaceutical industry, which has both economic and social importance. However, their IPR regime was not TRIPS compliant, so these countries were confronted with the issue of how to manage the continued viability of the local pharmaceutical industry while still providing access to affordable medicines and implementing TRIPS.

India, China, Brazil and South Africa have already implemented TRIPS-compliant patent laws[7] and introduced patent protection for both pharmaceutical products and processes.[8] Those countries' experiences of utilising TRIPS flexibilities and other possible policy mechanisms have important lessons for LDCs, such as Bangladesh, that are now making progress towards TRIPS compliance and adopting pharmaceutical patents.

This chapter analyses the policy options used by Brazil, China, India and South Africa in their transition to a TRIPS-compliant patent law and in their introduction of pharmaceutical patents.

Although the TRIPS Agreement allows flexibilities, these are ambiguous and therefore need to be dealt with and implemented at the national level by considering national developmental goals, the public interest and the stage of the country's development.[9] The experiences of Brazil, India and South Africa will be examined with respect to the available TRIPS flexibilities and other governmental interventions that do not conflict with TRIPS obligations, to determine legislative and other possible policy options that LDCs like Bangladesh might adopt.

---

7   Prabhu Ram, 'India's New "Trips-compliant" Patent Regime between Drug Patents and the Right to Health', *Chicago-Kent Journal of Intellectual Property* 5 (2006): 195; Luciano Martins Costa Póvoa, Roberto Mazzoleni and Thiago Caliari, *Innovation in the Pharmaceutical Industry in Brazil Post-TRIPS*, pp.1–5, http://www.elgaronline. com/view/9781782549468.00007.xml; Bernard Maister and Caspar van Woensel, 'Is Compliance Enough: Can the Goals of Intellectual Property Rights be Achieved in South Africa?', 2 (Leiden Law School Legal Studies Research Paper Series, Working Paper, 2013), http://papers.ssrn.com/sol3/papers.cfm?abstract_id=2213263

8   Ram, p.198; Catherine Tomlinson and Lotti Rutter, *The Economic and Social Case for Patent Law Reform in South Africa* (2014), http://www.tac.org.za/sites/default/files/ The Economic and Social Case for Patent Law Reform in South Africa.pdf

9   *The WTO and Developing Countries*; and *Intellectual Property Rights: A Critical History*.

3.2 The Journey Towards TRIPS and Obligations for Patent Law Reforms

Interpreting the TRIPS Agreement and defining precise obligations for national IP law reforms is a difficult process from various perspectives. The difficulty stems from the contradiction in the rationale of TRIPS, which represents the greater protection of monopoly, and the rationale of the General Agreement on Tariffs and Trades (GATT): free trade in goods without any discrimination between domestic industry and international trade in goods and services.

The interpretation of TRIPS also relates to the interpretation of pre-existing treaties on IP, which functioned under the system of the WIPO for a long time before being incorporated into TRIPS.[10] The assessment of compliance with TRIPS often requires the detailed examination of domestic IP law and, more particularly, the effectiveness of IP protection and enforcement systems. This task seems difficult given the divergence in the traditional grounds of national legal systems in dealing with the issue of IP. When a member implements TRIPS norms into their national legislation, it certainly needs to strike the balance between compliance with TRIPS and advancing the public interest and national developmental goals. This issue gained momentum particularly with regard to the effects of TRIPS on public health. On the one hand, each WTO member had to introduce pharmaceutical patents to protect product and process patents without discriminating between domestic and multinational pharmaceutical industries, thus reforming pharmaceutical regulations that protected local generic producers. On the other hand, however, each member also had to identify policy options to ensure access to affordable medicines and so save the local generic industry.

There has been much debate and controversy regarding the merits of pharmaceutical patents as required under the TRIPS Agreement, particularly from the point of view of developing countries and the

---

10   See Mohammed El-Said, 'The Road from TRIPS-Minus, to TRIPS, to TRIPS-Plus Implications of IPRs for the Arab World', *The Journal of World Intellectual Property* 4 (2001): 57; and Carlos Correa, 'The WTO Dispute Settlement Mechanism TRIPS Rulings and the Developing Countries', *The Journal of World Intellectual Property* 4 (2001): 253–54.

LDCs. There is an assumption that the introduction of product patent protection for pharmaceuticals will lead to substantially higher prices, which will have negative effects on both public health and generic-based pharmaceutical industries in developing countries. Predictions of higher prices are made on the basis of a comparison of drug prices between countries that do and do not offer pharmaceutical patent protection. However, these comparisons may involve mistaken assumptions, as it is not clear whether the comparisons consider other demand and supply side factors—notably differences in purchasing power, market structure, distribution margins, tariffs, taxes and exchange rate fluctuations—that may also drive prices.[11] Studies on the price increase effects of pharmaceutical product patent protection have estimated price increases of up to 67%.[12] One study estimated that the availability of therapeutic substitutes might limit price increases to a low of 12% or to a maximum of 68%.[13]

Some studies have argued that the introduction of product patents is unlikely to raise significantly the prices of pharmaceuticals, because most patented products have many therapeutic substitutes.[14] It has also been claimed that the absence of patent protection has been a disincentive for research-based global pharmaceutical companies to engage in research on diseases that disproportionately afflict the world's poor. The implication is that patent protection for pharmaceuticals will actually benefit developing countries by stimulating innovation and

---

11 For example, in two earlier studies, such comparisons are made in the case of price comparisons between India and Pakistan, both of which excluded pharmaceuticals from patent protection during the relevant period. See for details, Oxfam, *Cut the Cost–Patent Injustice: How World Trade Rules Threaten the Health of Poor People* (2001) and the Human Development Report (1999), United Nations Development Program (UNDP).

12 See Keith E. Maskus and Denise Eby-Konan, 'Trade-related Intellectual Property Rights: Issues and Exploratory Results', in *Analytical and Negotiating Issues in the Global Trading System*, ed. by Alan V. Deardorff and Robert M. Stern (Ann Arbor, MI: University of Michigan Press, 1994), pp.401–54; Arvind Subramanian, 'Putting Some Number on the TRIPS Pharmaceutical Debate', *International Journal of Technology Management* 10 (1995): 252–68.

13 Carsten Fink, 'How Stronger Patent Protection in India Might Affect the Behavior of Transnational Pharmaceutical Industries' (Working Paper No. 2352, World Bank, 2000), http://elibrary.worldbank.org/doi/abs/10.1596/1813-9450-2352

14 Subham Choudhuri, Pinelopi K. Goldberg and Panle Jia, *Estimating the Effects of Global Patent Protection in Pharmaceuticals: A Case Study of Quinolones in India* (Yale University, 2004), http://www.nber.org/papers/w10159

transfer of technology.[15] However, such claims are based on scanty evidence. Very little is known about the extent to which the prices of pharmaceutical products may increase as a result of the introduction of pharmaceutical patenting.

In Bangladesh, there is great apprehension that the introduction of pharmaceutical patents and TRIPS-compliant patent law will endanger the local pharmaceutical industry and have serious negative effects on access to medicines. One interview participant even claimed that because India and China have implemented pharmaceutical patents, there will be a sharp increase in pharmaceutical prices in Bangladesh because the local pharmaceutical industry is dependent on India and China for raw materials.[16]

The TRIPS Agreement incorporates the Paris Convention (the first international convention for the protection of industrial properties, including patents, in 1883)[17] and explicitly aims to supplement the protection of industrial property rights. The "Paris-plus" included in TRIPS is regarded as an international standard patent protection system,[18] which in fact reflects the practices of developed countries.[19] TRIPS clearly defines the normative criteria for protection of patents, which was not addressed in the Paris Convention.

The TRIPS Agreement contains a number of provisions on patents; for example, Article 27 provides for patentable subject matters, Article 28 stipulates the rights conferred by a patent, Article 33 determines the terms of patent protection, and so on. The basic criteria of patentability, protection and duration of patents set forth in TRIPS are regarded as notable achievements by developed countries in elevating and

---

15   Ibid.

16   Email interview with the CEO of a leading local pharmaceutical company, in Dhaka, Bangladesh, 11 March 2009.

17   See 'Paris Convention for Protection of Industrial Property of 20 March 1883', as revised in Brussels on 14 December 1900, in Washington on 2 June 1911, at The Hague on 6 November 1925, in London on 2 June 1934, in Lisbon on 31 October 1958 and in Stockholm on 14 July 1967, http://www.wipo.int/treaties/en/text.jsp?file_id=288514

18   See Carlos M. Correa, 'Patent Rights', in *Intellectual Property and international Trade: TRIPs Agreement*, ed. by Abdulqawi A. Yusuf and Carlos M. Correa (London: Kluwer Law International, 1998), pp.50–58.

19   J. H. Reichman, 'Universal Minimum Standards of Intellectual Property Protection under the TRIPs Component of the WTO Agreement', in *Intellectual Property and international Trade: TRIPs Agreement*, pp.23–31.

harmonising the minimum standards of patent protection, which was not within the scope of the Paris Convention.[20]

Therefore, the TRIPS Agreement substantially restrains the freedom of national legislation bequeathed by the pre-existing Paris Convention regarding patent protection. TRIPS imposes a series of obligations for patent law reform that will have implications for pharmaceutical regulation in the LDCs. As Brazil, China, India and South Africa have already implemented TRIPS-compliant patent laws, therefore, this section only addresses deficiencies and challenges for patent law reforms in Bangladesh.

3.2.1 Patentable Subject Matter

Article 27.1 of TRIPS defines in general terms three patentability criteria for inventions—novelty, inventive steps and industrial application—and leaves to national legislation the freedom to legislate the detailed requirements of such criteria.[21] However, the article requires that national legislation obey the rule of non-discrimination in patent protection. Therefore, while complying with the TRIPS Agreement, patent law and pharmaceutical regulation in Bangladesh should provide equal protection for domestic and foreign pharmaceutical patent applicants and inventors.

Article 27.1 also provides that patents "shall be available for any inventions, whether products or processes, in all field of technology". A further security is added to this provision: "patents shall be available and patent rights enjoyable without discrimination as to [...] the field of technology". The combined result of these provisions is that both product and process patents should be available for pharmaceutical technologies. As a product patent was not available for pharmaceutical invention and was largely excluded by most developing countries prior to TRIPS, this provision is considered a major achievement for the developed countries.[22]

---

20   Ibid.
21   See Chapter 4 of this study for further details on patentability criteria.
22   See for details, UNCTAD-ICTSD, 'Resource Book on TRIPS and Development' (Cambridge University Press, 2005).

Prior to TRIPS and during TRIPS negotiations, concerns about increased prices for patented pharmaceuticals and accessibility to pharmaceutical technology, and a strong campaign by NGOs and public interest groups, were the main reasons for the opposition of developing countries to patent protection for pharmaceutical products.[23]

However, under Article 27.1, national patent law can no longer justify this kind of exclusion from patentability due to the requirement for non-discrimination in the field of technology of invention. Pursuant to Article 27.1: "patents shall be available ... without discrimination as to the place of invention". Accordingly, any discrimination concerning patent applications made by nationals and foreigners is contradictory to the requirement of non-discrimination as to the place of the invention.

Although the Paris Convention does not mention patentability or particular exclusions from patentability, TRIPS enumerates concrete criteria for these contents.[24] Unlike the situation under the Paris Convention, national laws under TRIPS are required to conform to specific criteria regarding patent protection. With regard to this point, TRIPS removes much of the freedom conferred by the Paris Convention on national legislation.

Therefore, the *Patents and Designs Act, 1911* and the DCO 1982 of Bangladesh need to be altered to include clear provisions on pharmaceutical processes and product patent protection. In addition, existing pharmaceutical regulations must remove product restrictions on the multinational pharmaceutical industry.[25] However, the norms of patentability allow for some exceptions.[26] In addition to requirements of

---

23   See Mohammad Monirul Azam, *Intellectual Property, WTO and Bangladesh* (Dhaka: New Warsi Book Corporation, 2008).

24   The concept of *ordre public* under Article 27.2 of TRIPs is regarded as one of the grounds for permissible exclusion from patentability. Article 27.2 of TRIPS partly adopted the language of Article 4 of the Paris Convention in its last sentence for the general conditionality of the exclusion of patentability. Accordingly, the exclusion cannot be made merely because domestic law prohibits the exploitation. Article 4 of the Paris Convention refers to broader terms that are not only related to the granting of a patent, but also to its subsequent invalidation, in cases of restrictions or limitations resulting from domestic law. Additionally, Article 27.3 of TRIPS refers to the exclusion of methods for the treatment of humans and animals from patentability, which is regarded as not covering the apparatus used for diagnostics or treatment or to products like "diagnostic kits".

25   See Chapter 2 of this study for more details on the PDA and DCO 1982 of Bangladesh.

26   See for details on exceptions and policy options, Chapter 4 of this study.

non-discrimination for patentable subject matter and place of invention, national patent regulations may also need to review the existing rights and obligations of patentees in the context of the TRIPS Agreement.

3.2.2 Rights and Obligations of Patentees

While complying with patent provisions of the TRIPS Agreement, the Government of Bangladesh may need to review and adjust the rights and obligations of patentees in the pharmaceutical field. The provision in the last sentence of Article 27.1 of TRIPS, which refers to the requirement of non-discrimination between imported and locally produced products, generated huge debate, not least concerning the local working requirement.

Some scholars, such as J.H. Reichman, consider that the right to supply imports according to this provision (Article 27.1) overrides the obligation to work patents locally (manufacturing of patented products locally) under Article 5A of the Paris Convention.[27] Other experts argue that because this provision does not specify whose products it refers to (the patent holder or the patent infringer), when the patent confers only negative rights in accordance with Article 28.1 of TRIPS, the patent rights can be exercised with regard to the latter. If this is the case, the provision would not override the local production obligation of the patentee.[28] This question is yet to be answered precisely by the WTO panels.

With regard to the rights conferred by a patent, Article 28.1.b of TRIPS particularly provides for the exclusive rights of the holder of the product patent, including the right to supply the market with imports of the patented products. The protection of a patent process is extended to the product "obtained directly by that process" under Article 28.2.b of TRIPS. However, developing countries like India applied for a grant of compulsory patent licensing on the grounds that a non-working patent was recognised by the Paris Convention, which considers that it is applicable for the TRIPS Agreement as well.[29]

---

27   Reichman, 'Universal Minimum Standards', pp.51–52.
28   Correa, 'Patent Rights', pp.203–04.
29   See for details on local working, section 3.3 of this chapter and chapter 4 of this study.

In Bangladesh under the existing DCO 1982, multinationals are prevented from importing and selling certain pharmaceuticals in the local market: "On the commencement of this Ordinance, the registration or licence in respect of all medicines mentioned in the Schedules shall stand cancelled, and no such medicine shall, subject to the provisions of sub-section (2), be manufactured, imported, distributed, [stocked, exhibited or sold] after such commencement".[30] Further, Section 9 (1) of the DCO 1982 provides that no pharmaceutical raw material necessary for the manufacture of any medicine specified in any of the Schedules shall be imported. Only local generic companies are allowed to produce and sell some of the products listed in the Schedule of the DCO 1982.[31]

Therefore, even if a patent is granted for certain pharmaceuticals, the patentee of those pharmaceuticals may not be allowed to import and sell their products in Bangladesh. However, after the introduction of TRIPS-compliant patent law, the Government of Bangladesh may need to allow not only the granting of patents on pharmaceuticals but also certain monopoly rights to patentees, including the right to sell, import and distribute as per the TRIPS Agreement and the principle of non-discrimination. However, nothing in the TRIPS Agreement prevents a country from assigning the examination of patent applications in the pharmaceutical sector to the Ministry of Health or DDA, provided that assignment does not constitute a *de facto* discrimination as to the field of technology.[32] Another TRIPS requirement is the minimum term of patent protection, discussed in the next section.

3.2.3 The Term of Patent Protection

It is up to national legislation to decide the possible duration of patent protection under the Paris Convention. However, the TRIPS Agreement states in Article 33 that the term of patent protection shall not end before

---

30   Section 8(1), DCO 1982 (Bangladesh).
31   See for details and schedules, DCO 1982 (Bangladesh), http://bdlaws.minlaw.gov. bd/pdf/623___Schedule.pdf
32   See WTO document WT/TPR/M/75, 6 December 2000, para. 76. Brazil has adopted such a measure on the grounds that the patent office may lack the expertise "to examine all the complex technological elements involved in the pharmaceutical inventions".

the expiration of a period of 20 years, counted from the filing date. The patent law of Bangladesh provides for only 16 years of protection; this will need to be extended to 20 years.[33] This provision is considered one of the major successes of the developed countries during the Uruguay Round in internationalising their practices of patent protection.[34]

There was huge contention among members on how to implement the obligation under Article 33 in relation to Article 70 of TRIPS, which provides for the limitation and extension of the TRIPS effect in the protection of the existing subject matters.[35] The debate resulted in disputes regarding the national patent law of a WTO member and the term of protection for patents granted before the effective date of TRIPS.[36]

The WTO panels and the Appellate Body clarified that the provision of Article 33 is also applicable to patented inventions granted before the effective date of TRIPS. These are regarded as falling within the definition of existing subject matters under Article 70.2 of TRIPS.[37]

The Appellate Body in reviewing the panel's report argued that "the term of protection shall not end before 20 years counted from the date of filing of the patent application. The calculation of the period of 20 years is clear and specific. In simple terms, Article 33 defines the earliest date on which the term of protection of a patent may end. The earliest date is determined by a straightforward calculation: it results from taking the date of filing of the patent application and adding twenty years".

A growing number of low-quality patents and their protection for 20 years may put undue burden on the operation of the patent system and may prevent the diffusion of knowledge and competition. While a long period of protection may be justifiable in the case of major inventions, for minor improvements the optimal period of protection should be shorter and commensurate with the lower investment in skill,

---

33   Section 14, PDA (Bangladesh).
34   'Universal Minimum Standards', p.30.
35   See for details, 'Resource Book on TRIPS and Development'.
36   See WTO, Panel Report, Canada—Term of Patent Protection, WT/DS170/R, 5 May 2000.
37   See WTO, Panel Report, Canada—Patent, Complaint by US, at 6.56; Appellate Report, Canada—Term of Patent Protection, WT/DS170/AB/R, 11 August 2000.

time and resources made by the patentee.[38] Thus, patent offices in LDCs like Bangladesh need to devise strict qualifying criteria for inventions and hence a longer duration of protection; they also need to introduce separate mechanisms for weak innovation, rather than simply granting patents. While doing so, the Government of Bangladesh needs to craft carefully its TRIPS obligations for enforcement of IP rights.

3.2.4 Enforcement Obligations

Whereas the Paris Convention and other IP agreements under the WIPO leave the questions of enforcement to the domestic legislation of member states, TRIPS provides for specific enforcement obligations.[39] Although some pre-existing IP conventions have a number of provisions dealing with remedies against infringement, they do not impose the compulsory obligation to incorporate those remedies into the national laws of the member states, nor do they provide particular sanctions and remedies of enforcement.[40] However, TRIPS does impose on members the compulsory obligation of enforcement, and elaborates particular enforcement measures, remedies and procedures. This is quite different from the situation regarding pre-existing international IP conventions.

Article 41 of TRIPS states that enforcement procedures must "permit effective action" against present and future acts of infringement and be incorporated into the national legislation to become available in the domestic laws of the member states.[41] TRIPS also requires that judicial

---

38   The granting of utility models or petty patents for minor inventions may provide a way of approaching this issue. See for details, U. Suthersanen, 'Incremental Inventions in Europe: a Legal and Economic Appraisal of Second Tier Patents', *Journal of Business Law* (July 2001): 319–43.

39   See 'Provisions on Enforcement in International Agreements on Intellectual Property Rights, General Agreement on Tariffs and Trades' (GATT), Doc. MTN. GNG/NG11/W/18, 10 February 1988.

40   For example, Article 9 of the Paris Convention requires three specific types of remedy against goods unlawfully bearing a trademark or a trade name—seizure on importation; seizure in the country where the unlawful affixation occurred or in the country into which the goods have been imported; and prohibition of importation—but does not make the incorporation of such remedies into national law compulsory and provides that "until such time as the legislation is modified accordingly", the actions and remedies available to nationals shall apply.

41   See TRIPS Agreement, art. 41 (1).

authorities have the authority to require claimants to indemnify parties who are wrongly subjected to any of the provided procedures.[42] It further provides that preliminary injunctions to prevent future infringements and preserve relevant evidence must be available to judicial authorities.[43]

Counterfeiting and piracy are concretely defined and distinguished from the general infringements to be applied in the "Special Requirements Related to Border Measures"[44] elaborated in Articles 51–60 of TRIPS.[45] Competent national authorities may act *ex officio* to suspend the release of goods with respect to which the *prima facie* evidence of infringement is available.[46] The imposition of strict border control measures on imports of counterfeit goods is perceived as "a safety valve" in case enforcement at the source has been ineffective.[47] However, it is also argued that overbroad laws claiming to address the problem of fake or spurious medicines, but labelled as "anti-counterfeiting" laws, can seriously restrict the availability of generic HIV medicines.[48]

Thus, while adopting effective enforcement provisions complying with the TRIPS Agreement, the Government of Bangladesh may need to give due consideration to the exceptions and limitations available under the TRIPS Agreement so that enforcement provisions do not become a barrier to the realisation of public health goals.[49]

---

42 Ibid., art. 48
43 Ibid., art. 50.
44 Ibid., art. 51.
45 The right holder must have the right to take legal action to compel domestic customs authorities to suspend the release of imported goods into free circulation whenever complainants have valid grounds for suspecting that the items in question are counterfeit trademarks or pirated copyright goods.
46 TRIPS Agreement, art. 44 (1).
47 For details, see Pham Hong Quat, 'How to Comply with the TRIPS and WTO Law—The New Challenges to Vietnam's Patent Legislation from WTO Dispute Settlement Practice' (unpublished PhD thesis, Nagoya University, Japan, 2007).
48 See for details, Jennifer Brant with Rohit Malpani, Oxfam International, *Eye on the Ball Medicine Regulation—Not IP Enforcement—Can Best Deliver Quality Medicines* (2 February 2011), http://www.oxfam.org/sites/www.oxfam.org/files/eye-on-the-ball-medicine-regulation-020211-en.pdf
49 Mohammad Monirul Azam, *Effectiveness of the Intellectual Property Enforcement Mechanisms Under the TRIPS Agreement: The Context of Bangladesh* (World Intellectual Property Organization [WIPO] Academy—Turin Research Paper Series, 2007).

3.2.5 Exceptions and Limitations of Exclusive Rights

Although the Paris Convention does not provide the criteria for exceptions, but leaves them to national legislation, TRIPS provides in Article 30 limited exceptions from the exclusive rights conferred on patent holders. Article 30 refers only to "exceptions" to the exclusive rights derived from the patent rights. However, the limitations to patent rights are implied in the provisions on compulsory licensing, which are mentioned generally in Article 8 and particularly in Article 31 of TRIPS.

TRIPS refers to the limitations to exclusive patent rights with the phrase "other use without authorization of the right holder" in Article 31, rather than with "compulsory licenses" as provided in Article 5(A) of the Paris Convention. Accordingly, the requirements set forth in Article 31 aim at different types of compulsory licenses. The applicability scope of this article is broader than that of the rule provided in Article 5(A) (4) of the Paris Convention, which is only applicable to the type of compulsory licenses for non-working or insufficiently working patents.[50]Although the TRIPS Agreement permits compulsory licenses (CL), countries having no or low technical capacity cannot take the advantage of it as article 31(f) limits CL to drugs produced to meet domestic needs rather than exported to other countries. Para. 6 of the Doha Declaration suggested a possible solution, which was finally approved by the WTO General Council in August 2003 (August 30 Decision).[51]

3.2.6 Provisions on August 30 Decision (Implementation of Para. 6 of the Doha Declaration)

The August 30 Decision implemented para. 6, allowing the export of pharmaceuticals to countries having no or low manufacturing capacity.

The amendment includes five paragraphs and will come under Article 31 *"bis"* (as an additional sub-article to Article 31 after approval

---

50   For details on the different types of compulsory licenses, see Chapter 4 of this study.

51   WTO, 'Implementation of Paragraph 6 of the Doha Declaration on the TRIPS Agreement and Public Health. Decision of 30 August 2003' (WT/L/540. 2 September 2003).

by two-thirds of the WTO members).[52] Again, a new annex to the TRIPS Agreement has come as part of the amendment, which includes seven paragraphs setting out terms for using the system, and covers such issues as definitions, notification, preventing the pharmaceuticals being diverted to the wrong markets, developing regional systems to allow economies of scale, and annual reviews in the TRIPS Council.

The Decision is essentially comprised of three waivers from provisions in Article 31 with respect to pharmaceutical products:[53]

- First, it waives the obligation in 31(f) that CL shall be predominantly for supply to the domestic market,

- Second, it waives the obligation in 31(h) for the importing country to pay remuneration to the right holder and

- Third, it waives the obligation in 31(f) to the extent that re-export of the imported pharmaceuticals is allowed among members of a regional trade agreement, if at least half of these members are LDCs.

However, all LDCs are automatically eligible to use the system, while the developing country members are only eligible if they can show no or low manufacturing capacity and make a notification of their intention to the Council for TRIPS. The developed countries such as the U.S., the EU members, Japan and Australia voluntarily declared that they will not use the system for imports. Hong Kong, Israel, Korea, Kuwait, Macao, Mexico, Qatar, Singapore, Chinese Taipei, Turkey and the United Arab Emirates agreed that they would use the system for import only in situations of national emergency or extreme urgency. Any member (developed, developing or LDC) may be an exporter.

It is noting that all pharmaceutical products, including active ingredients, diagnostic kits and vaccines, are included in the system. There is no list of eligible diseases as the August 30 Decision refers to pharmaceuticals needed to address health problems, as recognised in the Doha declaration, para. 1: "We recognize the gravity of the public health problems afflicting many developing and least-developed countries, especially those resulting from HIV/AIDS, tuberculosis,

---

52   WTO, 'Members OK Health Amendment Permanent', 6 December 2005, https://www.wto.org/english/news_e/pres05_e/pr426_e.htm

53   Ibid.

malaria and other epidemics".[54] Therefore, epidemics are recognised as the core problem and other public health problems of similar gravity are also included.

The questions of using the August 30 Decision may be clarified by means of the following situations (in the context of supplying pharmaceuticals):

- First, if there is no patent on the particular pharmaceutical in either the exporting or importing country, supply can be met by regular import without reference to the August 30 Decision.[55] Therefore, being an LDC, Bangladesh can supply generic drugs to other LDCs or developing countries where such drugs are not patented without using the August 30 Decision.

- Second, in the case of having a patent in the importing country but not in the exporting country, the importer can issue a regular CL for import under Article 31 as the purpose would be to supply the domestic market.[56] Thailand and Brazil issued this kind of CL for imports in 2006 and 2007 respectively. Therefore, a pharmaceutical company in Bangladesh could also supply generic medicine to other developing countries, if any developing country was willing to issue a CL for import to receive medicines from Bangladesh.

- Third, the parties must use the Decision when there is a patent in the exporting country but not in the importing country. However, it is only the exporter that should issue a CL. On the other hand, if a particular product is patented in both countries, both of them have to issue CLs and proceed as per the August 30 Decision.[57]

There have been four initiatives to use the August 30 Decision. The first was an unsuccessful attempt by the NGO Médecins Sans Frontières/ Doctors Without Borders (MSF), acting on behalf of a country (the name of which was not disclosed) in 2004 to place an order to Canadian company to manufacture a combination pill of three HIV/AIDS medicines.[58] The second occurred in 2005 when Ghana declared an emergency situation with regard to HIV/AIDS and granted a government-use authorization

---

54   Para. 1 of the Doha Declaration.
55   Sekalala, p.11.
56   Ibid.
57   Ibid.
58   WIPO-WHO-WTO Trilateral Study, 'Promoting Access to Medical Technologies and Innovations—Intersection between Public health, Intellectual Property and Trade' (2013), pp.112–13.

order to import generic HIV/AIDS medicines.[59] It approached a Canadian company, where the products were patented. But Ghana later chose to import the products from generic manufacturers in India, where there was no patent, and hence it was not necessary to use the Decision. The third situation took place in September 2007 when one Indian pharmaceutical company filed an application as a potential supplier to the Indian patent office, requesting to manufacture and export to Nepal several anti-cancer pharmaceuticals patented in India, including *erlotinib*.[60] But the applicant later withdrew the applications. As an LDC, Nepal was automatically entitled to use the system approved under Aug 30 decision, but Nepal never informed the WTO regarding its intention to import the given patented medicines—a prerequisite for using the decision. The fourth initiative began in July 2007 "when Rwanda sent to the WTO a brief notification of its intention to import 260,000 packs of the triple-combination ARV, reserving the right to modify the estimated quantity".[61] In September 2007, a Canadian "company applied for a compulsory licence in Canada which, under the Aug 30 Decision, would allow it to export 15,600,000 tablets (the equivalent of 260,000 packs) over a two-year period. The compulsory licence was granted two weeks later. The Canadian government notified the WTO in October that it was using the System [under Aug 30 Decision] as an exporting country".[62] As per the August 30 Decision, "the tablets shipped to Rwanda were distinguished from the version manufactured for the domestic market by the mark 'XCL' and white colouring, instead of the standard blue. The packaging bore an export tracking number issued by the Canadian government. Details of the product and its distinguishing characteristics, as well as details of the shipment, were posted on the website. A royalty was payable by the Canadian company for the right to use the patent, but the patent holders waived payment".[63]

Although the August 30 Decision created an opportunity for countries with low or no manufacturing capacity to meet their health needs by importing medicines from overseas, it has not been used very much.

---

59   Ibid.
60   Ibid.
61   Ibid; see also, WTO, 'Notification of Rwanda', July 2007 (document IP/N/9/RWA/1).
62   Ibid; see also, WTO, 'Notification of Canada', October 2007 (document IP/N/10/CAN/1).
63   Ibid.

One should consider the complexity of the system and the "(potential) political or trade ramifications associated with the use of compulsory licensing".[64] The experiences of Brazil, China, India and South Africa could provide important lessons for the LDCs in how to utilise the options available under the TRIPS Agreement and while also dealing with potential political and trade risks associated with using additional governmental options (which are not conflicting with TRIPS).

3.3 The Experience of Brazil

Brazil's experience regarding TRIPS-compliant patent law for pharmaceuticals, and the societal and national obligation to ensure access to medicines, represents a situation in which exploitation by MNPCs was not only largely thwarted, but gave way to significant reforms in public health policy and reinstated local drug companies as viable contenders in the domestic market.[65]

Brazil's public health-oriented TRIPS compliance approach might be the perfect model for other developing countries and LDCs to utilise. Economic and technological collaboration between the public and private sectors could create favourable conditions for political alliance as well as a hospitable environment for balancing local pharmaceutical innovation and access to medicines.[66] Brazil has a population of over 180 million, so it is not only an important pharmaceutical market (with 2008 sales estimated at US$12.7 billion),[67] but also an important centre for R&D with clinical trial facilities, low development costs, and qualified professionals.[68] Although the pharmaceutical industry is dominated by MNCs, issues surrounding access to medicines have come to the forefront; affordability is one of the main problems in Brazilian healthcare.[69] Around 20% of the 370 established pharmaceutical

---

64   Ibid.
65   'Corporate Power and State Resistance', pp.149–50.
66   Kenneth C. Shadlen, 'The Politics of Patents and Drugs in Brazil and Mexico: The Industrial Bases of Health Policies', *Comparative Politics* 42.1 (2009): 41–58.
67   Business Wire Pharmaceutical, 'Research and Markets: Pharmaceutical Pricing and Reimbursement in Brazil: Population and Demand for Pharmaceuticals is Forecast to Increase in the Next 12 Years' (Press Release, 5 January 2010), http://www.reuters.com/article/2010/01/25/idUS147453+25-Jan-2010+BW20100125
68   Ibid.
69   Ibid.

companies in Brazil are foreign (mainly European or American), and it is estimated that they control around 70% of the pharmaceutical market in Brazil.[70] Given this tension, Brazil, within its IP regime, has attempted to create a balance between pharmaceutical innovation and access to medicines.

In 1883, Brazil was one of 16 countries that signed the Paris Convention.[71] This pre-TRIPS convention allowed countries to utilise the patent system as an instrument of economic and technological development. Under that convention, each country could establish its own IP regime in a way that would favour its national policy. Brazilian industrial property legislation granted patent protection for pharmaceutical processes and products until 1945.[72] In fact, Brazil was the fourth country in the world and the first in Latin America to protect the rights of inventors.[73]

Brazil's 1945 legislation was modified to exclude the protection of inventions related to foodstuffs, medicines, materials and substances obtained by chemical means or processes.[74] In 1969, a change in the Brazilian *Industrial Property Code* completely eliminated patenting in the pharmaceutical sector.[75] However, when Brazil became a member of the WTO,[76] it was required to implement a TRIPS-compliant patent regime, which included patent protection for both pharmaceutical products and processes. Brazil institutionalised the TRIPS Agreement by Presidential Decree in December 1994,[77] and its TRIPS-compliant regime came into effect on 14 May 1996, thereby introducing pharmaceutical product and process protection.[78]

Brazil began granting patents in the pharmaceutical sector in May 1997.[79] Given this early implementation, Brazil was criticised

---

70 *Intellectual Property in the Context of the WTO TRIPS Agreement: Challenges for Public Health*, ed. by Jorge A. Z. Bermudez and Maria Auxiliadora Oliveira (Rio de Janeiro: Centre for Pharmaceutical Policies and WHO, 2004); Kermani Faiz, *Brazil—Not a Market for Faint Hearted* (October 2005).

71 Bermudez and Oliveira, p.153.

72 Ibid., p.154.

73 Ibid., p.153.

74 Ibid., p.158.

75 Ibid.

76 Brazil has been a member of the WTO since 1 January 1995.

77 Bermudez and Oliveira, p.153.

78 Ibid.

79 Ibid.

by public health groups for implementing a TRIPS-compliant law in Brazil[80] that failed to fully utilise the flexibilities and safeguards in the TRIPS Agreement and thus ensure access to medicines.[81] In the face of this criticism, the Brazilian government took steps to facilitate access to drugs by introducing a number of amendments to the patent law, including a strong compulsory licensing regime.[82] MNPCs and developed countries, particularly the US, objected to these provisions,[83] and a WTO dispute was initiated by the US against Brazil.[84] Daya Shanker precisely noted the main points of contention between the US and Brazil: local working requirements in the Brazilian *Industrial Property Law*, parallel importing in the same law, and Brazil's request for consultation on the alleged violation of WTO provisions in the patent law of the US. Patents that are developed with the help of public funding need to be worked in the US.[85]

In its complaint, the US asserted that Article 68 of Brazil's *Industrial Property Law* had imposed a requirement that a patent either be subject to compulsory licensing if not applicable in the territory of Brazil, or not be used to manufacture the product in Brazil if the patented process was not used in Brazil.[86] In the view of the US, these provisions were in conflict with Articles 27.1[87] and 28.1[88] of the TRIPS Agreement. As Chakravarthi Raghavan has stated, "the Brazilian law also provided

---

80 Ibid.
81 Ibid., pp.151–53.
82 *Brazil—Not a Market for Faint Hearted*, p.22.
83 Bermudez and Oliveira. p.33.
84 On 8 January 2001, the US requested a WTO dispute settlement panel to resolve its differences with Brazil over Brazil's *Industrial Property Law, 1996*.
85 'Fault Lines in the World Trade Organization', p.33.
86 Article 68(1) of Brazil's *Industrial Property Law, 1996* provides that non-exploitation of the object of the patent within Brazilian territory will occasion a compulsory license for failure to manufacture the product, for incomplete manufacture of the product, or for failure to make full use of the patented process, except in cases where this is not economically feasible (and importation shall be permitted).
87 Article 27(1) of the TRIPS Agreement provides that "patents shall be available for any inventions, whether products or processes, in all fields of technology, provided that they are new, involve an inventive step and are capable of industrial application ... patents shall be available and patent rights enjoyable without discrimination as to the place of invention, the field of technology and whether products are imported or locally produced".
88 Article 28.1 of the TRIPS Agreement deals with the exclusive rights of the patent owner to prevent third parties not having the owner's consent for the acts of making, using, offering for sale, selling or importing the patented product.

that if a patent owner chose to exploit the patent through importation, others could either import the patented product or obtain the product from the patented process".[89]

In response to the complaint, Brazil contended that Articles 204[90] and 209[91] of the patent code of the US[92] had similar provisions; consequently, Brazil would initiate a dispute against the US over these provisions.[93] In the end, the complaint was withdrawn due to pressure from public health organisations and human rights groups both within and outside the US.[94] Shanker critically commented on the dispute:

> [t]he weakness of its position was known to the [US] but the main purpose of initiating the dispute appeared to be to communicate potential [US] displeasure and possible action against weak and poor countries of the Third World so that they would not incorporate such provisions in their

---

89   See Chakravarthi Raghavan, 'US to Withdraw TRIPS Dispute against Brazil', http://www.twn.my/title/withdraw.htm

90   The relevant provision is 35 USC § 204, entitled 'Preference for United States Industry', which provides that "[n]otwithstanding any other provision of this chapter, no small business firm or nonprofit organization which receives title to any subject invention and no assignee of any such small business firm or non-profit organization shall grant to any person the exclusive right to use or sell any subject invention in the United States unless such person agrees that any products embodying the subject invention or produced through the use of the subject invention will be manufactured substantially in the United States".

91   The relevant provision is 35 USC § 209, entitled 'Licensing Federally Owned Inventions', which provides that "in the case of an invention covered by a foreign patent application or patent, the interests of the Federal Government or United States industry in foreign commerce will be enhanced". It further adds that "[a] Federal agency shall normally grant a license ... to use or sell any federally owned invention in the United States only to a licensee who agrees that any products embodying the invention or produced through the use of the invention will be manufactured substantially in the United States".

92   US Patent Law 35 USC §§ 1 et esq., http://www.wipo.int/wipolex/en/details.jsp?id=5399

93   The US Patent Law, as consolidated in 2007, among other things, provides that when any patent is obtained, as a result of research funded by the US Government and its agencies, the patent should be worked in the US and cannot be licensed for production elsewhere. See ibid.

94   MSF and other public health groups, along with 120 Brazilian NGOs, requested that the US Government withdraw its request for a WTO dispute settlement procedure on the Brazilian patent law. The US brought a complaint before the DSB in Geneva, requesting measures that might handicap the successful Brazilian AIDS programme, which is largely based on Brazil's ability to manufacture affordable treatment. See Dispute Settlement, *Brazil: Measures Affecting Patent Protection*, WT/DS199/1, 5 July 2001, http://www.wto.org/english/tratop_e/dispu_e/cases_e/ds199_e.htm

patent Acts and should such provisions have already been incorporated in their patent acts, that they would not use them.[95]

Thus the success of the US action was evident from the fact that South Africa, Kenya and many other African countries refrained from using local working provisions to manufacture anti-AIDS pharmaceuticals, even when a substantial part of their populations was suffering from AIDS.[96]

However, Brazil has managed to obtain price reductions from big pharmaceutical companies by threatening to break patents through the issue of a compulsory license. For example, on 25 April 2007 Brazil decided to issue a compulsory license for the HIV drug Storcrin (the brand name for Efavirenz), after failure to secure a considerable discount from the patent owner.[97] The then Brazilian president signed a compulsory license on the grounds of public interest[98] for Efavirenz, which permitted the purchase of the patented pharmaceutical from generic suppliers.[99]

Brazil has also adopted a decree that establishes certain rules concerning the granting of compulsory licenses in cases of national emergency and public interest.[100] The definition of public interest is broad, including such matters as public health, nutrition, the protection

---

95   See Daya Shanker, 'India, the Pharmaceutical Industry and the Validity of TRIPS', *The Journal of World Intellectual Property* 5.3 (2002): 111.

96   See Daya Shanker (2002); see also Amir Attaran and Gillespie Lee, 'Do Patents for Antiretroviral Drugs Constrain Access to AIDS Treatment in Africa?', *Journal of the American Medical Association* 286 (2001): 1886.

97   For details on compulsory licenses issued in different countries, see James Packard Love, 'Recent Examples of the Use of Compulsory Licenses on Patents' (KEI Research Note 2007: 2), http://www.keionline.org/misc-docs/recent_cls.pdf

98   The definition of what falls into the public interest is of great importance. Public interest includes public health, nutrition, environmental protection, and elements of primordial importance for technological, social or economic development. The possibility of providing compulsory licensing in each of these cases implies that the fulfilment of the most basic needs would be covered for the public.

99   *Ministerial Ordinance No. 866*, dated 24 April 2007, declared that "there exists the possibility of compulsory licensing of patents in the public interest", as provided for in national laws, and decided "to declare public interest in relation to *Efavirenz* for the purposes of the granting of compulsory licensing for public non-commercial use, in order to guarantee the practicability of the National STD and AIDS Program, ensuring the continuity of universal and free access to all medicines necessary for the treatment of people living with HIV and AIDS".

100   Decree No. 3,201 of 6 October 1999, Diario Oficial da Uniao (Braz.) (translated into English).

of the environment, and elements of primordial importance for technological, social or economic development.[101] The possibility of being able to provide compulsory licensing in each of these cases implies that the fulfilment of the country's most basic needs would be covered. Thus, Brazil successfully utilised the compulsory license flexibility of TRIPS to protect public health.

In addition to compulsory license provisions, Brazilian law also utilised, within its TRIPS-compliant regime, other TRIPS flexibilities such as parallel importing,[102] experimental use, early working or Bolar exceptions,[103] and a strict novelty requirement.[104]

Using parallel import flexibility, Brazil permitted pharmaceuticals to be brought into the country if the patent holder or an authorised third party had previously commercialised the pharmaceutical in another country at a lower price than that offered in Brazil.[105]

The Brazilian *Industrial Property Law* also included a provision on experimental flexibility, which allowed the use of an invention without compensation for the patent holder.[106] The Bolar exception, as it applies in Brazil, allows a company to complete all of the procedures and tests that are necessary to register a generic product before the original patent expires.[107] Bolar flexibility allows the immediate marketing of a generic pharmaceutical after the patent has expired, thus promoting

---

101 Ibid.

102 Law No. 9,279 of 14 May 1996 (Industrial Property Law) (Braz.) (referencing Article 43).

103 This was introduced in Brazil by Law 10.196/2001 as an amendment to Articles 43 and 229 of Law No. 9,279.

104 Law No. 9,279 of 14 May 1996 (Industrial Property Law) (Braz.) (referencing Article 229 C).

105 In September 2003, Decree No. 4,830 also allowed for the importation of the object from countries where the product is not patented. Therefore, Brazil has the right to import products from any country, including those still using the transition period for pharmaceuticals, such as Bangladesh. Decree No. 4,830, 4 September 2003, Compulsory Licensing in the Case of National Emergency and Public Interest (translated into English).

106 Law No. 9,279 of 14 May 1996 (Industrial Property Law) (Braz.) (referencing Article 43).

107 Industrial Property Amendment Law No. 10,196 modified Articles 43 and 229 of Law No. 9,279. Article 43, which describes the limits of rights conferred to the patent holder (Exception to Rights Conferred), was amended to include the Bolar exception (early working) and allow local generic producers to complete all of the procedures and tests necessary to register a generic product before the original patent expires.

competition with the patent holder.[108] Another notable feature of the Brazilian *Industrial Property Law* is its innovative use of novelty flexibility.

In terms of novelty flexibility, the Brazilian National Institute for Industrial Property (INPI) is criticised by health activists, local generic producers and lawyers for adopting an overly broad definition of novelty. This results in many patent applications that are not new molecular entities (NMEs), but rather are simply revised versions of some existing patented NMEs. To avoid this problem, a 1999 Presidential Decree (converted into law in 2001) created and introduced a new provision requiring prior approval from the National Health Surveillance Agency (ANVISA or "the Agency") before granting a patent, thus ensuring that it will not endanger public health or create barriers for access to medicines.[109] Therefore, all pharmaceutical patent applications submitted to the INPI must go through the ANVISA review process, and patents can only be issued with prior consent from the ANVISA.[110] The Agency denies patents to drugs that lack genuine novelty and in cases where it judges that providing exclusive rights would be harmful to public health.[111] ANVISA uses its authority to prevent patents that, in its judgement, would extend the terms of existing patents.

Further, in December 2010, the Brazilian Senate approved the text of a new *Competition Act* that had been pending in the Brazilian Parliament since 2005 and finally entered into force on 29 May 2012 (Brazilian

---

108 This can ultimately lower the price of medicines. The WTO Panel in the EC–Canada case validated the Bolar exception as compatible with Article 30 of the TRIPS Agreement. See Panel Report, *Canada — Patent Protection of Pharmaceutical Products*, WT/DS114/R (17 March 2000), 2, 174, http://www.wto.org/english/tratop_e/dispu_e/7428d.pdf; see also Christopher Garrison, 'Exception to Patent Rights in Developing Countries' (Issue Paper No. 17, UNCTAD–ICTSD Project on IPR and Sustainable Development, 2006), http://www.unctad.org/en/docs/iteipc200612_en.pdf

109 See Maristela Basso, 'Intervention of Health Authorities in Patent Examination: The Brazilian Approach of the Prior Consent', *International Journal of Intellectual Property Management* 1 (2006): 54–74.

110 ANVISA's IP division established in 2001 and housed in the National Institute for Industrial Property's office building in Rio de Janeiro.

111 Bermudez Oliveira and Egleubia Oliveira, 'Expanding Access to Essential Medicines in Brazil: Recent Regulation and Public Policies', in *Intellectual Property in the Context of the WTO TRIPS Agreement: Challenges for Public Health*, ed. by Jorge A.Z. Bermudez and Maria Auxiliadora Oliveira (Rio de Janeiro: WHO, 2004), pp.129–52.

Competition Law, No. 12.529/2011).[112] It is expected that this law may help Brazil prevent both excessive pricing and abuse of the dominant position of the pharmaceutical industry.[113] However, the law has yet to be tested in the pharmaceutical sector.[114] Brazil has also adopted price control regulations, empowering the Ministry of Health to evaluate how far a new patented medicine can demonstrate a therapeutic advantage over an existing treatment and then to determine a price ceiling based on the lowest price of the drug in several countries, including the country of origin.[115]

Apart from public health-oriented TRIPS flexibilities, the local pharmaceutical sector in Brazil has also benefited from significant government investment in research and production through the Brazilian Ministry of Health.[116] Maurice Cassier and Marilena Correa stated that "[t]he Ministry of Health [of Brazil] acting as 'health entrepreneur' [as it] does not just purchase drugs but also takes an active role in their production".[117]

---

112 "On May 29, 2012, Law No. 12.529/11 took effect, significantly changing the landscape of antitrust enforcement in Brazil. The law (i) consolidates the investigative, prosecutorial, and adjudicative functions of Brazil's three competition authorities into one independent agency; (ii) introduces a mandatory pre-merger notification system; and (iii) introduces changes to the administrative and criminal sanctions applicable to anticompetitive conduct". See Ana Paula Martinez and Mariana Tavares de Araujo, 'Brazil's New Competition Law One Year after Taking Effect', 20 June 2013, http://www.lexology.com/library/detail.aspx?g=3155fa30-c311-45b5-8ced-a51f1bec14b0. See also Marco Botta, 'The Brazilian Senate Approves the Text of the New Competition Act' (15 December 2011), http://kluwercompetitionlawblog.com/2011/02/07/the-brazilian-senate-approves-the-text-of-the-new-competition-act

113 See Loraine Hawkins, 'WHO/HAI Project on Medicine Prices and Availability Review Series on Pharmaceutical Pricing Policies and Interventions' (Working Paper No. 4, Competition Policy, May 2011), p.14.

114 Ibid.

115 Brazil created a reference price regime for new patented products in 2003. Under this regime, the final price of a new drug in Brazil cannot exceed the lowest price among nine reference countries: Australia, Canada, Spain, the US, France, Greece, Italy, New Zealand and Portugal. See WHO, 'Pharmaceutical Pricing Policy' (2010), http://apps.who.int/medicinedocs/documents/s19585en/s19585en.pdf

116 The Government of Brazil invested in 18 public sector laboratories that mostly engage in formulation of final dosages and, to a lesser degree, of pharmaceutical inputs.

117 See Maurice Cassier and Marilena Correa, 'Intellectual Property and Public Health: Copying of HIV/AIDS Drugs by Brazilian Public and Private Pharmaceutical Laboratories', *RECIIS Electronic Journal of Communication, Information and Innovation in Health*,1.1 (2007): 83–90.

By using both the flexibilities inherent in the TRIPS Agreement and governmental investment in R&D, Brazil was able to balance the need for pharmaceutical innovation with the public health requirement of access to medicines. China and India had a similar vision, but took different paths towards TRIPS compliance.

3.4 The Experience of China

Patent law in modern China began with the promulgation of the *Patent Law of the People's Republic of China (PRC), 1984*.[118] Since then, China has amended its patent law four times: in 1992, 2000, 2008 and 2012.[119] The 1984 Chinese patent law excluded the protection of pharmaceutical product patents, and approved the granting of process patent only. It was not until 1992, when taking part in negotiations with the U.S. for accession to the WTO, that China amended its patent law of 1984 to comply with the TRIPS Agreement. Then, under Article 25 of the 1992 amended patent law, the Chinese government formally approved the granting of patent protection for pharmaceutical products.[120] The Chinese government introduced further changes to the patent law in 2000 to ensure full compatibility with the TRIPS Agreement prior to becoming a WTO Member in 2001. However, China also attempted to strike a balance between the interest of patent holders and public health, ratifying further amendment to the patent law in 2008 to adopt some public health-related measures, as approved by the Doha Declaration, and to encourage Chinese generic producers.[121] In 2012, the State Intellectual Property Office (SIPO) of China approved a fourth amendment to simplify public health-related measures (such as compulsory license procedure), which was enacted on 15 March 2012 and came into effect on 1 May 2012.[122]

---

118 State Intellectual Property Office (SIPO) of the People's Republic of China (PRC), Patent Law of the People's Republic of China, http://english.sipo.gov.cn/laws/lawsregulations/201101/t20110119_566244.html

119 Ibid.

120 Ibid.

121 Abbott, Correa and Drahos (2013).

122 See 'General Introduction to the Third Revision of the Patent Law of the People's Republic of China and its Implementing Regulations', http://english.sipo.gov.cn/laws/lawsregulations/201012/t20101210_553631.html

Among the public health-related measures, one important feature in the context of China is the disclosure requirement for traditional knowledge and genetic resources. The Chinese government supports and encourages research on local traditional knowledge and genetic resources. It therefore tried to preserve the interests of local producers and users by introducing strict requirements. Article 26 of the 2008 Patent Law adopted disclosure requirements, which require that the applicant disclose and explain the direct and original source of the genetic resource. If the applicant is not able to disclose the original source, the applicant must provide the reasons why.[123] However, Article 26 has some weakness in its implementation. For example, it is not clear how to define "direct source" and "original source", or acceptable and reasonable grounds for not disclosing the original source. This vagueness may create uncertainties and some companies may avoid the provision by using weak excuses.[124] The novelty provision is another important provision for the local generic producers in China.

Under the 2000 Patent Law of the PRC, novelty was not considered to be destroyed if an invention had already been used in foreign countries, provided it had not been used in China or published anywhere in the world before its filing in China.[125] That is why, in comparison to the Indian approach, Chinese patentability requirements were criticised for being weak and for allowing foreign pharmaceutical producers to exploit the law and keep their patent rights for a longer time than intended, delaying the entry of generics to the market.[126] Thus, China should raise the bar for medical patentability standards to prevent the patenting of medicines with small changes; the government could thereby encourage the production of generic drugs immediately after the expiry of patent.[127] However, the provision on novelty was amended

---

123 SIPO, 2008 Patent Law of the PRC, Art. 26.
124 Shruti Bhat, 'New Chinese Patent Law: What Does It Mean For Life Sciences Companies?', 6 February 2011, http://pharmaceuticalpatents.weebly.com/pharmaceutical-patents-and-intellectual-property-blog/new-chinese-patent-law
125 Ibid.
126 Sasha Kontic 'An Analysis of the Generic Pharmaceutical Industries in Brazil and China in the Context of TRIPS and HIV/AIDS', pp.9–12, https://www.law.utoronto.ca/documents/ihrp/HIV_kontic.doc
127 Elliot Hannon, 'How an India Patent Case Could Shape the Future of Generic Drugs', *Time World*, 21 August 2012, http://world.time.com/2012/08/21/how-an-indian-patent-case-could-shape-the-future-of-generic-drugs

under the Article 22 of the 2008 Patent Law of the PRC, which stipulates that "novelty" means the invention or utility model does not belong to prior art [disclosure or publication of the relevant invention anywhere in the world prior to patent application], which is also called "absolute novelty".[128] Therefore, patent examiners need to make the assessment that, prior to the date of filing, no other person shall have filed an application for an identical invention and that there is no evidence of public use either inside and outside of China. Adoption of an absolute novelty standard requires a higher pharmaceutical R&D capability, which could prevent patenting with minor changes and encourage the quick entry of cheaper generic medicines to the Chinese market.[129] However, when the supply and price of patented medicines go beyond sustainable limits, most countries have recourse to compulsory license.

It is noting that no CL has ever been granted in China even though Chapter VI of the 1984 Patent Law of the PRC had detailed CL provisions. Recognising the importance of CL in the context of public health challenges in China and the available flexibilities in the TRIPS Agreement, China revised its CL provisions during the third amendment to the patent law in 2008. According to Article 48 of the 2008 Patent Law, the SIPO may, upon the request of an entity or individual qualified for exploitation, grant a compulsory license to exploit a patent for an invention or utility model, when the patentee has not or has not sufficiently exploited it, without any justified reason, within three years of the granting of the patent right or four years of the filing for the patent. A compulsory license can also be granted to avoid or eliminate adverse effects on the competition in cases in which it has been legally determined that the enforcement of the patent right by the patentee constitutes a monopolistic act.[130] In addition, Article 50 of the 2008 Patent law permits the granting of a compulsory license for exporting medicines to countries with low or no manufacturing capacity with the aim of protecting public health, as per Para. 6 on the implementation mechanism of the Doha Declaration/August 30 Decision.[131]

---

128 SIPO, 2008 Patent Law of the PRC, Art. 22.
129 Ibid.
130 Ibid., Art. 48 (1)(2).
131 Ibid., Art. 50.

Articles 50 and 53 of the 2008 Patent Law of the PRC stipulate that for the purpose of promoting public health, in the case of countries without a manufacture capacity, patented medicines can be manufactured and exported with the CL granted by the patent administration department (of the PRC) to the LDCs and other WTO member states, provided they express the need to import the medicines according to the relevant provisions of the international treaties (i.e., the August 30 Decision of the TRIPS Agreement).[132] However, the CL mechanism permitted under the 2008 Patent Law of the PRC lacks safeguards with regard to how to regulate parallel importation and exportation to avoid imported medicines being re-imported to other countries, because it would affect the interests of patients that need cheaper medicine in the importing counties. Apart from these weaknesses on exporting medicines, there are other limitations regarding the CL mechanism's ability to meet local public health needs in China.

The SIPO adopted a further amendment to patent law in order to simplify measures on CL on 15 March 2012. The purpose of the adopted measures was to promote compulsory licensing in the pharmaceutical industry and to improve public health by bargaining for cheaper ARV second-line drugs for treating HIV/AIDS, drugs for which the patent rights are held by foreign pharmaceutical companies. Prior to 2012, the circumstances under which a person could apply for a compulsory license were (1) they had been unable to obtain a license after a reasonable period of negotiation based on fair and reasonable terms, if the implementation of an invention or utility model that constitutes a significant progress had to rely on the implementation of a patent previously granted; (2) in situations where public health is concerned; and (3) in a state of emergency.[133] The 2012 measures approved two more grounds: first if the patent has not been used for three years from the time of its granting, or four years from the time of application; and second, if the act of claiming the patent right is considered a violation of anti-monopoly law. With respect to public health, the field is thus significantly widened.[134] Under previous measures, it was limited to

---

132 Ibid., art. 50 and 53.
133 Article 4, 'Measures on Compulsory Licensing for Patent Exploitation', Order No. 31 of the SIPO (implemented on 15 July 2003).
134 Ibid., art. 5.

contagious diseases, but under the 2012 measures the contagious disease restriction does not exist.[135] Chinese patent law also includes provisions for Bolar exemptions, which is important for generic producers.

Article 69 (5) of the Chinese Patent Law of 2008 includes Bolar exemptions, and states that "Any person [who] produces, uses, or imports patented drugs or patented medical apparatus and instruments, for the purpose of providing information required for administrative examination and approval, or produces or any other person imports patented drugs or patented medical apparatus and instruments especially for that person" is excluded from infringement of the patent rights.[136] This provision is also consistent with Article 19 of the 2007 *Drug Registration Regulations* (DRR), which says that:

> for a drug patented in China, applicants other than the patentee may submit the application for registration two years prior to the expiry date of the patent. The State Food and Drug Administration (SFDA) shall review the drug application in accordance with the provisions, and after the expiry date of the patent, check and issue the drug approval number, Import Drug License or a Pharmaceutical Product License if the application conforms to the provisions.[137]

Before the establishment of Bolar exemptions by the 2008 Patent Law, when generic producers were trying to utilise Article 19 of the DRR handling the application, infringement lawsuits were always brought by patent holders. By shortening the application time spent on clinical trial, the provision relating to Bolar exemptions can be seen as encouraging the production of generics to reduce the price of patented medicines and improve accessibility to medicines.[138] Chinese patent law also allows parallel imports to ensure better accessibility and affordability of medicines, in case of excessive pricing of medicines in the local market.

---

135 Zhang Yan, 'New Measures for Compulsory Licensing of Patent', effective since 1 May 2012 (25 June 2012), http://www.lexology.com/library/detail.aspx?g=bef0d960-d8ae-4849-8750-2303eb70d982

136 'Third Revision of China's Patent Law, Legal Texts and Documents on Drafting Process', EU–China IPR2 Project, pp.5–6, http://www.lexisnexis.com/documents/pdf/20100211022732_large.pdf

137 Article 19, 'Provisions for Drug Registration', http://eng.sfda.gov.cn/WS03/CL0768/61645.html

138 Yafei Gao, 'The Conflict and Coordination between Biological Pharmacy's Intellectual Property Protection and Public Health' (in Chinese), October 2011, pp.20–30.

There is little ambiguity regarding parallel import provisions in China. Article 63(1) of the 2000 Patent Law allowed that "after the sale of a patented product that was made or imported by the patentee or the authorization of the patentee, or of a product that was directly obtained by using that patented process, any other person uses, offers to sell or sells the product".[139] Nevertheless, this led to different understandings of whether this provision actually adopted international exhaustion or whether "sell" in the provision meant within the country and therefore allowed domestic exhaustion. Thus, the 2000 Patent Law did not provide the specific legal basis for parallel importation. However, Article 69(1) of the 2008 Patent Law clarified the issue by stating that it would not constitute patent infringement after the product first entered the international market with the authorisation or consent of the patent owner. Nevertheless, China provided data exclusivity which may hamper the production of generic pharmaceuticals for the local market.

During its WTO accession process in 2001, China approved a six-year period of data exclusivity protection for pharmaceutical drugs containing a new chemical entity (NCE) under its *Provisions for Drug Registration*.[140] However, this protection can be excluded in two situations: where the public interest takes precedence, and where steps are taken to ensure the data are protected against unfair commercial use.[141]

It is estimated that data exclusivity increased China's health expenditure by an average of 45.55% per year from 2007 to 2009, while reducing accessibility to 267 types of medicines by 27.14% — a great negative impact on public health in China.[142] The six years of data exclusivity for all drugs, and the related policies, are too simplistic a measure, and some points need to be revised and clarified. Regarding Article 20 of the *Provisions for Drug Regulation* and Article 35 of the *Regulations for Implementation of the Drug Administration Law*, the

---

139 Article 63(1), Patent Law of The PRC (2000 Revision), adapted at the 17th Session of the Standing Committee of the Ninth National People's Congress on 25 August 2000, and announced by Order No. 36 of the President of the PRC.

140 Article 20, Provisions for Drug Registration (SFDA Order No. 28).

141 Article 35, Regulations for Implementation of the Drug Administration Law of the People's Republic of China, Decree of the State Council of the PRC No. 36.

142 S. Wu, S. Hang, J. Chen and L. Shi, 'Impact of Medical Data Protection on Drug Expenditure and Accessibility in China', *Chinese Journal of New Drugs* 21.20 (2012): 2353–55.

term "NCEs" needs to be defined clearly in the case of diverging opinions between China and developed countries. There should be more detailed requirements for experimental data, otherwise the protection scope of data exclusivity is difficult to understand. Further, the six-year exclusivity is too general: there should be a differential protection period for different kind of drugs, as is the case in Japan.[143] The provisions should add corresponding terms separately to NCEs, orphan drugs, paediatric drugs and so on. In this regard, the Indian approach for refusing to provide test data protection and dealing with other TRIPS flexibilities could be more viable for the LDCs, considering the embryonic stage of their industries in comparison to China and their weak financial and technical capacities.

3.5 The Experience of India

India's experience contrasts with that of Brazil. India entered the WTO in 1995 and went through a long process of amendments to have a TRIPS-compliant patent regime, which became effective on 1 January 2005.[144] The effect of stronger intellectual patent rights created problems for the larger Indian drug firms and greatly damaged smaller local firms' ability to meet the rising costs of remuneration for experienced and efficient pharmacists and other technical persons.[145]

---

143 In this regard, Japan could become a model for China. Japan incorporates data exclusivity into its post-marketing surveillance (PMS) process. By using a set of medical insurance and drug pricing mechanisms, the Japanese government has both complied with its obligation under TRIPS and successfully encouraged innovation by pharmaceutical companies. The PMS system practically affects the timing of generic entry. The PMS period is set for most new drug approvals, and until this period is over, generic companies cannot submit their applications for drug approvals. It is primarily intended to monitor efficacy and safety after the commercialisation of patented drugs and not to protect data. During the PMS period, the new drug's applicant can enjoy data exclusivity; thus, data exclusivity is imposed with the responsibility of the drug's applicant to ensure its safety and efficacy. The data exclusivity period varies from four (for medicinal products with new indications, formulations, dosages, or compositions with related prescriptions) to six (for drugs containing a new chemical element or medicinal composition, or requiring a new route of administration) to 10 years (for orphan drugs or new drugs requiring pharmaco-epidemiological study). See for details, 'Japanese Drug Regulations Related to Data Exclusivity (Excerpts)', *Kitamural Law*, http://kitamuralaw.com/publications/J_data_exclusivity_provisions.pdf
144 'India's New "Trips-compliant" Patent Regime'.
145 Ibid.

The Indian pharmaceutical industry, with its 8% share of global pharmaceutical production, "holds [the fourth] position in terms of volume and [the thirteenth] in terms of value of production".[146] It also enjoys a 20% share of the global generic market.[147] Indian pharmaceutical companies also play an important role globally by providing life-saving drugs at affordable prices. For instance, 70% of the ARV drugs procured to treat HIV/AIDS under the Global Fund to Fight HIV/AIDS, TB and malaria come from Indian companies and 70% of the UNICEF, International Development Association, and Clinton Foundation procurement is also from Indian companies.[148]

Drugs produced in India satisfy 95% of domestic demand, and two-thirds of the drugs produced in India are exported to the global market.[149] The exports of pharmaceuticals by the Indian pharmaceutical industry are around $5.3 billion.[150] Only two MNCs—GSK and Pfizer—figure in the top 10 pharmaceutical companies in India.[151] Although domestic companies in India now control 80% of the domestic market, this was not the case prior to patent policy reform in 1970, when Indian companies had only a 20% share.[152] Considering this, Indian patent policy reform provides LDCs with important lessons in utilising the transitional period for progress towards local pharmaceutical production and innovation, as well as moving towards TRIPS compliance.

146 See Planning Commission of India, *Report of the Working Group on Drugs and Pharmaceuticals for the Eleventh Five Year Plan (2007–2012)* 21 (2006), http://planningcommission.nic.in/aboutus/committee/wrkgrp11/wg11_pharma.pdf

147 Ibid.

148 Ellen t' Hoen, *The Global Politics of Pharmaceutical Monopoly Power* (AMB Publishers, 2009).

149 Based on data from the Directorate General of Foreign Trade, Government of India and Exim Bank, India reported by N. Lalitha, 'Access to Indian Generic Drugs: Emerging Issues', in *Intellectual Property, Pharmaceuticals and Public Health*, ed. by Kenneth C. Shadlen, Samira Guennif, Alenka Guzman and N. Lalitha (Cheltenham: Edward Elgar, 2011), pp.225–52. See Government of India, Directorate General of Foreign Trade, 'India—The Generics Pharma Capital of the World' (Pharmaceutical Exports Report, IDMA, Mumbai, India, 2010), http://dgftcom.nic.in

150 Reji K. Joseph, 'India's Trade in Drugs and Pharmaceuticals: Emerging Trends, Opportunities and Challenges' (Discussion Paper No. 159, Research Information System for Developing Countries, 2009).

151 Rasmus Alex Wendt, 'TRIPs in India' (unpublished PhD thesis, Roskilde University, 2007), pp.160–78.

152 Padmashree Gehl Sampath, *Economic Aspects of Access to Medicine After 2005* (UNU-MERIT, 2005, 22), p.22, http://www.who.int/intellectualproperty/studies/PadmashreeSampathFinal.pdf

India became an independent nation in 1947, after more than 100 years of British rule, and initially adopted the British *Patents and Design Act, 1911*.[153] Jawaharlal Nehru, India's first prime minister, was concerned about the influence and control of foreign companies over the Indian economy.[154] This concern was validated in two subsequent committee reports.

The 1948 Tek Chand Committee and the 1957 Ayyangar Committee both concluded that foreign interests were exploiting Indian patent protection to monopolise various markets, including the pharmaceutical market.[155] At the time of these reports, India was dependent on foreign sources for pharmaceuticals, including bulk chemicals and completed medicines. The great majority — some 90% — of the Indian pharmaceutical market was controlled by foreign companies.[156] Indian pharmaceutical prices at that time were among the highest in the world.[157] Initially, India sought to solve this problem by instituting high tariffs and price controls on pharmaceuticals.[158] India then amended its patent laws to encourage imitation and local pharmaceutical production. The change came with the passage of the *Patents Act, 1970*, eliminating product patents for pharmaceuticals and only allowing process patents, which gave protection for a maximum period of seven years.[159]

India thus encouraged the mass production of low-cost pharmaceuticals at the expense of innovation. Prime Minister Indira Gandhi, in her statement to the WHO Assembly in 1982, argued that "the idea of a better-ordered world is one in which medical discoveries will be free of patents and there will be no profiteering from life and death".[160] Given this focus, Indian pharmaceutical companies principally engaged themselves in the production of generic versions of name-brand pharmaceuticals through reverse engineering. By applying modified production processes, they successfully avoided conflict with

---

153 Stephen Barnes, 'Note: Pharmaceutical Patents and TRIPS: A Comparison of India and South Africa', *Kentucky Law Journal* 91 (2002–03).

154 Ibid.; David K. Tomar, 'A Look into the WTO Pharmaceutical Patent Dispute between the United States and India', *Wisconsin International Law Journal* 17 (1999).

155 'Note: Pharmaceutical Patents and TRIPS', p.920.

156 'A Look into the WTO Pharmaceutical Patent Dispute', p.582.

157 Ibid.

158 Ibid.

159 The Patents Act, No. 39 of 1970, § 53(1)(a) (India).

160 This quote comes from Indira Gandhi's message to the WHA at Geneva in 1982.

the original patent or having infringement claims made against them.[161] By "free riding" on others' inventions, Indian companies avoided R&D costs.[162] By focusing on existing pharmaceuticals, Indian pharmaceutical companies were able to offer generic alternatives at a fraction of the patented name-brand pharmaceutical cost, and thus India entered both the local and global pharmaceutical markets quickly.[163]

Its policy to exclude product patents for pharmaceuticals allowed the Indian pharmaceutical industry to grow rapidly. However, by joining the WTO, India agreed to adopt the requirements of the TRIPS Agreement. This required India to implement patent protection for pharmaceutical products and processes. After a three-stage amendment process in 1999, 2002 and 2005, India finally entered into a TRIPS-compliant patent regime on 1 January 2005, taking advantage of the entire transition period.[164]

The effect of stronger intellectual patent rights was felt by the larger Indian drug firms and damaged the smaller local firms' ability to meet the rising costs of production and the payment of royalties for patented pharmaceuticals.[165] The Indian TRIPS-compliant patent law was criticised by public health groups as being "likely to bring about a legal regime that is less favorable from the point of view of access to drugs for the people of [India]".[166] It was also argued that the new patent law in India generally provided stronger protection to patent holders, which implied that the balance of interests between inventors and the general public had shifted in favour of the inventor.[167]

However, India tried to preserve public health by limiting data protection and by incorporating into the TRIPS flexibilities much stricter patent standards, pre-grant and post-grant opposition procedures,

---

161 Susan Finston, 'India: A Cautionary Tale on the Critical Importance of Intellectual Property Protection (Essay)', *Fordham Intellectual Property, Media and Entertainment Law Journal* 12 (2002): 888–89.

162 Ibid., 889.

163 Ibid., 889, 894.

164 Janice Mueller, 'The Tiger Awakens: The Tumultuous Transformation of India's Patent System and The Rise of Indian Pharmaceutical Innovation', *University of Pittsburgh Law Review* 68.49 (2007): 491–641.

165 Ibid.

166 See Rajdeep Goswami, *Compliance of TRIPS in Indian Patent Law* (29 April 2012), http://www.legalservicesindia.com/article/article/compliance-of-trips-in-indian-patent-law-1103-1.html

167 Ibid.

compulsory licenses and government use, prior use exceptions, early working or Bolar exemptions, research and experimental use exceptions and parallel imports.[168]

The Indian patent opposition provision not only contains 11 grounds for pre-grant opposition but also permits post-grant opposition to be raised.[169] The Indian grounds for post-grant opposition[170] are broad enough to challenge novelty, inventive steps and the process of industrial application, the best method, claims and disclosure of origin, and even the use of indigenous or local knowledge. LDCs could do likewise, following the Indian model and adopting more extensive pre-grant grounds for objection and a process for post-grant opposition.

India also tried to set high thresholds with respect to the novelty of patent applications so that MNCs could not extend the life of a patent by "ever-greening".[171] In 2006, the Swiss-based pharmaceutical company Novartis AG challenged the constitutional validity of section 3(d) of the Indian *Patent Act, 2005*, which tried to exclude inventions that were not a "significant enhancement of the known efficacy" of the pharmaceutical. Novartis AG challenged the law on the grounds that the provision provided absolute power to the controller of the patent and denied the rights existing under Article 27[172] of the TRIPS Agreement that obliged WTO member states to provide patent protection to all fields of technology without discrimination.[173] The Indian High Court of Madras held that section 3(d) was not in violation of the Constitution of India and declined to rule on its incompatibility with the TRIPS Agreement.[174]

---

168   See generally, 'India's New "Trips-compliant" Patent Regime'.

169   The Patents (Amendment) Act, No. 15 of 2005, § 25 (India).

170   Archana Shanker and Neeti Wilson, *The Patent Opposition System in India* (8 July 2010), http://www.iam-media.com/Intelligence/IP-Value-in-the-Life-Sciences/2008/Articles/The-patent-opposition-system-in-India

171   The Patents (Amendment) Act, No. 15 of 2005, § 3(a), (d), (e), (p) (India).

172   Article 27(1) of the TRIPS Agreement states that "patents shall be available for any inventions, whether products or processes, in all fields of technology, provided that they are new, involve an inventive step and are capable of industrial application ... patents shall be available and patent rights enjoyable without discrimination as to the place of invention, the field of technology and whether products are imported or locally produced".

173   *Novartis A.G. v. Union of India and Others* (2006), 4 Madras L.J. 153 (India), http://www.scribd.com/doc/456550/High-Court-order-Novartis-Union-of-India

174   Ibid.

Government use is another effective means to curb abuse of patents. A government, or its authorised agent, can use a patent without the authorisation of the patent holder. The *Patent Act, 2005* provides for three types of government use. First, a patent is granted in India with the condition that the government can import the medicines for the distribution of pharmaceuticals in public sector hospitals or any other hospitals by making official notification through the government's *Gazette*.[175] Second, the government or authorised persons can use a patent against a royalty payment.[176] Third, the government can acquire a patent after paying compensation.[177] The government can exercise these powers at any time.[178] The patented article, as produced under government-use flexibility, can only be sold for non-commercial use.[179] However, the Act provides room for challenging the government's decision to use or acquire the invention in the High Courts.[180] This means that the patentee could delay such government use, because under the legislation the government has to prove its need before the court.[181]

Like Brazil, India has incorporated options concerning compulsory licenses for use in cases of public interest. India is also using compulsory licensing options to encourage local production in the cases of inadequate supply or excessive pricing, based its measures on the earlier experiences of Brazil, which has effectively and consistently managed to control the costs of several patented drugs by repeatedly threatening the use of the "national emergency" clause provided for under the TRIPS Agreement with regard to compulsory licensing.[182]

Further, the Indian Controller of Patents, while disposing of an application for a compulsory license in *Natco Pharma Ltd. v. Bayer Corporation*,[183] clarified the issue of the working of the patent in the territory of India. The controller noted that the phrase "worked in the

---

175 The Patents (Amendment) Act, No. 15 of 2005, § 47 (India).
176 Ibid., §§ 99, 100.
177 Ibid., § 102.
178 Ibid., § 100(1).
179 Ibid., § 100(6).
180 Ibid., §§ 100, 103.
181 The Patents (Amendment) Act, No. 15 of 2005, §§ 100, 103 (India).
182 'Access to Drugs in India', pp.8–9.
183 *Natco Pharma Ltd v. Bayer Corporation*, Compulsory Licensing Application No. 1 of 2011 (decided by the Controller of Patents, Indian Patent Office, 9 March 2012), http://www.cbgnetwork.org/downloads/BackgroundNexavar.pdf

territory of India" had not been defined in the *Patents Act, 2005* and thus needed to be interpreted with regard to "various International Conventions and Agreements in intellectual property", the *Patents Act, 1970* and legislative history.[184] The controller, using Article 27(1) of TRIPS and Article 5(1)(A) of the Paris Convention, interpreted it to mean that failure to manufacture in India was reason to grant a compulsory license to Natco, stating that "[p]atents are not granted merely to enable patentees to enjoy a monopoly for importation of the patented article" and that "the grant of a patent right must contribute to the promotion of technological innovation and to the transfer and dissemination of technology".[185]

Nevertheless, during the period 2005–10, only one application has been filed for the issuance of a compulsory license in India. This is due to the weakness in the compulsory license regime under the *Patents Act, 2005*.[186] For example, there are no clear guidelines with respect to the requirement to pay royalties.[187]

The Indian patent law amendment of 1999 provided for the early working or Bolar exemption provision to ensure quick entry of generics into the market for competition and hence reduce the price of medicines in India.[188] The 1999 amendment also included a provision on parallel importation by incorporating section 107(A) (b) into the existing Act. Under this provision, parallel importation is permitted for the "importation of patented products by any person from a person who was duly authorised by the patentee to sell or distribute the product".[189] However, this required authorisation from the patentee. The result was that a product could not be imported where it was produced under a compulsory license. This was resolved by a 2005 amendment to enable India to import pharmaceuticals even if the drugs were produced under a compulsory license.[190]

Indian patent law also contains a provision on research and experimental use that allows for the use of patented products for R&D

---

184   Ibid.
185   *Natco Pharma Ltd v. Bayer Corporation.*
186   'Product Patents and Access to Medicines in India', p.341.
187   Ibid.
188   The Patents (Amendment) Act, No. 17 of 2005, § 107(A) (India).
189   Ibid., § 107(A)(b).
190   The Patents (Amendment) Act, No. 17 of 2005, § 107(A) (India).

purposes.[191] Another feature of the Indian law is the provision under prior use exceptions, or the grandfather clause, that allows generic producers to continue the production and marketing of the generic product if they invested in it before the introduction of the product patent in India.[192] This means that if a generic producer can show that it has invested significantly in the production and marketing of a particular product before 1 January 2005, it can continue to operate in the same way even after the introduction of the product patent. However, if any prior use is approved, then the company is required to pay the patent holder a reasonable royalty.[193]

Further, India maintains a price control mechanism to ensure access to affordable medicines.[194] However, the taskforce formed by the Government of India to evaluate drug control mechanisms in India, popularly known as the "Dr Pronab Sen Taskforce", argued that drug control mechanisms in India are not effective. The taskforce claimed that "no price regulatory mechanism can be effective unless there is a credible threat of price controls being imposed and enforced. However, it is also felt that the present price control system is dysfunctional and its legislative authority inappropriate".[195]

The taskforce further recommended that price controls be imposed not on the basis of turnover, but on the "essentiality" of the drug and on strategic considerations regarding the effect of price control on the therapeutic class. The ceiling prices of controlled drugs should normally not be based on cost of production, but on benchmarks that can be readily monitored.[196] The taskforce also recommended that a process of active promotion of generic drugs be put in place, including mandatory de-branding for selected drugs, and that all public health facilities be required to prescribe and dispense only generic drugs, except in cases where no generic alternative exists.[197] It further recommended that in

---

191 The Patents Act, No. 39 of 1970, § 47 (India) (retained as it is in the TRIPS-compliant Indian Patent Law of 1999).

192 The Patents (Amendment) Act, No. 17 of 2005, § 11(A)(7) (India).

193 Ibid.

194 See 'Product Patents and Access to Medicines in India', p.341.

195 Ibid.

196 Ibid.

197 Pronob Sen, *Taskforce to Explore Options other than Price Control for Achieving the Objective of Making Available Life-saving Drugs at Reasonable Prices* (Department of Chemicals and Petrochemicals, India, 2005), pp.4–53.

the case of proprietary drugs—particularly anti-HIV/AIDS and cancer drugs—the government should actively pursue access programs in collaboration with drug companies with differential pricing and alternative packaging, if necessary.[198]

India also utilises the country's traditional medicinal knowledge to ensure access to affordable medicines. It has begun documenting traditional knowledge to prevent the misappropriation of that knowledge by MNCs.[199] MNCs have put pressure on India for the introduction of test data protection, which is submitted to obtain marketing approval; thus, these corporations have attempted to extend their monopoly pricing beyond the patent term. One study suggested that:

> an analysis of article 39 of TRIPS and its legislative history indicates that TRIPS speaks of data protection in a flexible manner, and does not mandate data protection to be implemented by bringing in a data exclusivity regime. Thus, the argument that data exclusivity must be provided for in Indian law for India to be in compliance with TRIPS is fallacious. Protection against "unfair commercial use" under TRIPS must be interpreted to mean protection through non-disclosure and prohibiting others from accessing test data for unfair commercial use. TRIPS gives member states the freedom to choose the nature and extent of protection they want to offer.[200]

This is why most Indian pharmaceutical companies claim that protection need not be in the form of data exclusivity, and why the Government of India provides no data exclusivity protection.[201] In 2002, the Indian government also introduced the *Competition Act, 2002*, which can be

---

198 Ibid., p.54.
199 V.K. Gupta, *Intellectual Property and Sustainable Development: Documentation and Registration of TK and Traditional Cultural Expressions* (12 December 2011), http://www.wipo.int/edocs/mdocs/tk/en/wipo_tk_mct_11/wipo_tk_mct_11_ref_t_5_1.pdf
200 Quoted in Animesh Sharma, 'Data Exclusivity with Regard to Clinical Data', *The Indian Journal of Law and Technology* 3 (2007): 82–104, http://ijlt.in/wp-content/uploads/2015/08/Sharma-Data-Exclusivity-with-regard-to-Clinical-Data-3-Indian-J.-L.-Tech.-82.pdf
201 Ibid. Shamnad Basheer reported that "After multiple deliberations spanning more than 3 years, a government committee has finally submitted its report on regulatory data protection and Article 39.3 of TRIPS. It finds that Article 39.3 does not require 'data exclusivity' and that, at the present moment, it may not be in India's national interest to grant 'data exclusivity' to pharmaceutical drug data. It relies heavily on the Doha Declaration to support this interpretation"; see Shamnad Basheer, 'Indian Government Committee Says "No" to Data Exclusivity' (6 June 2007), http://spicyip.com/2007/06/indian-government-committee-says-no-to.html

utilised to prevent excessive pricing as well as abuse of patents and of dominant market positions.[202]

The Indian experience of utilising TRIPS flexibilities and other government intervention options, such as price controls, could be utilised by LDCs like Bangladesh while still adopting TRIPS-compliant patent law. However, the South African struggle for access to medicines in the context of the TRIPS Agreement and pressure from the MNCs could also be an important consideration for LDCs, especially with respect to the issues of competition law.

3.6 The Experience of South Africa

Compared to India and Brazil, South Africa has a greater health crisis to deal with, including a large number of HIV/AIDS patients and severe problems of access to medicines. Hence, "the case of South Africa (economically the strongest African country) is particularly illustrative of [the] public health crisis and showcases the role domestic and international patent laws and policies may play in this context".[203]

South Africa has a large and highly developed pharmaceutical system, including considerable local production capacity. The South African Medicines Control Council (MCC) licensed 221 entities until 2009 in at least one of the categories of manufacturer, importer and exporter of medicines. Of these, 45 were locally registered subsidiaries or offices of MNPCs, including the major US and European innovators in this field. Africa imports 70% of the medicines it uses, including 80% of its ARV drugs used to treat HIV/AIDS.[204]

---

202 See Abhilash Chaudhary, 'Compulsory Licensing of IPRS and Its Effect on Competition', http://citeseerx.ist.psu.edu/viewdoc/download;jsessionid=3951F6A DF6A3C9DF40C1392A8DD2F8B7?doi=10.1.1.646.5309&rep=rep1&type=pdf. However, until now no successful attempt has been made to use competition law in the pharmaceutical sector. Having a national competition law, India may well embrace the South African experience and apply competition law to the pharmaceutical sector to prevent excessive pricing, if it were to arise in India. See Anand Grover, *Anti-competitive Practices in Patent Licensing Arrangements and the Scope of Competition Law/Policy in Dealing with them* (AMTC, National Workshop on Patent and Public Health, Ministry of Health, India, 11 April 2005).

203 'The South Africa AIDS Controversy', p.2.

204 African Leaders Call for Greater Industrialization of an Emerging Africa, UNAIDS (26 March 2013), http://www.unaids.org/en/resources/presscentre/ featurestories/2013/march/20130326cotedivoire/

South Africa has had patent legislation since at least 1916, and the existing law was promulgated in 1978.[205] South Africa undertook to become TRIPS-compliant in 1997 with the passage of the *Intellectual Property Laws Amendment Act, 1997*.[206] South Africa also became bound by the *Patent Cooperation Treaty* (PCT) in 1999. Further amendments to patent law were made in 2002 and 2005.[207] Although in principle "South Africa adopted TRIPS-compliant patent law, it was increasingly being contended that medicines already subject to a significant degree of regulation must be construed as public goods because of their critical public health and public interest impacts, and therefore TRIPS flexibilities should be used to ensure that patent law would not jeopardize public health concerns".[208] Countries such as South Africa and Brazil attracted the wrath of the US when they adopted TRIPS-compliant laws which used flexibilities in the TRIPS Agreement more broadly than the US wanted.[209]

The significance of the South African experience in dealing with pharmaceutical patent issues under the TRIPS Agreement, considering its national public health crisis, goes beyond doctrinal issues. South Africa used not only legislative approaches under its patent law but also competition law and other government interventions for price bargaining to encourage local generic production and R&D-based pharmaceutical industries. It has been stated that "it touches upon the more fundamental question of to what extent WTO member states— in general and particularly, developing countries—should be free to take legislative measures to deal with public health crises and to what extent the patent protection of pharmaceuticals required under TRIPS should limit the range of options available".[210] The South African

---

205 *Patents Act* 9 of 1916 (S. Afr.); Patents Act 57 of 1978 (S. Afr.).

206 *Patents Amendment Act* 38 of 1997 (S. Afr.).

207 *Patents Amendment Act* 20 of 2005 (S. Afr.); Patents Amendment Act 58 of 2002 (S. Afr.).

208 In Patrick Bond, 'Globalization, Pharmaceutical Pricing, and South African Health Policy: Managing Confrontation with U.S. Firms and Politicians', *International Journal of Health Services* 29 (1999): 765. See also Frederick M. Abbott, 'The Doha Declaration on the TRIPS Agreement and Public Health: Lighting a Dark Corner at the WTO', *Journal of International Economic Law* 5 (2002): 469–505.

209 See 'Globalization, Pharmaceutical Pricing, and South African Health Policy'; see also Abbott, 'The Doha Declaration on the TRIPS Agreement and Public Health'.

210 In 'The South Africa AIDS Controversy'.

experience brought the potential tension between patent protection for pharmaceuticals and public health concerns to the forefront of public awareness and triggered "a global debate about what should be allowed and what should be prohibited under TRIPS in order to preserve the incentives for investments in R&D of pharmaceuticals, while still allowing countries the flexibility to respond to public health crises as they deem fit".[211]

After apartheid, the vast majority of South Africans did not have access to healthcare at all, making healthcare reform one of the prime concerns for the post-apartheid government. This was in line with the mandate articulated within South Africa's newly adopted constitution to undertake substantial policy measures to ensure access to affordable healthcare for everyone.[212] To this end, the post-apartheid government appointed a National Drug Policy Committee to revamp South Africa's healthcare system.[213] After a series of investigations and consultations with relevant stakeholders, the committee found that among the most notable deficiencies were the lack of equity in access to essential drugs, the comparatively high prices for pharmaceuticals in the private sector and the loss of drugs through poor security in the public sector.[214]

The pharmaceutical companies in South Africa disapproved of the finding and argued that even lowering drug prices would not solve the access problem, as South Africa did not have adequate infrastructure for the distribution of drugs. The South African companies referred to India as an example of a country where access remains an issue despite the availability of generic versions of AIDS drugs.[215]

However, considering the excessive pricing of medicines by the MNCs in South Africa, the government inserted a new section 15C into the South African MRSCA.[216] The primary purpose of this amendment was to enable South Africa to benefit from lower prices abroad for the same drugs. The enactment of the MRSCA, with its provisions for parallel importation, attracted serious criticism from supporters of

---

211 Ibid.
212 Fisher and Rigamonti, pp.2–3, citing the 1996 South African Constitution.
213 'The South Africa AIDS Controversy', pp.2–3.
214 Ibid., citing 'National Drug Policy for South Africa', pp.9–10 (1996) (these page deals with drug pricing).
215 'New Crusade to Lower AIDS Drug Costs'.
216 *Medicines and Related Substances Control Amendment Act.*

patent protection for the pharmaceutical industry (as they considered it among the options for issuing compulsory licensing), whereas it received strong support from public health groups.[217] Regardless, the planned modifications, including section 15C, were signed into law by President Nelson Mandela on 12 December 1997.[218]

In an attempt to delay or halt the implementation of the amendments, the pharmaceutical companies took the matter to court and challenged the constitutionality of the amended MRSCA before the High Court of South Africa in February 1998.[219] While challenging section 15C, the plaintiffs argued (i) that the amended provision entailed an inappropriate delegation of powers to the executive branch of government, as the Minister of Health would be authorised to determine both the application of patent rights irrespective of the South African Patents Act and the conditions for the supply of more affordable medicines without any limiting guidelines; (ii) that it would empower the Minister of Health to deprive IP owners of their property without compensation in violation of Article 25 of the South African Constitution (which provides for the protection of property rights); and (iii) that it would violate obligations under Articles 44(4), 231(2) and 231 (3) of the South African Constitution and under Article 27 of the TRIPS Agreement, as South Africa had committed itself to meeting TRIPS obligations.[220]

However, the South African government defended its amended legislation, stating that section 15C was constitutional as it granted the Minister of Health only limited powers to abrogate patent rights, and under the South African Constitution the government had an obligation to protect its citizens' right to health.[221] Further, it claimed that section 15C was consistent with TRIPS, arguing that TRIPS allowed parallel

---

217 The planned modifications, including Section 15C, were signed into law by President Nelson Mandela on 12 December 1997. See ibid.

218 Ibid.

219 See 'Notice of Motion in the High Court of South Africa'.

220 Paragraphs 2.1, 2.3 and 2.4 of the 'Notice of Motion in the High Court of South Africa'; see also T. Kongolo, 'Public Interest Versus the Pharmaceutical Industry's Monopoly in South Africa', *Journal of World Intellectual Property* 4 (2001): 605–16.

221 See Holger Hestermeyer, 'Human Rights and the WTO: The Case of Patents and Access to Medicines' (Oxford Scholarship Online), http://dx.doi.org/10.1093/acpro f:oso/9780199552177.001.0001

imports and that section 15C did not address issues of compulsory licensing.[222]

The South African government alleged that it was being held to a "TRIPS-plus" standard, and therefore a higher level of patent protection beyond the requirements of the TRIPS Agreement, both by the US Government and the private plaintiffs in the lawsuit.[223] The constitutional challenge over the amended MRSCA had the effect of temporarily staying its implementation.

The contentious positions taken by public health activists and pharmaceutical companies regarding the MRSCA was explained in a study:

> while AIDS activists such as the South African Treatment Access Campaign (TAC) called for international protests against "drug profiteering" and claimed that delaying the implementation of the amended MRSCA would only cost additional lives, the pharmaceutical companies defended the court action on the grounds that "parallel importation of drugs would undermine the ability of pharmaceutical companies to charge different prices in different parts of the world" and that a "tiered pricing strategy allows wealthier countries to subsidize poorer ones, and the drug companies still get profits they need for research".[224]

Supporting the position of the South African government, the then Health Minister stated that "[w]e are not intending to bust any patents. We [are] not intending to break any treaties. All we want to do is to give health services to the people who are poor in this country, and to the people who have been denied those health services for centuries".[225]

But the pharmaceutical companies viewed section 15C as a threat to their business, and they feared that the explicit authorisation of parallel imports could turn into an example for other countries. The MNCs, mostly led by the US pharmaceutical industry, strongly opposed the

---

222 See Joint study by the WHO and the WTO Secretariats on 'WTO Agreements and Public Health' (2002), p.106, https://www.wto.org/english/res_e/booksp_e/who_wto_e.pdf

223 Fisher and Rigamonti (citing Statement by the South African Delegation, Minutes of the Council for TRIPS Special Discussions on Intellectual Property and Access to Medicines, IP/C/M/31 (10 July 2001)), p.27.

224 Quoted in 'The South Africa AIDS Controversy'. See also Steve Sternberg, 'Victims Lost in Battle Over Drug Patents', *USA Today* (May 24, 1999), 2D.

225 'The South Africa AIDS Controversy', p.7.

enactment of section 15C and argued that it was tantamount to a complete abrogation of patent rights and a violation of South Africa's obligations under the TRIPS Agreement.[226] As a representative of Bristol-Myers Squibb put it, "[p]atents are the lifeblood of our industry. Compulsory licensing and parallel imports expropriate our patent rights", adding that the only beneficiary of the erosion of patents would be the generic drug industry.[227]

The Pharmaceutical Research and Manufacturers of America, a trade group representing the US pharmaceutical industry, lobbied the US government and claimed the issue was sufficiently important to warrant putting pressure on South Africa to repeal the contested legislative measures. James Joseph, at that time the US ambassador to South Africa, wrote a letter to representatives of the South African government, strongly urging South Africa to alter section 15C and stating that "my Government opposes the notion of parallel imports of patented products anywhere in the world".[228] South Africa was also put on the *Special 301 Watch List*[229] in both 1998[230] and 1999[231] after the US Trade Representative determined that South Africa lacked adequate IP protection to an extent that merited bilateral attention. Being on the watch list meant it was possible for South Africa to have unilateral trade sanctions imposed on it by the US. However, the US did not bring a WTO case against South Africa due to a huge public health campaign both inside the US and beyond; the possible negative publicity was too great. The role of the-then Democratic presidential candidate Al Gore was also important, as he was co-chairman of the US/South Africa Binational Commission and had been actively involved in pressuring South Africa to give in to the demands of the pharmaceutical industry.

---

226 US subsidiaries accounted for 27% of the pharmaceutical market in South Africa, which was a higher share of the market than was accounted for by South Africa's local pharmaceutical industry. See 'Nkosazana Zuma'.

227 'The South Africa AIDS Controversy', p.5.

228 'South Africa's Health Committee Rejects MRSCA Bill Change', *Pharma Marketletter* (21 October 1997).

229 For details on this, see 19 USC. § 2411.

230 10 No. 6 J. Proprietary Rts. 19 (June 1998).

231 1999 US Trade Representative Special 301 Report (also stating that "South Africa's *Medicines Act* appears to grant the Health Minister ill-defined authority to issue compulsory licenses, authorize parallel imports, and potentially otherwise abrogate patent rights").

He consequently became one of the main targets of AIDS activists who had long urged the US government to change its policy towards South Africa.[232]

In April 2001, the pharmaceutical companies dropped their court challenge regarding section 15C and agreed to cover the South African government's legal expenses in the face of what has been described as a public relations nightmare.[233]

The situation leading to compromises between the South African government and the pharmaceutical companies was well stated by William W Fisher III and Cyrill P Rigamonti:

> the talks behind the scenes leading to the withdrawal involved Kofi Annan, the Secretary General of the United Nations, who was contacted by Jean-Pierre Garnier, the CEO of GlaxoSmithKline, on behalf of the largest pharmaceutical companies to broker a deal with Thabo Mbeki, the then President of South Africa. The EU and the WHO supported South Africa's position. As part of the deal, South Africa reiterated its pledge to comply with TRIPS when implementing the amendments to the MRSCA and invited the pharmaceutical industry to help draft future regulations.[234]

The position taken by South Africa was not only a reflection of the struggle between excessive pricing of patented medicines by the pharmaceutical companies and the government's societal and constitutional obligations to ensure access to medicines and the right to healthcare. It was also representative of the broader international struggle over the meaning of TRIPS, especially over the scope of and exceptions to internationally recognised IPRs.[235]

---

232 See for details, 'The South Africa AIDS Controversy'.

233 As one journalist put it, "Can the pharmaceuticals industry inflict any more damage upon its ailing public image? Well, how about suing Nelson Mandela?" Helene Cooper, Rachel Zimmerman and Laurie Mcginley., 'AIDS Epidemic Puts Drug Firms in a Vise: Treatment vs. Profits', *Wall Street Journal* (March 2, 2001). See also Rachel L. Swarns, 'Drug Makers Drop South Africa Suit over AIDS Medicine', *The New York Times* (20 April 2001), A1.

234 'The South Africa AIDS Controversy'. See also 'Drug Makers Drop South Africa Suit', and Ann M. Simmons, 'Firms Clear Way for Cheaper AIDS Drugs', *Chicago Tribune* (20 April 2001), 4.

235 'Pharmaceutical Production and Access to Essential Medicines in South Africa', p.29.

This South African case illustrates the fact that the issue of parallel imports is left to individual WTO member states to decide. Although the MRSCA provided an option for parallel imports, the South African patent law did not make explicit provisions for it.[236] Section 45(1) of the *Patents Act* states that the patent owner has the right to exclude others from importing the invention to which the patent relates during the duration of the patent.[237]

However, an amendment in 2002 added Section 45(2), which provides for the exhaustion of rights, although it does not contain any wording that would indicate that international exhaustion would apply—in other words, that parallel importation would be permitted.[238] Hence, South Africa issued a draft national IP policy on 4 September 2013, which proposed changing South Africa's IP laws to adopt a number of health safeguards, including a user-friendly parallel importation mechanism.[239] The non-existence of international exhaustion for parallel imports was confirmed by an announcement on 5 November 2013 by the Department of Trade and Industry of South Africa, which stated that "the *Patents Act* as it stands does not address issues of pricing of medicines, despite the fact that the National Policy on Intellectual Property seeks to address such matters".[240] It further stated that "South Africa will amend its legislation to address issues of parallel importation and compulsory licensing in line with the Doha Decision of the *WTO* on Intellectual Property and public health".[241]

---

236 This aspect was considered by the High Court in the case of *Stauffer Chemical Company v. Agricura Ltd* (1979) BP 168. The Judge confirmed that only national exhaustion was intended and found nothing that would induce (him) to depart from this principle.

237 Substituted by section 40 of Act no. 38 of 1997 (South Africa).

238 Section 45(2) provides as follows: "The disposal of a patented article by or on behalf of a patentee or his licensee shall, subject to other patent rights, give the purchaser the right to use, offer to dispose of and dispose of that article". See section 45(2), *Patent Act* no. 57 of 1978 (Sub-s(2) substituted by section 7 of Act No. 58 of 2002). For details, see http://www.wipo.int/wipolex/en/text.jsp?file_id=181330

239 See 'Draft National Policy on Intellectual Property 2013' (South Africa), http://ipasa.co.za/wp-content/uploads/2013/07/IPASA-Extracts-from-Submission-made-on-the-DRAFT-NATIONAL-POLICY-ON-IP....pdf

240 Quoted in 'South Africa "Seeks Balance" Between Intellectual Property, Public Health', http://www.bdlive.co.za/national/health/2013/11/06/south-africa-seeks-balance-between-intellectual-property-public-health

241 Ibid.

Most countries and commentators agree with South Africa that Article 6 of the TRIPS Agreement is based on a country-by-country approach to the exhaustion of IPRs and parallel imports.[242] This view is based on a plain reading of the TRIPS Agreement as well as on its drafting history. Although the issue of parallel imports was discussed by the TRIPS negotiators, they failed to reach a consensus on the subject. This is precisely because developing countries favoured international exhaustion, whereas the US advocated national exhaustion (and the EU tried to preserve the principle of EU-wide exhaustion).[243]

The South African controversy also centred on the question of whether it would be compatible with Articles 30 and 31 in the TRIPS Agreement for a WTO member state to grant compulsory licenses to lower drug prices to combat AIDS.

Articles 30 and 31 in the TRIPS Agreement set forth the conditions for the validity of a domestic compulsory licensing scheme.[244] To the extent that such a scheme does not "unreasonably conflict with the normal exploitation of the patent" and does not "unreasonably prejudice the legitimate interests of the patent owner", it is legal under Article 30 of the TRIPS Agreement.[245] If these general requirements are not met, however, the compulsory licensing mechanism is only permissible if it complies with the detailed prerequisites listed in Article 31 of the TRIPS Agreement. In the context of South Africa, the pharmaceutical companies feared that the Minister for Health could use the amended MRSCA to bypass these provisions to their detriment and to the benefit of South African manufacturers of generic drugs.

But in reality, this has rarely happened—despite the fact that, in addition to the MRSCA, the *South African Patents Act* of 1978 provides an avenue for the government and the courts to enforce compulsory

---

242 See 'Resource Book on TRIPS and Development' (portion on the drafting history of TRIPS, including parallel imports).

243 Ibid.

244 See TRIPS Agreement, art. 30, 31.

245 For example, in a case brought by the EU against Canada, the WTO Panel decided that Canada's "pre-expiration testing" exemption was consistent with Article 30 of TRIPS, while its "stockpiling" exemption was not. See *Canada—Patent Protection of Pharmaceutical Products*.

licenses.[246] Thus, despite having a huge health crisis and access problems, South Africa has never used compulsory licenses.[247]

However, the South African government has yet to make use of a statutory power that entitles it to "use an invention for public purposes".[248] The government must approach the court for assistance if the terms and conditions of government use—which include the licensing of generic companies as a mechanism for reducing drug prices—cannot be agreed upon.[249] There is little or no guidance on the terms and conditions associated with such compulsory licences in any reported judgements in South Africa. This almost certainly indicates that none have ever been granted.[250] The application for a compulsory license by local pharmaceutical companies requires huge legal and technical capacity as they will face legal battles with the larger competitors in the market. Vaver stated that "it is true that the risk that a licensee may

---

246 Sections 56(1) and 56(2), *Patents Act, 1978* (Act No. 57 of 1978, as last amended by *Patents Amendment Act, 2002*), South Africa.

247 See *Bayer's Attempt to Block Generic Production of Sorafenib Rejected; Case on India's First Compulsory License Still to be Heard in Court*, FIX THE PATENT LAWS (19 September 2012), http://www.fixthepatentlaws.org/?p=420

248 Section 4 Act 57 of 1978 (South Africa): "**State bound by patent**: A patent shall in all respects have the like effect against the State as it has against a person: Provided that a Minister of State may use an invention for public purposes on such conditions as may be agreed upon with the patentee, or in default of agreement on such conditions as are determined by the commissioner on application by or on behalf of such Minister and after hearing the patentee".

249 Section 56 Act 57 of 1978 (South Africa): "**Compulsory licence in case of abuse of patent rights** (1) Any interested person who can show that the rights in a patent are being abused may apply to the commissioner [a High Court judge] in the prescribed manner for a compulsory licence under the patent". In terms of section 56(2), the rights in a patent are deemed to be abused—if within a stated period of years there is without satisfactory reason inadequate or no commercial exploitation; if demand is not being met adequately and on reasonable terms; and if "by reason of the refusal of the patentee to grant a licence or licences upon reasonable terms, the trade or industry or agriculture of the Republic or the trade of any person or class of persons trading in the Republic, or the establishment of any new trade or industry in the Republic, is being prejudiced, and it is in the public interest that a licence or licences should be granted".

250 However, there are few reported decisions on court-granted compulsory licenses under section 56 of the South African Patent Act. Three cited cases in this regard are *Syntheta (Pty) Ltd (formerly Delta G Scientific (Pty) Ltd v. Janssen Pharmaceutica NV and Another* 1999 (1) SA 85 (SCA) at 88I, per Plewman JA; *Sanachem (Pty) Ltd v. British Technology Group plc* 1992 BP 276; and *Afitra (Pty) Ltd and Another v. Carlton Paper of SA (Pty) Ltd* 1992 BP 331. The court challenge under this provision has been used successfully in at least one matter to induce a major pharmaceutical company to grant a voluntary licence.

itself become the target of litigation may be an inhibition therefore non issuance of a compulsory license is primarily reluctance to antagonise large competitors. But if the regulatory framework was easier (and less risky) to use, there seems little doubt that such licenses will more readily be sought".[251]

Unlike Brazil and India, the South African Patent Office does not conduct a substantial patent examination=; therefore, it does not check novelty and non-obviousness of the invention.[252] It merely registers patents that fulfil the formalities set out for registration.

The absence of a local patent examination system means that patents are granted without substantive review or verification of whether they meet the patentability requirements provided for in the South African *Patents Act*. The Patent Office has no filter to ensure that patents are granted only when they are deserved. This undermines the country's ambition to provide free access to medicines and boost local production by its own generic industry.[253] This has been noted as a major drawback to the patent application system in South Africa, because setting high thresholds and requiring strict examination of novelty character could open up policy spaces for local generic producers to oppose patent applications for pharmaceuticals.[254] It is generally believed that the multinational pharmaceutical industry is fully exploiting this weakness in South Africa's legal and patent system to extend market exclusivity on key medicines that are nearing patent expiry.[255] According to one study, 2,442 pharmaceutical patents were registered in South Africa in a single year, 2008.[256]

Another loophole in the South African patent system is that South African legislation makes no provision for pre-opposition procedures and there appears to be a complete lack of transparency in the patent application process. The statute merely requires the registrar to conduct

---

251 See David Vaver, 'Intellectual Property Today: Of Myths and Paradoxes', *Canadian Bar Review* 69 (1990): 98–126.

252 'Why South Africa should Examine Pharmaceutical Patents' (TAC, MSF and RIS January 2013), http://donttradeourlivesaway.wordpress.com/2013/01/10/why-south-africa-should-examine-pharmaceutical-patents

253 Ibid.

254 Ethel Teljeur, *Intellectual Property Rights in South Africa: An Economic Review of Policy and Impact* (The Edge Institute, South Africa, 2003).

255 Ibid.

256 Ibid.

a formal tick-box approach to an application.[257] Based on simple tick-box examination of applications and specifications, the Registrar of Patents could grant patents if the applications merely comply with the requirements of the Act (Section 34). Due to a lack of pre-grant opposition and effective post-grant procedures, the South African opposition procedure may not be helpful for local generic producers.

The South African Patent Law of 1978 (Act No. 57 of 1978, as last amended by the *Patents Amendment Act, 2002*) covers the exclusions envisaged by TRIPS Article 27. These are exclusions of patents on inventions that encourage offensive or immoral behaviour as per Section 25(4) (a); on any variety of animal or plant or any essentially biological process for the production of animals or plants, not being a microbiological process or the product of such a process as per Section 25(4)(b); and on any surgical, therapeutic or diagnostic method of treatment of humans or animals as per Section 25(11). Further, it empowers the Registrar of Patents to refuse any application that is frivolous, or whose use encourages illegal, immoral and offensive behaviour, including publication or exploitation.[258] It is unclear how this provision is to be applied considering that the concepts of morality and offensive behaviour are relative, particularly in a diverse and evolving society such as South Africa.

South African patent law does not make explicit provision for educational, experimental or research exceptions.[259] One report stated that "the only indication in the Patents Act that the legislature may have intended to exclude non-commercial use from the definition of infringement is to be found in section 45(1) of the Act"[260] and:

---

257 Section 34 of the *Patent Act* (South Africa).

258 Ibid., § 36.

259 Esmé du Plessis, Report Q.202 (South Africa), AIPPI, https://www.aippi.org/download/commitees/202/GR202south_africa.pdf

260 Ibid., § 45(1) provides as follows: "45.(1) The effect of a patent shall be to grant to the patentee in the Republic, subject to the provisions of this Act, for the duration of the patent, the right to exclude other persons from making, using, exercising, disposing or offering to dispose of, or importing the invention, so that he or she shall have and enjoy the whole profit and advantage accruing by reason of the invention".

it could be argued that the reference to "the whole profit and advantage" in this provision could be indicative of an intention by the legislature to exclude other persons from carrying out the prohibited acts only insofar as those acts would have prejudicial commercial implications for the patent owner. However, South Africa courts have not yet considered this aspect to pronounce a clear principle (on the basis of section 45(1) or any other consideration) to the effect that non-commercial use of a patented invention (e.g. for research or experiment) would avoid infringement.[261]

Nevertheless, section 69A of the *Patents Act* was introduced by a legislative amendment in 2002 and provided for a Bolar-type exemption's.[262] As the definitions of experimental use exceptions and *Bolar*-type exemptions were not clear enough, the varied interpretations prevented the exemptions from being used by generic producers effectively and led to court cases for delaying generic entry in the market. It is also noted that stockpiling of products made or imported under section 69A (1) is prohibited by section 69A (2).[263]

On the other hand, there is no reference to test data protection in the *Patents Act*: protection of clinical trial data in South Africa predates its inclusion in the TRIPS Agreement.[264] In line with the practice of regulatory authorities worldwide, the MCC does not publicly disclose or share data submitted for registration purposes. However, when

---

261 Ibid.

262 Section 69A provides as follows: "69A (1) It shall not be an act of infringement of a patent to make, use, exercise, offer to dispose of, dispose of or import the patented invention on a non-commercial scale and solely for the purposes reasonably related to the obtaining, development and submission of information required under any law that regulates the manufacture, production, distribution, use or sale of any product. (2) It shall not be permitted to possess the patented invention made, used, imported or acquired in terms of subsection (1) for any purpose other than for the obtaining, development or submission of information as contemplated in that subsection".

263 Ibid.

264 The *Medicines and Related Substances Control Act, No 101 of 1965* controls the regulation of medicines in South Africa and does contain general confidentiality provisions related to medicines. Sections 22B and 34, read together, would suggest that there is general protection of information submitted with respect to the regulation of medicines against unfair commercial use. Again, section 22B permits the Director General of Health to disclose information relating to medicines where it is deemed "expedient and in the public interest". See http://www.wipo.int/edocs/lexdocs/laws/en/na/na018en.pdf

considering an application for the registration of a generic equivalent, the MCC does not require the applicant to furnish any new data on the safety and efficacy of the drug, but merely on the quality of the generic.[265]

Reviewing the basis of existing South African patent law reveals that competition law provides a more effective sanction than existing patent law against patent abuse in the form of an anti-competitive compulsory license, which is consistent with Article 31(k) of TRIPS.[266] The South African Competition Commission has already applied competition law successfully in the pharmaceutical sector to deal with restrictive practices and abuse of a dominant position.

In *Hazel Tau and Others v. GlaxoSmithKline and Boehringer Ingelheim*,[267] the prices set by the two litigating companies were considered to be an obstacle in accessing ARV medicines.[268] The Competition Commission ruled that the companies had violated the *Competition Act, 1998* in denying "a competitor access to an essential facility, [setting] excessive pric[es] and engag[ing] in an exclusionary act", whereas the pharmaceutical companies argued they were merely exercising the exclusive right they were granted through their patent, as they did in many other countries.[269] Nonetheless, the commissioner stated that:

> [o]ur investigation revealed that each of the firms has refused to license their patents to generic manufacturers in return for a reasonable royalty.

---

265 Ibid.

266 Ibid.

267 Dani Cohen and Jennifer Cohen, *Competition Commission Finds Pharmaceutical Firms in Contravention of the Competition Act* (Competition Commission, 2003), http://www.cptech.org/ip/health/sa/cc10162003.html

268 In brief, the fact is that the pharmaceutical companies GlaxoSmithKlein and Boehringer, patent owners of ARV (HIV/AIDS) drugs, set unjustifiably high prices for these drugs in South African markets. AZT (300 mg) is sold at US$0.92 as compared to the WHO generic price of US$0.25. Compulsory licensing negotiation under the *South African Patent Act* proved futile as the companies demanded a 25% royalty on sales, compared with the international rate of 4–5%. The Competition Commission took action under Section Eight of the South African Competition Act, which prohibits "a dominant firm to charge an excessive price to the detriment of the consumers", ordering the issuance of licenses to market generic versions of the patented ARV drugs in return for the payment of a reasonable royalty to be decided by the Competition Tribunal.

269 Ibid.

We believe that this is feasible and that consumers will benefit from cheaper generic versions of the drugs concerned. We further believe that granting licenses would provide for competition between firms and their generic competitors. We will request the Tribunal to make an order authorizing any person to exploit the patents to market generic versions of the respondent's patented medicines or fixed dose combinations that require these patents, in return for the payment of a reasonable royalty.[270]

Even though GlaxoSmithKline and Boehringer Ingelheim denounced the complaint as unfounded, they sided with the commission and granted voluntary licenses to produce a generic version of their patented pharmaceuticals. Since this case was decided, there has been huge progress in South Africa towards providing access to anti-HIV and AIDS pharmaceuticals.[271]

The South African model of competition law could be utilised by developing countries and LDCs including Bangladesh to prevent excessive pricing of medicines.

3.7 Comparative Review and Lessons for the LDCs, including Bangladesh

This analysis highlights that India, Brazil and South Africa have used different options in their transition to a pharmaceutical patent regime and TRIPS-compliant patent law. India and Brazil substantially revised their national patent laws using the flexibilities present in the TRIPS Agreement. These flexibilities are also available to LDCs as they move towards TRIPS compliance. The issues for LDCs are which flexibilities to adopt and at what stages during the transition process to use them. The different policy options taken by these countries are represented diagrammatically in Table 3.1.

---

270 Rachel Roumet, 'Access to Patented Anti-HIV/AIDS Medicine: The South African Experience', *European Intellectual Property Review* 3 (2010): 137, 140, citing 'South African Competition Finds GSK and BI Responsible for "Excessive Pricing" and "Abuse of Market Position"', in *HIV Treatment Bulletin* (December 2003/January 2004), http://i-base.info/htb/12424

271 'Access to Patented Anti-HIV/AIDS Medicine'.

Table 3.1: Policy options used by Brazil, India and South Africa

TRIPS stage	Legislative position	India	Brazil	South Africa	China	Remarks
Pre-TRIPS	1. No patent protection for pharmaceuticals. 2. Process patent only. 3. Limited duration for pharmaceutical patent protection.	To encourage the generic production of drugs and to develop imitating capacity, India prohibited product patents and allowed only process patents for pharmaceuticals. Process patent for pharmaceuticals granted only for seven years.	Eliminated both process and product patents for pharmaceuticals.	Provided both product and process patents for pharmaceuticals in the pre-TRIPS period without any substantive examination.	Did not grant process and product patents for pharmaceuticals until 1984. The 1984 patent law amendment introduced granting of patent protection on process, and the 1992 amendment introduced granting of patent protection on pharmaceutical products.	India allowed process patents only during the pre-TRIPS regime, whereas Brazil eliminated patent protection for pharmaceuticals altogether; South Africa provided both product and process patenting even during the pre-TRIPS period.
Transitional period: until 1 January 2005 for developing countries and until 1 January 2016 for LDCs (extended to 1 July 2021)	Utilisation of full transition period.	Utilised the full transition period and introduced TRIPS-compliant patent law in 2005.	Approved a TRIPS-compliant patent law (Industrial Property Law 9.279) in 1996 and implemented it in May 1997.	Undertook to become TRIPS-compliant in 1997.	Officially became a WTO member on 11 December 2001 and during accession negotiations committed itself to reforming its IPR regime. Accordingly, it adopted TRIPS-compliant patent law on 25 August 2000, which entered into force on 1 July 2001.	Brazil and South Africa introduced TRIPS-compliant law several years before the 2005 deadline, whereas India waited until the expiration of the whole period.

Flexibilities under TRIPS-compliant patent law and other available policy options				
Strict patentability requirements: absolute novelty and high level of disclosure. Early working or Bolar exemption and research & experimental use. Pre- and post-grant opposition. Compulsory license and government use. Parallel imports. Prior use exception. Limit test data protection. Price control. Utilisation of traditional medicinal knowledge. Competition law.	Included all legislative options in its national patent law.	Included all provisions in its national patent law, especially compulsory licensing; but use of traditional medicine is not significant and test data protection is not limited as it is in India.	Included some TRIPS flexibilities such as compulsory licensing and parallel imports; has competition law and price control mechanism; but has no substantive patent examination system, pre-grant opposition, or clear rules on experimental use and prior use. However, it does provide test data protection.	Included all the flexibilities by a three-step amendment process in 2000, 2008 and 2012, creating a strong legal base for compulsory licensing. But China provides data exclusivity due to pressure from the US government and to satisfy investors in the pharmaceutical sector.	A combination of the Brazilian and Indian approaches may be useful to balance innovation and public health. In addition, the South African experience of price control and competition law could be useful for LDCs. China as a big market power has strong bargaining capacity to reduce prices, which may not be the case for the LDCs.

The requirement to move towards TRIPS has created apprehension within Bangladesh, where the fear is that the price of pharmaceuticals in the local market will increase and local pharmaceutical companies may not survive, due to the high cost of royalties for patented medicines and the need to compete with MNCs.[272] In this regard, the experiences of Brazil, India and South Africa, in their utilisation of the TRIPS flexibilities and other alternative measures to balance innovation and access to pharmaceuticals, should be considered by LDCs including Bangladesh.

The present patent regime in Bangladesh has no effective provisions for utilising the TRIPS flexibilities in the way that India, Brazil and South Africa have done. Importantly, to utilise the flexibilities, it is necessary to amend Bangladesh's *Patents and Designs Act, 1911.*[273] In addition to utilising TRIPS flexibilities, the Government of Bangladesh could adopt a competition law based on the experience of South Africa and could also revise its price control mechanisms based on the experiences of India and Brazil.

The Government of Bangladesh enacted its *Competition Act, 2012* in June 2012.[274] According to one study, "A draft bill for such a law was first proposed in 1996; however, it took 16 years to finally come to fruition".[275]

The progress of the bill was delayed because "the political will to implement a competition law is limited, and there is some opposition from business groups".[276] "Indeed, competition problems are potentially more serious in a country [such as Bangladesh] with a weaker private sector, where one or a few dominant firms can take control" and abuse their dominant position.[277] "The media coverage ... suggests [that] Bangladesh may suffer from significant competition problems, with

---

272 'Pharmaceutical Patent Protection', pp.1–4.
273 For details, See, *History of Indian Patent System*. For details about required patent law reform options for Bangladesh, see Mohammad Monirul Azam, 'Globalising Standard of Patent Protection in WTO and Policy Options for the LDCs', *Chicago-Kent Journal of Intellectual Property*, 13.2 (2014), pp.402–88.
274 Rafia Afrin with Daniel Sabet, 'Will Bangladesh's New Competition Law Prove Effective?' (1 July 2012), http://ces.ulab.edu.bd/wp-content/uploads/sites/18/2015/07/Competition_law_07-12.pdf
275 Ibid.
276 Ibid.
277 Ibid., p.2.

substantial costs to consumers"[278] and to the public health sector of Bangladesh, more specifically.

However, it is suggested that taking lessons from South African competition law, the Competition Commission of Bangladesh should rectify the weakness by empowering the Competition Commission to issue compulsory licenses, to recommend fixed royalty rates, and to expressly allow for the export of products produced under compulsory licenses to maintain sustainable investment.[279] In addition, LDCs like Bangladesh may also stipulate in national competition law that compulsory licensing could be granted in cases of anti-competitive behaviour, such as in the case of the patent holder's unilateral refusal to grant a license (refusal to deal).[280] Competition law could also be applied in the case of obtaining pharmaceutical patents in an unjustified and fraudulent manner.[281] Again, the issues of "poor quality" and "frivolous" patents and regulatory practices, such as marketing approval and data exclusivity, can be controlled under competition law.[282]

Further, research has shown that despite having an impressive sales and export growth, the local pharmaceutical industry in Bangladesh, particularly after the introduction of the DCO 1982, helped Bangladesh ensure the supply of generic medicines at a lower price, but limited the local industrial development of innovative capacity for basic research and patenting of new medicines.[283] On the other hand, lack of proper monitoring by the DGDA in Bangladesh raises the question of quality

---

278 Ibid.

279 See 'Globalising Standard of Patent Protection', p.462; see also T. Avafia, J. Berger and T. Hartzenberg, 'The Ability of Select Sub-Saharan Africa Countries to Utilize TRIPS Flexibilities and Competition Law to Ensure a Sustainable Supply of Essential Medicines: A Study of Producing and Importing Countries' (tralac Working Paper, No. 12/2006, August 2006), pp.4–5, http://www.section27.org.za/wp-content/uploads/2010/10/Avafia-Berger-and-Hartzenberg.pdf

280 See Carlos M. Correa, *Intellectual Property and Competition Law: Exploration of Some Issues of Relevance to Developing Countries* (International Centre for Trade and Sustainable Development, 2007), p.20, http://www.iprsonline.org/resources/docs/corea_Oct07.pdf

281 In fact, these patents should never be granted in the first place. However, lack of proper resources, expertise and proper examination in LDCs may allow for such fraudulent registrations. In these situations, competition law could play an important role.

282 See Correa (2007).

283 Azam and Richardson (2010a), p.6.

medicines.[284] Also, a lack of expertise and required resources in the Patent Office of Bangladesh raises doubts over its capability to deal with pharmaceutical patents and TRIPS-compliant patent law.[285]

3.8 Concluding Remarks

This chapter has identified options used by Brazil, India and South Africa during their transitions to a TRIPS-compliant patent regime. These options enabled them not only to promote the local pharmaceutical industry but also to maintain access to medicines. The experiences of India, Brazil, China and South Africa will have important lessons for LDCs like Bangladesh. Brazil, India, China and South Africa utilised TRIPS flexibilities in their process of transition to TRIPS-compliant patent law. This study revealed how these countries utilised these options in order to locate the right balance between the interests of the pharmaceutical industry and the increased demand by the public for affordable medicines. On this basis, the author's current position is that LDCs will need to utilise the benefit of the transition period of the TRIPS Agreement, consider their technological and infrastructural limitations, and together to lobby for further extension of the transition period for the introduction of pharmaceutical patents.[286] The future of the pharmaceutical industry in the LDCs follows from the legislative and policy intervention options taken by the Bangladeshi government to implement TRIPS-compliant patent legislation, and the extent to which local industry can utilise the TRIPS waiver to develop technological and innovative skills for transitioning from a copycat into an innovative nation.[287]

---

284 Ibid., pp.11–14.
285 Ibid., p.10.
286 Ibid., pp.1–2.
287 Ibid.

4. The Globalising Standard of Patent Protection in WTO Law and Policy Options for the LDCs: The Context of Bangladesh

4.1 Introduction

This chapter analyses the globalising standard of patent protection as adopted under the TRIPS Agreement of the WTO and measures it against the experiences of Brazil, India and South Africa in order to identify possible options for the LDCs,[1] with special reference to pharmaceutical patent issues. The developed member states of the WTO negotiated mandatory protection for pharmaceutical products and processes in the TRIPS Agreement, on the basis that such mandatory protection would provide the incentive for continued pharmaceutical innovation. In contrast, the developing countries and LDCs argued that enacting patent laws that comply with the TRIPS Agreement would restrict production and supply of low-cost generic medicines by their local pharmaceutical industries or by the pharmaceutical industries in other developing countries, and hence could increase the price of pharmaceuticals to the point that they become inaccessible to their populations.

During the TRIPS negotiations, it was argued that the principle of a balance of rights and obligations was required because IP owners needed to undertake certain obligations in return for the exclusive rights conferred on them, and also to allow governments to take remedial

---

1   See for details, *Criteria for Identification and Graduation of LDCs*, UN-OHRLLS, http://unohrlls.org/about-ldcs/criteria-for-ldcs

     http://dx.doi.org/10.11647/OBP.0093.04

measures in the case of non-fulfilment of these obligations so that IPRs could promote industrial creativity to benefit society in general.[2] This principle was generally recognised in pre-existing IP conventions and in the national laws of many countries:[3] "The acceptance of this principle was aimed at assuring the access of developing countries to modern technology, eliminating non-use, misuse or abusive use of IPRs, especially with a view to avoiding trade distortions, and allowing the flexibility in the intellectual property protection for the public interest and the developmental and technological needs of developing countries" and LDCs.[4]

Therefore, the principle of balance of rights and obligations could be used while also employing other flexibilities of the TRIPS Agreement. It was further suggested that the TRIPS Agreement should take into account the application of the GATT principle of securing a balance of rights and obligations among parties.[5] However, as in the case of the principle of public interest, the application of the principle of balance of rights and obligations was adopted with the lock of the consistency test. As worded in TRIPS Article 8.2, any measure taken under the umbrella of this article must be "consistent with" the provisions of the TRIPS Agreement.[6] Moreover, the extents to which a practice is regarded as "unreasonably" restraining trade or "adversely" affecting the international transfer of technology and to which a national response against such practices is regarded as an appropriate measure are ambiguous under article 8.2. These unclear conditions leave room for interpretation, and create difficulties in applying the principle of balance of rights and obligations. Considering the room for interpretation of TRIPS flexibilities and practices for countries like India, Brazil and

---

2   GATT, Negotiating Group on TRIPs, 'Including Trade in Counterfeit Goods', *Meeting of Negotiating Group of 11–13 September 1989*, GATT Doc. MTN.GNG/ NG11/15 (26 October 1989), p.20, https://www.wto.org/gatt_docs/English/ SULPDF/92080131.pdf

3   See Michael Blakeney, *Trade Related Aspects of Intellectual Property Rights: A Concise Guide to the TRIPS Agreement* (Intellectual Property in Practice) (1998).

4   'How to Comply with the TRIPS and WTO Law', p.42.

5   See Negotiating Group on TRIPs, 'Including Trade in Counterfeit Goods', *Meeting of Negotiating Group of 10–21 September 1990*, MTN.GNG.NG11/25, p.8, http://www. wto.org/gatt_docs/English/SULPDF/92110158.pdf

6   TRIPS Agreement, art. 8.2.

South Africa, this chapter explores possible options for Bangladesh while it complies with patent provisions under the TRIPS Agreement.

Brazil, India and South Africa used TRIPS flexibilities in different ways to modify their national patent regimes to become TRIPS-compliant,[7] though they experienced some difficulties with respect to the legislative measures they enacted.[8] However, the legislative provisions were found to be within the scope of the flexibilities of the TRIPS Agreement. Bangladesh, as an LDC, faces similar public health challenges but also has the potential to become a substantial (global) producer of generic medicines. The need to balance these competing interests (pharmaceutical innovation and access to pharmaceuticals) means that there are good grounds for Bangladesh to use the Indian, Chinese, Brazilian and South African experiences as a way to guide

---

7   For example, Brazil implemented a system of compulsory licensing. See 'The Politics of Patents and Drugs in Brazil and Mexico', p.41. India's experience was very different. It entered the WTO in 1995 and went through a long amendment process to institute a TRIPS-compliant patent regime, which became effective on 1 January 2005. See 'India's New "Trips-compliant" Patent Regime', p.95. The effect of stronger intellectual patent rights created problems for the larger Indian drug firms and greatly damaged the ability of smaller local firms to meet the rising costs of royalties and remuneration of experienced and efficient pharmacists and other technical people. See 'Note: Pharmaceutical Patents and TRIPS', pp.911, 924–25.

8   For example, the DSB of the WTO established a panel, as requested by the US, to look into the complaint about the patent laws of Brazil in 2001, which the US claimed illegally required the local working of patents and enabled compulsory licensing of the patent, or the authorisation of imports of the patented product (parallel imports), without the authorisation of the patent holder. See WTO, *Brazil: Measures Affecting Patent Protection*, Dispute Settlement: Dispute DS199, http://www.wto.org/english/tratop_e/dispu_e/cases_e/ds199_e.htm. However, due to massive public pressure and campaigns by public health groups, both parties negotiated it outside the DSB. See ibid. In contrast, Indian patent law was challenged even in the Indian courts by an MNPC, Novartis, claiming that it was inconsistent with some of the provisions of the TRIPS Agreement. Rajshree Chandra, 'The Role of National Laws in Reconciling Constitutional Right to Health with TRIPS Obligations: An Examination of the Glivec Patent Case in India', in *Incentives for Global Public Health—Patent Law and Access to Essential Medicines*, ed. by Thomas Pogge, Mathew Rimmer, and Kim Rubenstein (Yale University, 2010). Another major concern is the confiscation of generic Indian medicines used to treat illnesses such as AIDS and hypertension in several European countries, regarding which India and Brazil complained to the WTO, saying that the European Union (EU) had wrongfully confiscated generic medicines. See Jennifer M. Freedman, 'India, Brazil Complain at WTO over EU Drug Seizures', *Business Week* (12 May 2010), http://web.archive.org/web/20100515054911/http://www.businessweek.com/news/2010-05-12/india-brazil-complain-at-wto-over-eu-drug-seizures-update3-.html (accessed by searching the Internet Archive index).

Bangladesh's legislative transition to a TRIPS-compliant patent regime. It is crucial for Bangladesh to use these experiences to develop IPR policies that preserve the full complement of TRIPS flexibilities. In this regard, a comment by Rochelle Cooper Dreyfuss is worth noting: "These practices [of India, Brazil, South Africa, and other developing countries] achieve international recognition as they are defended in international courts and put on the agendas of international organizations".[9] Therefore, "domestic actors then may interpret the law in a particular way that allows them to offer a new approach that others may choose to emulate".[10] While evaluating the possible policy options for LDCs to balance pharmaceutical innovation and access to medicines against the experiences of Brazil, India and South Africa in complying with the TRIPS-compliant patent law, relevant discussions, policies and recommendations as formulated in the WHO will also be indicated. The discussions here do not use the experience of China, because China has a very strong technological base, critical bargaining capacity and substantial market power; therefore the Chinese perspective is not relevant for the LDCs.

This chapter explores possible legislative and government intervention options for Bangladesh, utilising the experiences of Brazil, India and, to some extent, South Africa (as the South African patent law has yet to introduce a substantive patent examination process, some of the important policy options such as disclosure, high threshold, novelty, pre-grant and post-grant requirements have not been well tested in South Africa). It also reflects on the relevant policy issues and recommendations from the WHO. This chapter uses legal doctrinal analysis, comparative review and field research in Bangladesh, by way of surveys and interviews aimed at understanding stakeholders' perceptions of the various policy options available under the TRIPS Agreement. The field research in Bangladesh analysed in depth the

---

9   Rochelle C. Dreyfuss, 'The Role of India, China, Brazil and Other Emerging Economies in Establishing Access Norms and Intellectual Property and Intellectual Property Law Making' (IICJ Working Paper, 2009), http://papers.ssrn.com/sol3/papers.cfm?abstract_id=1442785

10   Susan K. Sell, 'TRIPS Was Never Enough: Vertical Forum Shifting, FTAS, ACTA and TPP', *Journal of Intellectual Property Law* 18 (2011): 447, 476. http://infojustice.org/download/tpp/tpp-academic/Sell - TRIPS Was Never Enough - June 2011.pdf

situation at the DPDT[11] and the DGDA[12] to understand the ongoing roles of these two important regulatory bodies during the TRIPS waiver period and their possible roles in a post-TRIPS setting.

4.2 Legislative Options for Bangladesh

Drawing on the Brazilian, Indian and South African experiences, a number of legislative options should be considered by Bangladesh in introducing TRIPS-compliant patent law to help preserve its local pharmaceutical industry and to promote innovation and access to medicine. For the purposes of this chapter, the legislative options include (i) having a high threshold for patentability and exclusion from patentability provisions, (ii) having a best mode patent disclosure and disclosure of origin, (iv) narrowing the scope of patent claims, (iv) providing exceptions to product patent rights such as early working, parallel imports, and research and experimental use exceptions, (v) having a strong compulsory licensing mechanism, (vi) having prior use exceptions, (vii) having pre-grant and post-grant oppositions, (viii) making the duration of patent protection subject to exceptions and (ix) not adopting overprotective enforcement provisions. Each of these options will be examined in turn.

4.2.1 A High Threshold and Exclusion Clause

Under the TRIPS Agreement, patent protection must be granted for products and processes that are *new*, involve an *inventive step* and are *industrially applicable*.[13] The definition of an *invention* itself constitutes a key aspect of any patent policy with implications in other areas, such as industrial and public health policies. Therefore, with countries that are net importers of technologies, their priority should be to focus on narrowing the scope of patentability and incorporating as many exceptions as possible under the national patent law to facilitate

---

11   See DPDT, http://www.dpdt.gov.bd
12   See *Assessment of the Regulatory Systems* (2012).
13   TRIPS Agreement, art. 27.1 (providing that "patents shall be available for any inventions, whether products or processes, in all fields of technology, provided that they are new, involve an inventive step and are capable of industrial application").

development of a viable technological base. This also applies in the case of pharmaceutical products.

The TRIPS Agreement did not define the criteria for patent protection; therefore, these criteria can be interpreted and applied by member states in accordance with their national priorities and developmental goals.[14] For example, the TRIPS Agreement "does not specify the patenting of new uses of known products, including pharmaceutical drugs, thus allowing member countries the possibility of rejecting these new uses for lack of novelty, inventive step or industrial applicability".[15]

The TRIPS Agreement considers novelty to mean that the invention is not already part of an existing invention and involves an inventive step.[16] Considering the importance of having a high threshold for patentability in countries like Bangladesh, Tony VanDuzer states:

> It is a common practice of patent owners in the pharmaceutical sector to seek to extend the effective duration of patent protection by obtaining a second later patent on a new mode of delivery of a patented drug (such as capsules instead of tablets) or some other small change in a patented product. Setting high standards for novelty and inventive step would help to ensure that a patent on a product was not, in effect, extended by a subsequent patent on a trivial improvement.[17]

Justifying the non-granting of patents for new uses or second uses, Correa remarks:

---

14   See Mohammed El Said, 'The Implementation Paradox: Intellectual Property Regulation in the Arab World', *Journal of International Trade Law and Policy* 9 (2010): 221, 228.

15   Ibid., 229.

16   See ibid., Article 27.1, which reads:
Subject to the provisions of paragraphs 2 and 3, patents shall be available for any inventions, whether products or processes, in all fields of technology, provided that they are new, involve an inventive step and are capable of industrial application. Subject to paragraph 4 of Article 65, paragraph 8 of Article 70 and paragraph 3 of this Article, patents shall be available and patent rights enjoyable without discrimination as to the place of invention, the field of technology and whether products are imported or locally produced.

17   Tony VanDuzer, 'TRIPS and Pharmaceutical Industry in Bangladesh: Towards a National Strategy' (Paper No. 24, CPD, April 2003), http://www.bdresearch. org/home/attachments/article/nArt/TRIPS_and_the_Pharmaceutical_Industry_ in_Bangladesh.pdf. See generally Rajnish Kumar Rai, 'Patentable Subject Matter Requirements: An Evaluation of Proposed Exclusions to India's Patent Law in Light of India's Obligations under the TRIPS Agreement and Options for India', *Chicago-Kent Journal of Intellectual Property* 8 (2008).

Such an invention relating to the use of a product may be deemed as non-patentable because it consists of the discovery of an existing property rather than a new development, or because it falls under the exclusion from patentability (allowed by the [TRIPS] Agreement and most national laws) of therapeutical methods.[18]

It is feared that awarding protection to new uses of medicines will stifle innovation and restrict the ability of pharmaceutical companies in developing countries and LDCs to produce advanced medications needed for eradicating local disease.[19] This requirement could also block the introduction of generics, particularly in those countries where pharmacy laws do not permit generic substitution and/or generic prescribing.[20] This will have anti-competitive consequences and result in higher prices for medications.

In this regard, the CIPIH Report provides that:

Governments should take action to avoid barriers to legitimate competition by considering developing guidelines for patent examiners on how properly to implement patentability criteria and, if appropriate, consider changes to national patent legislation.[21]

Again, the UK IPR Commission recommends that:

Most developing countries, particularly those without research capabilities, should strictly exclude diagnostic, therapeutic and surgical methods from patentability, including new uses of known products.[22]

On the one hand, "there is no agreed international standard of absolute novelty, and, within limits, the developing countries may pick and choose from among the different approaches recognized in the domestic

---

18 *Intellectual Property Rights, The WTO and Developing Countries*, p.56.

19 See Carlos Correa, 'Guidelines for the Examination of Pharmaceutical Patents: Developing a Public Health Perspective — A Working Paper' (2006), pp. iv–v, http://ictsd.net/downloads/2008/04/correa_pharmaceutical-patents-guidelines.pdf

20 See Ibid., p.1.

21 WHO, 'Public Health, Innovation, and Intellectual Property Rights: Report of the Commission on Intellectual Property Rights, Innovation and Public Health' (2006) (the "CIPIH Report"), p.133, http://www.who.int/intellectualproperty/documents/thereport/ENPublicHealthReport.pdf

22 Commission on Intellectual Property Rights, 'Integrating Intellectual Property Rights and Development Policy' (2002), p.50, http://www.iprcommission.org/papers/pdfs/final_report/CIPRfullfinal.pdf. Clare Short, the then British Secretary of State for International Development, established the Commission on Intellectual Property Rights in May 2001.

patent laws",[23] but on the other, the manner of dealing with the issue of the scope of patentability differs from one country to another because this issue relies heavily on each country's level of progress, development and technological capability.

Further, in addition to the flexibility awarded in drafting its patentability criteria, the TRIPS Agreement provides for a number of exemptions that may be excluded from patentability. Article 27.2 of TRIPS states:

> Members may exclude from patentability inventions, the prevention within their territory of the commercial exploitation of which is necessary to protect *ordre public* or morality, including to protect human, animal or plant life or health or to avoid serious prejudice to the environment, provided that such exclusion is not made merely because the exploitation is prohibited by their law.[24]

The fact that the TRIPS Agreement does not define "protect *ordre public* or morality" gives member states additional room for flexibility.

The existing patent law of Bangladesh, the PDA, contains no legislative provision regarding the patentability of a pharmaceutical product and no provision detailing excluded categories of inventions. By defining thresholds to impose a significant requirement for novelty, Bangladesh could ensure that trivial improvements in technology do not receive patent protection. India adopted such an approach in its amended *Patent Act, 2005*.[25] The *Patent Act, 2005* restricts the scope for granting patents based on frivolous claims[26] and clarifies that an "inventive step" means a feature of an invention that "involves technical advances as compared to the existing knowledge or having economic significance or both".[27] It also provides a definition for "pharmaceutical substance" as being "a new entity involving one or more inventive steps",[28] and that "the mere

---

23   J.H. Reichman, 'From Free Riders to Fair Followers: Global Competition under the TRIPS Agreement', *New York University Journal of International Law and Politics* 29 (1997): 11, 30.

24   TRIPS Agreement, art. 27.2.

25   See Reichman (1997), p.93.

26   'Product Patents and Access to Medicines in India', pp.326, 334.

27   The *Patents Act, 1970*, § 2(ja), No. 39, Acts of Parliament, 1970 (India).

28   Ibid., § 2(ta).

discovery of a new form of a known substance which does not result in the enhancement of the known efficacy" is not patentable.[29]

In an attempt to ensure access to medicine, section 3(b) of the Indian *Patent Act, 2005* excludes from patentability "an invention the primary or intended use or commercial exploitation of which could be contrary to public order or morality or which causes serious prejudice to human, animal or plant life or health or to the environment".[30] Section 3(p) excludes patenting of "an invention which, in effect, is traditional knowledge or which is an aggregation or duplication of known properties of traditionally known component or components".[31] This provision is an attempt to avoid bio-piracy and ensure that traditional knowledge, whether handed down or developed, is incapable of being captured by patents. One interview participant commented that Section 3 of the *Patent Act, 2005* is a powerful instrument to prevent frivolous patents and the abuse of traditional knowledge and resources in India.[32]

Given the absence of patentability and exclusion clauses in the existing patent law of Bangladesh, such legislative provisions should be considered by Bangladesh as it moves towards TRIPS compliance. These provisions comply with the TRIPS Agreement, and are justified on the basis that limiting the availability of patents should promote competition in the local market.[33] However, the *Draft Patents and Designs Act, 2010* of Bangladesh (the Draft PDA)[34] includes provisions on patentable

---

29 Ibid., § 3(d).

30 The *Patents (Amendment) Act, 2005*, § 3(b), No. 15, Acts of Parliament, 2005 (India).

31 Ibid., § 3(p).

32 Email Interview with a patent law academic in Delhi, India, 10 March 2012.

33 See generally 'Trips Compliant Patent Law', p.141.

34 In 2001, a draft patent law was prepared by the Law Commission of Bangladesh in consultation with the WIPO. It was not considered until 2007. Meanwhile, for LDCs, the transition period for the introduction of TRIPS-compliant intellectual property law, including patent law, was extended until July 2013, and the obligation to introduce pharmaceutical patents was extended until 1 January 2016. See WTO, *Developing Countries' Transition Periods*, 'Fact Sheet: TRIPS and Pharmaceutical Patents', http://www.wto.org/english/tratop_e/trips_e/factsheet_pharm04_e.htm. This draft was reviewed lightly in 2007, and was under consideration by the Ministry of Law and Parliamentary Affairs of Bangladesh as the *Draft Patents and Designs Act, 2010*. It was translated by the Law Commission and Ministry of Law into the national language "Bangla" with little revision and adopted as a separate draft Act in "Bangla" for patents only, as *Bangladesh Patent Ain, 2012* (*Bangladesh Patent Act, 2012*). Unless this draft is approved by the Parliament of Bangladesh, the existing PDA, 1911 will remain in force.

inventions[35] and exclusion from patentability.[36] Unlike the Indian patent law provisions, these provisions fail to utilise the high threshold of patentability options effectively because they lack a provision covering pharmaceutical substances, an exclusion clause pertaining to mere improvement and protection from abuse of traditional knowledge. The Draft PDA tries to extend the ambit of prior art under the definition of novelty:

> prior art in the case of an invention shall be taken to comprise-(a) all matter, whether a product, a process, information about either, or anything else, made available to the public anywhere in the world, by written or oral description, by use or in any other way, at any time prior to the filing or, as the case may be, the priority date, of the application for patent claiming the invention.[37]

However, this provision may not be effective without a specific exclusion clause; therefore, these provisions should be revised in light of the Indian *Patent Act, 2005*.

Local pharmaceutical companies in Bangladesh view this provision as very important for generic producers and consumers because it will increase competition in the local market.[38] However, MNPCs argue that a high threshold for patentability will exclude local inventions, which would not benefit society.[39] The middle ground would suggest that such a provision will balance the need to maintain and support innovation with the need for access to pharmaceuticals.

4.2.2 Best Mode Disclosure and Disclosure of the Source of Genetic Resources and Traditional Knowledge

As the aim of the patent regime is the disclosure of information and spread of knowledge, a "[l]ack of sufficient disclosure may be a reason for refusal result in the rejection of an application or invalidation of

---

35 *Draft Patents and Designs Act, 2010* § 3, 2010 (Bangl.).
36 Ibid., § 4.
37 Ibid., § 5(2).
38 Based on the survey data, this position has been supported by the majority of large, medium and small local pharmaceutical companies in Bangladesh.
39 This has been remarked on by the CEO of an MNPC operating in Bangladesh.

a patent".[40] Correa stresses that "[t]his requirement has particular importance in the chemical and pharmaceutical fields to enable the reproduction of the invention during the patent term (for instance, in the case of a compulsory license) or after patent's expiry".[41]

Article 29 of the TRIPS Agreement requires that an applicant for a patent disclose the invention "in a manner sufficiently clear and complete for the invention to be carried out by a person skilled in the art",[42] which "may also require the applicant to indicate the best mode for carrying out the invention known to the inventor at the filing date".[43]

The absence of strong disclosure requirements will have long-term negative implications for innovation, technology transfer and the dissemination of technology in the pharmaceutical sector in developing countries.[44] It will likely strengthen the monopolistic position of MNPCs by preventing local pharmaceutical companies from benefiting from the disclosed technical information and by precluding efforts in R&D based on that information.[45]

Section 4(2) of Bangladesh's PDA simply states that "a complete specification must particularly describe and ascertain the nature of the invention and the manner in which the same is to be performed".[46] Bangladesh should take advantage of Article 29 of the TRIPS Agreement by requiring disclosure of the best known mode for carrying out the invention and also stipulating that the disclosure enable the execution of all embodiments of the invention.

During an interview, one participant argued that given the weakness of the existing provisions, patent applications in Bangladesh are typically ambiguous. Often it is difficult to ascertain a precise description of the invention, which ultimately frustrates the objective of granting a patent

---

40   Correa (2006), p.4.

41   Ibid.

42   TRIPS Agreement, art. 29.

43   Ibid.

44   Ibid.

45   See generally Bingbin Lu, 'Best Mode Disclosure for Patent Applications: An International and Comparative Perspective', *Journal of Intellectual Property Rights* 16 (2011): 409, http://papers.ssrn.com/sol3/papers.cfm?abstract_id=1938859

46   PDA, § 4, effective 26 March 1971 by virtue of the Laws Continuation and Enforcement Order of 25 March 1971, and adaptation of Existing Bangladesh Law Order of 1972. The PDA is the same as the Indian PDA (No. II of 1911 (10 Pat. & T.M. Rev. 3697)).

in exchange for sufficiently disclosing the invention to contribute to technical learning and teaching.[47] One participant argued that the ultimate benefit of disclosing an invention is the further development of that particular invention, which leads to increased competition in the marketplace; thus, after the expiry of the patent term, competitors can enter the market with more viable options.[48]

Both India and Brazil have adopted the best mode disclosure approach. Section II, Article 24 of the Brazilian *Industrial Property Law* provides that the "specifications shall clearly and sufficiently describe the object, so as to permit its reproduction by a technician versed in the subject, and shall indicate, when applicable, the best way of doing it".[49] On the other hand, section 10(4) of the Indian *Patent Law, 1970* requires that every complete specification shall:

1) fully and particularly describe the invention and its operation or use and the method by which it is to be performed;

2) disclose the best method of performing the invention which is known to the applicant and for which he is entitled to claim protection.[50]

Therefore, Bangladesh should adopt a similar requirement to facilitate innovation and the development of competing products. It is worth noting that section 11 of the Draft PDA of Bangladesh includes a provision demanding that every complete specification shall:

1) fully and particularly describe the invention and the method by which it is to be performed

2) disclose the best method of performing the invention which is known to the applicant and for which he is entitled to claim protection.[51]

Adoption of this provision would help the DPDT of Bangladesh to reject patent applications if the inventions are not sufficiently disclosed.

---

47   Interview with a pharmacist from a leading local pharmaceutical company, in Dhaka, Bangladesh, 3 March 2009.

48   Interview with an examiner at the DPDT, in Dhaka, Bangladesh, 1 March 2009.

49   Lei No. 9.279 art. 24, de 14 de maio de 1996, Diario Oficial Da Uniao [DOU] de 15.05.1996. (Braz.), translated in Brazil: *Industrial Property Law*, 14/05/1996, No. 9.279, http://www.wipo.int/wipolex/en/details.jsp?id=515

50   The *Patents Act, 1970*, § 10(4), No. 39, Acts of Parliament, 1970 (India), http://ipindia.nic.in/ipr/patent/patent_2005.pdf

51   *Draft Patents and Designs Act, 2010* § 11, 2010 (Bangl.).

However, best mode disclosure does not necessarily require disclosure of origin, and hence may not prevent abuse of genetic resources and traditional knowledge. This has led a number of developing countries, including Brazil and India,[52] to debate in the WTO the question of "whether and how patent applicants should be obliged to disclose the origin or source of the genetic resource and traditional knowledge used in an invention and provide evidence of prior informed consent and benefit sharing".[53] As TRIPS Article 29 does not specifically require disclosure of origin, developing countries are requesting amendments to the TRIPS Agreement to ensure that the necessary requirements are incorporated into patent application procedures.[54]

Switzerland also made proposals relating to disclosure of origin to the WTO/TRIPS Council,[55] to the WIPO Working Group on Reform of the *Patent Cooperation Treaty, 1970* (PCT 1970)[56] and to the WIPO Intergovernmental Committee on Intellectual Property and Genetic

---

52   See WTO Council for TRIPS, 'Elements of the Obligation to Disclose the Source and Country of Origin of Biological Resource and/or Traditional Knowledge Used in an Invention' (IP/C/W/429) 2 (21 September 2004), http://docsonline.wto.org/imrd/directdoc.asp?DDFDocuments/t/IP/C/W429.doc

53   See WTO Public Symposium, 'Disclosure Requirements: Incorporating the CBD Principles in the TRIPS Agreement on the Road to Hong Kong' (21 April 2005), p.1, http://ictsd.org/downloads/2008/12/meeting-report.pdf

54   Tove Iren S. Gerhardsen, 'Developing Countries Propose TRIPS Amendment on Disclosure', *Intellectual Property Watch* (1 June 2006): 1344, http://www.ip-watch.org/2006/06/01/developing-countries-propose-trips-amendment-on-disclosure

55   See WTO Council for TRIPS, Article 27.3(b), 'Relationship Between the TRIPS Agreement and the CBD, and the Protection of Traditional Knowledge' (IP/C/W/400/Rev.1), 18 June 2003, http://docsonline.wto.org/imrd/directdoc.asp?DDFDocuments/t/IP/C/W400R1.doc; see also WTO Council for TRIPS, 'Further Observations by Switzerland on its Proposals Regarding the Declaration of the Source of Genetic Resources and Traditional Knowledge in Patent Applications' (IP/C/W/433) (25 November 2004), http://docsonline.wto.org/imrd/directdoc.asp?DDFDocuments/t/IP/C/W433.doc

56   Working Group on Reform of the Patent Cooperation Treaty (PCT), WIPO, International Patent Cooperation Union, Proposals by Switzerland Regarding the Declaration of the Source of Genetic Resources and Traditional Knowledge in Patent Applications (PCT/R/WG/4/13) (5 May 2003), http://www.wipo.int/edocs/mdocs/pct/en/pct_r_wg_4/pct_r_wg_4_13.pdf; Working Group on Reform of the Patent Cooperation Treaty (PCT), WIPO, International Patent Cooperation Union, Proposals by Switzerland Regarding the Declaration of the Source of Genetic Resources and Traditional Knowledge in Patent Applications (Doc PCT/R/WG/5/11 Rev.), 19 November 2003, http://www.wipo.int/edocs/mdocs/pct/en/pct_r_wg_5/pct_r_wg_5_11_rev.pdf

Resources, Traditional Knowledge and Folklore.[57] In Switzerland's opinion, "the provisions of the TRIPS Agreement provide for adequate flexibility with regard to a formal requirement to disclose the source. Accordingly, Switzerland does not consider it necessary to amend the TRIPS Agreement".[58] Consequently, it can be said that TRIPS Article 29 does not prevent the introduction of the requirement to disclose the source within the national legislation.[59] In the context of Bangladesh, one interviewee argued that "in the absence of qualified and experienced examiners, best mode disclosure and disclosure of origin provisions would have little effect".[60]

In Bangladesh, neither the existing PDA nor the Draft PDA includes any provision on the disclosure of origin. However, the *Draft Patent Law, 2012* states under section 15 that patents on genetic resources or traditional knowledge could be granted provided that the procedure of "relevant authority and related rules" is followed, and, before such patents are granted, due consideration must be given to the issues of public order and morality.[61] There is no explanation or indication in the draft law regarding "relevant authority and rules", nor is there an

---

57   See WIPO Intergovernmental Committee on Intellectual Property, and Genetic Resources, Traditional Knowledge, and Folklore, Further Observations by Switzerland on Its Proposals Regarding the Declaration of the Source of Genetic Resources and Traditional Knowledge in Patent Applications (WIPO/GRTKF/IC/7/INF/5) (18 October 2004), http://www.wipo.int/edocs/mdocs/tk/en/wipo_grtkf_ic_7/wipo_grtkf_ic_7_inf_5.pdf

58   Felix Addor, WTO Public Symposium, ICTSD/CIEL/IDDRI/IUCN/QUNO, 'Dialogue on Disclosure Requirements: Incorporating the CBD Principles in the TRIPS Agreement On the Road to Hong Kong: Switzerland's Proposals Regarding the Declaration of the Source of Genetic Resources and Traditional Knowledge in Patent Applications and Switzerland's views on the Declaration of Evidence of Prior Informed Consent and Benefit Sharing in Patent Applications' (21 April 2005), p.5, http://www.iprsonline.org/ictsd/docs/DOO6_Addor.pdf

59   "A number of countries ... have already [incorporated] disclosure of origin requirements (in different forms and conditions) in their domestic legislation, including in the Andean Community (Bolivia, Colombia, Ecuador, Peru and Venezuela), Brazil, Costa Rica, Denmark, India, Nepal, Norway and the African Union (53 African countries)". *Disclosure Requirements: Ensuring Mutual Supportiveness Between the WTO TRIPS Agreement and the CBD*, ed. by Martha Chouchena-Rojas, Manuel Ruiz Muller, David Vivas, and Sebastian Winkler (IUCN: Gland and Cambridge; International Centre for Trade and Sustainable Development [ICTSD], Geneva, 2005).

60   Interview with an IP lawyer working as a legal adviser and practitioner at the Supreme Court, in Dhaka, Bangladesh, 27 December 2009.

61   See *Draft Patent Ain (Law), 2012* § 15, 2012 (Bangl.).

existing authority in Bangladesh that deals with the issues of genetic resources or traditional knowledge. Therefore, Bangladesh should amend the proposed law, preferably to include disclosure of origin as part of patent application requirements rather than in a separate provision.

In addition to high-level disclosure, limiting the scope of patent claims may also be useful for Bangladesh.

4.2.3 Narrowing the Scope of Patent Claims

In a 2003 report, VanDuzer states:

> The broader the claims that an inventor can make under [a patent] law, the wider the monopoly the inventor can obtain. Broad claims reduce the scope for competing products in the market, whereas narrow claims create greater opportunities for innovation and competition. National laws vary in the nature and breadth of claims permitted. In relation to pharmaceutical products claims can be restricted to the chemical structure or composition of a new product ... The TRIPS Agreement is silent on the form of and limits on allowable claims and so Bangladesh would be free to adopt a patent law that requires that pharmaceutical patent claims be limited to the precise chemical composition of the product.[62]

Section 4(3) of the PDA of Bangladesh provides that a specification, whether provisional or complete, must commence with the title, and in the case of a complete specification must end with a distinct statement of the invention claimed.[63] Based on this provision, the law is not able to facilitate the narrowing of coverage of pharmaceutical patents, but rather encourages applications for broad patents. By way of comparison, Brazilian legislation provides that "[t]he claims shall be substantiated in the specifications, characterizing the particulars of the application, and clearly and precisely defining the subject matter that is the object of the protection".[64] During an interview, one participant argued that most of the pharmaceutical patents granted in Bangladesh

---

62 'TRIPS and Pharmaceutical Industry in Bangladesh', p.33.

63 PDA § 4(3), 1911 (Bangl.).

64 Lei No. 9.279 art. 25, de 14 de maio de 1996, Diario Oficial Da Uniao [DOU] de 15.05.1996. (Braz.), translated in Brazil: *Industrial Property Law*, 14/05/1996, No. 9.279, http://www.wipo.int/wipolex/en/details.jsp?id=515

prior to the suspension of pharmaceutical patents in 2008 were based on broad claims, which in the future may restrict the production of generic pharmaceuticals.[65] Therefore, Bangladesh should adopt provisions similar to those of Brazil that narrow the ability to claim a pharmaceutical patent on broad claims. However, to encourage further development and innovation on any patented product, additional exceptions are necessary to facilitate generic competition and cheaper products for consumers. Such exceptions include early working, a research and experimental use exception, and parallel imports.

4.2.4 Exceptions to Product Patent Rights

Patent rights are not absolute but are subject to certain limitations and exceptions. These limitations and exceptions are often designed to foster and promote technology transfer, to prevent the abuse of IP, to foster research and innovation, and to protect public policy priorities including public health.

Article 30 of the TRIPS Agreement permits member countries to "provide limited exceptions to the exclusive rights conferred by a patent".[66] That article does not list the specific acts for which exceptions can be provided. What it says is that such exceptions should satisfy certain conditions that do not "unreasonably conflict with a normal exploitation of the patent and do not unreasonably prejudice the legitimate interests of the patent owner, taking account of the legitimate interests of third parties".[67] The TRIPS Agreement does not contain any explanation of the terms "limited exceptions", "unreasonably conflict", "legitimate interests" and "hence the use of this provision depends on the interpretation of these conditions".[68] There are two exceptions used by India and Brazil

---

65   Interview with a pharmaceutical researcher at the University of Dhaka, in Dhaka, Bangladesh, 12 March 2009.

66   TRIPS Agreement, art. 30.

67   Ibid.

68   Mohammad Monirul Azam and Yacouba Sabere Mounkoro, *Intellectual Property Protection for the Pharmaceuticals: An Economic and Legal Impacts Study with Special Reference to Bangladesh and Mali*, LE GRIOT DU DEVELOPPEMENT § 7.1.2 , June 1, 2012, http://legriotdudeveloppement.blogspot.co.uk/2012/06/intellectual-property-protection-for.html

in their legislative framework: (i) early working (Bolar exemptions), and research and experimental use; and (ii) parallel importing.

4.2.5 Early Working (or Bolar Exceptions), Research and Experimental Use

The early working exemption is commonly referred to as the "Bolar" provision or exception, as it derives from *Roche Products, Inc. v. Bolar Pharmaceutical Co.*,[69] which concerned the manufacturing of generic pharmaceuticals. Bolar Pharmaceutical was the generic drug manufacturer and Roche Products was the pharmaceutical company that made and sold Valium, the active ingredient of which was patented.[70] Before the patent expired, Bolar used the patented chemical in experiments to determine if its generic product was the bioequivalent to Valium, and thus could be given US Food and Drug Administration (FDA) approval for its generic version.[71] Bolar argued that its use of the patented product was not an infringement based on the experimental use exception and that public policy favoured the availability of generic drugs immediately following a patent's expiration.[72]

The Court of Appeals for the Federal Circuit "rejected Bolar's contention holding that the experimental use exception did not apply because Bolar intended to sell its generic product in competition with Roche's Valium after patent expiration and, therefore, Bolar's experiments had a business purpose", and did not qualify for the statutory exception.[73] The court recognised that any change to the patent law needed to be made by Congress.[74]

Shortly after the Bolar Pharmaceutical case was decided, Congress passed a law permitting the use of patented products in experiments

---

69 *Roche Prods., Inc. v. Bolar Pharm. Co.*, 733 F. 2d 858 (Fed. Cir. 2006); see Anshull Mittal, 'Patent Linkage in India: Current Scenario and Need for Deliberation', *Journal of Intellectual Property Rights* 15 (2010).

70 *Bolar Pharm.*, 733 F.2d at 861.

71 Ibid., 861–62.

72 Ibid., 862.

73 'Patent Linkage in India', p.193.

74 See ibid.

for the purpose of obtaining US FDA approval.[75] As a result of this change, exceptions for early working gained momentum and now Bolar exceptions have been enacted in most jurisdictions.[76]

Importantly, the WTO Dispute Panel upheld the use of the Bolar exception as conforming to the requirements of the TRIPS Agreement in the Canada–EU dispute.[77] Supporting the inclusion of an early use exception, the CIPIH Report recommended that "Countries should provide in national legislation for measures to encourage generic entry on patent expiry, such as the 'early working' exception, and more generally policies that support greater competition between generics,

---

75 *Drug Price Competition and Patent Term Restoration Act of 1984*, Pub. L. No. 98–417, 98 Stat. 1585 (codified as amended at 15 USC §§ 68(b)–(c), 70(b) (1994); 21 USC §§ 301, 355, 360cc (1994); 28 USC § 2201 (1994); 35 USC §§ 156, 271, 282 (1994)).

76 In the US, this exemption is also technically called the § 271(e)(1) exemption or Hatch–Waxman exemption. K. Suresh Kumar et al., 'Patent Laws and Research Exemption Imperative—Do Scientists Have Enough Freedom to Operate?', *Current Science* 99 (2010): 1488, 1524. The US Supreme Court considered the scope of the Hatch–Waxman exemption in *Merck v. Integra*, Merck KGaA v. Integra Lifesciences I, Ltd., 545 US 193 (2005):
The Supreme Court held that the statute exempts from infringement *all* uses of compounds that are reasonably related to submission of information to the government under any law regulating the manufacture, use or distribution of drugs. In Canada, this exemption is known as the Bolar provision or Roche–Bolar provision, named after the case *Roche Products v. Bolar Pharmaceutical*. In the European Union, equivalent exemptions are allowed under the terms of EC Directives 2001/82/EC (as amended by Directive 2004/28/EC) and 2001/83/EC (as amended by Directives 2002/98/EC, 2003/63/EC, 2004/24/EC and 2004/27/EC).
Research Exemption, Wikipedia, http://en.wikipedia.org/wiki/Research_exemption

77 'Intellectual Property Protection for the Pharmaceuticals'; see also *Canada—Patent Protection of Pharmaceutical Products*:
Article 30 of the TRIPS Agreement authorizes limited exceptions to patent rights for such things as research, prior user rights, and pre-expiration testing. Often called the 'research exception', the provision is commonly used by countries to advance science and technology by allowing researchers to use a patented invention to gain a better understanding of the technology. In addition, countries also use the provision to allow manufacturers of generic drugs to apply for marketing and safety approval without the patent owner's permission and before the patent protection expires. The generic producers can then market the drug. This practice, often called the 'regulatory exception' or 'Bolar' provision, has been upheld as conforming to the TRIPS Agreement. ... [The Panel also found] that manufacturing and stockpiling patented drugs prior to the exhaustion of patent protection is not a 'limited exception' which can be exempted under Article 30.
Bryan Mercurio, 'The Impact of the Australia–United States Free Trade Agreement on the Provision of Health Services in Australia', *Whittier Law Review* 26 (2005): 1051, 1065 (footnote and citation omitted).

whether branded or not, as an effective way to enhance access by improving affordability".[78]

In addition to the Bolar exception, the "exception for research or experimental use of an invention also falls under the Article 30 category of exceptions".[79] This exception is extensively used in many national patent laws around the world.[80] It "allows the use of a patented product in experimentation, for both scientific as well as commercial purposes, without the consent of the patent holder. This exception plays a significant role in the process of encouraging innovation, dissemination of knowledge and transfer of technology".[81]

This kind of exception is important for maintaining and developing efficient alternatives to protect public health and to encourage innovation within the industry. The opportunity to use patented products for R&D purposes will enable indigenous firms to be ready with efficient processes and use these whenever they are permitted to do so.

The existing patent law of Bangladesh under section 21 provides for experimental use exceptions. However, the language and process as mentioned in the existing PDA are so ambiguous and complicated that it will have no positive effect. The law must be amended to simplify the entry of generic pharmaceuticals into the market. The research and experimental provision "is very important for generic entry. It permits generic entry soon after the patents expire and hence allows

---

78 CIPIH Report, p.24.
79 Mohammed K. El Said, *Public Health-related TRIPS-Plus Provisions in Bilateral Trade Agreements: A Policy Guide for Negotiators and Implementers in the WHO Eastern Mediterranean Region* (2010), p.153, http://applications.emro.who.int/dsaf/dsa1081. pdf. See for details, Carlos Correa, *Integrating Public Health Concerns into Patent Legislations in Developing Countries* (Geneva: South Centre, Chernin du Charnpd' Anier, pp.17, 1211, 2000), http://apps.who.int/medicinedocs/pdf/h2963e/h2963e. pdf
80 Ibid. According to Oh and Musungu, "[n]ational laws reviewed in Latin American and Caribbean countries all contained provisions relating to the research or experimental use exception; in Asia, 85% of the national laws reviewed provided for this exception, although the figure is lower in Africa at 59%". Cecilia Oh and Sisule Musungu, 'The Use of Flexibilities in TRIPS by Developing Countries: Can They Promote Access to Medicines?' (Commission on Intellectual Property Rights, Innovation and Public Health [CIPIH], Study 4C), 12 October 2010, http://www. who.int/intellectualproperty/studies/TRIPSFLEXI.pdf
81 El Said, *'Public Health Related TRIPS-Plus Provisions'*; see also 'Exception to Patent Rights in Developing Countries', pp.46, 49.

the consumers to benefit from competition and lower prices without delay. In the absence of it, generic companies will have to wait till[sic] the patents actually expire before they can start the tests necessary for getting regulatory approval".[82]

It will take time to get such approvals and without such an exception, "the patentee will effectively enjoy monopoly status even though there are no legal barriers to entry".[83] However, the Draft PDA tries to simplify the process, stating that:

> [A]ny machine, apparatus or other article in respect of which the patent is granted or any article made by the use of the process in respect of which the patent is granted, may be made or used, and any process in respect of which the patent is granted may be used, by any person for the sole purpose merely of experiment or research including the imparting of instruction to pupils.[84]

Nonetheless, the exemption as laid down in the Draft PDA may not be enough if a generic producer wants to use it for experimental purposes leading to the collection of data to be submitted to the drug approval authority for the production of on-patent drugs.[85] In the context of the terms of the legislative provision itself, guidance can be sought from section 107A(a) of the Indian *Patent Act, 2005*, which declares:

> [A]ny act of making, constructing, using, selling or importing a patented invention solely for uses reasonably related to the development and submission of information required under any law for the time being in force, in India, or in a country other than India, that regulates the manufacture, construction, use, sale or import of any product ... shall not be considered as an infringement of patent rights.[86]

In Bangladesh there are diverging opinions within the pharmaceutical industry regarding this. During interviews, most representatives of the local pharmaceutical industry[87] strongly supported the inclusion

---

82   'Intellectual Property Protection for the Pharmaceuticals'.

83   Ibid.

84   *Draft Patents and Designs Act, 2010* § 48(c), 2010 (Bangl.).

85   See Shamnad Basheer, 'India's Tryst with TRIPS: *The Patents (Amendment) Act, 2005', Indian Journal of Law and Technology* 1 (2005): 15, 30, http://papers.ssrn.com/sol3/papers.cfm?abstract_id=764066

86   *Patent (Amendment Act), 2002,* § 107A(a), 2002 (India).

87   During surveys, most local pharmaceutical companies in Bangladesh, irrespective of size, supported this provision.

of this provision to benefit generic producers, whereas MNPCs[88] thought it might discourage investment and technology transfer in the pharmaceutical sector. One interview participant argued that in the absence of a research and experimental use provision, generic producers in Bangladesh would be restricted from experimenting with patented products.[89]

Arguably, the absence of a research and experimental use provision encourages the high pricing of pharmaceuticals, given the monopoly of a patent holder. Therefore, the present provision in Bangladesh needs to be extended to include a similar provision to that of India to facilitate the generic entry of patented drugs as early as possible after the introduction of pharmaceutical patents in Bangladesh. As part of the transition to a TRIPS-compliant regime, the legislative option of including both an early working and a research and experimental use exemption should be considered.

A further exemption that demands attention is the practice of permitting parallel imports.

4.2.6 Parallel Imports

The TRIPS Agreement provides that the patent owner has the exclusive right to prevent others not only from making, using or selling the invented product or process in the country, but also from importing the product from other countries.[90] However, this right is subject to Article 6 of the TRIPS Agreement, which deals with the principle of "exhaustion"[91] and states that "once patent holders have sold a patented product, they cannot prohibit the subsequent resale [or import] of that product since their rights in respect of that market have been exhausted by the act of selling the product".[92] With respect to patent exhaustion as it relates to parallel imports, Sudip Chaudhuri writes:

---

88   In the survey feedback, MNPCs did not answer this question, but during interviews they opposed the provision and considered that, in the long term, it would provide no benefits for Bangladesh.

89   Interview with an official from a public health NGO, in Dhaka, Bangladesh, 9 February 2009.

90   TRIPS Agreement, art. 28.1(a).

91   TRIPS Agreement, art. 6.

92   WHO, 'Intellectual Property Protection: Impact on Public Health', *WHO Drug Information* 19 (2005): 236, 240, http://apps.who.int/medicinedocs/pdf/s7918e/s7918e.pdf

Such imports of patented products without the consent of the patent holder in the importing country are known as parallel imports. This is very important in the pharmaceutical industry because the same patented medicine is often sold at different prices in different countries and hence parallel imports permit a country to shop around for the lowest price. The underlying justification of allowing parallel imports is that since the innovator has been rewarded through the first sale of the product, its patent rights have been "exhausted" and hence it should have no say over the subsequent re-sale.[93]

Article 6 of the TRIPS Agreement was further clarified by the Doha Declaration, which stipulated that each country was "free to establish its own regime for such exhaustion without challenge".[94]

There are three kinds of exhaustion regimes for the purpose of parallel imports: national, regional and international.[95] The US has adopted "a national exhaustion principle whereby the patent owner has no control over the product once it is placed in the domestic market"; however, the patent holder "can exercise his rights outside the US market regarding the price and quantity of the product".[96] In contrast, the EU has adopted a "regional exhaustion principle whereby the rights are exhausted within" the boundaries of the EU.[97] By comparison, international exhaustion has no jurisdictional limit; the rights of the patent owner are exhausted once he has sold his product.[98] International exhaustion is consistent with the objective of Article 7 of the TRIPS Agreement.[99] The advantage of international exhaustion is that developing countries

---

93   Sudip Chaudhuri, 'Indian Generic Companies, Affordability of Drugs and Local Production in Africa with Special Reference to Tanzania, IKD' (Working Paper No. 37, September 2008), http://oro.open.ac.uk/26384/2/

94   Doha Declaration, art. 5(d); Sudip Chaudhuri (2008).

95   See generally Marco C.E.J. Bronckers, 'The Exhaustion of Patent Rights under World Trade Organization Law', *Journal of World Trade Law* 32 (1998): 137–38.

96   N. Lalitha, 'Doha Declaration and Public Health Issues', *Journal of Intellectual Property Rights* 13 (2008): 401, 404, http://nopr.niscair.res.in/bitstream/123456789/2026/1/JIPR 13(5) 401-413.pdf

97   Ibid.

98   Ibid.

99   Ibid. A submission to the World Health Organization stated:
Article 7 is a key provision that defines the objectives of the TRIPS Agreement. It clearly establishes that the protection and enforcement of intellectual property rights do not exist in a vacuum. They are supposed to benefit society as a whole and do not aim at the mere protection of private rights" and should be utilized in a way for "the mutual advantage of producers and users of technological knowledge; social and economic welfare; and the balance of rights and obligations.

can scout for lower-priced patented products anywhere in the world.[100] Research conducted in a number of countries supports this claim. In Kenya, for example, it was found that "parallel importation reduced the price of first-line ARV medicines to one-third of the price of the patented version".[101] In this regard, the Report on the Commission of Intellectual Property Rights (UK) states:

> Developing countries should not eliminate potential sources of low cost imports from other developing or developed countries. In order to be an effective pro-competitive measure in a scenario of full compliance with TRIPS, parallel imports should be allowed whenever the patentee's rights have been exhausted in the foreign country. Since TRIPS allows countries to design their own exhaustion of rights regimes (a point restated at Doha), developing countries should aim to facilitate parallel imports in their legislation.[102]

Moreover, the CIPIH Report, Recommendation 4.19, declares that "[d]eveloping countries should retain the possibilities to benefit from differential pricing, and the ability to seek and parallel import lower-priced medicines".[103]

In the context of Bangladesh, one pharmaceutical market expert argued that "international exhaustion will be of no benefit for Bangladesh; rather, it will increase counterfeiting and low-quality

---

Council Discussion on Access to Medicines, TRIPS, Developing Country Group's Paper—Submission by the Africa Group, Barbados, Bolivia, Brazil, Dominican Republic, Ecuador, Honduras, India, Indonesia, Jamaica, Pakistan, Paraguay, Philippines, Peru, Sri Lanka, Thailand and Venezuela (IP/C/W/296) 18 (19 June 2001), http://www.wto.org/english/tratop_e/trips_e/paper_develop_w296_e.htm. Therefore:
[e]ach provision of the TRIPS Agreement should be read in light of the objectives and principles set forth in Articles 7 and 8. Such an interpretation finds support in the Vienna Convention on the Law of Treaties (concluded in Vienna in 23, May 1969), which establishes, in Article 31, that "[a] treaty shall be interpreted in good faith in accordance with the ordinary meaning to be given to the terms of the treaty in their context and in the light of its object and purpose". Ibid., 17.

100 Lalitha (2008).
101 Rohit Malpani, 'All Costs, No Benefits: How TRIPS-plus Intellectual Property Rules in the US–Jordan FTA Affect Access to Medicines' (Oxfam Briefing Paper No. 102, 21 March 2007), p.11, http://www.oxfam.org/sites/www.oxfam.org/files/all costs, no benefits.pdf
102 'Integrating Intellectual Property Rights', p.52.
103 See CIPIH Report, p.124.

medicine in the local market".[104] He also indicated that allowing cheaper medicines from alternative sources may jeopardise the entire pharmaceutical market in Bangladesh with regard to the institutional and infrastructural limitation of the DDA, because it would open the flood gates for different products, making it impossible for the DDA to inspect and monitor all the possible cheaper pharmaceutical products.[105] However, one public health activist in Bangladesh argued that fear of counterfeiting is not reason enough to shut the door to opportunities; rather, counterfeiting can be prevented if the proper steps are taken.[106] She further remarked that in the absence of parallel imports, a monopoly will result and may threaten the adequate supply of and access to affordable pharmaceuticals.[107]

The PDA of Bangladesh does not contain any provisions dealing with the legality or otherwise of parallel imports. Brazilian patent law does not support international exhaustion either.[108] However, the Indian *Patent Act, 2005* (under section 107) allows parallel imports and permits the import of patented drugs at the lowest available price in the global market (international exhaustion). Section 107A(b) of the Indian *Patent Act, 2005* provides that "Importation of patented products by any person from a person who is duly authorised under the law to produce and sell or distribute the product, shall not be considered as an infringement of patent rights".[109]

The Draft PDA of Bangladesh, section 92 includes the following provision:

---

104 This remark was made by an official from a leading MNPC operating in Bangladesh during an interview, Dhaka, Bangladesh, 1 February 2009.

105 Ibid.

106 Interview with a policy analyst from an international NGO working in Bangladesh, Dhaka, Bangladesh, 1 March 2012.

107 Ibid.

108 See Esther M. Flesch et al., Report Q 156 in the name of the Brazilian Group: International Exhaustion of Industrial Property Rights (XXXVIIIth World Intellectual Property Congress in Melbourne, 23–30 March 2001), https://www.aippi.org/download/commitees/156/GR156brazil.pdf; see also Shamnad Basheer and Mrinalini Kochupillai, 'TRIPS, Patents and Parallel Imports: A Proposal for Amendment', *Indian Journal of Intellectual Property Law* 2 (2009), http://www.nalsar.ac.in/IJIPL/Files/Archives/Volume 2/4.pdf

109 *2005 Patent (Amendment) Act*, No. 15 § 92(1), 2005 (India).

Meaning of Use of Invention for Purposes of Government

1) For the purposes of this chapter, an invention is said to be used for the purposes of government if it is made, used, exercised or vended for the purposes of the government or a government undertaking.

2) Without prejudice to the generality of the provisions of sub-section (1) of this Section:

    a) the importation, by or on behalf of the government, of any invention being a machine, apparatus or other article covered by a patent granted before the commencement of this Act, for the purposes merely of its own use; and

    b) the importation, by or on behalf of the government, of any invention being a medicine or drug covered by a patent granted before the commencement of this Act:

        i)   for the purpose merely of its own use; or

        ii) for the purpose of distribution in any dispensary, hospital or other medical institution maintained by or on behalf of the government or in any other dispensary, hospital or other medical institution that the government may, having regard to the public service that such other dispensary, hospital or medical institution render, specify in this behalf by notification in the Official Gazette, shall also be deemed, for the purposes of this Chapter, to be use of such invention for the purposes of Government.[110]

Draft Patent Ain (Law), 2012 of Bangladesh also includes a similar provision, which authorised individuals to parallel import with permission from a duly empowered authority, provided the individuals comply with the rules framed for such authorisation.[111]

> This provision is ambiguous and only allows government institutions and duly authorised institutions or individuals to make use of parallel imports. The existing Patent Act of Bangladesh (the PDA 1911) and the Draft PDA require notification from a duly empowered authority or government, whereas the *Draft Patent Law, 2012* requires compliance with clumsy administrative rules for obtaining permission for parallel imports. Considering the bureaucratic hurdles and delayed procedures typically faced when making a notification or obtaining an authorisation,

---

110 *Draft Patent and Designs Act, 2010* § 92, 2010 (Bangl.).
111 *Draft Patent Ain (Law), 2012* § 31, 2012 (Bangl.).

along with the fact of dysfunctional government health services, this provision will have no positive effect on the availability or accessibility of cheaper generic drugs in Bangladesh. Therefore, Bangladesh should permit parallel importing by anyone, based on the principle of international exhaustion, and should adopt clear and transparent procedures for granting parallel imports within a reasonable time.

The Indian parallel imports regime has some defects; for example, the "importation of patented products by any person from any person who is duly authorised under the law to produce and sell or distribute the product".[112] Therefore, it may restrict the importation of cheaper drugs unless the exporter is duly authorised by law to produce, sell or distribute such drugs. Shamnad Basheer explains this problem using an example: suppose India's patent laws prohibit production of a drug that is under a valid patent, but Bangladesh's laws do not. These drugs are available via import from a Bangladeshi drug producer because there is no pharmaceutical patent in Bangladesh; therefore, the drug producer in Bangladesh does not need any authorisation from the patent holder.[113] However, under the existing provision in India, an Indian importer may be barred from importing from Bangladesh because of a potential violation of Article 28 of the TRIPS Agreement,[114] as the goods produced in Bangladesh by a third party did not have authorisation from the patent holder, were not distributed by the patent holder and the patent right has not been exhausted. In this situation, there will be complications when trying to import drugs from cheaper sources that may also trigger unnecessary legal hurdles and litigation for violation of the TRIPS provisions. Therefore, Basheer suggests the following amendment be included as section 107B in India's *Patent Act, 2005*:

107B. Exhaustion of Rights

1) For the purposes of this Act, the rights of a patentee or anyone claiming through such patentee shall be exhausted after a patented article has been sold once anywhere in the world (including within India), by or with the authorization of such patentee.[115]

---

112 *2005 Patent (Amendment) Act* § 107A(b), 2005 (India).

113 'TRIPS, Patents and Parallel Imports', pp.66–74.

114 See TRIPS Agreement, art. 28.1 (stating in a pertinent part that "a patent owner shall have the exclusive right to prevent third parties not having the owner's consent from the acts of: making, using, offering for sale, selling, or importing for these purposes that product").

115 'TRIPS, Patents and Parallel Imports', pp.84–85.

This suggestion seems to be more logical because the first sale[116] of a product anywhere in the world by the patent holder would be considered an exhaustion of rights, and therefore it could be imported from anyone and from anywhere in the world. Bangladesh should use this approach when drafting its parallel importation to ensure access to medicine at the best possible price. Allowing for the parallel import of pharmaceuticals may be an effective tool to force patent holders to sell their protected pharmaceuticals at reasonable and affordable prices.[117]

In addition to research exceptions and parallel imports, a strong compulsory licensing regime is important for ensuring access to affordable medicines.

4.2.7 Strong Compulsory Licensing Mechanism

The issues of compulsory licensing were "brought to the forefront of the international debate about intellectual property and public health policy in January 1998, after the Executive Board of the World Health Assembly adopted a resolution urging the member states to put public health above commercial interests and to review their options under TRIPS to safeguard access to essential drugs".[118]

Although the TRIPS Agreement does not use the term "compulsory license", Article 31 of TRIPS permits "use without authorization of the right holder" and includes both use by third parties and the government.[119] The Doha Declaration clarified the WTO's position on compulsory licensing by providing that "each member has the right to grant compulsory licenses and the freedom to determine the grounds upon which such licenses are granted".[120]

---

116 "Exhaustion of rights, or the doctrine of first sale, is inherent to IPRs and a necessity in bringing about legal certainty in downstream markets". Thomas Cottier, 'The Exhaustion of Intellectual Property Rights - A Fresh Look', *IIC International Review of Intellectual Property and Competition* 39 (2008): 755.

117 See Krithpaka Boonfueng, 'Parallel Imports in Pharmaceuticals: Increase Access to HIV Drugs', *Thailand Law Forum* (2010), http://www.thailawforum.com/articles/hivdrugs1.html

118 'The South Africa AIDS Controversy', p.12; see also WHA Executive Board Res., WHO, 'Revised Drug Strategy' (EB 101/R.24), 2 (27 January 1998), http://apps.who.int/gb/archive/pdf_files/EB101/pdfangl/angr24.pdf

119 TRIPS Agreement, art. 31.

120 Doha Declaration, at 5(b).

Article 31 of the TRIPS Agreement dealing with compulsory licensing does not clarify the grounds on which a compulsory license can be given. However, as stated elsewhere:

[C]ertain conditions listed in the Article will have to be satisfied. These include: (i) that authorization of such use will have to be considered on its individual merits, (ii) that before permitting such use (except in such cases as situations of national emergencies, extreme urgency, public non-commercial use), the proposed user will have to make efforts over a reasonable period of time to get a voluntary license on reasonable commercial terms, (iii) that the legal validity of the compulsory licensing decision and the remuneration will be subject to judicial or other independent review, and (iv) that the compulsory licenses can be terminated if and when the circumstances which led to it cease to exist and are unlikely to recur.[121]

Nevertheless, there are some "[l]ess controversial grounds for issuing compulsory licences as contemplated in TRIPS itself", such as "[t]o correct anticompetitive practices ... [n]ational emergenc[ies] or other situations of extreme urgency, including public health crises, and ... [p]ublic non-commercial use, such as to provide health care to the poor".[122] In all these circumstances, "TRIPS Article 31 permits a Member to grant compulsory licences without first having to make efforts to obtain a licence from the patent owner [under] reasonable commercial terms and conditions".[123] However, even in these cases the TRIPS Agreement requires the payment of "adequate remuneration in the circumstances of each case, taking into account the economic value of the [licence]".[124]

In the PDA of Bangladesh, there is also a provision dealing with the issue of compulsory licenses. Section 22 of the PDA provides that:

1)   Any person interested may present a petition to the government which shall be left at the Department of Patents, Designs and Trade Marks, together with the prescribed fee, **alleging that the demand for a patented article in Bangladesh is not being met to an adequate**

---

121 'Intellectual Property Protection for the Pharmaceuticals'; TRIPS Agreement, art. 31.
122 'TRIPS and Pharmaceutical Industry in Bangladesh', p.36.
123 Ibid.
124 Ibid. (quoting TRIPS Agreement, art. 31). For details, see Swarup Kumar, 'Compulsory Licensing Provision under TRIPS: A Study of Roche vs Natco Case in India vis-à-vis the Applicability of the Principle of *Audi Alteram Partem*', *SCRIPT-ed* 7.1 (2010).

> extent and on reasonable terms and praying for the grant of a
> compulsory license, or, in the alternative, for the revocation of the
> patent.
>
> 2) The government shall consider the petition, and **if the parties do not
> come to an arrangement between themselves** the government may,
> as it thinks fit **either dispose of the petition itself or refer it to the
> High Court Division for a decision** [author's emphasis].[125]

There are some limitations within section 22 (see the passages in bold
above) in the context of meeting the needs of the local pharmaceutical
industry and in ensuring access to medicine. The first limitation is that
the section only applies where a situation is one of inadequacy and
unreasonable terms. These terms are not defined in the PDA, so there
is uncertainty as to their scope. The second limitation is that there is
no expert body to deal with a compulsory license application; there is
only a referral to the High Court Division. The third limitation is that
the section only applies to domestic need. Therefore, local generic
producers in Bangladesh may not take the opportunity to export to
countries that have no manufacturing capacity or those in extreme need
of pharmaceuticals. The fourth limitation is that the section does not
provide any clear indication as to royalties or a ceiling on the royalties
in the case of a compulsory license. The absence of a clear provision
on royalties may give rise to higher claims for royalties and related
litigation,[126] which could arguably create a degree of uncertainty. The
fifth limitation is that the section does not prescribe any time limit
for the conclusion of the proceedings. The sixth limitation is that the
section does not provide that a compulsory license can be issued on
the grounds of public interest, a health emergency or for public non-
commercial use. Further, section 23(3) of the PDA states that "No order
revoking a patent shall be made … which is at variance with any treaty,
convention, arrangement or engagement with any foreign country".[127]
Such a provision could be used to prevent the issue of a compulsory
license or the revocation of a patent, facilitating the argument that

---

125 The PDA § 22, 1911 (Bangl.) (emphasis added).
126 See generally F.M. Scherer and Jayashree Watal, 'Post-TRIPS Options for Access
to Patented Medicines in Developing Countries' (Working Paper Series, Paper No.
WG4:1, Commission on Macroeconomics and Health [CMH]), http://library.cphs.
chula.ac.th/Ebooks/HealthCareFinancing/WorkingPaper_WG4/WG4_1.pdf
127 The PDA § 23(3), 1911 (Bangl.).

Bangladesh is breaching the TRIPS Agreement or any other bilateral free trade and investment agreement. Thus, patent holders could take advantage of the cumbersome procedure and frustrate the efforts of interested enterprises in getting compulsory licenses. Despite having provisions for compulsory licenses, the Government of Bangladesh has never issued a compulsory license for patented drugs.[128]

These limitations should be removed and the PDA amended to incorporate a viable compulsory licensing mechanism. In this regard, the legislative examples of India and Brazil may be useful. Both countries have included compulsory licensing mechanisms within their legislative regimes. Such legislation has the potential to not only ensure access to medicines, but also enable local generic producers to export and supply generic pharmaceuticals to other poor countries, countries without manufacturing capacity and those in urgent need of medicines.[129]

Bangladesh should adopt a provision similar to the Indian provision that permits the issue of a compulsory license in the case of a national emergency or health crisis, or for public non-commercial use. For example, section 92(1) of the Indian *Patent Act, 2005* provides that:

> 4.2.1   If the Central Government is satisfied, in respect of any patent in force, in circumstances of national emergency or in circumstances of extreme urgency or in case of public non-commercial use, that it is necessary that compulsory licences should be granted at any time after the sealing thereof to work the invention, it may make a declaration to the effect, by notification in the *Official Gazette*.[130]

To allow exports under a compulsory license, section 92A of the Indian *Patent Act, 2005* states:

> 1)   Compulsory licenses shall be available **for the manufacture and export of patented pharmaceutical products to any country having insufficient or no manufacturing capacity** in the pharmaceutical sector for the concerned product to address public-health problems, provided compulsory licences have been granted by such country or such country has, by notification or otherwise, allowed importation

---

128 Interview with a deputy registrar from the DPDT, in Dhaka, Bangladesh, 7 March 2012.

129 See generally 'The Use of Flexibilities in TRIPS by Developing Countries'.

130 *2005 Patent (Amendment) Act* § 92(1), 2005 (India).

of the patented pharmaceutical products from India [author's emphasis].[131]

Bangladesh should adopt a similar provision to allow local generic producers to exploit the opportunity to export cheap generic medicines to other countries that have no manufacturing capacity or that are facing an extreme health emergency. It is also interesting to note that the Indian *Patent Act, 2005* includes a provision listing the prime objectives for granting a patent for pharmaceuticals. In the event of a violation of any of these provisions, grounds for the issue of a compulsory license could be raised. In this regard, section 83 of that Act provides:

Without prejudice to the other provisions contained in this Act, in exercising the powers conferred by this Chapter, regard shall be had to the following general considerations, namely:

1) that patents are granted **to encourage inventions and to secure** the **Public-health Safeguards in Indian Patents Act** that the inventions are worked in India on a commercial scale and to the fullest extent that is reasonably practicable without undue delay;

2) that they are not granted merely to enable patentees to enjoy a monopoly for the importation of the patented article;

3) **that the protection and enforcement of patent rights contribute to the promotion of technological innovation and to the transfer and dissemination of technology, to the mutual advantage of producers and users of technological knowledge and in a manner conducive to social and economic welfare, and to a balance of rights and obligations;**

4) that **patents granted do not impede protection of public health and nutrition and should act as instruments to promote public interest,** especially in sectors that are of vital importance for the socioeconomic and technological development of India;

5) that patents granted do not in any way prohibit Central Government in taking measures to protect public health;

6) that the patent right is not abused by the patentee or person deriving title or interest on-patent from the patentee, and the patentee or a person deriving title or interest on-patent from the patentee does not resort to practices which unreasonably restrain trade or adversely affect the international transfer of technology; and

---

131 Ibid., § 92A (emphasis added).

7)   that patents are granted to make the benefit of the patented invention available at reasonably affordable prices to the public [author's emphasis].[132]

By inserting the above section, the Indian government validated its present actions and any future actions as a measure to protect the public interest. In particular, sections 83(d) and (e) are adopted from the objectives and principle clause of the TRIPS Agreement,[133] which validates government actions based on the socioeconomic conditions of the country. Bangladesh should adopt a similar provision as a proactive measure so that it can validate future actions to protect the public interest, and the socioeconomic interest and developmental goals of the country.

However, commentary on the Indian compulsory licensing regime has highlighted a limitation of the section: there is no clear detail regarding the requirement to pay royalties. Gopakumar states that "gaps in the law take away the effectiveness of a compulsory license regime under the Patents Act. As a result, during the last five years only one application was filed for the issuance of a compulsory license in India".[134]

In this respect, either an administrative body should be created to speed up the process of issuing compulsory licenses in the case of an emergency situation, or a provision should be enacted to empower the government itself to issue a compulsory license without application. In this respect, Article 71 of the Brazilian *Industrial Property Law* provides that "In cases of national emergency or of public interest, as declared in an act of the Federal Executive Power, and provided the patent holder or his licensee does not fulfil such need, a temporary and non-exclusive compulsory license for exploiting the patent may be granted, ex officio, without prejudice to the rights of the respective titleholder".[135]

This provision empowers the Brazilian government to issue a compulsory license if negotiations between parties fail.[136] Such a

---

132   Ibid., § 83 (emphasis added).
133   TRIPS Agreement, arts. 7–8.
134   'Product Patents and Access to Medicines in India', pp.326, 341.
135   Lei No.9.279 art. 71, de 14 de maio de 1996, Diario Oficial Da Uniao [DOU] de 15.05.1996. (Braz.), translated in Brazil: Industrial Property Law, 14/05/1996, No. 9.279, http://www.wipo.int/wipolex/en/details.jsp?id=515 (emphasis added).
136   Brazil used this provision to threaten compulsory licenses to gain substantial price reductions on several occasions. See 'Fault Lines in the World Trade Organization'.

legislative option should be considered by Bangladesh as part of its TRIPS-compliant legislative regime. In the Draft PDA, Bangladesh tried to use the Indian option, but the provision needs clarification[137] because it is not clear whether exports can be made to non-WTO member countries and to those that do not have pharmaceutical patents or patents of a particular drug.[138] As the law currently stands, the issue of compulsory licenses is still determined by the courts, as in India, rather than by any specific executive body, as in Brazil. The court procedure in Bangladesh is overly long, costly and complicated; thus, it may discourage potential applicants from applying for compulsory licenses.

In this regard, the IPR Commission in the UK has stated that "an important barrier to compulsory licensing in developing countries is the absence of straightforward legislative and administrative procedures to put it into effect".[139] In addition, the CIPIH Report recommends that "Countries should provide in their legislation powers to use compulsory licensing, in accordance with the TRIPS agreement, where this power might be useful as one of the means available to promote, inter alia, research that is directly relevant to the specific health problems of developing countries".[140]

Bangladesh should follow the Brazilian approach of issuing compulsory licenses and establish an expert body to deal with compulsory licensing issues in the shortest possible time, speeding up the production of generic drugs in cases of public health crises. As the TRIPS Agreement does not prohibit administrative decision-making on compulsory licenses and government use of patents, the establishment of an expert administrative body could speed up the issue of compulsory licenses and also avoid prolonged litigation, as the legal systems in most

---

137 *Draft Patents and Design Act, 2010*, § 84, 2010 (Bangl.).

138 Although it is not clarified in the *Draft Patents and Design Act, 2010*, the *Draft Patent Ain, 2012* under section 14(18) provides that compulsory licenses can be granted for pharmaceutical exports to countries having inadequate or no manufacturing capacity. However, the draft law of 2012 included a separate provision in section 30 stipulating that compulsory licenses including pharmaceutical export licenses could not be granted in Bangladesh unless the 30 August TRIPS amendment becomes effective in Bangladesh; see *Draft Patent Act, 2012* and Azam, 'Globalising Standard of Patent Protection in WTO Law and Policy Options for the LDCs', *Chicago-Kent Journal of Intellectual Property*, 13.2 (2014).

139 'Integrating Intellectual Property Rights', p.8.

140 CIPIH Report, p.176.

developing countries and LDCs, including Bangladesh, are already overburdened.

Further, the issue of reasonable remuneration is not clearly defined; bargaining over this issue may also unnecessarily delay the procedure of issuing compulsory licenses. In this case, Bangladesh could perhaps adopt, with slight modification, the Canadian approach of fixing royalties based on the UN's Human Development Index (HDI).[141] The same formula should be used based on the ranking of the country in which the manufactured drugs under the compulsory license are to be exploited (the Canadian model only accounts for exports based on the destination of the drugs—the importing country).[142] Bangladesh still holds a very low ranking in the HDI, and most of the exporting

---

141 "The Human Development Index (HDI) is a measure of life expectancy, literacy, education, and standard of living for countries worldwide. It is a standard means of measuring well-being, especially child welfare". Centre for Environment Education, *Sustainable Development: An Introduction* 17 (2007). The HDI is used to determine whether the country is a developed, a developing or an under-developed country, and to measure the effect of economic policies on quality of life (Ibid.). The origins of the HDI are found in the annual Human Development Reports of the UNDP; Sakiko Fukuda-Parr, 'The Human Development Paradigm: Operationalizing Sen's Ideas on Capabilities', *Feminist Economics* 9 (2003): 301, 303. It was devised by economist Mahabub-ul Haq in 1990 with the explicit purpose of shifting "the focus of development economics from national income accounting to people centered policies" (ibid., citation omitted). For more information, see *Human Development Index (HDI)*, Human Development Reports, UNDP, http://hdr. undp.org/en/statistics/hdi

142 According to James Love:
In 2005, Canada proposed royalty guidelines for the export of medicines under the Jean Chrétien Pledge to Africa Act, which implements the WTO waiver of Article 31(f) of the TRIPS Agreement. The Canadian royalty guidelines are a sliding scale of the generic sales price. The rate depends entirely upon the location of the importing market and the rank of the importing country in the [United Nations Human Development Index] (UNHDI). The formula is one, plus the number of countries on the UNHDI, minus the importing country's rank on the UNHDI, divided by the number of countries on the UNHDI, multiplied by 0.04. The rate is then applied to the generic sales price. With 177 countries currently in the UNHDI index, the royalty rate can be expressed as: Royalty rate = $0.04 \times [(178) -$ rank importing country]/177. (James Love, 'Remuneration Guidelines for Non-voluntary Use of a Patent on Medical Technologies' (2005), p.72, http://www.who.int/medicines/areas/ technical_cooperation/WHOTCM2005.1_OMS.pdf.) During the time of adoption of this royalty approach in 2004, the top rate was 4% of the generic sales price for Norway, as it was the number one country in the HDI in 2004, and the lowest rate was 0.02% for Sierra Leone as the lowest ranking country in the HDI in 2004 (ibid.). See for details, Mohammad Monirul Azam, 'Revisiting the Climate Change Negotiation under the UNFCCC: In Search of Effective Framework for Negotiation and Technology Transfer' (2009), http://www.conference.unitar.org/yale/sites/ conference.unitar.org.yale/files/Paper_Azam.pdf

destinations of Bangladeshi pharmaceutical products are also in the lower levels of the HDI.[143] With this modification, Bangladesh would be able to produce drugs locally using compulsory licenses, or it could use compulsory licenses for export by paying the minimum fixed royalties without any cumbersome bargaining.

Further, the Government of Bangladesh may need to modify existing provisions that regulate "local working" of the patent or related provisions concerning patented processes or products used or manufactured outside of Bangladesh. Section 23 of the PDA provides that:

1) At any time not less than four years after the date of a patent granted under this Act, any person may apply to the Government for relief under this section on the ground that the patented article or process is manufactured or carried on exclusively or mainly outside Bangladesh.

2) The Government shall consider the application, and, if after inquiry it is satisfied-

   a) that the allegations contained therein are correct; and

   b) that the applicant is prepared, and is in a position, to manufacture or carry on the patented article or process in Bangladesh; and

   c) that the patentee refuses to grant a license on reasonable terms, then, subject to the provisions of this section, and unless the patentee proves that the patented article or process is manufactured or carried on to an adequate extent in Bangladesh, or gives satisfactory reasons why the article or process is not so manufactured or carried on, the Government may make an order; and

   d) revoking the patent[144]

The existing patent law of Bangladesh does not contain any definition of the clause "manufactured or carried on exclusively or mainly outside Bangladesh" as articulated in section 23 of the PDA. This absence of a definition may result in varied and ambiguous interpretations. Again,

---

143 The ranking of Bangladesh in the HDI of 2010 was 129. UNDP, 'Human Development Report 2010, The Real Wealth of Nations: Pathways to Human Development' (2010), p.145, http://hdr.undp.org/sites/default/files/reports/270/hdr_2010_en_complete_reprint.pdf. For the HDI of other countries, see ibid., pp.143–46.

144 The PDA § 23, 1911 (Bangl.).

section 23 of the PDA requires that four years should lapse from the date of granting of a patent before one can apply for its revocation on the grounds of "non-working in the territory" of Bangladesh.[145] Therefore, the ambiguity of the existing provision and the four-year requirement will delay the entry of cheaper local pharmaceuticals. This will allow the MNPCs to enjoy a monopoly for their patented pharmaceuticals without any transfer of technology and investment for local manufacture, since they will rely on manufacturing facilities outside Bangladesh. In this regard, section 84 of the Indian *Patent Act, 2005*[146] and Article 68 of the Brazilian *Industrial Property Act, 1996*[147] may be models for Bangladesh, because so far they have successfully resisted the pressure of the US and the MNPCs.[148]

The Indian Controller of Patents, while disposing of an application for compulsory license in *Natco Pharma Ltd. v. Bayer Corp.*,[149] clarified the issue of the working of the patent in the territory of India. The controller noted that the term "worked in the territory of India" had not been defined in the Indian *Patent Act, 2005*, and so he needed to

---

145 Ibid.

146 *2005 Patent (Amendment) Act* § 84, 2005 (India):
   Compulsory licences. –
   (1) At any time after the expiration of three years from the date of the grant of a patent, any person interested may make an application to the Controller for grant of compulsory licence on patent on any of the following grounds, namely –
   (a) that the reasonable requirements of the public with respect to the patented invention have not been satisfied, or (b) that the patented invention is not available to the public at a reasonably affordable price, or (c) that the patented invention is not worked in the territory of India.

147 Lei No.9.279 art.68, de 14 de maio de 1996, Diario Oficial Da Uniao [DOU] de 15.05.1996. (Braz.), translated in Brazil: *Industrial Property Law*, 14/05/1996, No. 9.279, http://www.wipo.int/wipolex/en/details.jsp?id=515:
   (1) The following also occasion a compulsory license:
      I. non-exploitation of the object of the patent within the Brazilian territory for failure to manufacture or incomplete manufacture of the product, or also failure to make full use of the patented process, except cases where this is not economically feasible, when importation shall be permitted; or
      II. commercialization that does not satisfy the needs of the market.

148 See generally 'India, the Pharmaceutical Industry and the Validity of TRIPS'; see also Daya Shanker, 'Brazil, Pharmaceutical Industry and the WTO', *Journal of World Intellectual Property* 5 (2002): 53.

149 Compulsory License Application No. 1 of 2011, Application for Compulsory License Under Section 84(1) of the *Patents Act, 1970* in Respect of Patent No. 215758, *Natco Pharma Ltd. v. Bayer Corp.* (9 March 2012), http://www.ipindia.nic.in/iponew/compulsory_license_12032012.pdf

interpret the term with regard to "various International Conventions and Agreements in intellectual property", the *Patent Act, 1970* and the legislative history.[150] The controller, using Article 27(1) of the TRIPS Agreement and Article 5(1)(A) of the Paris Convention, interpreted it to mean that failure to manufacture in India supported the grant of a compulsory license to Natco, stating that: "[p]atents are not granted merely to enable patentees to enjoy a monopoly for importation of the patented article" and that "the grant of a patent right must contribute to the promotion of technological innovation and to the transfer and dissemination of technology".[151]

Therefore, considering the experience of India, the author consider that Government of Bangladesh could adopt the following provision on the working of the patent in the territory of Bangladesh:

> Compulsory License for Non-working in the territory of Bangladesh: At any time after the expiration of three years from the date of the grant of a patent, any person interested may make an application to the Department of Patents, Designs and Trademarks or to the duly authorised office for grant of a compulsory license on patent on any of the following grounds, namely –
>
> 1) that the reasonable requirements of the public with respect to the patented invention have not been satisfied . . .
>
> 2) the demand for the patented article has not been met to an adequate extent or on reasonable terms . . .
>
> 3) that the patented invention is not available to the public at a reasonably affordable price
>
> 4) that the patented invention is not worked in the territory of Bangladesh.

This section is to be applied to the extent that due consideration is given to the fact that patents are not granted merely to enable patentees to enjoy a monopoly on importation of the patented article: the grant of a patent right must contribute to the promotion of technological innovation and to the transfer and dissemination of technology.

---

150 Ibid., pp.39–45.
151 Ibid., p.43.

During interviews, most participants argued that Bangladesh should have strong compulsory licensing mechanisms.[152] However, one participant argued that compulsory licenses are not a viable option as they will discourage technology transfer and FDI in Bangladesh.[153] Another participant commented that the provision alone would not be enough if the procedure was complicated and resulted in an inordinate delay in the issuance of compulsory licenses.[154] Including a compulsory license provision in its future amended patent law that avoids clumsy and complicated procedures will help Bangladesh ensure access to pharmaceuticals in the event of a public health emergency and provide a competitive advantage to its local pharmaceutical industry when exporting to countries that have low or no manufacturing capacity.

Similarly, Bangladesh should include a prior use exception to protect local producers within the pharmaceutical industry.

4.2.8 Prior Use Exceptions

Given the number of local generic producers in Bangladesh and the magnitude of investment made in the area of cheap generics, the prior use exception should be incorporated into Bangladesh's TRIPS-compliant patent law. In a study by the World Bank, the Indian example of prior user rights is referred to as a "grandfather clause" or automatic compulsory license and described as follows: "Generic versions of patented medicine can continue to be manufactured in India provided that: (1) the generic manufacturer was producing and marketing the product prior to January 1, 2005; (2) the generic manufacturer made significant investment in the production and marketing for the product; and, (3) a reasonable royalty is paid to the patent holder".[155]

During the author's field studies in Bangladesh, the majority of participants strongly supported the inclusion of a prior use rights

---

152 During interviews, compulsory licensing was supported by most of the executives of local pharmaceutical companies, irrespective of size. That support was echoed by public health NGOs and local researchers.

153 Interview with a policy analyst from an MNPC operating in Bangladesh, in Dhaka, Bangladesh, 9 March 2012.

154 Interview with a policy analyst from an international NGO working in Bangladesh, in Dhaka, Bangladesh, 10 March 2012.

155 'Public and Private Sector Approaches'.

provision similar to India's.[156] However, one participant argued that this kind of provision would discourage FDI and transfer of technology to Bangladesh.[157]

The Indian example of prior user rights has some weaknesses. It may be challenged by the patent holder on a number of grounds. If it was not exploited prior to 1 January 2005, or prior to the introduction of pharmaceutical patents, investment alone is not sufficient (as there is no indication in the law), and the degree of investment that can be considered sufficient, as well as the reasonable royalty rate, may be challenged. These weaknesses may create barriers for generic production. In this case, Bangladesh should perhaps replicate the Brazilian provision, which has no such limitations. Such an exception is contained in Article 45 of Brazil's *Industrial Property Law* and provides that "A person who in good faith, prior to the filing or priority date of a patent application, was exploiting the object thereof in this country, shall be assured the right to continue the exploitation, without onus, in the same manner and under the same conditions as before".[158]

Although the above legislative options help define the matters of patentability and exceptions, a provision related to the patent application objection procedure should also be included.

4.2.9 Pre-grant and Post-grant Opposition

Pre-grant and post-grant opposition "is an important way to assist and encourage public interest groups and local generic pharmaceutical companies to oppose attempts by others" who seek patents.[159] An opposition provision is currently contained in section 9(1) of the PDA:

> Any person may, on payment of the prescribed fee, at any time within **four months from the date of the advertisement of the acceptance of an**

---

156 This was mentioned by representatives from a number of large, medium and small pharmaceutical companies in Bangladesh, and was supported by officials at the Patent Office and DGDA, Bangladesh.

157 Interview with the CEO of an MNPC operating in Bangladesh, in Dhaka, Bangladesh, 9 March 2012.

158 Lei No.9.279 art. 45, de 14 de maio de 1996, Diario Oficial Da Uniao [DOU] de 15.05.1996. (Braz.), translated in Brazil: *Industrial Property Law*, 14/05/1996, No. 9.279, http://www.wipo.int/wipolex/en/details.jsp?id=515

159 'Pharmaceutical Patent Protection', pp.1, 8.

application, give notice at the Department of Patents, Designs and Trade Marks of opposition to the grant of the patent on any of the following grounds, namely:

1)   that the applicant obtained the invention from him, or from a person of whom he is the legal representative or assign; or

2)   that the invention has been claimed in any specification filed in Bangladesh which is or will be of prior date to the patent, the grant of which is opposed; or

3)   that the nature of the invention or the manner in which it is to be performed is not sufficiently or fairly described and ascertained in the specifications; or

4)   that the invention has been publicly used in any part of Bangladesh or has been made publicly known in any part of Bangladesh; or

5)   that the complete specification describes or claims an invention other than that described in the provisional specification, and that such other invention either forms the subject of an application made by the opponent for a patent, which if granted would bear a date in the interval between the date of the application and the leaving of the complete specification, or has been made available to the public by publication in any document published in Bangladesh in that interval; **but on no other ground** [author's emphasis].[160]

As emphasised above and in a study by Azam and Richardson, objections to the provision are limited by two conditions. The first is that "the objection must be made within four months of the advertisement of the acceptance of the application".[161] The second is that the objection can only be based on the grounds provided by section 9(1).[162] Azam and Richardson further state that "[i]f defects in the patent application are revealed, or identified after the four-month period, no objection can be raised against the patent application. In other words, the existing legislative regime does not permit any type of post-grant opposition".[163] They add that "This is in contrast to the legislative equivalent in India which not only contains eleven grounds for pre-grant opposition but also permits post-grant opposition".[164]

---

160 The PDA § 9(1)), 1911 (Bangl.) (emphasis added).
161 Azam and Richardson (2010a), p.8.
162 Ibid.
163 Ibid.
164 Ibid., 8.

The Indian grounds for post-grant opposition are "broad enough to challenge novelty, inventive steps and the process of industrial application, best method, claims and disclosure of origin and even the use of indigenous or local knowledge".[165] Given this comparison, it is clear that the existing Bangladeshi provision is not sufficient and should be amended to include more extensive pre-grant heads of objection, as well as a process for post-grant opposition.

In taking such a legislative step, Bangladesh should ensure "that the heads of objection should be as wide as possible so that the twin aims of ensuring access to medicine with the aim of promoting innovation within the pharmaceutical industry are not hampered".[166] During the author's field studies in Bangladesh, the majority of participants opined that the Indian example of pre-grant and post-grant opposition would need to be replicated in Bangladesh.[167] However, one participant argued that the local pharmaceutical industry and public health organisations in Bangladesh lack adequate expertise and resources to effectively exploit pre-grant and post-grant opposition; they should prepare themselves to use this option effectively.[168] Another participant also criticised the lack of accessible online information about ongoing patent applications in Bangladesh and the fact that even a paper copy of DPDT's journal is not distributed regularly. This means that interested parties will have extreme difficulties in collecting the required information to oppose any patent application or granted patent.[169] Therefore, simply including this provision may not be enough unless access to information regarding patent applications and granted patents is regularly updated and available for review by interested parties. One interviewee, however, argued that this provision may open the flood gates to unnecessary opposition and may even frustrate investment in the pharmaceutical sector.[170]

The issue of how long a patent should last also needs consideration.

---

165 Ibid.; see also *The Patent Opposition System in India*, p.14.

166 Azam and Richardson (2010a), pp.8–9.

167 During interviews, this view was echoed by most of the officials of pharmaceutical companies in Bangladesh, irrespective of size, and was also supported by local IP academics and public health NGOs.

168 Interview with an IP academic from the University of Chittagong, in Chittagong, Bangladesh, 5 March 2012.

169 Ibid.

170 Interview with the CEO of an MNPC operating in Bangladesh, in Dhaka, Bangladesh, 7 March 2012.

4.2.10 Duration of Patent Protection

Under section 14 of the PDA of Bangladesh, patent protection is available for 16 years. The TRIPS Agreement requires that patent protection be available for 20 years. The Brazilian *Industrial Property Law* simply indicates that patent protection shall be for 20 years from the date of filing.[171] Indian patent law extends the duration to 20 years subject to patent legislation in India, and states that the duration is to be counted from the date of filing:

> Subject to the provisions of this Act, the term of every patent granted, after the commencement of the Patents (Amendment) Act, 2002, and the term of every patent which has not expired and has not ceased to have effect, on the date of such commencement, under this Act, shall be twenty years from the date of filing of the application for the patent.[172]

Although the TRIPS Agreement limits the ability of Bangladesh to explicitly reduce a patent period, the legislative amendment should contain a qualification. To that extent, this study suggests that while amending the PDA to be TRIPS-compliant, Bangladesh could add that the "duration of protection is subject to exceptions as included in this Act or to be included by any future amendments". Such an extension may provide the government with some freedom to act as times change and TRIPS compliance is assessed. It will also permit the government to act immediately in case of a health emergency or the public interest. During interviews, some participants considered this kind of reservation to be useful in limiting patent protection, if necessary, on public interest grounds.[173] However, one participant argued that limiting patent protection will discourage investment in the pharmaceutical sector; he argued instead that 20 years is not sufficient to recover investment and

---

171 Lei No.9.279 art. 40, de 14 de maio de 1996, Diario Oficial Da Uniao [DOU] de 15.05.1996. (Braz.), translated in Brazil: *Industrial Property Law*, 14/05/1996, No. 9.279, http://www.wipo.int/wipolex/en/details.jsp?id=515 ("An invention patent shall remain in force for a period of 20 (twenty) years, and a utility model patent for a period of 15 (fifteen) years from the date of filing").

172 *2005 Patent (Amendment) Act*, § 53(1), 2005 (India).

173 From interview data (this has been supported by many large, medium and small local pharmaceutical companies in Bangladesh).

that the duration should be extended to 30 years in the pharmaceutical sector.[174]

The US and the EU (driven and supported by their MNPCs), while negotiating bilateral investment agreements with the developing countries and the LDCs including Bangladesh, insisted on the inclusion of an extended period for pharmaceutical patents beyond 20 years to compensate the originator of the drug for the time lost during the patent application and drug registration procedures.[175] The US and the EU considered this a legitimate right that should be granted to "compensate" their pharmaceutical companies for "unreasonable" delays throughout the patent examination or registration processes.[176] However, "[t]he costs of patent term extension are grave".[177] For example:

> a recent study in the Republic of Korea concluded that the extension of patent terms is likely to cost the Korean National Health Insurance Corporation ... 504.5 billion won (US$529 million) for extending drug patents for three years and 722.5 billion won (US$757 million) if it has to agree to a four-year extension as proposed under [Free Trade Agreement] negotiations with the US.[178]

The TRIPS Agreement "is clear regarding this term of protection. It does not specify that a member state is obliged to extend the patent protection term for any reason (including delays in registering drugs or issuing patents) beyond the term prescribed under Article 33".[179]

In this regard, the CIPIH Report states that "[b]ilateral trade agreements should not seek to incorporate TRIPS-plus protection in ways that may reduce access to medicines in developing countries".[180]

---

174 Interview with an executive from an MNPC operating in Bangladesh, in Dhaka, Bangladesh, 9 March 2012.

175 See Emily Jones, 'Signing Away the Future: How Trade and Investment Agreements Between Rich and Poor Countries Undermine Development' (Oxfam Briefing Paper No. 101, March 2007), http://www.oxfam.org/sites/www.oxfam.org/files/Signing Away the Future.pdf

176 Ibid.

177 El Said (2010), p.145.

178 Ibid.; see also 'US FTA May Cost Drug Industry $1.2 Billion: Gov't', *the hankyoreh*, 17 October 2006, http://english.hani.co.kr/arti/english_edition/e_business/165065.html

179 El Said, p.144; see 'Resource Book on TRIPS and Development'. It should be noted that patent term extensions were proposed by the developed countries and rejected by the developing countries during the Uruguay Round.

180 CIPIH Report, p.182.

Therefore, LDCs such as Bangladesh should not adopt patent term extensions under the patent regime and should not agree in any future free trade agreements (FTAs) to patent terms beyond the TRIPS Agreement. Again, the Government of Bangladesh needs to craft enforcement provisions in such a way as not to erect barriers to the production and supply of generic drugs.

4.2.11 Do Not Adopt Overprotective Enforcement Provisions

LDCs such as Bangladesh should be aware that the TRIPS Agreement only sets minimum requirements with respect to the enforcement of IPRs. However, there has been an increased focus on strengthening mechanisms for the enforcement of IPRs, far beyond what is required by the TRIPS Agreement, through so-called "anti-counterfeiting" initiatives.[181] The developing countries and LDCs are increasingly under pressure to place criminal sanctions on a wide array of IPR violations, including patent infringement.[182] However, placing criminal sanctions on patent infringement (e.g., considering generic medicines

---

181 See generally 'Global Communication on HIV and the Law, Regional Issues Brief: Intellectual Property Rights and Access to Medicines' (17 February 2011), p.22, http://www.hivlawcommission.org/resources/aprd/IssuesBrief_IPR.pdf. For example:
In 2008, Kenya enacted its *Anti-counterfeit Act*, purportedly designed to address the problem of counterfeit goods, including substandard and spurious medicines. It attached harsh criminal sanctions related to counterfeiting. However, according to the definition of the Act safe, effective and legitimate generic medicines were also considered "counterfeit". By conflating the issues of safety, quality and efficacy, and the separate field of intellectual property, the Act potentially criminalized the manufacture, import, export, possession or sale of perfectly safe generic medicines. Kenya's *Anti-counterfeit Act* was challenged before the High Court in July 2009 by three petitioners living with HIV on the basis that impinges on their constitutional right to health. The Court passed preliminary judgment in favour of petitioners on 23 April, 2010 and suspended powers of Anti-counterfeit Agency to interfere with importation and distribution of generics pending ruling on the substance.
UNDP, 'Good Practice Guide: Improving Access to Treatment by Utilizing Public Health Flexibilities in the WTO TRIPS Agreement' (2010), p.47, http://content.undp.org/go/cms-service/stream/asset/?asset_id=3259443

182 See generally Ermias Biadgleng and Viviana Tellez, 'The Changing Structure and Governance of Intellectual Property Enforcement' (South Centre Research Paper No. 15, January 2008), http://papers.ssrn.com/sol3/papers.cfm?abstract_id=1210622; Susan Sell, 'The Global IP Upward Ratchet, Anti-counterfeiting and Piracy Enforcement Efforts: The State of Play' (PIJIP Research Paper Series. No. 15, American University Washington College of Law, 2010), http://digitalcommons.wcl.american.edu/research/15

"counterfeit")[183] can restrict access to medicines and "could have a chilling effect on generic manufacturers' willingness to enter the market with affordably priced generic medicines".[184]

On the other hand, "overbroad powers granted to customs officials, have already been used to hinder the legitimate trade of affordable generic medicines" under the pretext of counterfeiting and infringement.[185] For example, in 2009, Dutch authorities seized a shipment in transit of the generic drug Abacavir, produced in India, purchased by the NGO UNITAID[186] and on its way to Africa, on the grounds that the generic version of the medicine violated patent rights in Europe.[187]

The use of the term "counterfeit" medicines became more controversial when the WHO–IMPACT meeting in December 2008 suggested that a medical product is counterfeit when there is false representation in relation to its identity, history or source, or to its container, packaging or other labelling information.[188] However, the 66th meeting of the WHO

---

183 See generally Carlos Correa, Centre for Interdisciplinary Studies on Industrial Property and Economics, 'The Push for Stronger Enforcement Rules: Implications for Developing Countries' (2007); Michael Blakeney, 'International Proposals for the Criminal Enforcement of Intellectual Property Rights: International Concern with Counterfeiting and Piracy', *Intellectual Property* Q.1 (2009).

184 UNDP, p.46.

185 Ibid.; see Henning Grosse Ruse-Khan and Thomas Jaeger, 'Policing Patents Worldwide? EC Border Measures Against Transiting Generic Drugs Under EC and WTO Intellectual Property Regimes', *International Review of Intellectual Property and Competition Law*, 40 (2009): 502; see also *Eye on the Ball Medicine Regulation*.

186 UNITAID is the first global health organisation that "uses innovative financing to increase funding for greater access to treatments and diagnostics for HIV/AIDS, malaria and tuberculosis in low-income countries". *About Unitaid*, UNITAID, http://www.unitaid.eu/en/who/about-unitaid. It is "[b]ased in Geneva and hosted by the World Health Organization, approximately half of UNITAID's finances come from a levy on air tickets". It was "established in 2006 by the governments of Brazil, Chile, France, Norway and the United Kingdom as the 'International Drug Purchasing Facility'" (Ibid.). It is now backed by an expanding north-south membership, including Cyprus, Korea, Luxembourg, Spain, Cameroon, Congo, Guinea, Madagascar, Mali, Mauritius and Niger, along with philanthropic organisations like the Bill and Melinda Gates Foundation.

187 See Frederick M. Abbott, 'Seizure of Generic Pharmaceuticals in Transit Based on Allegations of Patent Infringement: A Threat to International Trade, Development and Public Welfare', *WIPO Journal* 1 (2009): 43–50, http://papers.ssrn.com/sol3/papers.cfm?abstract_id=1535521

188 The International Medical Products Anti-counterfeiting Taskforce (IMPACT) is a global coalition of stakeholders including NGOs, enforcement agencies, pharmaceutical manufacturers associations, and drug and regulatory authorities. IMPACT, Summary Report for Third IMPACT General Meeting (3–5 December 2008), http://apps.who.int/impact/resources/IMPACTthirdgeneralmeeting_report.pdf

Regional Committee for South-East Asia rejected the WHO-IMPACT definition of counterfeit drugs. Recognising the need to separate IP issues from quality and safe medical products, the draft resolution urged member countries to refrain from IP enforcement that compromises access to medicines.[189] In this regard, the Indian Pharmaceutical Alliance argued that the references to "history" and "source" in the WHO-IMPACT definition suggest patent infringement and that this might affect exports of generics (from India) because it wrongly leads the public to believe that generics are counterfeits.[190] Therefore, India requested that the original WHO definition of counterfeit medicines be maintained: "A counterfeit medicine is one which is deliberately and fraudulently mislabelled with respect to identity and/or source. Counterfeiting can apply to both branded and generic products and counterfeit products may include products with the correct ingredients or with the wrong ingredients, without active ingredients, with insufficient active ingredients or with fake packaging".[191]

However, the TRIPS Agreement does not require the criminalisation of patent infringement, and it limits criminalisation obligations to wilful trademark counterfeiting and copyright piracy on a commercial scale.[192]

Neither Brazil nor India has adopted overprotective enforcement mechanisms that could criminalise generic production and supply. Therefore, while instituting TRIPS-compliant enforcement obligations within domestic patent law and pharmaceutical regulations, the Government of Bangladesh, rather than adopting overprotective

---

189 For details, see 'Access to Indian Generic Drugs: Emerging Issues', pp.225–52.

190 See 'Why did the Government of India oppose the 'counterfeit drug' definition proposed by IMPACT?', http://spicyip.com/2009/03/why-did-government-of-india-oppose.html

191 See WHO, *Counterfeit Drugs. Guidelines for the development of measures to combat counterfeit drugs*, http://apps.who.int/medicinedocs/en/d/Jh1456e/

192 See TRIPS Agreement, art. 61. It states:
Members shall provide for criminal procedures and penalties to be applied at least in cases of *wilful trademark counterfeiting or copyright piracy on a commercial scale*. Remedies available shall include imprisonment and/or monetary fines sufficient to provide a deterrent, consistently with the level of penalties applied for crimes of a corresponding gravity. In appropriate cases, remedies available shall also include the seizure, forfeiture and destruction of the infringing goods and of any materials and implements the predominant use of which has been in the commission of the offence. Members may provide for criminal procedures and penalties to be applied in other cases of infringement of intellectual property rights, in particular where they are committed wilfully and on a commercial scale.

provisions that would hamper the supply of generic medicines, should focus on efforts to strengthen drug regulatory authorities; promote rational use and encourage the public not to sell, buy or distribute any fake or counterfeit medicines; and should not include 'patent infringement' as a possible ground under the term of 'counterfeiting of medicines'.

In addition to the above legislative options, the Government of Bangladesh should consider additional interventions to ensure access to medicines and to promote pharmaceutical innovation in the process of moving towards a TRIPS-compliant regime.

4.3 Government Intervention Options

Although the patenting of pharmaceuticals and the consequent effect on pharmaceutical price do not constitute the only issue affecting access, it is considered a significant barrier and one that is common to all developing countries, whatever their stage of development.[193] Most interviewees in this study echoed the belief that simply using the flexibilities available in the TRIPS Agreement when drafting national patent laws will not improve access to medicines in Bangladesh, especially when the country's economic development, health infrastructure, drug distribution and drug availability are in disarray.[194] There is also the fear that the achievements made thus far through the local production of pharmaceuticals will not continue if MNPCs and developed countries put pressure on Bangladesh to refrain from producing and exporting cheaper generic drugs that compete with the more expensive patented brands produced by the MNPCs.[195]

Nonetheless, MNPCs and developed countries are not yet pressuring Bangladesh for pharmaceutical patents. As an LDC, Bangladesh can still waive compliance with the pharmaceutical patents of the TRIPS Agreement. Additionally, Bangladesh is not yet a competitive threat because it is not a country that promises huge profits.[196] Despite its

---

193 See 'Access to HIV/AIDS Treatment in Developing Countries', Interagency Coalition on AIDS and Development (August 2001), http://www.icad-cisd.com
194 Interview with officials at the DGDA and public health NGOs, in Dhaka, Bangladesh, 12–15 March 2012.
195 *Make Vital Medicine Available for People*, p.5.
196 Ibid.

population of more than 150 million people, the average wage, life expectancy and literacy rate are among the lowest in the world, and its local pharmaceutical industry is incapable of making the raw materials for new drugs; hence, MNPCs are not interested in putting pressure on Bangladesh.[197] In 1997, the US Embassy in Bangladesh reported that "Intellectual property infringement is common, but is currently of relatively limited significance for US firms".[198] One study suggested that "this attitude may change soon, as it has happened in other poor countries such as Ghana and Uganda where multinational companies have already acted to stop them importing cheaper generic drugs, which compete with the more expensive patented brands of medicine".[199] Therefore, apart from reforming patent law, Bangladesh may need to consider other alternative government intervention options to ensure access to medicines.[200]

Supporting alternative measures to market-based instruments, Zafarullah Chowdhury remarks that:

> Medicines are one commodity you can't leave to market forces. The market is simply not competent. It makes for monopolies and cartels, not competition. And every drug is, by definition, essential. If you have a malfunctioning liver and only one drug can save your life, that to you is the most essential drug in the world. Allowing the global drug market to be controlled by foreign firms (with lengthy periods of patent control) is not going to help us.[201]

Chowdhury further adds that "local drug firms have no innovative technology, therefore when Bangladesh is bound to honor foreign patents on new drugs that could be our collapse".[202]

Another renowned public health activist in Bangladesh, Farhad Mazahar, remarks that "the impact of pharmaceutical patent on Bangladesh will be huge because most of our raw materials [for new and existing drugs] come from India and our companies are only pharmacies, really [not a pharmaceutical industry]".[203] Therefore, considering the

---

197 Ibid.
198 Ibid.
199 Quoted in *Make Vital Medicine Available for People*.
200 Email interview with a patent law academic, in New Delhi, India, 11 March 2012.
201 *Make Vital Medicine Available for People*, p.6.
202 Ibid.
203 Ibid.

delicate state of public health infrastructure, the low level of access to medicines and lack of innovation in its local pharmaceutical industry, Bangladesh should adopt some alternative measures based on the examples of Brazil, India and South Africa. These are (i) controlling drug prices; (ii) national competition law; (iii) introducing a patent prize system; (iv) limiting data protection; (v) developing a patent pool on country-specific diseases; (vi) avoiding TRIPS-plus requirements in any future Bilateral Investment Treaties (BITs) or under FTAs with developed countries, particularly the US and the EU; (vii) lobbying for a further extension to the transitional period for pharmaceutical patents; (viii) introducing process patents only for limited periods and adopting a utility model law; and (ix) instituting a special investment protection regime, open source drug innovation and a social business model in the pharmaceutical sector.

4.3.1 Drug Price Control

The affordability of medicines by individual patients in the LDCs is an important factor influencing access to care and treatment.[204] However, control over the cost of medicines exists in one form or another in most countries. For example, in Australia, "new drugs with no advantage over existing products are offered at the same price",[205] and "Where clinical trials show superiority, incremental cost effectiveness is assessed to determine whether a product represents value for money at the price sought".[206] In the UK, the pharmaceutical price regulation scheme—a voluntary agreement between the Department of Health and the Association of the British Pharmaceutical Industry—exists so that companies negotiate profit rates from sales of drugs to the UK National

---

204 See generally, World Health Organization (WHO), *Drugs and Money Prices, Affordability and Cost Containment*, ed. by M.N.G. Dukes, C.P. de Joncheere et al. (2003) http://www.euro.who.int/__data/assets/pdf_file/0011/96446/e79122.pdf

205 Amit Sen Gupta, 'Should Drug Prices be Controlled?', *Economic Times* (6 August 2002), http://articles.economictimes.indiatimes.com/2002-08-06/news/27340990_1_drug-prices-price-controls-drug-companie

206 Jan Swasthya Abhiyan, National Coordination Committee, 'Access to Essential Medicines', p.37 (February 2007), http://www.healthpolicy.cn/rdfx/jbywzd/gjjy2/yd/yjwx/201002/P020100227572014659949.pdf. See generally Jon Sussex, Koonal K Shah and Jim Butler, 'The Publicly Funded Vaccines Market in Australia' (Consulting Report No. 10/02, Office of Health Economics [OHE], 25 October 2010).

Health Service.[207] In France, Italy and Belgium, prices are set in relation to the relative cost and contribution made to the national economy.[208]

In Bangladesh, there is no drug price control mechanism under the existing Patent Act. However, the DCO 1982 provides for the fixing of prices by a government-appointed committee.[209] The committee mostly deals with essential medicines, as listed by the DGDA. Accordingly, these listed drugs can be circulated without such pricing controls.[210]

This is an important guarantee that the prices of pharmaceuticals, whether produced nationally or imported from the outside, will not increase without prior government authorisation.[211] Further, it is within the government's purview to refuse the registration of any pharmaceuticals that are regarded as unaffordable.[212]

In 1982, 150 pharmaceuticals were defined as essential pharmaceuticals[213] and any changes to their prices were decided by the DCC. However, since 1993, the number of price-controlled pharmaceuticals has declined to 117 primary healthcare pharmaceuticals.[214] The DCO 1982 empowered the government to determine the Minimum Retail Price (MRP) of these 117 essential drugs/chemical substances. The MRP consists of trade price (75.5%), wholesale commission (2.3%), retail commission (12.0%) and VAT (12.5%) for local products.[215] The breakdown for imported products is trade price (88.9%) and retail commission (11.11%).[216]

---

207 The pharmaceutical price regulation scheme regulates profits to within 17–21% on historic capital or the initial capital used to begin the venture, with 25% variation on either side. Companies are free to set prices, provided the rate of return is within the regulation band. If the profits are higher, the companies have to reduce them the next year, and if they are lower they can raise their prices. For details, see Kevin A Hassett, *Price Controls and the Evolution of Pharmaceutical Markets* (American Enterprise Institute, 2004), http://www.who.int/intellectualproperty/news/en/Submission-Hassett.pdf

208 See Alan Maynard and Karen Bloor, 'Dilemmas in Regulation of the Market for Pharmaceuticals', *Health Affairs* 22.3 (2003).

209 See Azam and Richardson (2010b).

210 See *Study on the Viability of High Quality Drugs Manufacturing*.

211 No drug can be introduced into the market without prior approval from the Drug Control Committee and price fixation by the Drug Price Committee as per the DCO 1982 § 9(2), 1982 (Bangl.).

212 DCO 1982, § 6(1) (Bangl.).

213 See *Study on the Viability of High Quality Drugs Manufacturing*.

214 Interview with an official from the DDA, in Dhaka, Bangladesh, 26 February 2012.

215 See Sanjay Kathuria and Mariem Mezghenni Malouche, *Toward New Sources of Competitiveness in Bangladesh: Key Insights of the Diagnostic Trade Integration Study*, https://openknowledge.worldbank.org/handle/10986/22712

216 Ibid.

Non-essential drugs are priced through a system of indicative prices. The rule is applicable only in the case of locally produced goods. A fixed percentage of mark-up is applied to the cost and freight price of finished goods to determine the MRP of imported finished goods. This applies to both essential and non-essential products. Therefore, the manufacturer is able to set the price for pharmaceuticals that do not fall into the controlled category. In principle, this does not mean that an exorbitant price can be set by a manufacturer, as the price must be approved (but not controlled) by the DCC;[217] however, in practice, the committee accepts the pricing offered by manufacturers or importers for products that are not on the list of essential medicines. No other stakeholders have a say in fixing the price.[218] The result is that sometimes manufacturers or importers demand higher prices if the product is not on the essential medicines list in Bangladesh, and the DCC will not object to or criticise the pricing.

The list needs to be updated from time to time, as some older listed medicines may not work and thus patients may need expensive new medicines that are often exempt from price control. One such situation occurs with multi-drug resistance, in which the older drugs are not working and yet the patient cannot afford the newer expensive drugs. Zaman Khan explains the situation in Bangladesh:

> we have recently lost four patients to multi-drug resistance disease. Eventually there will be new drugs but they will be even more expensive than the antibiotics we use now, Cefrazidine from Glaxo, for instance, at 450 taka (US$8) a dose or Ceftriazone from Roche, at 500 taka ($9). Very few people can even afford the drugs we have got. We ask patients about their economic history and then we decide who can and can't afford drugs. But I would say 70% of the people we see cannot afford to buy medicines. Even the cheaper versions are often beyond them.[219]

This account is corroborated by Khurshid Talukder of the Institute of Child and Mother Health in Bangladesh:

> We just want the best possible answers to treat all diseases. Simply, we must have the drugs here when they are available in developed countries. And they have to be affordable for poorer people to buy.

---

217 DCO 1982, § 4(2) (Bangl.).
218 Interview with a policy analyst from an international public health NGO, in Dhaka, Bangladesh, 23 February 2012.
219 *Make Vital Medicine Available for People*, p.4.

> People are often too poor to buy the correct drugs needed to cure an illness or cannot complete the full course of medicines, which in turn leads to more resistance.[220]

Public health activists and generic producers in Bangladesh who are concerned about the possible negative effect of TRIPS on the public health situation in Bangladesh say that "people of Bangladesh could be very seriously affected. It is an alarming and dismal picture".[221] Thus, most of the public health NGOs and experts in Bangladesh believe that the government should establish a permanent price control mechanism and make it accessible to the general public and public health groups.[222] Any individual or public health group would then be permitted to challenge or review the pricing of medicines on social or health grounds.[223] Another concern is the number of pharmacies that operate in Bangladesh without a license and sell pharmaceuticals to customers without a prescription and at a higher price.[224]

The DCC should be given jurisdiction to deal with these issues, and public health interest groups should be able to access the committee.[225] An example of a body that operates in such a fashion is the Canadian Patented Medicine Prices Review Board (PMPRB), established under the *Patent Act, 1987* as an independent quasi-judicial tribunal that limits the prices set by manufacturers for all patented medicines—new and existing—sold in Canada under prescription or over the counter, thus ensuring that pricing is not excessive.[226] As an independent quasi-judicial body, the PMPRB carries out its mandate independently of other organisations such as Health Canada—which approves drugs for safety and efficacy—and public drug plans, which approve the listing of drugs on their respective formularies for reimbursement purposes.[227]

The PMPRB has a dual role in regulating and reporting.[228] Its regulatory role is to protect consumers and contribute to Canadian healthcare by

220 Ibid.
221 Ibid.
222 Interview with public health NGOs and pharmaceutical researchers, in Dhaka, Bangladesh, 12 March 2012.
223 Ibid.
224 Interview with a public health activist, in Dhaka, Bangladesh, 23 December 2009.
225 Ibid.
226 See *About PMPRB*, Patented Medicine Prices Review Board, http://www.pmprb-cepmb.gc.ca/about-us
227 Ibid.
228 Ibid.

ensuring that prices charged by manufacturers for patented medicines are not excessive.[229] Its reporting role contributes to informed decisions and policymaking by reporting on pharmaceutical trends and on the R&D spending by pharmaceutical patentees.[230] The PMPRB is unique in the sense that it was set up exclusively to monitor the prices of patented drugs. In addition, it analyses the therapeutic contribution of patented pharmaceuticals and documents pharmaceutical R&D investment in Canada. A similar mechanism should be considered by Bangladesh as it moves towards a TRIPS-compliant patent regime.

It is interesting to note here that, in contrast to some small pharmaceutical companies, the leading local pharmaceutical companies in Bangladesh, as well as the MNPCs operating there, all oppose the price control mechanism.[231] One interviewee argued that "some companies are trying to seize the market with low price, low-quality products, which may become a real threat for public health".[232] This was echoed by another participant who claimed that price control might encourage both cheap drugs and, in a way, low-quality counterfeited pharmaceuticals.[233] The CEO of one small pharmaceutical company argued that the "withdrawal of price control will become a threat for access to medicines and for their (small pharmaceutical companies) survival" as well. He added that "it is better to have price control to encourage local competition and ensure affordability of pharmaceuticals for the local people".[234] The BAPI made no comment on this issue, which it considered contentious from both legal and political perspectives, and admitted that there is a conflict of

---

229 Ibid.

230 Ibid.

231 The surveys indicated that 50% of pharmaceutical companies operating in Bangladesh strongly agreed with the withdrawal of price control and 27% also agreed with the withdrawal (this represents all multinational, large and medium-sized companies that participated in the survey). In contrast, 18% strongly disagreed and 5% disagreed with the proposition (all of them small pharmaceutical companies).

232 Interview with an official from a large local pharmaceutical company, in Dhaka, Bangladesh, 13 March 2012.

233 This view of large pharmaceutical companies was also supported by an official from a medium-sized local pharmaceutical company during an interview, in Dhaka, Bangladesh, 13 March 2012.

234 Interview with the CEO of a local pharmaceutical company, in Dhaka, Bangladesh, 28 December 2009 (confirming the notion that small pharmaceutical companies support price control measures because they derive greater benefits, given their low production range, which is limited to certain products only).

opinion among its members.[235] Nonetheless, public health NGOs and IP academics in Bangladesh support a broadening of the role of price control and believe any attempt to withdraw price control will be a disaster.[236] One official at the DPDT in Bangladesh argued that "reality shows that even the government is not able to control price effectively with the present ordinance. So the non-existence of price control would definitely lead towards a real disaster in terms of access to drugs".[237] He further added that "in the absence of it, the price of drugs would be sky-high, which would ultimately lead towards the real obstacle in order to access to drugs".[238]

India's National Pharmaceutical Pricing Authority was established under the *Drugs (Prices Control) Order, 1995*[239] and is entrusted to fix or revise the prices of controlled bulk drugs and formulations (bulk drugs are price controlled like the essential medicines list in Bangladesh), and to enforce prices and availability of medicines in India. It has also been empowered to recover amounts overcharged by manufacturers of controlled drugs for consumers, and to monitor the prices of decontrolled drugs to keep them at reasonable levels. However, drug control mechanisms in India are considered to be ineffective by the government-backed Dr Pronab Sen Taskforce.[240] The taskforce argued that "no price regulatory mechanism can be effective unless there is a credible threat of price controls being imposed and enforced. However, it is also felt that often the present price control system is inappropriate, inadequate, cumbersome, and time consuming".[241]

---

235 Interview with an official from BAPI, in Dhaka, Bangladesh, 23 January 2009.
236 Interviews with IP academics and public health activists, in Dhaka, Bangladesh, 14 March 2012.
237 Interview with a deputy registrar from the DPDT, in Dhaka, Bangladesh, 22 January 2009.
238 Ibid.
239 The DCO was first passed in 1970 and then revised in 1979, 1987 and 1995. See for details, 'National Pharmaceuticals Pricing Policy, 2012', http://apps.who. int/medicinedocs/en/d/Js20106en. See also, Government of India, National Pharmaceutical Pricing Authority, http://www.nppaindia.nic.in/index1.html
240 'Recommendations of the Task Force Constituted Under the Chairmanship of Proneb Sen to Explore Issues Other than Price Control to Make Available Life-saving Drugs at Reasonable Prices' (2005), http://www.drugscontrol.org/pdf/f_recom2005.pdf
241 Ibid., 1.1.

The taskforce further recommended that "[p]rice controls should be imposed not on the basis of turnover, but on the 'essentiality' of the drug and on strategic considerations regarding the impact of price control on the therapeutic class. This must be a dynamic process".[242] It declared that "The ceiling prices of controlled drugs should normally not be based on cost of production, but on readily monitor-able market-based benchmarks".[243] Some other recommendations of the taskforce that may also be relevant for Bangladesh are:

- A process of active promotion of generic drugs should be put in place, including mandatory debranding for selected drugs.

- All public health facilities should be required to prescribe and dispense only generic drugs, except in cases where no generic alternative exists.

- In the case of proprietary drugs, particularly anti-HIV/AIDS and cancer drugs, the government should actively pursue access programmes in collaboration with drug companies with differential pricing and alternative packaging, if necessary.

- Public sector enterprises involved in the manufacture of drugs should be revived where possible and used as key strategic interventions for addressing both price and availability issues. Arrangements may need to be made to ensure their continuing viability.

- Fiscal incentives should be provided on a long-term assured basis to R&D activities in drugs.[244]

One public health activist remarked that the Government of Bangladesh should also appoint a taskforce to review its drug control mechanism and that it would benefit immensely from the Indian taskforce suggestion to restructure the existing mechanism.[245] However, another participant remarked that the Canadian approach is free from the problems identified by the Indian taskforce, and therefore an agency such as that in Canada—empowered as recommended by the Dr Pronob Sen Taskforce, particularly regarding the promotion of generic drugs and revival of public sector enterprises such as Essential Drugs Limited,

---

242 Ibid., 1.2.
243 Ibid., 1.5.
244 *Taskforce to Explore Options*, pp.53–54.
245 Interview with a public health activist and policy analyst working with a public health-based international NGO, in Dhaka, Bangladesh, 11 February 2012.

a government pharmaceutical manufacturing facility in Bangladesh—may help Bangladesh to develop a unique mechanism to maintain access to medicines, to assess R&D investment in the pharmaceutical sector and to feed information back to the government on such matters as incentives like tax exemption and other policy measures.[246] Some researchers, such as AK Monawar Uddin Ahmad, consider that the withdrawal of price controls for many pharmaceutical products do not lead to any rise in the price level, and that the MRP of some finished formulations actually decline due to competitive bulk drug pricing.[247]

Price control also has some built-in limitations or problems. There is the possibility that it could disrupt the balance between supply and demand in the market. If prices are held below natural levels, resources such as talent and investor capital leave an industry to seek a better return elsewhere.[248] There will be less discovery and innovation, and fewer new drugs will become available to consumers.[249] Although supply and demand shift constantly according to the price of raw materials, production costs and local needs, the government price will change only after a lengthy political and bureaucratic process. Thus, the government price will effectively never be an equilibrium price: it will be either too high or too low.[250] Price control could also affect the openness of competition and the availability of alternatives, which would tend to discourage rapid entry of generic medicines.[251]

In the context of Bangladesh, one important element that needs serious consideration is that the majority of drug costs are privately paid for in the absence of an effective health insurance system that provides

---

246 Interview with an IP lawyer working as an in-house legal counsel and regulatory affairs adviser at a local pharmaceutical company, in Dhaka, Banglesh, 13 February 2012.

247 A.K. Monaw-war Uddin Ahmad, 'Competition, Regulation and the Role of the State: The Case of Bangladesh', *Journal of Asiatic Society of Bangladesh* 53 (2008): 199, 211.

248 Fiona M. Scott Morton, 'The Problems of Price Controls', *Regulation* (2001), p.50, http://object.cato.org/sites/cato.org/files/serials/files/regulation/2001/4/morton.pdf

249 Ibid.

250 Ibid., p.53.

251 See Patricia Danzon and Michael Furakawa, 'Prices and Availability of Pharmaceuticals', *Health Affairs* 27 (2005): 221, 225.

access and availability to all.[252] Price regulation in most countries involves the government purchasing medicines for delivery through the public health system or fixing reimbursement rates against insurance claims, but rarely fixing prices prevailing in the open market.[253] Leading large and medium pharmaceutical companies are now more interested in exporting to other countries than in supplying the local market, due to low profits from price-controlled products.[254] Similarly, MNPCs operating in Bangladesh are not interested in supplying products in the local market that are under price control and have low profit margins.[255] In the absence of production by MNPCs and in the face of inadequate supply from leading local companies, small pharmaceutical companies with inadequate quality control are trying to seize an opportunity. Unless the price control mechanism works efficiently and in a timely manner with proper information about the market and relevant products, excessive price control in the long run will not give optimal results for public health in Bangladesh; rather, it could create a market for low-quality, cheaper products. Considering the limitations of price control, competition law may be an additional instrument for Bangladesh.

4.3.2 National Competition Law

When implementing the TRIPS Agreement, members can prevent the abuse of IPRs and control anti-competitive practices either by integrating competition rules into the national IP law or by framing

---

252 See generally Wendy J. Werner, 'Micro-insurance in Bangladesh: Risk Protection for the Poor?', *Journal of Health, Population and Nutrition* 27 (2009): 563, http://www.ncbi.nlm.nih.gov/pmc/articles/PMC2928102/pdf/jhpn0027-0563.pdf

253 For example, in the UK, "public health and insurance takes care of 83.4 percent of the spending on medicine, and in Germany, it is 78.5 percent". S. Narayan, 'Some Approaches to Pricing Controls for Patented Drugs in India', *ISAS Insights* 41 (1 December 2008): 1, 2, http://mercury.ethz.ch/serviceengine/Files/ISN/94707/ipublicationdocument_singledocument/f8515305-e6a3-4b13-9ba4-27d9ba38b937/en/42.pdf

254 Interview with patent lawyers and pharmaceutical researchers, in Dhaka, Bangladesh, 14 March 2012.

255 Interview with public health activists, in Dhaka, Bangladesh, 16 March 2012. All activists supported the notion that MNPCs operating in Bangladesh are not interested in supplying products in the local market that are under price control and have low profit margins.

a separate competition law to prevent abusive monopoly practices or the abuse of a dominant position.[256] Article 8.2 of the TRIPS Agreement permits WTO members to adopt "[a]ppropriate measures ... to prevent the abuse of intellectual property rights ... or ... practices which unreasonably restrain trade or adversely affect the international transfer of technology", while Article 40 of the TRIPS Agreement recognises the possible link between IP laws and competition policy.[257] Therefore, the use of competition law and policy could provide developing countries with several advantages, including[258] (i) countries will have flexibilities under the TRIPS Agreement to use a competition framework appropriate to their socioeconomic condition; (ii) countries will have the freedom to define what constitutes anti-competitive behaviour; (iii) competition law and policy are well suited for implementation by an independent competition authority vested with extensive investigative powers; and (iv) competition law and policy have already been used successfully by South Africa to reduce the price of essential medicines.

A World Bank study emphasising the importance of developing and institutionalising appropriate competition policy for developing countries and LDCs stated that "Unless developing countries rapidly establish adequate competition frameworks and regulatory institutions that also address monopoly abuse of [intellectual property rights], it is possible that increasing [intellectual property right] protection could result in welfare losses from monopoly behavior".[259]

Therefore, the Government of Bangladesh should consider enacting a national competition law to prevent the abuse of monopoly pricing during the post-TRIPS patent regime. Brazil introduced a new

---

256 Sislu F. Musungu, Susan Villanueva and Roxana Blasetti, *Utilizing TRIPS Flexibilities for Public Health Protection through South-South Regional Framework* (South Centre, 2004), http://www.iprsonline.org/resources/docs/trips-health-southcentre2004.pdf

257 TRIPS Agreement, art. 8.2; see ibid., art. 30; Thomas Cottier and Ingo Meitinger, 'The TRIPS Agreement without a Competition Agreement' (Paper presented at the Trade and Competition in the World Trade Organization [WTO] and Beyond, Venice, 4–5 December 1998).

258 'The Ability of Select Sub-Saharan Africa Countries to Utilize TRIPS Flexibilities and Competition Law', pp.2–4.

259 The World Bank, 'World Development Report: Building Institutions for Markets' (2002), p.147, https://openknowledge.worldbank.org/handle/10986/5984

competition law in December 2010,[260] and India, in 2002.[261] However, these countries have yet to effectively use competition law or policy for the pharmaceutical sector, whereas South Africa has already successfully implemented and tested its competition law in the pharmaceutical sector; therefore South African competition law appears to have a viable role to play in reducing the price of medicines[262] and its model should be adapted to suit Bangladesh's unique national circumstances.

In South Africa, the *Medicines and Related Substances Control Amendment Act, No. 90 of 1997*[263] created the grounds for using competition law to ensure access to medicines in cases of excessive pricing and abuse of a dominant position. This Act was introduced in response to the HIV/AIDS crisis the country had been facing and the lack of access to pharmaceuticals due to cost. Section 15C, considered controversial by the MNPCs, reads:

> Section 15C - Measures to ensure supply of more affordable medicines. The Minister may prescribe conditions for the supply of more affordable medicines in certain circumstances so as to protect the health of the public, and in particular may -
>
> 1)   notwithstanding anything to the contrary contained in the Patents Act, 1978 (Act 57 of 1978) determine that the rights with regard to any medicine under a patent granted in the Republic shall not extend to

---

260   In Brazil, a competition law, *Law No. 8,884/94*, was replaced by an updated *Competition Act, Law No. 12,529/11*, which came into force on 29 May 2012. Ana Paula Martinez, 'Abuse of Dominance: The Third Wave of Brazil's Antitrust Enforcement?', *Competition Law International* 9 (2013): 169, 170. Article 1 of the Brazilian competition law states that the statute's objective is to set out "antitrust measures in keeping with such constitutional principles as free enterprise and open competition, the social role of property, consumer protection, and restraint of abuses of economic power". *Federal Law No. 8,884 of 11 June 1994* (Braz.).

261   In India, the *Competition Act* was enacted in 2002 to replace the *Monopolies and Restrictive Trade Practices (MRTP) Act, 1969*. Terry Calvani and Karen Alderman, 'BRIC in the International Merger Review Edifice', *Cornell International Law Journal* 43 (2010): 73, 74. It established the Competition Commission of India to "eliminate practices having adverse effect on competition, to promote and sustain competition, protect the interests of consumers and ensure freedom of trade carried on by other participants" in markets. Vinod Dhall, 'Competition Law in India', *Antitrust* 21-SPG (2007): 73.

262   See generally Carina Smit, *The Rationale for Competition Policy: A South African Perspective* (2005), http://econex.co.za/wp-content/uploads/2015/04/econex_researcharticle_10.pdf

263   *Medicines and Related Substances Control Amendment Act.*

acts in respect of such medicine which has been put onto the market by the owner of the medicine, or with his or her consent;

2)   prescribe the conditions on which any medicine which is identical in composition, meets the same quality standard and is intended to have the same proprietary name as that of another medicine already registered in the Republic, but which is imported by a person other than the person who is the holder of the registration certificate of the medicine already registered and which originates from any site of manufacture of the original manufacturer as approved by the council in the prescribed manner, may be imported.[264]

The above provision authorises the South African government to determine the extent to which a specific drug patent will apply. This provision was a direct challenge to the pharmaceutical industry.[265] Such an enactment demonstrates that in becoming TRIPS-compliant, a nation may avail itself of some latitude within the flexibilities allowed under the TRIPS Agreement, particularly in pursuance of the imperative of public welfare.

The South African Competition Commission has already applied competition law successfully in the pharmaceutical sector to deal with restrictive practices and abuse of a dominant position. In *Hazel Tau and Others v. GlaxoSmithKline and Boehringer Ingelheim*, the prices set by these two companies were considered an obstacle to access to ARV medicines.[266] The Competition Commission ruled that they had violated the *Competition Act, 1998* by "1. Den[ying]a competitor access to an essential facility[,]2. Excessive pricing[,] and 3. Engag[ing] in an

---

264 Ibid., § 15C.

265 According to *Court Case Between 39 Pharmaceutical Firms and The South African Government*, CPTech, http://www.cptech.org/ip/health/sa/pharma-v-sa.html:
A group of 39 pharmaceutical companies has dropped its lawsuits against the government of South Africa. They had taken South Africa to court over its Medicines and Related Substances Act. The main issue was Amendment 15(c) which would allow TRIPS-compliant compulsory licensing and parallel imports of medicines in South Africa. The suit was first filed on February 18, 1998.
On March 6, 2001, the South African court hearing the case ruled that the Treatment Access Campaign (TAC) would be granted a friend of the court role. It also adjourned the case until April 18, bowing to threats from the PMA to file an appeal on the grounds that they needed additional time to response [sic] to the new evidence and issues raised by TAC.
On April 19, 2001, the pharmaceuticals companies, under an extremely high amount of international pressure, dropped their case.

266 See *Competition Commission Finds Pharmaceutical Firms.*

exclusionary act", whereas the pharmaceutical companies claimed they were merely exercising the exclusive right granted through their patent as in many other countries.[267] However, the commissioner stated:

> Our investigation revealed that each of the firms has refused to license their patents to generic manufacturers in return for a reasonable royalty. We believe that this is feasible and that consumers will benefit from cheaper generic versions of the drugs concerned. We further believe that granting licenses would provide for competition between firms and their generic competitors. We will request the Tribunal to make an order authorising any person to exploit the patents to market generic versions of the respondents' patented medicines or fixed dose combinations that require these patents, in return for the payment of a reasonable royalty.[268]

Even though the two companies denounced the complaint as unfounded, they compromised by adopting voluntary licenses to produce a generic version of their patented pharmaceuticals. Since this case, there has been substantial progress in South Africa towards providing access to pharmaceuticals for anti-HIV and AIDS.[269]

Bangladesh now has a competition law to prevent the abuse of monopoly pricing during the post-TRIPS patent regime. The Government of Bangladesh enacted the *Competition Act, 2012* in June 2012.[270] One study stated that "A draft bill for such a law was first proposed in 1996; however, it took sixteen years to finally come to fruition".[271] The progress of the bill has been delayed: "the political will to implement a competition law is limited, and there is some opposition from business groups".[272]

Indeed, competition problems are potentially more serious in a country such as Bangladesh, which has "a weaker private sector, where one or a few dominant firms can take control" and abuse their dominant position.[273] The media coverage suggests that "Bangladesh may suffer from significant competition problems, with substantial

267 Ibid.
268 'Access to Patented Anti-HIV/AIDS Medicine'.
269 Ibid.
270 'Will Bangladesh's New Competition Law Prove Effective?'.
271 Quoted in Will Bangladesh's New Competition Law Prove Effective?'.
272 Karen Ellis Rohit Singh, Shaikh Eskander, and Iftekharul Huq, *Assessing the Economic Impact of Competition: Findings from Bangladesh* (ODI, 2010), http://www.odi.org.uk/sites/odi.org.uk/files/odi-assets/publications-opinion-files/6058.pdf
273 Ibid., p.2.

costs to consumers" and to the public health sector of Bangladesh, more particularly.[274]

The Government of Bangladesh should utilise competition law so that its objective is the welfare of its population. Despite the enactment of the competition law in 2012, it is yet to be implemented, as the Ministry of Commerce in Bangladesh has not adopted the rules to enforce it.[275]

When considering weaknesses in the South African competition law, it is suggested that in any future Bangladeshi competition law, "to increase its effectiveness as a tool for reducing prices of essential medicines", a competition commission should be empowered with the authority to issue compulsory licenses, recommend fixed royalty rates and expressly allow for the export of products produced under compulsory licenses to maintain sustainable investment.[276] In addition, LDCs such as Bangladesh may also stipulate in national competition law that compulsory licensing could be granted in cases of anti-competitive behaviour, such as in the case of the patent holder's unilateral refusal to grant a license (refusal to deal).[277] Competition law could also be applied in the case of obtaining pharmaceutical patents in an unjustified and fraudulent manner.[278] Issues of "poor quality" and "frivolous" patents and regulatory practices such as marketing approval and data exclusivity can also be controlled under competition law.[279]

One interviewee argued that the use of competition law would be a viable tool for Bangladesh to prevent excessive pricing and to allow generic production of particular pharmaceutical products if there is any abuse of dominant position, as it would be extremely difficult for Bangladesh to allow a compulsory license under patent law due to

---

274 Ibid.
275 Shakhawat Hossain, 'No Enforcement of Laws on Food Adulteration, Children, Fair Trade', *New Age* (Dhaka) (19 May 2014), http://newagebd.net/12634/ no-enforcement-of-laws-on-food-adulteration-children-fair-trade/#sthash.IMYI3 DvK.dpuf
276 'The Ability of Select Sub-Saharan Africa Countries', p.6.
277 See *Intellectual Property and Competition Law: Exploration of Some Issues*.
278 See ibid., pp.13–19. In fact, these patents should never have been granted in the first place. Lack of proper resources, expertise and proper examination in the LDCs may allow for such fraudulent registrations. In these situations, competition law plays an important role.
279 See ibid., pp.13–16.

political pressure from the developed countries.[280] In contrast, another participant argued that even the use of competition law may also face political pressure, and that the competition authority should moreover have enough expertise and resources to guide its reasoning.[281]

Another alternative government intervention mechanism is a prize system.

4.3.3 Patent Prize System

The use of patent prizes as an alternative to patents, proposed by some scholars such as Joseph E. Stiglitz, could address the lack of incentive with respect to problems such as disease in developing countries, and it would provide immediately affordable pricing for products still under patent protection.[282] In a prize system, "[i]nstead of authorizing drug developers to exclude competitors, the government would pay successful developers", and therefore "[o]ther firms, including generic drug manufacturers, would be free to make and sell the drugs in question".[283] Some studies further suggest that many drug companies spend much of the money earned through patents on marketing and advertising, as opposed to research for new drugs.[284]

However, "[t]he controversy between a patent and prize systems [sic] reaches as far back as the nineteenth century", when "commentators proposed 'bonuses' [be] granted to inventors by the government, professional associations financed by private industries,

---

280 Interview with an IP academic from the University of Chittagong, in Chittagong, Bangladesh, 18 January 2012.

281 Interview with a public health activist, in Dhaka, Bangladesh, 23 January 2012.

282 See Joseph E. Stiglitz, 'Scrooge and Intellectual Property Rights', *British Medical Journal* 333 (2006): 1279–80; see also Joseph E. Stiglitz and Arjun Jayadev, 'Medicine for Tomorrow: Some Alternative Proposals to Promote Socially Beneficial Research and Development in Pharmaceuticals', *Journal of Generic Medicines* 7(3): pp.217–26.

283 William W. Fisher and Talha Syed, 'A Prize System as a Partial Solution to the Health Crisis in the Developing World' (Discussion Paper No. 5, Petrie-Flom Center for Health Law Policy, Biotechnology and Bioethics at Harvard Law School, 2009), https://www.law.berkeley.edu/files/Fisher_Prizes12.pdf

284 See generally Mayer Brezis, 'Big Pharma and Health Care: Unsolvable Conflict of Interests Between Private Enterprise and Public Health', *Israel Journal of Psychiatry and Related Sciences* 45 (2008): 83, http://publichealth.doctorsonly.co.il/wp-content/uploads/2011/12/2008_2_3.pdf

intergovernmental agencies, or an international association funded by private industries".[285] Michael Polanvyi trumpeted the idea of prizes as a means of patent reform in 1944, stating that "[i]n order that inventions may be used freely by all, we must relieve inventors of the necessity of earning their rewards commercially and must grant them instead the right to be rewarded from the public purse".[286] However, these suggestions did not garner much support.

The Royal Academy of Science in Paris had a prize system that "served as a model for scientific societies in other countries during the eighteenth and nineteenth centuries. The lack of a central authority or specific policy for prize distribution" made the prize system contentious and, some claimed, corrupt.[287] "Academy members were at odds when trying to determine which fields should receive general prizes", and "[s]uch disputes were only partly resolved by commissions represented by multiple disciplines. At the same time, prizes were becoming increasingly a matter solely of money, not honor".[288] The "ultimate question of whether the costs outweigh the benefits of a prize system over a patent system remains open" and is one that "can only be answered empirically".[289] Few studies have focused on the economic effects of prizes,[290] and there is no consensus on how prize systems should be designed.[291]

Nevertheless, a prize system may be designed to encourage local pharmaceutical companies and MNPCs to invest in R&D for the diseases most prevalent in Bangladesh. A prize system is justified on the grounds that granting patents stimulates a monopoly rather than the R&D necessary to deal with the particular problems of a country without

---

285 Marlynn Wei, 'Should Prizes Replace Patents? A Critique of the Medical Innovation Prize Act of 2005', *Boston University Journal of Science and Technology Law* 13.1 (2007), http://www.bu.edu/law/central/jd/organizations/journals/scitech/volume131/documents/Wei_WEB.pdf

286 Michael Polanvyi, 'Patent Reform', *Review of Economic Studies* 11 (1944): 61, 65 (emphasis omitted).

287 'Should Prizes Replace Patents?', p.29 (footnote omitted).

288 Ibid.

289 Ibid., p.31.

290 See generally Lee N. Davis, *Should We Consider Alternative Incentives for Basic Research? Patents vs. Prizes* (Paper presented at the DRUID Summer Conference, 6–8 June 2002), http://www.druid.dk/conferences/summer2002/Papers/DAVIS.pdf

291 Michael Abramowicz, 'Perfecting Patent Prizes', *Vanderbilt Law Review* 56 (2003): 115, 121.

resources such as Bangladesh, or of inventing something where there is no hope of a huge profit.[292] Further, it is important to acknowledge the criticism that "the patent system and other exclusive rights contribute to high drug prices, global health inequities, limited access to potentially life-saving medicines and medical technologies, and the production of drugs that have little incremental therapeutic value".[293] In a system that rewards patent owners, pharmaceutical companies will target only affluent patients who can pay more or significantly higher prices that cover the cost of R&D and marketing; therefore, "pharmaceutical companies have little incentive to invest in R&D for low-return ... neglected diseases, or other 'non-profitable' diseases".[294] The WHO estimates that approximately 10 million lives could have been saved with access to existing medicines and vaccines. The deadweight loss of monopoly pricing of drugs is anywhere between US$3 billion and $30 billion annually in the US drug market alone.[295] In this context, a prize system has three underlying goals: (i) to provide incentives for R&D in new, significantly better medicines; (ii) to enhance access to medicines; and (iii) to focus more resources on non-profitable, neglected diseases.[296]

Considering potential benefits and limitations, Bangladesh could introduce a prize system while initially maintaining the patent system, rather than preventing patents altogether. The prize system should have as its principle criteria: (i) the number of patients benefited by the invention/innovation; (ii) "the incremental therapeutic benefits

---

292 See generally *Should We Consider Alternative Incentives for Basic Research?*
293 'Should Prizes Replace Patents?', p.26 (footnote omitted). Many authors have criticised the growing numbers of "me-too" drugs on the market, products that duplicate the therapeutic value of already existing drugs. See Aidan Hollis, 'An Efficient Reward System for Pharmaceutical Innovation' (10 June 2004) (unpublished manuscript), p.6, http://www.who.int/intellectualproperty/news/ Submission-Hollis6-Oct.pdf; Youngme E. Moon and Kerry Herman, *Marketing Antidepressants: Prozac and Paxil* (Harvard Business School Case 502-055, October 2005). For an argument favourable towards "me-too" drugs for creating competition, see Thomas H. Lee, '"Me-too" Products: Friend or Foe?', *New England Journal of Medicine* 350 (2004).
294 'Should Prizes Replace Patents?', p.26. Only 10% of the world's expenditure on R&D is spent on targeting 90% of the disease burden (citing Amy Kapczynski Samantha Chaifetz, Zachary Katz and Yochai Benkler, 'Addressing Global Health Inequities: An Open Licensing Approach for University Innovations', *Berkeley Technology Law Journal* 20 (2005)).
295 'Should Prizes Replace Patents?', pp.26–27 (footnotes omitted).
296 Ibid., p.28 (footnotes omitted).

of the innovation; (iii) the degree to which the innovation addresses healthcare needs, including global infectious diseases, orphan illnesses, and neglected diseases affecting the poor in developing countries; and (iv) '[t]he improved efficiency of manufacturing processes for drugs'".[297]

During WHA 60.30, "The governments of Bolivia, Suriname and Bangladesh present[ed] for discussion a proposal concerning the possible use of prizes as a new incentive mechanism for innovation in new cancer treatments and vaccines that would separate rewards to innovation from the price of the products". This proposal is based on an earlier one presented by the governments of Barbados and Bolivia in April 2008 during the WHO Intergovernmental Working Group on Public Health, Innovation and Intellectual Property.[298] As the proposal declares, "[a]ccess to new cancer treatments and vaccines in developing countries is limited, due to several factors including, but not limited to: poor medical infrastructure; inadequate screening; and the high costs of oncology equipment, services and medicines".[299] It also mentions that "[h]igh prices for new cancer drugs and vaccines either discourage use completely, or place enormous burdens on the healthcare budgets of developing countries. Treatments for several new cancer drugs exceed [US]$50,000 per completed course".[300]

However, this was not a proposal for a global prize fund; rather, it suggested that "national governments in developing countries introduce a new system of rewarding the development of new medicines and vaccines for cancer".[301] Specifically, it proposed "that

---

297 Ibid., p.34; see also 'A Prize System as a Partial Solution'.

298 'Proposal by Bolivia, Suriname and Bangladesh: Prizes as a Reward Mechanism for New Cancer Treatments and Vaccines in Developing Countries' (15 April 2009), p.1, http://www.who.int/phi/Bangladesh_Bolivia_Suriname_CancerPrize.pdf. The proposal stated:

According to the WHO, of the more than 8 million persons who died from cancer in 2008, 5.7 million, or 71 percent, lived in developing countries. Cancer is a leading cause of death worldwide. According to the WHO, the percentage of total deaths attributed to cancer is expected to decline in developed countries, but to increase in all developing country regions.

See also Krista L. Cox, 'The Medicines Patent Pool: Promoting Access and Innovation for Life-saving Medicines through Voluntary Licenses', *Hastings Science and Technology Law Journal* 4 (2012): 291.

299 'Proposal by Bolivia, Suriname and Bangladesh', p.2.

300 Ibid.

301 Ibid.

developing countries de-monopolize the entire sector of medicines and vaccines for cancer, and permit free entry by generic suppliers".[302] The proposal further stated that "[i]n return for ending the monopoly, developing country governments would offer to provide a domestic system of rewards for developers of new medicines and vaccines for cancer that is based on a fixed percentage of the national budget for cancer treatments".[303]

It was argued that such a proposal was consistent with the TRIPS Agreement as developing countries "can eliminate the exclusive rights to use patented inventions, in cases where patent owners receive remuneration or compensation".[304] However, there has been no outcome from this proposal despite the fact that "[o]n February 24, 2005, some 162 leading medical researchers, NGOs, parliamentarians, government officials, and other stakeholders submitted a letter to the [WHO] asking that it evaluate a proposal for a new global treaty to support medical R&D".[305] The letter proposed "to deal with higher drug prices for consumers in developed and developing countries by introducing a Medical R&D Treaty Framework that could ultimately replace existing or planned trade agreements that focus on patents or drug prices".[306]

According to Andrew Farlow:

> In late 2005 Kenya formally submitted a resolution to the WHO's Executive Board (WHO EB) asking for the creation of a working group of member states to consider the [Medical R&D Treaty (MRDT)]. In January 2006 Brazil co-sponsored the resolution. Subsequently, the WHO EB approved a heavily bracketed version of a draft resolution. That draft was debated at the World Health Assembly (WHA) in late May 2006.[307]

---

302 Ibid.
303 Ibid. (emphasis omitted).
304 Ibid., p.3; see also TRIPS Agreement, arts. 30, 31, 44.
305 CPTech, 'Proposal for Treaty on Medical Research and Development' (February 2005), http://www.cptech.org/workingdrafts/rndtreaty.html
306 Ibid.
307 Andrew Farlow, 'A Global Medical Research and Development Treaty: An Answer to Global Health Needs?' (2007) (IPN Working Paper on Intellectual Property, Innovation and Health), p.12, http://www.andrewfarlow.com/global_medical_research_treaty.pdf; see WHO, '[Global Framework on] Essential Health Research and Development', in *Executive Board, 117th Session, Resolutions, Decisions, and Annexes* (27 January 2006), p.20, http://apps.who.int/gb/ebwha/pdf_files/EB117-REC1/B117_REC1-en.pdf

The MRDT would require all countries—rich and poor—to pledge to spend a fixed percentage of their GDP on medical R&D.[308] The WHO Consultative Expert Working Group (CEWG) Report also proposed the creation of a new binding agreement to provide billions of dollars annually for R&D to address the special healthcare needs of poor persons living in developing countries, and to introduce new approaches to funding R&D that included open innovation models, the delinking of R&D costs from product prices, and technology transfer and capacity building in developing countries.[309] However, the CEWG Report also stated that "[w]e see a convention not as a replacement for the existing intellectual property rights system, but as a supplementary instrument where the current system does not function".[310]

On the other hand, there was contention regarding suitability of the WHO as a forum to negotiate a relevant treaty. That is why it was stated that "although the sponsors believe that a treaty on MRDT would considerably 'transform the landscape of biomedical innovation to incorporate needs-driven health research and development', several developed country members, primarily the US and the EU, said that the WHO was not an appropriate forum for discussing the treaty".[311] Finally, the WHO negotiations on MRDT ended without any concrete action; instead, the WHO deferred the issues until 2016 by deciding to convene another open-ended meeting of member states prior to the 69th WHA in May 2016 in order to assess progress and continue discussions on the remaining issues in relation to monitoring, coordination and financing for health R&D.[312] Public health groups like Knowledge Ecology International (KEI) criticised the outcome:

---

308 Ryan Abbot, 'Potential Elements of the WHO Global R&D Treaty: Tailoring Solutions for Disparate Contexts', *Intellectual Property Watch* (29 January 2013), http://www.ip-watch.org/2013/01/29/potential-elements-of-the-who-global-rd-treaty-tailoring-solutions-for-disparate-contexts

309 Ibid.

310 WHO, 'Research and Development to Meet Health Needs in Developing Countries: Strengthening Global Financing and Coordination' (5 April 2012), http://www.who.int/phi/CEWG_Report_5_April_2012.pdf

311 'WHO Tackles Intellectual Property, R&D Treaty', *Bridges Weekly Trade News Digest* (27 May 2009): 1, 3, http://www.ictsd.org/sites/default/files/review/bridgesweekly/bridgesweekly13-19.pdf

312 See James Love, 'WHO negotiators propose putting off R&D treaty discussions until 2016', Knowledge Ecology International (KEI) (28 November 2012, 8:22 PM), http://keionline.org/node/1612

A treaty on R&D financing would have not have cost the United States any money, while creating obligations on other countries to pay more for global health R&D projects. The only reason for blocking this initiative was to protect the existing drug development business model. The existing model benefits big pharma the most, and exploits consumers and marginalizes the poor.[313]

On the basis that there is no international scheme, Bangladesh could try a country-specific prize fund picking on the most preventable diseases in Bangladesh. During the author's surveys of pharmaceutical companies in Bangladesh, no one showed any interest in the prize system. However, pharmaceutical researchers and public health NGOs who were interviewed considered it a viable option.[314]

Limiting data protection is another policy position in need of consideration by the Government of Bangladesh.

4.3.4 Limit Data Protection

To gain marketing approval for any newly developed pharmaceuticals, companies are required to submit test and clinical data relating to safety and efficacy to national health authorities.[315] The data exclusivity provisions "refer to a practice whereby, for a fixed period of time, national drug regulatory authorities prevent and block the registration files of an originator to be used to register a therapeutically equivalent generic version of that medicine without obtaining the consent of the patent holder unless the generic manufacturer actually conducts the clinical trials again".[316]

Supporters of data exclusivity provisions consider it important to compensate for inordinate delays in granting patents and also to recover

---

313 Ibid.

314 Based on interview responses from pharmaceutical academics and researchers.

315 Carlos M. Correa, *Protecting Test Data for Pharmaceutical and Agrochemical Products under Free Trade Agreements, UNCTAD-ICTSD Dialogue on Moving the Pro-development IP Agenda Forward: Preserving Public Goods in Health, Education and Learning* (United Nations Conference on Trade and Development [UNCTAD], 29 November to 3 December 2004), http://www.iprsonline.org/unctadictsd/bellagio/docs/Correa_Bellagio4.pdf

316 "Data exclusivity was first introduced in 1987 in a number of European countries to compensate for insufficient product patent protection. However, product patents for twenty years are now available in all 27 EU member states. The rules on data exclusivity have been changed in the EU pharmaceutical laws adopted in 2004". *Public Health Related TRIPS-Plus Provisions*, p.186.

investment and research costs for innovators. On the other hand, generic companies believe:

> Data exclusivity has nothing to do with protecting research data. Long after the data exclusivity period has expired, the originator documentation remains protected by copyright laws and other legal provisions. Data exclusivity merely extends the originator company's market monopoly over a product by not allowing the authorities to process an application for marketing authorisation.[317]

Therefore, "[d]ata exclusivity can be a barrier to generic entry irrespective of whether the drug was patented, or if the patent period has expired".[318]

In India, when generic companies apply for approval of a pharmaceutical, they are not required to conduct their own studies and submit independent data.[319] Rather, companies can rely on the safety and efficacy data submitted by the innovator company to obtain marketing approval for their products.[320]

Article 39.3[321] of the TRIPS Agreement is being interpreted by some MNCs and some developed countries, particularly the US, "to mean that WTO member countries are required to grant data exclusivity for a specified period of time".[322] However, after tracing the history and text of Article 39, scholars "have concluded that the protection need not be in the form of data exclusivity".[323] If data exclusivity "were the

---

317 *Data Exclusivity*, European Generic Medicines Association, http://www.cptech.org/ip/health/dataexcl

318 'Integrating Intellectual Property Rights', p.62.

319 Animesh Sharma, 'Data Exclusivity with Regard to Clinical Data', *The Indian Journal of Law and Technology* 3 (2007): 82–104, http://ijlt.in/wp-content/uploads/2015/08/Sharma-Data-Exclusivity-with-regard-to-Clinical-Data-3-Indian-J.-L.-Tech.-82.pdf

320 Ibid., p.84.

321 Article 39.3 of the TRIPS Agreement states:
Members, when requiring, as a condition of approving the marketing of pharmaceutical or of agricultural chemical products which utilize new chemical entities, the submission of undisclosed test or other data, the origination of which involves a considerable effort, shall protect such data against unfair commercial use. In addition, Members shall protect such data against disclosure, except where necessary to protect the public, or unless steps are taken to ensure that the data are protected against unfair commercial use.

322 Sudip Chaudhuri, 'TRIPS and Changes in Pharmaceutical Patent Regime in India' (Indian Institute of Management Calcutta, Working Paper No. 535, January 2005), p.19.

323 Ibid.

intention then the terms 'exclusive rights' would have been used as in Article 70.9" of the TRIPS Agreement.[324] Article 39.3 requires countries to "protect data against 'unfair commercial use'"[325] and countries "have the discretion to [protect data] not through data exclusivity but by proscribing situations where a competitor obtains the results of testing data through fraud, breach of confidence or other 'dishonest' practices and derive a commercial advantage".[326] Thus, "[p]rotection is not necessary if regulatory authorities do not require the submission of such data for marketing approval or if the data are already public".[327]Protection should only be required for new chemical entities so that each country can have considerable freedom "in defining what is 'new', and may exclude the different formulations based on the same chemicals".[328]

Thus, the TRIPS Agreement requires "data protection" but does not require data exclusivity, as there is a clear distinction between these two concepts. Data exclusivity involves a monopoly right over test data for a certain period of time, whereas data protection only requires authorities to keep the data confidential. A WHO study quite clearly states that:

> Given the negative impact on public health and access to medicines of providing for data exclusivity, it is important that developing countries try to avoid it. If unable to avoid data exclusivity, countries should limit the duration of data exclusivity as well as its scope (e.g., only for new chemical entities, and only for undisclosed data). Countries should also consider creating exemption mechanisms by which they can exempt products from data exclusivity provisions if necessary.[329]

Moreover, the CIPIH Report reaffirms this under Recommendation 4.20, which states:

> Developing countries need to decide in the light of their own circumstances, what provisions, consistent with the TRIPS agreement, would benefit public health, weighing the positive effects against the negative effects. A public health justification should be required for data

---

324 Ibid.
325 Ibid.; see TRIPS Agreement, art. 39.3.
326 Sudip Chaudhuri, p.19.
327 Ibid.
328 Ibid., 20.
329 WHO, *Intellectual Property Rights and Access to Medicines: A South-East Asia Perspective on Global Issues* (2008), http://apps.searo.who.int/pds_docs/B3468.pdf

protection rules going beyond what is required by the TRIPS agreement. There is unlikely to be such a justification in markets with a limited ability to pay and little innovative capacity. Thus, developing countries should not impose restrictions for the use of or reliance on such data in ways that would exclude fair competition or impede the use of flexibilities built into TRIPS.[330]

During the surveys for this study, all but one participant argued that Bangladesh should not give any test data protection.[331] They also believed that it would be beneficial to follow the Indian approach and allow generic competition.[332] One participant argued that granting test data protection over clinical and pre-clinical trial data could restrict entry of generic medicines, given that local pharmaceutical companies in Bangladesh lack the financial and technical resources to conduct original clinical trials.[333] However, one MNPC remarked in the survey that "test data protection may encourage foreign direct investment and technology transfer in Bangladesh".[334]

As an LDC, Bangladesh is still enjoying the Doha waiver for pharmaceutical patents; therefore, it currently has no test data protection system. Bangladesh should maintain that position to help local generic producers, while working towards creating a patent pool in cooperation with other countries and private organisations.

4.3.5 Patent Pool on Country-specific Diseases

A patent pool is an agreement between two or more patent owners to license one or more of their patents to one another, or to third parties, whether they are transferred directly by the patentee to license, or through any medium—such as a joint venture—set up specifically to

---

330 CIPIH Report, p.126.

331 In the surveys, representatives from all the local pharmaceutical companies, regardless of their size, supported the Indian position, whereas one MNPC supported test data protection, and the other MNPCs did not disclose their position on the issue.

332 Ibid.

333 Interview with an academic from the University of Dhaka, in Dhaka, Bangladesh, 13 March 2009 (discussing pharmaceutical technology).

334 From a survey response by one MNPC, Dhaka, Bangladesh, 22 January 2009.

administer the patent pool.[335] Therefore, a patent pool is a mechanism through which various patents held by different entities such as companies, universities and research institutions are made available to others for production or further development.[336] The patent holders receive royalties for the use of the patent not from the user directly, but from the pool management.[337] Patent pools are increasingly seen as a useful tool for tackling barriers to access to medicines in developing countries through the sharing of knowledge and technologies.[338]

The rationale for creating a patent pool is that it helps lower the price of pharmaceuticals and enhances innovation by considering particular local health needs.[339] Further, "[a] patent pool that licenses patents in several countries can ensure that generic manufacturers operate in efficient economies of scale" and can provide enhanced capacity to manage legal issues in the face of a multitude of patents, potential claims of infringement, variance of national laws, complexity of international treaties and national patent laws, and "complicated rules for the export of medical technologies under compulsory licenses present barriers for the expanded use of generic medicines".[340] Patent pool managers "have the expertise and capacity to manage issues that arise on behalf of governments, donors, public health agencies, patent owners and generic manufacturers".[341] It is also worth noting that collective management of the patent pool "will help [establish] global 'best practice' norms for licensing on such issues as quality control, remuneration, open competition, etc".[342]

---

335 See Steven C. Carlson, 'Note, Patent Pools and the Antitrust Dilemma', *Yale Journal on Regulation* 16 (1999): 352–9.

336 See Robert P. Merges, 'Institutions for Intellectual Property Exchange: The Case of Patent Pools', in *Intellectual Products: Novel Claims to Protection and their Boundaries*, ed. by Rochelle Dreyfuss (2001).

337 Manisha Singh Nair, *Rationality of a Patent Pool* (12 December 2009), http://ipfrontline.com/2009/04/rationality-of-a-patent-pool

338 Ibid.

339 Ibid.

340 WHO, KEI, Intergovernmental Working Group Submission on Collective Management of Intellectual Property — 'The Use of Patent Pools to Expand Access to Needed Medical Technologies' (30 September 2007), p.3, http://www.who.int/phi/public_hearings/second/contributions_section2/Section2_ManonRess-PatentPool.pdf

341 Ibid.

342 Ibid.

The WHA discussed patent pools back in 2008 and later in the CEWG Report, and considered it a feasible mechanism to accelerate the availability of newer, low-cost medicines in developing countries.[343] However, the possibility of creating a Medicines Patent Pool (MPP) was first proposed to UNITAID in 2006 by KEI and Médecins Sans Frontières following a proposal by KEI at the International AIDS Conference in 2002.[344] UNITAID played an instrumental role in the creation of the MPP and decided to explore the possibility of establishing a MPP in July 2008. Finally, UNITAID decided in December 2009 to create and fund a patent pool focusing on increasing access to HIV medicines in developing countries; this became a reality in July 2010. It has been endorsed by the WHO, the UN High Level Meeting on AIDS, and the Group of 8 as a promising approach to improving access to HIV medicines.

The MPP negotiates with patent holders to license to the MPP.[345] This means that the patent holder allows other producers to manufacture and sell low-cost, high-quality versions of patented medicines in developing countries, or to develop adapted formulations under certain terms and conditions. The MPP seeks licenses that push the status quo in the direction of greater access to medicines — covering more countries, and under public health-oriented terms and conditions — with the ultimate aim of ensuring all people living with HIV in developing countries can access the treatment they need at affordable prices.

Once the license is signed with the original patent holder, the MPP proceeds to make sub-licenses with low-cost generic manufacturers and other entities. The manufacturer is then free to develop, produce and sell the medicine in the agreed countries under strict quality assurance. It is stated that "[t]he MPP will particularly ease the development and production of fixed dose combination drugs (FDCs) that have proven to simplify treatment for people living with HIV and facilitate treatment scale-up in developing countries, and medicines suited for the specific

---

343 David de Ferranti, 'Can Patent Pools Get More AIDS Drugs to Patients?', *Huffington Post* (9 April 2012), http://www.huffingtonpost.com/david-de-ferranti/aids-drugs_b_1404218.html

344 Ibid.

345 For details about the working procedure of the Medicines Patent Pool (MPP), see *About the MPP*, Medicines Patent Pool, http://www.medicinespatentpool.org/about/

needs of children".[346] In this way, more people can be treated for the same cost, which is crucial in a climate of increasing needs and funding challenges: "Patent holders can get a small royalty on the sales of the medicines, and people living with HIV get access to affordable, adapted treatment they need at prices they can afford".[347] Figure 4.1 depicts the working procedure of the MPP.

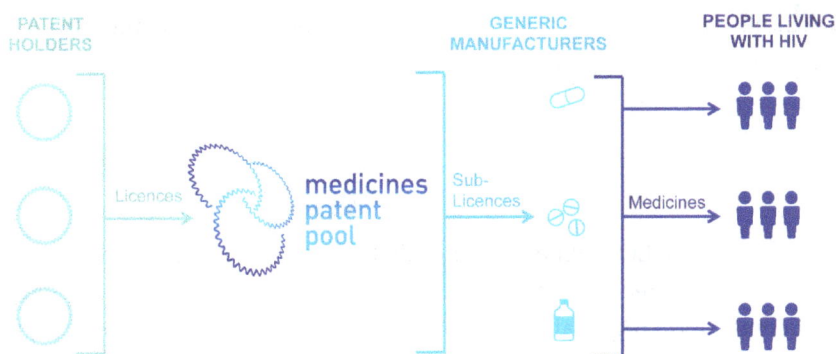

Figure 4.1: Working procedure of the Medicines Patent Pool[348]

In analysing the importance of the MPP, it was remarked in the *Huffington Post*:

> As of today, the history of the MPP is still being written. It will be important to see over the coming year whether this patent pool will become large enough to effectively accelerate the production of low-cost generic versions of new AIDS drugs and the creation of the fixed dose combinations. Millions of patients in countries around the world will be affected by what happens.[349]

Bangladesh could consider a patent pool structure for prevalent diseases in consultation with other countries needing such pharmaceuticals. This

---

346 Ibid.
347 Ibid.
348 *How it Works*, Medicines Patent Pool, http://www.medicinespatentpool.org/wp-content/uploads/how-it-works-diagram.png
349 'Can Patent Pools Get More AIDS Drugs to Patients?'.

could be accomplished by using Articles 66.2[350] and 67[351] of the TRIPS Agreement to seek technical and financial cooperation from developed countries for developing a patent pool for specific diseases. During the surveys, none of the pharmaceutical companies expressed any interest in a patent pool. However, some interviewees argued that this option may help Bangladesh gain technological and financial assistance from developed countries on country-specific diseases.[352]

Further, Bangladesh should avoid entering any agreements that limit flexibilities allowed under the TRIPS Agreement or that could impose any TRIPS-plus obligations.

4.3.6 Avoiding Bilateral Investment Treaties or Free Trade Agreements that Erode TRIPS Flexibilities

The ability of LDCs like Bangladesh to utilise the flexibilities of the TRIPS Agreement "is being slowly eroded away through various bilateral and regional negotiations with developed countries".[353]

---

350 Article 66.2 of the TRIPS Agreement provides that "Developed country Members shall provide incentives to enterprises and institutions in their territories for the purpose of promoting and encouraging technology transfer to least-developed country Members in order to enable them to create a sound and viable technological base". As Carlos Correa states, "This article puts an *obligation* on developed Member countries to provide incentives to enterprises and institutions. However, the precise nature of the incentives is not established; only their end is spelled out: to enable LDC members 'to create a sound and viable technological base'". Carlos Correa, 'Intellectual Property in LDCs: Strategies for Enhancing Technology Transfer and Dissemination' (UNCTAD The Least Developed Countries Report 2007, Background Paper No. 4, 2007), pp.3, 18, http://unctad.org/Sections/ldc_dir/docs/ldcr2007_Correa_en.pdf

351 "Article 67 of the TRIPS Agreement sets out developed countries' commitments on technical cooperation. This Article provides that developed country members must provide, on request and on mutually agreed terms and conditions, technical and financial cooperation in favour of developing and least-developed country members to facilitate TRIPs implementation. Such assistance can include assistance in drafting laws and regulations to protect IPRs as well as the establishment or reinforcement of domestic enforcement agencies". Farhana Yamin, 'Globalisation and the International Governance of Modern Biotechnology: IPRs, Biotechnology and Food Security', Foundation for International Environmental Law and Development, p.25, http://www.sristi.org/mdpipr2004/other_readings/OR 42.pdf

352 During interviews, this was supported by IP academics, pharmaceutical researchers and public health activists working with national and international NGOs that were involved in the public health sector in Bangladesh.

353 'Good Practice Guide', p.49, http://content.undp.org/go/cms-service/stream/asset/?asset_id=3259443

High-income and industrialised countries—particularly the US and the EU—put pressure on developing countries and LDCs to introduce TRIPS-plus provisions: for example, commitments beyond those specified by TRIPS and providing more extensive protection than TRIPS.[354] TRIPS-plus provisions are "introduced through bilateral agreements, such as free trade agreements (FTAs) and investment treaties".[355] Between 2001 and 2010, "72 FTAs with intellectual property clauses have been announced to the WTO. Of specific concern are the FTAs between developed countries and markets, most notably the US and the EU with low and middle income countries", because extensive patent provision in the FTAs restricts utilisation of TRIPS flexibilities and hence presents barriers to the access of essential pharmaceuticals.[356] More recently, serious concerns have been raised regarding the Trans-Pacific Partnership Agreement (TPP)[357] and the Anti-Counterfeiting Trade Agreement (ACTA),[358] due to the inclusion of TRIPS-plus patent provisions that may have serious effects on public health. LDCs like Bangladesh should be aware of the various TRIPS-plus provisions that can have a negative effect on the use of TRIPS Agreement flexibilities and subsequently on access to affordable medicines. Some of the most common TRIPS-plus provisions related to public health and access to medicines are:

---

354 Peter Drahos, 'BITS and BIPS: Bilateralism in Intellectual Property', *Journal of World Intellectual Property* 4 (2001): 791, 800–01, https://www.anu.edu.au/fellows/pdrahos/articles/pdfs/2001bitsandbips.pdf

355 'Good Practice Guide', p.49; Drahos, p.802.

356 'Global Communication on HIV and the Law', p.25; see also 'Good Practice Guide' and 'TRIPS-plus Free Trade Agreements and Access to Medicines', p.41.

357 The Trans-Pacific Partnership Agreement (TPP) was based on an agreement originally concluded in 2005 between Brunei, Chile, New Zealand and Singapore, and now also negotiated between Australia, Malaysia, Peru, the US and Vietnam. See 'TRIPS Was Never Enough', p.447.

358 The Anti-Counterfeiting Trade Agreement (ACTA) is a multinational treaty that aims to establish an international intellectual property framework targeting primarily counterfeit goods, generic medicines and copyright infringement on the Internet. It would create a new governing body outside existing forums such as the WTO, the WIPO and the UN. It has yet to come into effect. ACTA has been criticised by MSF for endangering access to medicines in developing countries. See 'A Blank Cheque For Abuse: ACTA and Its Impact on Access to Medicines', Médecins Sans Frontières Access Campaign (17 February 2012), http://www.msfaccess.org/sites/default/files/MSF_assets/Access/Docs/Access_Briefing_ACTABlankCheque_ENG_2012.pdf

- waiving the LDC exception as allowed under the TRIPS Agreement[359]
- defining "innovation" for the purposes of determining patent protection to include minor "me-too" molecular variations
- restricting patent oppositions
- extending patent terms beyond 20 years for delayed marketing approval
- limiting parallel imports of patented drugs
- restricting grounds for compulsory licensing
- imposing "data exclusivity" rules
- linking patent systems to drug regulatory systems.[360]

These TRIPS-plus provisions, if adopted by developing countries and LDCs, will outweigh the benefits of the TRIPS flexibilities for the country concerned and will have severe consequences for access to medicines.[361] The pressure to adopt more extensive protection than required by the TRIPS Agreement has also led to a floor vs. ceiling debate regarding an eventual international IP regime.

Annette Kur and Henning Grosse Ruse-Khan argue that advancing the concept of a ceiling for the TRIPS Agreement would protect flexibilities from encroachment by "IP maximalists":[362]

> [T]he concept of maximum rights or "ceiling rules" which provide for a binding maximum amount of IP protection that WTO Members can offer in their national laws ... [to] maintain a balanced approach towards IP

---

359 LDCs may need to adopt TRIPS-compliant national law, including pharmaceutical patents, despite the fact that they are entitled to a transition period until 1 January 2016 to fully implement patent protection for pharmaceuticals—and as per the decision of June 2013, have a further exemption until 1 July 2021 for general TRIPS obligations and possibly a separate extension for pharmaceutical patents beyond 2021.

360 See Gaelle P. Krikorian and Dorota M. Szymkowiak, 'Intellectual Property Rights in the Making: The Evolution of Intellectual Property Provisions in US Free Trade Agreements and Access to Medicine', *Journal of Intellectual Property Law* 10 (2007): 388; see also 'Good Practice Guide'.

361 'Trading Away Health: How the US's Intellectual Property Demands for the Trans-Pacific Partnership Agreement Threaten Access to Medicines', Médecins Sans Frontières Access Campaign, 12 (August 2012), http://aids2012.msf.org/wp-content/uploads/2012/07/TPP-Issue-Brief-IAC-July2012.pdf

362 See Annette Kur and Henning Grosse Ruse-Khan, 'Enough is Enough: The Notion of Binding Ceilings in International Intellectual Property Protection' (Max Planck Institute for Intellectual Property, Competition and Tax Law, Research Paper Series No. 09-01, 8 December 2008), p.44, http://ssrn.com/abstract=1326429

protection, and to protect member states' autonomy in preserving public policy goals vis-à-vis pressure exerted against them in bilateral trade negotiations.[363]

According to them, TRIPS Article 1:1 provides that "[M]ore extensive protection may only be granted 'provided that such protection does not contravene the provisions of this Agreement'. In spite of that, the general perception in international IP regulation so far has been that above the prescribed minimum standards there is no ceiling or limit other than the sky".[364]

On the other hand, J.H. Reichman states that with the mandates, the TRIPS Agreement has established a floor for global IP norms.[365] Reichman contends that "states must accord to the nationals of other member states those international minimum standards of intellectual property protection that are comprised within 'the treatment provided for in this Agreement'".[366] The US Government and its industry lobbyists argue that the TRIPS Agreement should not only be preserved as the "floor" for global standards, but that more attempts need to be made to strengthen the TRIPS Agreement and other agreements to upgrade legal systems and enforcement mechanisms in the field of IP.[367]

To date, there has been no debate at the WTO or other international bodies regarding the introduction of a ceiling or maximum protection restriction, nor any proposal in support of it from the developing countries or the LDCs. In the absence of any maximum limit, a country could frame its IP law based on its comparative advantage in a specific (R&D-based) area of innovation or imitation. Additionally, considering the importance of other societal values and public good beyond those of commercial interest, as well as the country's stage of development, LDCs and developing countries may need distinct types of ceilings. Any binding international regime on the ceiling, at least if placed within the WTO, could potentially open the door to further complex legal disputes under the WTO dispute settlement body and could further jeopardise

---

363 Ibid., p.1.
364 Ibid.
365 See generally 'Universal Minimum Standards', p.345.
366 Ibid., p.351.
367 See Global Intellectual Property Center, 'TRIPS: Floor Versus Ceiling?' (26 January 2010), p.4, http://www.theglobalipcenter.com/sites/default/files/reports/documents/TRIPS_FloorVsCeiling_WP_1_10_2.pdf

the ongoing process of developing policy space for access to medicines and other developmental goals in the LDCs.

Therefore, LDCs such as Bangladesh need not adopt any ceiling on IPRs at the national level, but instead can keep the space open to strengthen IPRs in future, if local industry matures and engages in innovation. Bangladesh should try to avoid any TRIPS-plus obligations in free trade and investment agreements with the US, the EU or any other developed countries, and it may need to be aware of and try to mitigate TRIPS-plus obligations in various bilateral and regional free trade or investment agreements.[368] Although avoiding TRIPS-plus obligations will allow LDCs like Bangladesh the freedom to utilise TRIPS flexibilities, LDCs could also lobby for further extension of the TRIPS waiver in general and of pharmaceutical patent waivers in particular.

4.3.7 Utilisation of the Transitional Period for Pharmaceutical Patents

In light of the vulnerable position of LDCs due to their socioeconomic conditions and weak public health infrastructures, the introduction of pharmaceutical patents will further marginalise LDCs in terms of coping with the prevailing situation. Bangladesh, in cooperation with other LDCs, lobbied for a further extension of the transitional period for pharmaceutical patents beyond 2016 to give the LDCs more time to develop their infrastructure and local pharmaceutical industry for dealing with public health problems in a post-TRIPS setting. The prime minster of Bangladesh has argued that it is necessary for LDCs like Bangladesh to receive another 15-year extension because of their weak

---

368 Since 2003, Bangladesh has been negotiating a Trade and Investment Framework Agreement (TIFA) with the US to include provisions on IP. It was finalised for ratification in 2009 and then revised further in 2012, but ratification was postponed by the Government of Bangladesh with an eye to the upcoming election. There is an assumption that the proposed TIFA text could impose TRIPS-plus obligations on Bangladesh. When requested to disclose the draft TIFA text for the sake of avoiding controversies, an official of the US mission in Dhaka said that Washington was not in a position to make the draft public before signing the agreement, and that "There are other drafts of TIFA and this one is similar to that". See Khawaza Main Uddin, 'Govt Inching Closer Towards Signing TIFA with US', *Business Info Bangladesh* (7 November 2009), https://web.archive.org/web/20101120054050/http:// bizbangladesh.com/business-news-2758.php (accessed by searching the Internet Archive index).

infrastructure and vulnerable health conditions, and the nascent stage of their pharmaceutical industry.[369] During her speech to the 64th WHA (17 May 2011), Bangladeshi Prime Minister Sheikh Hasina reiterated that the flexibilities accorded within the existing IP regime, in particular the patent waiver for LDCs for pharmaceuticals, must be extended further.[370]

In this respect, Bangladesh argued that the socioeconomic situation, low level of development, and health and technical infrastructure at the time of the original transitional period are still prevalent in LDCs; therefore, graduation to a pharmaceutical patent regime will have a huge negative effect on Bangladesh.[371] Unless there is considerable progress in the social and economic development of the LDCs, growth of health infrastructure, and an increase in the accessibility and availability of medicines, Bangladesh should argue for the continuation of the waiver for pharmaceutical patents under the principle of special and differential treatment for the derogation from commitment.[372]

On 11 November 2011, on behalf of the LDC Group, the delegation of Bangladesh to the WTO submitted to the TRIPS Council an elements Paper on the extension of the TRIPS transition period for LDCs. The Paper mentioned that LDCs are facing serious economic, financial and

---

369 Sheikh Hasina, Prime Minister of Bangladesh, Speech to the 64th WHA (17 May 2011), http://www.who.int/mediacentre/events/2011/wha64/sheikh_hasina_speech_20110517/en/index.html

370 Ibid.

371 "Special and Differential Treatment" (S&D) may be sought to extend the transition period until graduation to a higher level of social and economic development and, hence, an ideal situation for the introduction of pharmaceutical patents case by case or under a country-driven approach with recourse to the WTO. See Thomas Cottier, 'From Progressive Liberalization to Progressive Regulation in WTO Law', *Journal of International Economic Law* 9.4 (2006): 414–19.

372 S&D is a set of GATT provisions (GATT 1947, Article XVIII) that exempts developing countries from the same strict trade rules and disciplines of more industrialised countries. For example, in the Uruguay Round Agreement on Agriculture, LDCs are exempt from any reduction commitments and developing countries are given longer to phase in export subsidy and tariff reductions than the more industrialised countries. Using this principle, exemption from introducing pharmaceutical patents may also be extended as long as problems of access to pharmaceuticals and a low level of social and economic development persists in the particular country. See, for example, Javier Lopez Gonzalez, Maximillano Mendez Parra and Anirudh Shingal, 'TRIPS and Special and Differential Treatment — Revisiting the Case for Derogations in Applying Patent Protection for Pharmaceuticals in Developing Countries' (Draft Working Paper No. 2011–37, NCCR Trade Regulation, 2011), https://www.sussex.ac.uk/webteam/gateway/file.php?name=wp-2011-37.pdf&site=261

administrative constraints on their efforts to bring their domestic legal systems into conformity with the TRIPS Agreement.[373]

Most of the survey participants in Bangladesh argued that the Government of Bangladesh, along with those of other LDCs, should lobby for a further extension for pharmaceutical patents until graduation from the LDC category.[374] However, the MNPCs that participated in the surveys argued that a further extension of the waiver for pharmaceutical patents would not benefit Bangladesh; rather, it would hamper technological development and further investment in the sector.[375] In contrast, one interviewee argued that the local pharmaceutical sector in Bangladesh is yet to achieve sufficient R&D to compete with the MNPCs; therefore, a further extension will help them to engage in R&D and prepare themselves for the transition to a pharmaceutical patent regime.[376] One expert from the DPDT commented that, in light of the technical and infrastructural limitations of the DPDT, it would be better to have a transition period until graduation from LDC status for the introduction of pharmaceutical patents.[377] The Government of Bangladesh, in cooperation with other LDCs, strongly lobbied for further extension of pharmaceutical patents, considering their present stages of technological capability and infrastructural development.

However, a simple extension of the transitional period without any concrete steps to promote the advancement of the pharmaceutical industry would be useless. Therefore, LDCs such as Bangladesh should use the transitional period as part of a national strategy aimed at encouraging pharmaceutical production and investment in R&D-based industry for progression towards innovation and TRIPS compliance. One such strategy is to introduce a process patent and utility model law

---

373 WTO Council for TRIPS, 'Elements Paper on the Extension of the Transition Period under Article 66.1 of the TRIPS Agreement', IP/C/W/566 (11 November 2011), https://docs.wto.org/dol2fe/Pages/FE_Search/DDFDocuments/41380/Q/IP/C/W566.pdf&usg=AFQjCNHwAYKL_So9eXKC_QSxp9a-k5O5-w&cad=rja

374 This position was supported by all the large, medium and small local pharmaceutical companies in Bangladesh that participated in the survey.

375 During the surveys, this position was supported by all the MNPCs operating in Bangladesh.

376 Interview with an expert at the DDA in Bangladesh, in Dhaka, Bangladesh, 12 January 2012.

377 Interview with a deputy registrar from the DPDT, in Dhaka, Bangladesh, 22 January 2012.

to encourage weak or low-level national innovation and, consequently, promote technological learning and progress on basic research.

4.3.8 Provision for Process Patent during the Transitional Period and Adoption of a Utility Model Law

Before adoption of the TRIPS Agreement, many countries provided only process—not product—patents because process patents would still allow for the manufacture of patented products using a different process or method. This has enabled manufacturers in certain countries, including India, to make and become global suppliers of generic versions of patented drugs.[378]

Despite having a long tradition of drug manufacturing, India's patent law (*Patent Act, 1911*) until 1970, placed constraints on its ability to use the full potential of its local industry. By introducing only process patents along with other supporting industrial policies, India was able to dislodge the MNPCs from their position of dominance and become a major pharmaceutical-producing nation. As Chaudhuri states, "India emerged as a global pharmaceutical supplier due to: the development of process technology by indigenous enterprises; the externalities associated with the setting up of two major public enterprises; the close association between manufacturers and government laboratories; and the patent and industrial policies since the 1970s supporting process patent".[379]

Bangladesh still adheres to the *Patent Act, 1911* (as did India, until 1970), but the country should follow in India's footsteps by introducing process patents and encouraging the local pharmaceutical industry to invest in R&D. Local pharmaceutical industry could also work in cooperation with local research institutions and universities.

In addition to process patents, the Government of Bangladesh could introduce a utility model law. This could play a very important role in promoting innovative activity not only in the pharmaceutical sector but also in emerging local industries in the fields of information technology,

---

378 See WHO (19 WHO Drug Info), p.238.
379 See Sudip Chaudhuri, 'The WTO and India's Pharmaceutical Industry' (2005); 'TRIPS and Changes in Pharmaceutical Patent Regime'.

textile manufacturing, telecommunications and biotechnology. In Bangladesh, there are many small- and medium-sized enterprises (SMEs), including pharmaceutical companies with inventive ideas; however, they often do not file patent applications due to the high cost of acquiring a patent, bureaucratic hurdles, long delays in acquiring a patent and a lack of confidence in their ability to satisfy high patentability requirements.

However, the surveys show that most local pharmaceutical companies believe a simple system that could grant protection quickly would help them to grow and further innovate.[380] Bureaucratic delays and expensive filings could be avoided if a simple system were in place. Such a system could, given a broad scope, help in overcoming the lack of incentives for inventions excluded from patent protection.[381] It is important to require relative, rather than absolute, novelty for a utility model and also decrease the amount of time it takes to review and grant patents, which currently stands at up to five years. Adopting relative novelty will ensure that innovators achieve utility model protection quickly by way of simple examination, even if the patent application contains only weak innovation—such as if there is at least one difference between the invention and the prior art.

A utility model law, along with the introduction of process patents, would play an important role in filling the gap in law for promoting local—albeit weak—inventions, while also encouraging further research and innovation. However, it would be better for Bangladesh to introduce process patents under the existing patent law and to adopt a separate law on utility models to encourage local innovation, as local industries are yet to attain adequate technical capacity and financial resources for basic research and, hence, for product patents. In addition to the process patent and utility model, the Government of Bangladesh could also consider introducing special investment protection measures for the pharmaceutical industry to promote further investment, joint ventures, technology transfer and basic research.

---

380 Based on the survey data from local large, medium and small pharmaceutical companies in Bangladesh. However, MNPCs made no comments on this.
381 See Uma Suthersanen, 'Utility Models and Innovation in Developing Countries' (February 2006), pp.5–7, http://unctad.org/en/Docs/iteipc20066_en.pdf

4.3.9 Special Investment Protection Regime, Open Drug Innovation Model and Promotion of Social Business Model in the Pharmaceutical Sector

LDCs such as Bangladesh need to introduce some alternative ways of promoting innovation for country-specific diseases and attracting investment during the TRIPS-waiver periods, as in the absence of patent protection there might be little desire for innovation or investment in the pharmaceutical sector. It was stated in a study that "there is a lack of new medicines for the 'neglected diseases'—those that primarily affect populations with little purchasing power, and therefore offer an insufficient incentive for industry to invest in R&D".[382] Therefore, developing countries and LDCs should devise a special investment regime to encourage investment in research related to country-specific neglected diseases and urge local research institutions to join an open drug innovation model in the absence of huge financial resources for basic research. Basheer proposed a comprehensive investment protection regime based on the compensatory liability model, which would grant comprehensive market exclusivity for new drugs against free riders until such time as the investment in the discovery and development of that drug is recouped. He considered that it might be more preferable to a patent regime.[383] He further recommended a reimbursement model in which the costs of drug discovery and development could be reimbursed through public funding and prizes.[384] Unlike patents and data exclusivity for uniform periods of protection, the proposed regime would reward a rate of return on investment dependent, *inter alia*, on the health value of the drug.[385]

However, Basheer considers that his proposed investment protection regime is better suited to fostering cures for developed country diseases

---

382 Suerie Moon J. Bermudez, E. 't Hoen, 'Innovation and Access to Medicines for Neglected Populations: Could a Treaty Address a Broken Pharmaceutical R&D System?', *PLoS Med* 9.5 (2012), e1001218, http://dx.doi.org/10.1371/journal.pmed.1001218

383 See Shamnad Basheer, 'The Invention of an Investment Incentive for Pharmaceutical Innovation', *Journal of World Intellectual Property* 15 (2012): 305, http://ssrn.com/abstract=2203440

384 Ibid., pp.46–48.

385 Ibid.

prevalent in the US and the EU.[386] Considering the huge cost of basic research and drug development, and the minimal financial resources of consumers in LDCs like Bangladesh, this kind of investment regime could be of limited help to generate investment in LDC-specific diseases.

Most developing countries and LDCs such as Bangladesh have clearly different pharmaceutical demands to those of developed countries: "The diseases of the poor attract very little R&D efforts by the large pharmaceutical industry, since they are not promising income generators. R&D is driven by market considerations. R&D targeting diseases found in developing countries is marginal".[387]

Despite the lack of patent protection for pharmaceuticals in Bangladesh until the patent waiver for LDCs expires, the Government of Bangladesh could introduce a special investment protection regime to encourage investment and technology transfer in the pharmaceutical sector by providing "exclusive marketing rights" for the same duration as a patent. The government could also provide tax incentives for a certain period of time. In this regard, Bangladesh could set two preconditions for getting special investment protection: (i) investment and/or technology transfer in an area of neglected diseases or diseases prevalent in Bangladesh; and (ii) any drugs produced under the investment or by way of technology transfer—if intended for offer in the local market—must satisfy requirements for licensing and market authorisation by the DGDA in Bangladesh.[388]

The Government of Bangladesh could also encourage local research institutions and pharmaceutical companies to engage in the development of a new open source drug innovation model and to participate in existing open source drug discovery models.[389] These

---

386 Ibid., p.309.
387 Carlos Correa, 'TRIPS and R&D Incentives in the Pharmaceutical Sector' (Communication on Macroeconomics and Health, Working Paper No.WG2:11, November 2011), p.19, http://library.cphs.chula.ac.th/Ebooks/HealthCareFinancing/WorkingPaper_WG2/WG2_11.pdf
388 See generally *Globalization and Access to Drugs*.
389 Open source is "a way of sharing data, expertise, and resources to increase collaboration, transparency, and cumulative public knowledge. It has been used in the software field since its infancy half a century ago, and tried in the bio-pharma field over the last decade". Hassan Masum and Rachelle Harris, *Open Source for Neglected Diseases: Magic Bullet or Mirage?* (Washington, DC: Results for Development Institute, 2011), http://healthresearchpolicy.org/sites/healthresearchpolicy.org/files/assessments/files/OS_for_NTDs_Consultation

models are based on the idea that the sharing of medical information and international collaboration among scientists will advance medical research and, ultimately, help patients all over the world who are suffering from neglected diseases.[390] As an example, Bangladesh could follow the Indian *Open Source Drug Discovery* (OSDD) project to encourage research on the diseases prevalent in Bangladesh. The Indian OSDD project works with a collaborative online platform where contributors can collectively discover new therapies for neglected diseases, beginning with TB research. It began in 2008 with US$12 million in funding provided by the Indian government, which also gave a commitment to invest US$35 million total in the project. In a similar vein, the Government of Bangladesh could provide some initial funding and encourage local research institutions and pharmaceutical companies to form collaborative drug innovation projects on country-specific diseases, later seeking the financial and technical cooperation of international organisations such as the WHO, UNIDO, MNPCs and transnational research institutions, as well as funding from philanthropic organisations like the Bill & Melinda Gates Foundation. Other open source initiatives in the pharmaceutical sector, such as the *Tropical Diseases Initiative,*[391] *TDR Targets,*[392] *Collaborative Drug Discovery*[393] and

---

Draft.pdf. In addition, a number of open source initiatives have been launched in the medical field, such as India's Council of Scientific and Industrial Research, which is working on open source drug discovery to develop drugs for the treatment of drug-resistant tuberculosis (TB). See Council of Scientific and Industrial Research, 'NMITLI Achievements', http://www.csir.res.in/External/Heads/collaborations/sa%20old%20new.pdf. "In the long run, it may help minimize duplication of effort, and create a 'commons' of knowledge and data from which future innovation can grow". *Open Source for Neglected Diseases*, p.3.

390 See Stephen M. Maurer A. Rai, and A. Sali, 'Finding Cures for Tropical Diseases: Is Open Source an Answer?', *PLoS Med* 1.3 (2004), e56, http://dx.doi.org/10.1371/journal.pmed.0010056

391 "The Tropical Diseases Initiative (TDI) modelled itself explicitly on open source approaches as early as 2004 and produced a set of potential drug targets from pathogen genomes that have been released under a Creative Commons license for further work". *Open Source for Neglected Diseases*, p.7.

392 "TDR Targets is a WHO/TDR database that facilitates prioritization of potential drug targets across tropical disease areas". It "brings together information on genomics, structural data, inhibitors and targets, and drug ability". Ibid.

393 Collaborative Drug Discovery is a California-based company that has "created a platform for selective sharing of collaborative drug discovery data … It allows preclinical biological and chemical drug discovery data to be securely stored, shared, analysed, and collaborated upon through a web interface". Ibid., p.6.

the *Lilly TB Drug Discovery Initiative*,[394] could also be examined by LDCs to gain an understanding of their working procedures, and then used to develop more effective open source drug innovation projects targeting the health needs of the LDCs.

Further, LDCs such as Bangladesh could devise a different strategy to encourage multinationals to invest in Bangladesh's pharmaceutical sector under a "social business model"[395] as part of their social corporate responsibility and humanitarian goals. Thus, they could help ensure that newly patented drugs, which are necessary but not produced by the Bangladeshi pharmaceutical companies, are available at affordable prices. This could be done either in collaboration with local research institutions or through a joint venture with local pharmaceutical companies. The Government of Bangladesh could provide "special exclusive marketing rights" for pharmaceuticals produced under a social business regime for a certain period and in consultation with the DGDA and prospective investors. In deciding to grant this exclusivity, LDCs could consider factors such as the nature of the investment, the necessity of the medication and the local demand. The exclusivity could be conditional on the requirement that the company continues to provide an adequate supply of the drug at an affordable price.

4.4 Conclusion

This chapter examined the possible options for legislative change and government interventions for developing countries and LDCs such as

---

394 The *Lilly TB Drug Discovery Initiative* is a not-for-profit public-private partnership headquartered in Seattle, Washington, with a mission to accelerate early-stage drug discovery and help identify the TB drugs of the future. It has opened access to its drug discovery expertise and scientific resources—such as its proprietary library of 500,000 compounds and innovative chemistry research tools—to be applied to the search for new drugs to fight TB. See *About the Initiative*, Lilly TB Drug Discovery Initiative, https://www.lilly.com/About/default.aspx

395 A social business is a non-loss, non-dividend company designed to address a social objective. Muhammad Yunus, *Building Social Business: The New Kind of Capitalism That Serves Humanity's Most Pressing Needs* (Public Affairs, 2010). In this type of business organisation, profits are used to expand the company's reach and improve the product or service to a greater extent than in a traditional for-profit corporation. Thus, investors receive no dividends or extra payments apart from their initial investment. See Muhammad Yunus, *Creating a World without Poverty: Social Business and the Future of Capitalism* (Public Affairs, 2008). The main organisations promoting and incubating social businesses are the Yunus Centre in Bangladesh and the Grameen Creative Lab in Germany.

Bangladesh by comparing them with the options used in Brazil, India and South Africa. It further explained some of the drawbacks and limitations of existing patent laws. In light of the limitations of patent law, this chapter explored possible government intervention options that could be used to facilitate access to medicines, such as drug price control, national competition law, patent prizes, patent pools, process utility patents, investment protection regimes and social business models.

This chapter also explored the option of lobbying to extend the transitional period for the introduction of pharmaceutical patents and recommended that developing countries and LDCs reject BITS/FTAs that contain TRIPS-plus provisions that result in the erosion of TRIPS flexibilities. However, a country cannot gain substantial benefits from an extended transitional period or from TRIPS flexibilities unless it has attained a certain level of technological capacity and developed a strong generic pharmaceutical industry.[396] Even a compulsory licensing mechanism will be of little use without the technological capability to produce generic pharmaceuticals and a well-developed local pharmaceutical industry.[397] Hence, the creation of sound competitive market structures through competition law and enforcement could be more effective both in enhancing access to medical technology and fostering innovation in the pharmaceutical sector.[398] This could serve as a corrective tool if IPRs hinder competition and create a potential barrier to innovation and access.[399] While adopting a TRIPS-compliant patent law, LDCs need to ensure that their IP protection regimes do not run counter to their public health policies, but are consistent with and supportive of such policies.

---

396 See Bryan Mercurio, 'Resolving the Public Health Crisis in the Developing World: Problems and Barriers of Access to Essential Medicines', *Northwestern University Journal of International Human Rights* 5 (2006): 1, 40.

397 Ibid.

398 WHO, 'Promoting Access to Medical Technologies and Innovation: Intersections between Public Health, Intellectual Property and Trade' (2012), p.53, http://www.wto.org/english/res_e/booksp_e/pamtiwhowipowtoweb13_e.pdf

399 Ibid., p.14.

5. Has the TRIPS Waiver Helped the Least Developed Countries Progress Towards Innovation and Compliance?

This chapter analyses the issue of waivers for the LDCs under the TRIPS Agreement in the context of how waivers help these countries graduate from the LDC category and progress towards TRIPS compliance. It also identifies the technical and infrastructural development and changes required as LDCs move towards TRIPS compliance, using the case study of Bangladesh.

5.1 Background: TRIPS Waivers for the LDCs and Designing a Plan of Action for Graduation and Progression Towards Innovation and Compliance

WTO members have agreed to extend the transition period for LDCs to implement the TRIPS Agreement until July 2021; it was previously due to end on 1 July 2013. Haiti submitted a request on 5 November 2012 and on behalf of the LDC group to extend the transition period further — specifically, until a given member graduates from being a LDC.[1] That proposal, among others, mentioned that "the situation of LDCs has not changed significantly since the last extension decision in 2005 ... [and

---

1   WTO, 'Communication from Haiti on Behalf of the LDC Group: Request for an Extension of the Transitional Period under Article 66.1 of the TRIPS Agreement' (5 November 2012) (IP/C/W/583).

      http://dx.doi.org/10.11647/OBP.0093.05

they] have not been able to develop their productive capacities and have not beneficially integrated with the world economy".[2] The Joint United Nations Programme on HIV/AIDS (UNAIDS), the United Nations Development Program (UNDP) and civil society organisations widely supported the proposal to give urgent consideration to the continued special needs and requirements of LDCs with respect to their social and economic development.[3] UNAIDS pointed out that "an extension would allow the world's poorest nations to ensure sustained access to medicines, build up viable technology bases and manufacture or import the medicines they need".[4]

There is thus a fair amount of consensus that LDCs should be allowed to suspend implementation of the TRIPS Agreement until graduation from the LDC category, or be given provision for voluntary compliance, considering economic, financial and administrative constraints and the need for these countries to enjoy flexibility in creating a "sound and viable technological base".[5] The finally-agreed extension allowed them a transitional period up until 1 July 2021. The LDCs also received separate extensions for pharmaceutical patent waivers until 1 January 2033. It is now important to evaluate when and how LDCs like Bangladesh might graduate from the LDC category and progress towards TRIPS compliance, which includes the introduction of pharmaceutical patents.

Without proper utilisation of the extended period and with continuation of inadequate institutional and infrastructural capacity, building programmes will simply result more time wasted with no progress towards a viable technological base in the LDCs.[6] It is necessary to explore the extent to which the transition period has helped LDCs to become technologically advanced and transition from

---

2   Ibid.
3   UNAIDS press release, 'UNAIDS and UNDP Back Proposal to Allow Least Developed Countries to Maintain and Scale up Access to Essential Medicines', Geneva, 26 February 2013.
4   Ibid. (stated by Michel Sidibé, executive director of UNAIDS, Geneva, 26 February 2013).
5   Omolo Joseph Agutu, 'Least Developed Countries and the TRIPS Agreement: Arguments for a Shift to Voluntary Compliance', *African Journal of International and Comparative Law* 20.3 (2012): 423–47.
6   South Centre and CIEL, 'Extension of the Transition Period for LDCs: Flexibility to Create a Viable Technological Base or Simply (A Little) More Time?', *Intellectual Property Quarterly Update* (2006).

copycat to innovative nations. This chapter uses doctrinal research and a case study, deriving from surveys and interviews, on the pharmaceutical sector in Bangladesh. It explores challenges for public and health and the promotion of innovation in the pharmaceutical sector during progression towards TRIPS compliance. Bangladesh was chosen for the case study because it has greater technological capacity in the pharmaceutical sector and a stronger presence in international negotiations than other LDCs.

5.2 Extending the LDC Transition Period: Is it a Measure for Making a Viable Technological Base or Simply a Waste of Time?

While the initial deadline for transition to full compliance for LDCs was 1 January 2006, the TRIPS Agreement provides that the TRIPS Council[7] "shall, upon duly motivated request by a LDC Member, accord extensions of this period".[8] Accordingly, there have been three subsequent extensions in favour of the LDCs. The first was particularly related to pharmaceutical patents and lasted until 1 January 2016. The second was approved by the TRIPS Council on 29 November 2005, and meant that LDCs would not have to apply TRIPS provisions (in general, not just as they apply to pharmaceuticals) other than Articles 3, 4 and 5 until 1 July 2013; this was again extended to 1 July 2021 by a TRIPS Council decision on 11 June 2013. The Doha waiver that specifically addressed pharmaceutical patents was further extended until January 2033 on the basis of a request from the LDC group. To this end, LDCs on several occasions requested an unconditional extension to the transitional period unless or until a particular member country graduates from LDC status. One important question arises as to whether the transition period is a measure for creating a viable technological base in the LDCs—including facilitating graduation from

---

7   Open to all members of the WTO, the Council for TRIPS is the body that is responsible for administering the TRIPS Agreement, and in particular monitoring the operation of the Agreement, http://www.wto.org/english/tratop_e/trips_e/intel6_e.htm

8   Article 66(1), TRIPS Agreement.

the LDC category—or whether granting extension after extension is simply wasting more time.

Considering the danger of extension without any concrete steps, one study suggested that "the experience of the last decade strongly indicates that an extension alone would not lead to any IP-related improvements in LDCs. On the contrary, an unconditional extension would not resolve anything but would only further postpone the implementation of TRIPS by LDCs".[9]

The extensions granted to the LDCs based on Article 66.1 aim to provide them not merely with more time to comply, but are also meant to help LDCs develop their national policies and economies to ensure that the eventual implementation of the TRIPS Agreement will promote rather than undermine their social, economic and environmental wellbeing.[10]

The 2005 TRIPS Council decision to extend the transitional period for the LDCs acknowledged the continuing needs of LDCs for technical and financial cooperation, "to enable them to realize the cultural, social, technological and other developmental objectives of intellectual property protection" as laid down in Articles 7 and 8 of the TRIPS Agreement.[11]

Technical and financial cooperation have an important role to play in allowing LDCs to build a sound technological base. However, the extension decisions made to date do not seem to be linked or even relevant to supporting the development and dissemination of technologies in LDCs. For example, the 2005 decision refers to technical cooperation under Article 67, which has no other objective than to allow implementation of the TRIPS Agreement.[12] Yet, it makes no reference to Article 66.2, which requires developed country members to "provide incentives to enterprises and institutions in their territories for the

9   Arno Hold and Bryan Christopher Mercurio, 'Transitioning to Intellectual Property: How Can the WTO Integrate Least Developed Countries into TRIPS?' (Working Paper No. 2012/37, World Trade Institute [WTI], October 2012).

10   'Extension of the Transition Period for LDCs'.

11   Council for TRIPS, 'Extension of the Transition Period under Article 66.1 for Least-developed Country Members', 30 November 2005, WTO document IP/C/40.

12   Ibid.

purpose of promoting and encouraging technology transfer to [LDCs] in order to enable them to create a sound and viable technological base".[13]

It was also remarked that the language of Article 66.2 is vague and there is disagreement about the nature and quantity of the incentives that should be provided to the private sector to encourage such transfers.[14] A study conducted by Surie Moon concluded it was unclear whether Article 66.2 had led to *any* increase in incentives for technology transfer to LDCs.[15]

Article 67 requires developed country WTO members to provide "technical and financial assistance" in favour of developing country and LDC members "in order to facilitate the implementation" of the Agreement.[16] However, the language used in Article 67 is also vague, and therefore the exact contours of the obligations it contains are unclear.[17] Official WTO documents provide little guidance as to the exact meaning or interpretation of the terms in Article 67, and to date no dispute over the transitional arrangements in Part VI of TRIPS has been brought before the WTO's dispute settlement body.[18]

Therefore, both Articles 66.2 and 67 of the TRIPS Agreement have so far failed to deliver the expected positive outcomes for the LDCs.[19] However, the TRIPS Council decision of 2005 established a process in which LDCs were requested to provide information on what they considered priorities for the technical and financial assistance that would enable them to successfully implement the TRIPS Agreement. Although all LDC members were originally requested to provide

---

13 Ibid.

14 Mohammad Monirul Azam, 'Climate Change Resilience and Technology Transfer: The Role of Intellectual Property', *Nordic Journal of International Law* 80.4 (2011).

15 For details, see Suerie Moon, 'Does Article 66.2 Encourage Technology Transfer to LDCs? An Analysis of Country Submissions to the TRIPS Council (1999–2007)', UNCTAD/ICTSD Project on IPRs, and Policy Brief Number 2 (2008).

16 Article 67 of the TRIPS Agreement shall include, but is not limited to, "assistance in the preparation of laws and regulations on the protection and enforcement of intellectual property rights as well as on the prevention of their abuse, and support regarding the establishment or reinforcement of domestic offices and agencies relevant to these matters, including the training of personnel".

17 'Transitioning to Intellectual Property'.

18 Ibid.

19 Ibid.

the TRIPS Council with this information by 1 January 2016, only 9 of the 34 LDC members (including Bangladesh) have submitted their assessments.[20] Bangladesh submitted its priority needs assessment on 23 March 2010.[21]

Some NGOs and other commentators criticised the priority needs assessment as merely a delaying tactic used by developed country members to further postpone honouring their promises for assistance.[22] These critics also claimed that the assessment would force LDCs to spend already scarce resources on collecting data and information regarding the status of their implementation of TRIPS.[23] As there are no specific guidelines for the appropriate scope, depth, breadth and criteria for the priority needs assessment, those submitted so far differ significantly in quality, scope, analytical reasoning and structure.[24]

It is also apparent that some of the priority needs assessments contained requests that go beyond achieving compliance with TRIPS obligations and are designed to contribute to the establishment of a national IP system beneficial to the country's socioeconomic development (e.g., Bangladesh's priority needs assessment requested US$14.5 million for community-based museums and for conducting research on traditional knowledge).[25] Some potential donor countries believe that technical and financial assistance should be exclusively targeted at bringing LDCs' IP laws and institutions into compliance with the obligations under TRIPS.[26] However, the six LDCs that have so far submitted assessments have received little response from developed country members, and too little funding to make substantial technical and infrastructural progress for possible graduation from the LDC category and progression towards TRIPS compliance.

Therefore, the submission of priority needs assessments has not triggered any substantive additional technical and financial assistance.[27]

---

20   See for details, WTO, 'Intellectual Property: Least Developed Countries', https://www.wto.org/english/tratop_e/trips_e/ldc_e.htm

21   See for details, WTO, 'Council for TRIPS, Priority Needs for Technical and Financial Co-operation: Communication from Bangladesh' (23 March 2010) (IP/C/W/546).

22   'Extension of the Transition Period for LDCs'.

23   Ibid.

24   'Transitioning to Intellectual Property'.

25   For details, see 'Council for TRIPS, Priority Needs'.

26   'Transitioning to Intellectual Property'.

27   Ibid.

Considering the inadequate technical and financial cooperation from other WTO members, the lack of a positive attitude towards innovation and R&D by the national industries, and the lack of a proper plan of action by the LDCs at the national level during the transitional period, the question arises—have the LDCs such as Bangladesh gained from their LDC status and from the transitional period?

5.3 The Case of Bangladesh: Has the Country Gained from its LDC Status and the Transition Period?

Bangladesh has been an LDC for almost four decades, even after the three-decade long *Programs of Action* adopted by the UN in the 1980s to support the development and eventual graduation of the LDCs.[28] LDCs have enjoyed a transitional period granted by the WTO in which they do not need to comply with the TRIPS Agreement, and a waiver for pharmaceutical patents lasting more than 15 years. The question arises: what has Bangladesh gained from its LDC status and waiver from TRIPS obligations, including the pharmaceutical patent waiver? Bangladeshi economist Wahiduddin Mahmud considers that most LDCs have failed to gain from their status for two reasons First, international plans and commitments have not only proved inadequate to addressing the structural handicaps that affect the LDCs, but their implementation has also fallen short of targets relating to aid, trade and WTO provisions. Second, the capacity to take advantage of international support measures is often severely constrained by weak institutional and governance structures—particularly in politically fragile and conflict-torn LDCs.

However, without these support measures, the LDCs might have fared even worse, and the measures have provided at least some limited benefits. For example, Bangladesh has been able to benefit from LDC-specific support measures, particularly with respect to trade preferences. A large part of Bangladesh's garment export, for example, has gained from the duty-free access of LDC exports to the markets of the EU and the U.S.[29] In the last 15 years, Bangladesh's share of apparel exports to

---

28 Wahiduddin Mahmud, 'Has Bangladesh Gained from its LDC status?', *The Daily Star* (28 May 2010).

29 'Bangladesh's Ready-made Garments Landscape: The Challenge of Growth' (2011), http://www.mckinsey.de/sites/mck_files/files/2011_McKinsey_Bangladesh.pdf

the EU and the U.S. has more than doubled, and it is now third among exporters to the EU and fourth among exporters to the U.S.[30]

Further, utilising the TRIPS waiver for pharmaceutical patents, Bangladesh gained from pharmaceutical exports earning US$46.0 billion in 2011, an increase of 16.1% over the US$39.6 billion of sales in 2010.[31] Bangladesh also gained self-sufficiency in the pharmaceutical sector and now supplies almost 97% of medicines for the local market.[32]

However, Bangladesh devoted too much of its developmental efforts and economic diplomacy to exploiting the benefits of its LDC status and TRIPS waiver, including for pharmaceutical patents. The textile and pharmaceutical sectors in Bangladesh devoted too much effort to gaining quick cash by way of increasing exports rather than engaging in basic development. The textile sector in Bangladesh engaged in producing cheaper garments, defying international labour standards and social compliance, and even creating building and infrastructural security issues, which resulted in the collapse of a building that killed more than two thousand garment workers.[33]

Leading pharmaceutical companies in Bangladesh are concentrating mainly on producing generic medicines and gaining quick cash by exporting to non-WTO members, LDCs and other developing countries where these medicines are off-patent. Although the NDP tried to encourage the twin goals of ensuring access to medicines and investing in basic research, most local pharmaceutical companies in Bangladesh are not interested in basic research.[34]

There is even criticism that leading pharmaceutical companies in Bangladesh are more interested in exports than in supplying the local

---

30   Ibid.
31   An Overview of the Pharmaceutical Sector in Bangladesh'.
32   Ibid.
33   'Bangladeshi Factory Deaths Spark Action among High-street Clothing Chains', *The Guardian*, http://www.guardian.co.uk/world/2013/jun/23/rana-plaza-factory-disaster-bangladesh-primark
34   During surveys, few pharmaceutical companies in Bangladesh disclosed their ratio of investment to basic research. However, by analysing the annual reports of leading pharmaceutical companies in Bangladesh, the author found that all the leading pharmaceutical companies invested less than 1% in research and development (R&D).

market.[35] The field studies undertaken in Bangladesh for the current study revealed that some important medicines for treating diabetes and cardiovascular disease are either not available or are in short supply in retail pharmacies; thus, a patient needs to go from one pharmacy to another in search of a particular medicine, and may need to pay more than the retail price.

In the absence of strong regulatory bodies and a proper plan of action, the gains made by Bangladesh in the pharmaceutical sector during the initial pharmaceutical patent waiver period could not provide the country with any further benefit that might help it graduate from the LDC category and transition from a copycat to an innovative nation. A leading pharmaceutical businessman in Bangladesh remarked that by putting restrictions on the MNCs in 1982 (after which all of the leading global pharmaceutical companies either closed or suspended their manufacturing operations in Bangladesh) and encouraging only imitation in the pharmaceutical sector, Bangladesh missed the opportunity to build an innovative pharmaceutical sector.[36]

Bangladesh has already reached a stage of development where it should pay more attention to improving production efficiency, skills and entrepreneurial capabilities rather than merely seeking preferential LDC treatment. In the pharmaceutical sector, it should pay more attention to basic research, production efficiency and collaboration with global research institutions and other global pharmaceutical companies for joint research and technology transfer, rather than simply relying on off-patent imitated medicines and requesting further extensions of the pharmaceutical patent waiver. In the long run, without acquiring advanced technological skills and investing in basic research, Bangladesh cannot serve the growing local market for patented medicines.

Of course Bangladesh should take advantage of its LDC status and TRIPS waiver as much as possible, but it should also begin to plan for how and when it might graduate from LDC status and achieve innovation and TRIPS compliance.

---

35 This concern was raised and supported by a number of the interviewees in Bangladesh.

36 Stated by Shamson H. Chowdhury, CEO of Square Pharmaceuticals in Bangladesh (Speech during Pharma Expo, Dhaka, 2009).

5.4 Progress Towards Graduation and Compliance

Bangladesh successfully used its LDC status to gain economic benefits for its textile sector, but that gain has not been realised in regulatory development, improvement of quality of life, investment in education and public health, maintenance of international labour standards, or social and security compliance. Simply by making a quick profit in one sector, a country cannot graduate from LDC status – not without a proper plan of action for development, integrating all relevant criteria for graduation.

Bangladesh has become self-sufficient in the pharmaceutical sector and its pharmaceutical companies export generic medicines to more than 107 countries. However, due to the lack of any plan of action for encouraging investment in basic research, and the absence of institutional and infrastructural capacity building, the country remains in a similar situation to 1995, when the transitional period was introduced for LDCs under the TRIPS Agreement, in terms of IPR administration and basic research in the pharmaceutical sector. Even after a decade and a half of transitional periods under the TRIPS Agreement, LDCs like Bangladesh are still facing institutional, infrastructural, social, technological and public health constraints, despite some progress in the pharmaceutical sector. Without a proper plan of action, Bangladesh will neither gain from LDC status nor achieve long-term benefits from waiver periods for general obligations or pharmaceutical patents under the TRIPS Agreement.

5.4.1 When and How Might LDCs Graduate from this Category?

Although originally including 25 countries, the current LDC list comprises 49 countries: 33 are in Africa, 13 in Asia Pacific and one in Latin America. Three eligible countries declined to become LDCs: Ghana, Papua New Guinea and Zimbabwe. Since its inception, only four countries have graduated from the LDC list: Botswana on 19 December 1994, Cape Verde on 20 December 2007, Maldives on 1 January 2011 and Samoa on 1 January 2014. Bangladesh joined the LDC category in 1975 and remains on the list, although it has shown more economic development than other low-income LDCs.

A country may be designated as an LDC if it meets the following three criteria:

- "low income", based on Gross National Income (GNI) per capita (a three-year average), with thresholds of US$905 for cases of addition to the list.

- "human assets weakness", based on a composite index (the Human Assets Index, HAI) that consists of indicators on nutrition, health, school enrolment and literacy.

- "economic vulnerability", based on a composite index (the Economic Vulnerability Index, EVI) that includes indicators on natural shocks, trade shocks, exposure to shocks, economic smallness and economic remoteness.

Low-income countries with populations greater than 75 million are not eligible for inclusion.

Although initially there was no criteria for graduation from LDC status, in 1991 it was suggested that a country would be recommended for immediate graduation if it met at least two of the three criteria in relation to income, human assets and economics, in two consecutive triennial reviews.[37] In 2006, the criteria for recommendation for graduation were revised to include exceptional cases in which the GNI per capita of a country is at least twice the graduation threshold levels.[38]

Compared to the typical small LDC, Bangladesh is considered more resilient to shocks and has the ability to diversify its economy by taking advantage of the economies of scale supported by a relatively large domestic market. This is why Bangladesh is considered one of the least economically vulnerable LDCs as measured by a composite index reflecting various structural features of the economy, such as the share of primary production, exposure to shocks and export instability. In terms of its EVI, which is one of the three criteria for LDC classification, Bangladesh easily qualifies for graduation. In terms of the LDC criterion relating to HAI, which reflects the health and educational status of a

---

37   The list of LDCs is reviewed every three years by the Economic and Social Council of the UN, drawing on recommendations by the Committee for Development Policy.

38   See for details, 'Criteria for Identification and Graduation of LDCs', http://unohrlls. org/about-ldcs/criteria-for-ldcs

population, Bangladesh has been making good progress and is ahead of some non-LDC countries like Pakistan, although its score is still somewhat below the threshold level for graduation.

The other criterion is GNI per capita, for which Bangladesh is mid-ranking among LDCs. Therefore, it would be difficult to fulfil this criterion for graduation in the short term unless there is rapid progress in industrial development, commercialisation of research or development of strong creative industries (which are knowledge-based, rather than requiring a huge investment base, which is the case for information technology and IP-based industries).

Considering the above criteria for graduation from LDC status, it is interesting to consider how the competitiveness of local industry and a proper plan for human development may qualify Bangladesh for graduation and support its progression towards innovation and TRIPS compliance.

5.4.2 Competitiveness of the Local (Pharmaceutical) Industry and a Plan for Graduation from the LDC Category and Progress towards TRIPS Compliance: The Context of Bangladesh

Bangladesh has already met the EVI threshold and therefore needs to meet only one of the remaining two criteria to graduate from LDC status:

- Under a business-as-usual scenario, Bangladesh will meet the graduation threshold for lower-middle-income country by 2047 (based on an average growth rate of 5.9%).[39]

- Under a recent performance-based scenario (2007–10), Bangladesh will meet the graduation threshold for a lower-middle-income country by 2039 (based on an average growth rate of 6.3%).[40]

The large population size in Bangladesh is limiting per capita income. Therefore, if it is possible to increase investment in health, education, skill development, and the supply of efficient and skilled people in industry,

---

39 Debapriya Bhattacharya and Lisa Borgatti, 'An Atypical Approach to Graduation from LDC Category: The Case of Bangladesh', *South Asia Economic Journal* 13.1 (2012): 1–25.

40 Ibid.

to create employment and advance industrialisation, Bangladesh could meet the graduation threshold in the next 15–20 years.

A study by Debapriya Bhattacharya and Lisa Borgatti showed that Bangladesh could graduate in the next 15–20 years if it emphasised substantial improvement in its human capital, particularly reducing two worsening indicators: child mortality rate and secondary school enrolment ratio.[41] Bangladesh could meet the graduation threshold by 2027 and graduate by 2033 if it improved its HAI and continued its progress in the EVI.[42]

While planning for graduation from LDC status, it is important for Bangladesh to take into account issues relating to the TRIPS Agreement in general and pharmaceutical patents in particular. If Bangladesh qualifies for graduation before the expiration of the transitional period for LDCs, it may need to implement the TRIPS Agreement despite having regulatory bodies such as the Patent Office (DPDT). Local industries like the pharmaceutical industry may not be ready to cope with pharmaceutical patent issues. Thus, it may be important to make an integrated plan for graduating from LDC status and graduating from the TRIPS waiver together.

In the context of the WTO, the principle of *graduation* as illustrated by Cottier seeks to provide an added flexibility to the international system, making implementation of WTO provisions contingent on overcoming a set of identified graduating constraints. Taking into account social and economic development, it could also be commensurate with the level of competitiveness of the industries and sectors concerned.[43] Countries that fall below a chosen threshold would be entitled to derogations.[44] The threshold could be used to define the application of a particular agreement or a particular rule to a particular industry in a country.[45] Here, an attempt is made to define the threshold for pharmaceutical patents under the TRIPS Agreement in the context of the pharmaceutical sector in Bangladesh.

---

41 Ibid.
42 Ibid.
43 'From Progressive Liberalization to Progressive Regulation'.
44 Ibid.
45 Ibid.

There is little or no research on whether the introduction of an IP regime in general and pharmaceutical patents in particular might help a country meet the criteria for graduation from LDC status. In the case of two countries that to date have graduated from LDC status, there is no genuine link between graduation and the introduction of an IP regime. Rather, Maskus argued that the presence of onerous patenting provisions may impede the growth of the necessary industrial capabilities of developing countries.[46] Developing countries might attain industrial and technical capabilities by "imitating" pharmaceutical production, which could provide important benefits with respect to further development of R&D, as was the case in the Indian pharmaceutical sector.[47] Through this process, countries could develop their domestic capacity so that firms would demand the presence of a fully functioning patenting mechanism to protect their innovative activities.[48]

Cottier suggested that countries need to consider not only international competitiveness, but also the domestic competitive environment and the interplay between domestic and foreign sources for pharmaceuticals.[49] The nature of the WTO obligations can be subsumed into regulation of the competitive environment between domestic and imported products; hence, graduation should be contingent on competitive shortfalls, where commitments kick in after international competitiveness is attained.[50]

Cottier further added that countries, regardless of their qualification, would be obliged to introduce patent protection for a particular sector once their domestic industry had achieved a level of competitiveness defined on the basis of economic factors and data.[51] However, below this threshold, industries would be allowed to develop in accordance with domestic needs and engage in producing generics irrespective of

---

46   See Keith E. Maskus, 'Intellectual Property Rights and Economic Development', in *Beyond the Treaties: A Symposium on Compliance with International Intellectual Property Law* (Fredrick K. Cox International Law Center, Case Western Reserve University, 2000).

47   See J. Watal, 'Pharmaceutical Patents, Prices and Welfare Losses: Policy Options for India under the WTO TRIPS Agreement', *The World Economy* 23 (2000): 733–52.

48   See Keith E. Maskus, 'Intellectual Property Rights and Economic Development'.

49   See, Thomas Cottier, 'From Progressive Liberalisation to Progressive Regulation in WTO Law', *Journal of International Economic Law* 9.4 (2006): 779–821.

50   Ibid.

51   Ibid.

patent protection abroad.[52] Many countries in the past (e.g., India and Italy) have followed that path and built their industrial base.[53] Thus, it would be a viable solution for the LDCs to engage in technological and institutional development, and introduce pharmaceutical patents once they have attained a certain level of competitiveness.

However, further research is needed on how to measure defined levels of competitiveness and the threshold for graduation. Using country-specific data, economists could create a composite index specific to a particular sector to determine competitiveness and therefore obligations to introduce patent protection for that sector. Cottier and colleagues,[54] in a study based on earlier work,[55] developed a checklist that included large market size, local demand, highly skilled labour forces and abundant natural resources.

Further, Lopez Gonzalez et al. created a composite index for graduating thresholds that could apply in the pharmaceutical sector.[56] The authors identified three broad categories for a procedural test: access to required pharmaceuticals, capacity to meet health priorities in developing countries and the incidence of disease in these countries.[57] Based on these criteria, the study developed a list of countries including Bangladesh that should be exempted from TRIPs provisions for patent protection in the pharmaceutical sector.[58]

As the LDCs are in a transitional period for TRIPS general obligations and enjoy a pharmaceutical patents waiver based on their institutional, administrative and financial constraints, the author of this study

---

52   Ibid.
53   Ibid.
54   Thomas Cottier, Shaheeza Lalani and M. Temmerman, 'Use it or Lose it? Assessing the Compatibility of the Paris Convention and TRIPS with Respect to Local Working Requirements', Working Paper (18 February 2013), World Trade Institute, University of Bern, Switzerland.
55   See, K.E. Maskus, 'The Role of Intellectual Property Rights in Encouraging Foreign Direct Investment', *Duke Journal of Comparative & International Law* 9 (1998); and J.H. Dunning, 'Trade, Location of Economic Activity and the MNE: A Search for an Eclectic Approach', in *The International Allocation of Economic Activity*, ed. by B. Ohlin et al. (London: Macmillan, 1977).
56   J. Lopez Gonzalez et al., 'TRIPS and Special & Differential Treatment – Revisiting the Case for Derogations in Applying Patent Protection for Pharmaceuticals in Developing Countries', NCCR Trade Regulation Working Paper No. 2011/37, May 2011.
57   Ibid.
58   Ibid.

considers that the following issues need special attention. Moreover, further research is required to determine competitiveness and readiness to introduce for patent protection for the pharmaceutical sector:

- The ability of local pharmaceutical production facilities and pharmaceutical imports to meet local needs, and the ratio of pharmaceutical exports, if any, by the domestic pharmaceutical industry.

- Strong local market and export opportunities for economies of scale to recover investment costs and make profits for reinvestment in R&D.

- The nature, quality, safety and efficacy of domestic pharmaceutical production measured in light of a number of WHO pre-qualified pharmaceutical plants based on GMP, U.S. FDA-approved manufacturers and certification for exports by highly regulated markets like the EU, Australia and Canada.

- Health infrastructure and healthcare facilities in particular LDCs, and out-of-pocket expenditure for health. Despite having local pharmaceutical production and cheaper medicines, citizens in the LDCs may have access problems, considering 100% out-of-pocket expenditure for medical treatment and the absence of health insurance. Therefore, the additional cost for patented medicines may make these inaccessible to them. To evaluate this, healthcare and public health data from the WHO could be utilised.

- Prevalent diseases and the ratio of off-patent and patented medicines used for treatment in the particular country. This needs to be evaluated with respect to the extent to which local production facilities could supply medicines (both generic and patented) for those diseases in the country concerned.

- The level of local innovation and progression of R&D as evidenced by increasing the number of patents by local industries and research institutions in the pharmaceutical sector. National patent office data from individual LDCs and global patent applications from a particular country, under the PCT system of the WIPO, could be used to classify levels of innovation. However, all 24 LDCs that are party to the PCT are from Africa.[59] None of the Asia Pacific, Latin American or Caribbean LDCs are members of the PCT. In the absence of PCT data, patent applications by citizens of a particular

---

59 'Summary Table of Membership of the World Intellectual Property Organization (WIPO) and the Treaties Administered by WIPO, plus UPOV, WTO and UN', http://www.wipo.int/treaties/en/summary.jsp

country to the patent offices of the EU, Japan and U.S. could be used.

- Competition between domestic and foreign companies in the local market, which could be determined based on the ratio of shares in the pharmaceutical sales and on comparison of selected product prices.

- Technical capacity and facilities for basic research at national research institutions and local companies as evidenced by their research results, successful applications for product and process patents, research articles in internationally reputable journals, use of technologies, and cooperation and joint research with global research institutions and pharmaceutical companies.

- Financial strength and the ratio of investment for R&D as reflected in the annual reports of the leading local pharmaceutical companies. The financial constraints of a particular LDC must also be examined based on economic data.

- An adequate supply of technically skilled and efficient human resources for the pharmaceutical industry, drawn from science and technology graduates of national higher education institutes.

- Strong and efficient regulatory bodies. National patent offices need to be equipped with modern technologies and should have efficient patent examiners; a patent information system for the status and description of existing, expired and pending patent applications; an online patent database; and an efficient adjudication system to deal with pharmaceutical patent applications and analyse substantive and procedural requirements. The DGDA needs continuous supervision to maintain the quality of medicines produced and imported for the local market. The DGDA should have adequate expertise to identify counterfeit medicines.

- Infrastructural facilities such as cost-effective and adequate energy supplies, efficient local transport, port facilities for export and import, and international transportation. As infrastructural facilities could reduce cost of production, and facilitate the efficient import of raw materials and export of medicines, this needs to be taken into consideration for determining the competitiveness of the local industry.

- Working conditions (job security, standard wages for employees and other labour costs, safety standards, unemployment benefits, health and accident insurance, etc.) need to be considered for the long-term sustainability of local industry.

- Although low wages and the low cost of employment conditions may provide short-term profits for the local industry, in the long run this will not help it become a sustainable business competitor and attract technical and skilled people. Thus, LDCs need to have in place employment and labour laws ensuring safe, comfortable and fair working conditions for the long-term sustainability and competitiveness of the local industry.[60]

If the above conditions are evaluated—along with existing indexes such as the HDI,[61] World Bank data on basic infrastructure, the High Technology Infrastructure Index and the Residents Patent Index—to create an innovation capability and competitiveness index, this would be useful in determining the status of the pharmaceutical sector, a possible plan of action and support measures, and the time required to attain competitiveness and hence achieve compliance.[62]

Based on the above criteria, LDCs such as Bangladesh may be encouraged to submit reports on their pharmaceutical sectors (and in turn on other sectors of vital importance) to the TRIPS Council along with their general technology needs assessment and a sector-specific

---

60 For example, although Bangladesh is the second largest apparel exporter in the world after China, poor working conditions and a lack of adequate safety measures led to the collapse of a garment factory in April 2013, killing over one thousand workers. This sparked a huge debate and a good number of importers of apparel from Bangladesh suspended their orders. This will have serious negative impacts for the stability of the industry.

61 The Human Development Index (HDI) is a composite statistic of life expectancy, education, and income indices used to rank countries into four tiers of human development, a concept of well-being based on a capability approach. It was created by the Mahbub ul Haq in 1990. In his capacity as Special Advisor to the UNDP Administrator, Haq initiated the concept of Human Development and the Human Development Report as its Project Director. He engaged other renowned experts, such as Paul Streeten, Inge Kaul, Frances Stewart, Amartya Sen and Richard Jolly, to prepare annual Human Development Reports. See Mahbub ul Haq, *Reflections on Human Development* (Oxford University Press, 1996).

62 However, using World Bank data Rajah Rasiah analysed capability building in the developing countries in the context of the TRIPS Agreement. He based his analysis on the Basic Infrastructure Index, the High Technology Index and the Resident Patent Data Index. He concluded that LDCs are seriously disadvantaged as they lack the high technology infrastructure to participate actively in the innovation process; yet achieving even adequate basic infrastructure and fulfilling the TRIPS Agreement may hinder technological capability building and competitiveness for the LDCs (he classified them as less industrialized developing economies, or LIDE). See for details, Rajah Rasiah, 'TRIPS and Capability Building in Developing Economies: Critical Issues', *Journal of Contemporary Asia* 33.3: 338–62.

needs assessment, such as for technology in the pharmaceutical sector. Based on such reports, technological and financial assistance could be requested from the developed countries, utilising Articles 66.2 and 67 of the TRIPS Agreement,[63] and also from the WIPO, WHO, UNIDO and other relevant international organisations.[64] The TRIPS Council and the developed countries could also provide access to their reports on when and how the pharmaceutical sector in a particular LDC would be ready for graduation, and the nature of financial and technical cooperation needed to make such progress towards TRIPS compliance. Technical and financial cooperation will, therefore, be a key element in ensuring that LDC members of the WTO are prepared to apply TRIPS in a manner appropriate to their socioeconomic condition and to the stage of technological development and competitiveness of a particular sector.[65] This could be replicated to some extent in other sectors that have patent-intensive industries.

Although patent protection on the price of pharmaceuticals has likely contributed to a lack of access to affordable medicines, its elimination would not be a silver bullet, nor would it solve these countries' major health issues.[66] Even in countries where patent laws have been permissive or levels of enforcement are low, access to medicines remains suboptimal.[67]

Therefore, determining the competitiveness of its local pharmaceutical industry and identifying thresholds for graduation based on the above criteria should help determine the ideal time for the introduction of pharmaceutical patents, as well as the capability of a particular LDC

---

63 Article 67 of the TRIPS Agreement places an obligation on developed country WTO members to provide, on request and on mutually agreed terms and conditions, technical and financial cooperation in favour of developing and least-developed WTO members.

64 The WTO–WIPO Cooperation Agreement of 22 December 1995 stipulates that legal and technical assistance and technical cooperation relating to TRIPS be provided to developing countries by the WIPO. See the text of the Agreement at http://www.wto.org/english/tratop_e/trips_e/intel3_e.htm

65 Duncan Matthews and Viviana Munoz-Tellez, 'Bilateral Technical Assistance and TRIPS: The United States, Japan and the European Communities in Comparative Perspective', *The Journal of World Intellectual Property* 9.6 (2006): 629–53.

66 See, J. Watal, 'Pharmaceutical Patents, Prices and Welfare Losses: Policy Options for India under the WTO TRIPS Agreement', *The World Economy* 23 (2000): 733–52.

67 Amir Attaran, 'How Do Patents and Economic Policies Affect Access to Essential Medicines in Developing Countries?', *Health Affairs* 23.3 (2004): 155–66.

to deal with administrative, institutional and financial constraints in general and public health problems in particular.

In the course of transitioning from the patent waiver period to the introduction of patent protection, developed country members are expected to "provide incentives to enterprises and institutions in their territories" for the purpose of promoting and encouraging technology transfer to the LDCs, thus ensuring the achievements of the objectives and principles of the TRIPS Agreement as set out in Articles 7 and 8. It is also important that LDCs themselves initiate capacity-building programmes targeting their domestic institutional and infrastructural constraints.

5.5 Progress towards Graduation and Compliance: Institutional and Infrastructural Issues in Bangladesh

Developing appropriate plans of action and introducing adequate capacity-building initiatives within a range of institutions for progression towards innovation and TRIPS compliance, and at the same time meeting local societal and developmental goals such as incentives for the local pharmaceutical industry and ensuring that access to medicines is long term, are very challenging tasks for LDCs. However, they are essential for implementing the objectives, principles, rights and obligations of the TRIPS Agreement in a manner conducive to the social and economic development goals of LDCs. The alternative is a narrow approach focused only on compliance with the TRIPS provisions.[68] On the other hand, the IPR and pharmaceutical sector-related institutional and infrastructural solutions that are often used in developed countries may differ from those best suited to the needs of the LDCs. Bangladesh may need additional institutional and infrastructural capacity-building initiatives, considering its low level of technological development, bureaucratic hurdles, lack of access to information and culture of

---

68   See M. Leesti and T. Pengelly, 'Assessing Technical Assistance Needs for Implementing the TRIPS Agreement in LDCs', ICTSD Programme on Intellectual Property Rights and Sustainable Development, International Centre for Trade and Sustainable Development, Geneva, Switzerland (2007).

non-cooperation between bureaucrats, policymakers, academic institutions and local industries.[69]

The necessity of technical and infrastructural development was supported by a number of interviewees in this study. One remarked that:

apart from policy options for patent law reform, the Government of Bangladesh may need to take technical and infrastructural steps for the effective outcome and promote pharmaceutical research and ensure access to medicines in the country. Ultimately technical capacity building in the pharmaceutical sector and greater public-private partnership for R&D can make a balance. Simply making patent law either weak or TRIPS compliant can make no difference.[70]

Another expert commented that:

The DDA and patent office should have adequate expertise to deny any patent registration and registration of pharmaceuticals respectively if it considers little improvement and may become a threat to public health in the country. There should be greater public access to the patent office to gain information about patent applications, expired patents and granted patents in the field of pharmaceuticals.[71]

Also showing dissatisfaction with the existing facilities and lack of proper action on the part of the Government of Bangladesh, one industry expert commented on the "inordinate delay for the establishment of the Active Pharmaceutical Ingredients (API) Park and no proper initiative for the establishment of a bio-equivalency lab at the DDA with all modern facilities is a sign of sheer negligence on the part of the government ... we want action in practice not in words".[72]

It is clear that Bangladesh needs to seriously consider technical and infrastructural capacity-building issues to better serve its pharmaceutical industry, promote innovation and ensure access to medicines, while

---

69   See Mohammad Monirul Azam, 'Establishment of the WTO and Impacts on the Legal System of Bangladesh', *Macquarie Journal of Business Law* 3 (2006).

70   Email interview with an IP law academic, in Brazil, 12 March 2012.

71   Interview with a policy analyst from a leading public health NGO, in Dhaka, Bangladesh, 7 March 2012.

72   Interview with the CEO of medium-sized local pharmaceutical company in Bangladesh, in Dhaka, Bangladesh, 25 January 2012.

making the transition towards a TRIPS-compliant patent regime. Some important technical and infrastructural policy issues will now be discussed.

5.5.1 Capacity Building in the Department of Patents, Designs and Trademarks, and Intellectual Property-related Institutional and Infrastructural Issues

The functions of the Patent Office (under the DPDT in Bangladesh) will increase rapidly after the implementation of a TRIPS-compliant patent regime. The DPDT needs adequate expertise to ensure that an invention is absolutely new and not similar to any previously granted patents. To perform this function, the DPDT must be equipped with adequate technical resources and professional staff with experience in the relevant fields. Its present workforce does not meet these requirements: its current total number of 112 staff consists of 1 registrar, 4 deputy registrars, 9 assistant registrars, 25 examiners and 73 support staff.[73] Of the 112 officials, less than 50% work in the field of patents. Arguably, the present number of 25 examiners is not sufficient to ensure timely assessment of patent applications; one interviewee suggested that the existing examiners also lack the proper training and technical facilities to deal with complex applications in the field of pharmaceuticals.[74]

It is relevant that neither the present patent law nor the Draft PDA 2010 and *Draft Patent Law, 2012* deal with the human-resource issues of the DPDT. Fortunately, the need to modernise the DPDT has been recognised: in 2009, Bangladesh initiated two relevant projects with the technical and financial assistance of WIPO.[75] Unfortunately, however, neither project delivered any meaningful suggestions for the development of the DPDT due to a lack of coordination between local experts and technical staff at the DPDT, the traditional and procrastinating bureaucratic process in Bangladesh, a lack of integrated

---

73   Email interview with a deputy director of the Patent Office of Bangladesh (anonymous), in Dhaka, Bangladesh, 27 September 2010.

74   Email interview with a patent examiner (anonymous), in Dhaka, Bangladesh, 27 September 2010.

75   The projects are the *Modernization and Strengthening of Patents and Designs Systems in Bangladesh* and the *Nationally Focused Action Plan for the Government of Bangladesh for Modernization of the Patent Office*.

approaches and a lack of interest from the WIPO in engaging local experts.

The joint *EU–WIPO Programme on IP* (2008–11) tried to support modernisation of the national IP legislative system, and to raise awareness about the importance of IP protection in the public and private sectors.[76] However, due to slow bureaucratic processes, lack of inter-ministry coordination in Bangladesh, and lack of understanding on the donors' part about local priorities and bureaucratic processes, a Swiss–Bangladeshi project on IP capacity-building remained dysfunctional.[77] Without an understanding of local priorities, the needs of local people, the necessity of local inventors, institutions, industry and the engagement of experts with an understanding of IP law and institutions in Bangladesh, no bilateral capacity-building project can deliver meaningful results for IP in Bangladesh. Based on the field studies and perceptions of stakeholders in Bangladesh, a number of IP-related institutional and infrastructural issues have been identified in this study that seem to be very important for Bangladesh during the post-TRIPS patent regime. They are discussed below.

Patent Information System. A database is required of patents, non-working patents and expired patents. In Bangladesh there is currently no patent information system at the DPDT, and public access to the patent database is mostly restricted and subject to slow bureaucratic processes. Further, as the DPDT to date has used a paper-based patent application system, it is difficult to extract patent information about any particular invention without personally visiting the DPDT and going through the long bureaucratic process to gain access to the required information. From the perspective of the local generic producers in Bangladesh, it is vital to highlight the increased importance of making use of inventions that have entered the public domain. To ascertain

---

76 See 'WTO Trade Policy Review', Bangladesh, 2012; and 'Council for TRIPS, Priority Needs'.

77 The Swiss report to the WTO stated that "The Bangladeshi-Swiss Intellectual Property Project (BSIP) was approved by Switzerland in 2011. Approval from Bangladesh, however, was left pending until 30 June 2015, at which time the dedicated project funds were forfeited and the project was cancelled accordingly". See, WTO (document no. IP/C/W/610/Add.3), Communication from Switzerland (23 September 2015) p.2, https://docs.wto.org/dol2fe/Pages/FE_Search/DDF Documents/134826/q/IP/C/W610A3.pdf

information about such inventions, it is necessary to know about patents that have entered into the public domain. In a study by the WHO, it was mentioned that due to the lack of adequate administrative and legal infrastructure in developing countries, it is difficult to determine the patent status of pharmaceuticals.[78] It is recommended that an authority, be it governmental (such as the DPDT) or non-governmental, be created or be given sufficient competence to search for expired patents and declare that such patents are freely available to interested parties for future exploitation. Such an authority should cooperate with other regional or international organisations (such as the WHO) to achieve the greatest possible advantage that an expired patent can bring.

It is recommended that a free online database be developed for all educational and research institutions in Bangladesh. The database should classify patented inventions, non-working patents and expired patents, and also provide information about the particular sector and about inventions. Such a database would provide local inventors with technical knowledge about different inventions, and allow them to make plans for the use of expired patents and non-working patents. Publication of non-worked inventions and expired patents enables various players and manufacturing companies in diverse industry segments to understand how and when they can make use of unused technology and expired technology, which may be more efficient and cost-effective for the industry and local population. During the author's field research in Bangladesh, public health NGOs, pharmaceutical researchers and IP academics argued that this kind of database would help immensely with technological teaching and learning, and also with the immediate generic production of expired patented pharmaceutical products.[79] Bangladesh may also need to develop a traditional knowledge database to encourage local inventors to exploit such knowledge further, and at the same time to prevent abuse.

Traditional Knowledge Database. The Government of Bangladesh could develop a separate publicly accessible online database detailing available

---

78   WHO, 'Intellectual Property Rights and Access to Medicines: A South-East Asia Perspective on Global Issues' (2008), p.20.
79   Based on interview data from IP academics, pharmaceutical researchers and public health activists involved with NGOs in Bangladesh.

traditional knowledge, medicinal plants and biological resources in Bangladesh to prevent bio-piracy and abuse of these resources for patenting. In this regard, Bangladesh could follow the existing models of India and China. China has developed a database on traditional Chinese medicines,[80] and India has developed a broad-based traditional knowledge digital library derived from old scriptures and available archival information.[81] Bangladesh may also need to take initiatives to inform different stakeholders regarding IPRs.

Considering the low level of IP awareness in Bangladesh, it is necessary to establish information centres around the country with support policies for SMEs.

Further, given existing workforce and technical resource issues in the patent area, Bangladesh should consider joining the PCT 1970 to outsource patent examinations.[82] This would enable Bangladesh to extend patent protection for local inventions all over the world and would pave the way for foreigners to apply to Bangladesh through the international application system under the PCT.[83] The advantage of relying on PCT preliminary examination reports to determine whether to award a national patent (as opposed to relying on foreign patent proxies under a re-registration scheme) is that developing countries are assured access to the underlying analysis on which the patentability was determined, as well as to the relevant body of prior work that was considered. However, Bangladesh could adopt the Brazilian model of forwarding pharmaceutical patent applications to any public health-related IP review body (as ANVISA was established under the Ministry of Health in Brazil) for review before pharmaceutical patents are granted in Bangladesh.[84]

---

80 See Traditional Chinese Medicines Integrated Database, http://www.megabionet.org/tcmid

81 See Traditional Knowledge Digital Library, http://www.csir.res.in/External/Utilities/Frames/career/main_page1.asp?a=tkdl_topframe.htm&b=tkdl_left.htm&c=../../../Heads/TKDL/main.htm

82 The PCT is a WIPO-administered treaty concluded in 1970. It provides patent applicants with the opportunity of filing an international patent application. Instead of filing separate applications in different countries, the applicant can file a PCT application with the International Bureau of WIPO, or any national or regional patent office. The date of this international filing is deemed as the date of filing in all national offices.

83 'Pharmaceutical Patent Protection'.

84 See 'Intervention of Health Authorities in Patent Examination'.

To attain the optimum benefits of any patent information system, it is necessary to take steps for the promotion of R&D. Unfortunately, in Bangladesh there appears to be a lack of imperatives to increase and encourage investment in R&D. The DPDT could take initiatives to promote innovation and patenting practices among local SMEs and research institutions. One interviewee pointed out that there are no government initiatives in place to support or promote R&D.[85] Another argued that the failure to support and promote R&D is a major barrier for the post-TRIPS survival of the pharmaceutical industry in Bangladesh.[86] It is highly recommended that an ongoing policy for R&D based on domestic raw materials and traditional plant varieties be adopted. In this regard, one participant commented that it is important to establish new scientific research centres whose goal is to take part in modernising the domestic pharmaceutical industry and creating new pharmaceuticals for the public at reasonable prices.[87] To promote R&D in local research centres and pharmaceutical companies, it is crucial to improve the quality of services at the DGDA.

5.5.2 Capacity Building in the Directorate of Drug Administration and Public Health-related Institutional and Infrastructural Issues

The incapacity of the DGDA to monitor properly the standard of pharmaceuticals in Bangladesh was revealed during the Rid Pharmaceutical scam in July 2009, when several people died from using low-quality medicines distributed by Rid Pharmaceutical, a local small company.[88] The DGDA itself admitted that it has insufficient manpower and technical facilities to monitor all domestic manufacturers. Moreover, the industry is against taking strict action.[89]

Considering the adverse opinion of rigorous measures and the low financial and technical strength of local companies, Bangladesh could

---

85 Interview with a pharmaceutical researcher working in an MNC with a manufacturing plant in Bangladesh, 7 March 2012.

86 Interview with an IP lawyer working as in-house counsel for a local medium-sized pharmaceutical company, 8 March 2012.

87 Interview with an academic working on pharmaceutical technology at the Department of Pharmacy, University of Dhaka, Bangladesh, 27 February 2012.

88 See Azam and Richardson (2010b).

89 Ibid.

adopt the responsive regulations theory (RRT) in the enforcement framework of the DGDA in an attempt to encourage gradual development in the pharmaceutical sector and to fulfil the twin goals of promoting pharmaceutical innovation and safety, on the one hand, and banning counterfeit, fake and low-quality medicines on the other.[90] This theory is based on allowing flexibility in the regulatory approach to promote gradual development and ensure continuous supervision; in other words, "soft words before hard words, and carrots before sticks".[91] This approach recognises the need for a diversity of regulatory strategies and for all strategies to be practically grounded and context-appropriate.[92]

The RRT proposes a Regulatory Enforcement Pyramid of Sanctions (REPS) that targets the achievement of a maximum level of regulatory compliance by persuasion and advice.[93] Therefore, persuasion, motivation, education, advice, training and so forth are situated at the base of the pyramid. If this does not work, the regulators could proceed to an escalation in the pyramid and issue a warning letter for improvement as per required regulatory standards. If the warning letter also fails to secure compliance, the DGDA may then impose a civil monetary penalty in an attempt to prompt compliance. The next step is criminal prosecution. If all these steps fail, the DGDA can move to shut down a particular manufacturing plant or issue a temporary suspension of the licence for the pharmaceutical company concerned: it can order them to withdraw from the market all the low-quality pharmaceuticals

---

90 The responsive regulations theory was first developed by John Braithwaite and Ian Ayres in their book *Responsive Regulation: Transcending the Deregulation Debate* (Oxford University Press, 1992). However, it is important to emphasise that the development of responsive regulation as a theory has been and continues to be a collective effort, contributed to by numerous scholars and institutions, the most important early development being by Neil Gunningham, Peter Grabosky and Darren Sinclair in their *Smart Regulation* (Clarendon Press, 1998), with further contributions by John Braithwaite, 'Responsive Regulation and Developing Economies', *World Development* 34.5 (2006): 884–98; John Braithwaite, *Regulatory Capitalism: How it Works, Ideas for Making it Work Better* (Edward Elgar, 2008); and Valerie Braithwaite's *Defiance in Taxation and Governance* (Edward Elgar, 2009).

91 See J. Healy and John Braithwaite, 'Designing Safer Health Care through Responsive Regulation', *The Medical Journal of Australia* 184.10 (Suppl.) (2006), https://www.mja.com.au/journal/2006/184/10/designing-safer-health-care-through-responsive-regulation

92 See M. Sparrow, *The Regulatory Craft: Controlling Risks, Managing Problems and Managing Compliance* (Brookings Institute, 2000).

93 See 'Designing Safer Health Care'.

they produce and supply. Finally, if the temporary suspension of licence does not work, the DGDA could escalate to the final step of the pyramid and revoke the licence of the pharmaceutical producer, prohibiting sales and distribution of their products. Figure 5.1 demonstrates the REPS under the RRT.

License revocation

License suspension

Criminal penalty

Civil penalty

Warning letter and improvement notice

Persuasion, training and education

Figure 5.1: Regulatory Enforcement Pyramid of Sanctions under the responsive regulations theory for application in the pharmaceutical regulatory sector. Source: Based on Ayres and Braithwaite (1992), pp.35–38.

It is expected that the application of REPS may facilitate a gradual improvement in all manufacturing plants in Bangladesh. However, to apply REPS in the pharmaceutical sector of Bangladesh and to improve the capacity of the DGDA to deal with post-TRIPS challenges, the DGDA needs more manpower and technical facilities. The most pressing problem is one of manpower deficiency, which compromises to a great extent the DGDA's ability to maintain regular inspections, and ensure the safety and efficacy of pharmaceuticals produced in Bangladesh.[94] A large pharmaceutical industry requires a large DRA. The DGDA itself estimated that they need 700 staff members to adequately carry out the necessary work, and has requested the appointment and approval of a budget for this number of staff.[95] However, as of 2012, they have

---

94   See 'Bangladesh Pharmaceuticals in Health Care Delivery Draft Mission Report', 24 October–3 November 2010 (WHO Regional Office for South East Asia: New Delhi, 2010).

95   *Assessment of the Regulatory Systems.*

only 370 approved posts, and of these only 135 are filled and 235 stand vacant.[96] No clinical pharmacologists are employed. Thus, the DGDA must urgently hire qualified staff.

The pharmaceutical sector falls under the Ministry of Health and Family Welfare in Bangladesh; in other countries, the Ministry of Industry and Commerce or the Ministry of Science and Technology are responsible for this area. One option may be for the pharmaceutical sector in Bangladesh to be split between different ministries under a coordination cell, in order to meet the dual goals of technological development in the sector and societal demands for ensuring access to pharmaceuticals. In addition to this, the Government of Bangladesh should address the health-related institutional and infrastructural issues, for example by promoting investment in R&D and encouraging local pharmaceutical companies to develop an excipient-based industry.

Investment in R&D. As Bangladesh has an opportunity to manufacture patented drugs for its local needs as well as export them to other LDCs, the industry needs to invest in its R&D so that it can manufacture patented drugs by reverse engineering. Also, as it must follow TRIPS-compliant patent provisions after the expiration of the transitional period, Bangladesh needs to be well supplied with the entire range of patented drugs for this period, and will need to be sufficiently technologically developed to face the challenges after pharmaceutical patents are introduced. In the meantime, the country could contribute to the invention and discovery of new drug molecules on the basis of "learning by doing" during the transitional period. During surveys, 63% of participants strongly agreed and 32% agreed that pharmaceutical companies in Bangladesh should invest in R&D, whereas 5% disagreed.[97] The Government of Bangladesh could follow the model of the Brazilian Health Ministry and invest in pharmaceutical research and production, with a concentration on local pharmaceutical needs and country-specific diseases.

In addition to investment in R&D, pharmaceutical companies need to develop standards.

---

96 Ibid.
97 Based on the findings of survey data, small pharmaceutical companies argued that it is in fact not possible for them to make the huge investments required for new invention and basic pharmaceutical research.

Developing Standards for Pharmaceutical Companies. Many pharmaceutical companies in Bangladesh cannot boast of complying with GMP and other national and international standards. Modifications are essential for the development of manufacturing plants and infrastructure that would ensure the production of quality pharmaceuticals. One interviewee argued that maintaining GMP status is extremely important for the reputation of pharmaceutical products from Bangladesh and thus for expanding pharmaceutical exports.[98] Another participant argued that maintaining standards is essential not only to the production of quality medicines and exports but also to competing with MNCs.[99] Another participant remarked that the DGDA of Bangladesh does not regularly monitor standards of pharmaceutical companies, which the occurrence of low-quality cheaper medicines in the local market.[100] The DGDA will need to strictly monitor modifications and improvements to seize the opportunity for export. The Government of Bangladesh may approach the WHO for assistance. Thus, there may need to be improvements in the DGDA. While improving standards in the pharmaceutical sector, the government may need to encourage the setting up of excipient-based pharmaceutical companies.

Setting Up Excipient-based Pharmaceutical Companies. One interviewee noted that at present, almost all excipients are imported to Bangladesh by local companies.[101] Arguably, locally manufactured pharmaceutical excipients would be much cheaper, and the overall production cost for finished products substantially reduced. The setting up of the local pharmaceutical industry to produce excipients and other additives would be profitable for Bangladesh and would remove the deficiency of pharmaceutical excipients/additives that are most required for the production of finished products. Another issue for Bangladesh that needs attention is the lack of modern test facilities to facilitate international certificates for export.

International Certificates for Export, and Modern Test Facilities. One interviewee mentioned that to acquire export registration it is necessary

---

98   Mentioned by an official from a large local pharmaceutical company during interview.

99   Stated by an official from a medium-sized local pharmaceutical company during interview.

100 Mentioned by an official from an MNC with a manufacturing plant in Bangladesh during interview.

101 Interview with an official from BAPI, 8 March 2012.

to have bio-equivalence, bio-availability tests and clinical trial reports.[102] The costs associated with implementing such a testing and documentary system are high. One participant argued that this is a major drawback for pharmaceutical SMEs in Bangladesh.[103] The availability of pharmaceutical-related testing facilities is an ongoing challenge that will need to be met before Bangladesh is able to engage effectively and competitively in a post-TRIPS environment.

Bangladesh has only two pharmaceutical testing laboratories: one in Dhaka and one in Chittagong. These two laboratories are not equipped with sufficiently modern instruments to carry out all the tests required for pharmaceutical products.[104] Put simply, these two laboratories are insufficient to monitor and check the quality status of the products of a large number of pharmaceutical companies in Bangladesh, which is why most Bangladeshi companies are facing problems in undertaking such testing and export registration.[105] The Government of Bangladesh needs to consider a programme of building these facilities, which are required not only for compliance but to maintain any momentum garnered as Bangladesh takes the opportunities afforded to it during the transition period.

As one interviewee argued, in addition to building facilities, the government and the BAPI will need to work together to encourage local pharmaceutical companies to seek international certification, and assist them to understand the requirements of particular countries with the help of Bangladeshi foreign missions in those respective countries.[106]

In addition to these technical and infrastructural initiatives, the Government of Bangladesh may need to adopt development-centred IP policies and national health strategies, and to promote university-industry-government cooperation and public-private partnerships to achieve its long-term goals of transforming into an innovative nation

---

102 Interview with an official from a large local pharmaceutical company, 9 March 2012.

103 Interview with an official from a small local pharmaceutical company, 10 March 2012.

104 Such as bio-equivalency tests, bio-availability tests and the conduct of clinical trials.

105 It should be noted that among local pharmaceutical companies in Bangladesh, very few obtained export registration and only Beximco and Square have gained registration for export to highly regulated countries like the U.S., the UK, Austria and Australia.

106 Interview with an official from BAPI, in Dhaka, Bangladesh, 11 March 2012.

and securing proper healthcare and affordable medicine for the vast majority of its population.

5.6 Adopting a National Development-centred Intellectual Property Policy and a National Health Strategy Integrating Long-term Innovation and Access Objectives

Bangladesh could adopt a national IP policy in consultation with different stakeholders, integrating national developmental goals such as public health, unemployment and poverty reduction, climate change mitigation and adaptation. The ultimate objective of such a policy would be to promote innovation in sectors of vital importance for the country, by local universities and public and private institutions; develop technologies on country-specific needs; address local problems; and acquire affordable solutions. There are still no technology transfer offices in local universities and research institutions. As part of its IP policy, Bangladesh could adopt broader policy goals to promote IP creation and commercialisation through start-ups, venture capital, SMEs and university technology commercialisation centres. To do this, the government could adopt a special IP and innovation fund, incentives mechanism, patent fee waiver and reward schemes.

Lowering drug prices is crucial, but it is just one element. As the WHO's director general stated, "It would be naive, however, to think that the cutting of prices of medicines is enough. The prospect of cheaper medicines stimulates demand for care, and this will actually increase the need for resources".[107] To ensure access to necessary drugs, countries need to formulate and implement national health strategies (NHSs), integrating long-term innovation and access objectives. The Government of Bangladesh should take initiatives for improving healthcare services and should give priority to building local innovation capacity, while considering long-term public health objectives and present and future access needs for medicines that treat country-specific diseases. An NHS to ensure regular access to essential drugs for the population and promote long-term innovation should include:

---

107 See for details, G. Brundland, 'Cheaper Drugs Offer Hope in the War Against AIDS', *International Herald Tribune* (14 February 2001).

- Transparency and sustained participation of all stakeholders in the formulation, implementation and regular review of the NHS, considering unmet needs.

- Sound drug supply management and distribution systems, supported by strengthened human resources development. Rather than simply using a government-controlled top-down approach as currently employed in Bangladesh, a mechanism could be adopted for efficient drug supply using a mix of public, private and NGO sectors in the national drug supply and distribution systems.[108]

- Cost-effective selection of essential drugs and rational use of medicines. Many highly effective medicines are—or can be—made available at very low cost. Fully acceptable and affordable treatments can be found if one chooses well. Thus, the rational use of medicines is very important for improving the public health situation in a country. A rational selection of medicines includes defining which medicines are most needed and identifying the most cost-effective treatments for particular conditions while taking full account of their quality and safety, and ensuring that they are used effectively.[109]

- Use of generic names. It is crucial to ensure that the generic medicines on sale are of guaranteed quality and that the population is strongly aware of this. Typically, people who cannot afford high prices buy costly branded medicines in the belief that they are superior to generic equivalents.[110]

- Special investment protection measures for joint venture and the promotion of R&D by governmental investment for pharmaceutical research and production, utilising the experiences of Brazil and India.

- Centralised, pooled bulk purchasing of generic drugs through fully accessible and transparent international tenders.

- Effective drug pricing policies as explained in this chapter, giving due consideration to limitations.[111]

- National patent law and pharmaceutical regulation should include all the possible TRIPS flexibilities as outlined in this chapter.

---

108 See WHO, 'Public-private Roles in the Pharmaceutical Sector. Implications for Equitable Access and Rational Drug Use, Health Economics and Drugs', DAP series no. 5. WHO/DAP/97.12 (Geneva, 1997).

109 See *Drugs and Money Prices.*

110 Ibid.

111 See drug price control option in chapter 4 of this study.

- Elimination of tariffs, duties and taxes for certain periods: the WHO, the WTO and other public health organisations advocate the elimination of import duties (>30% in some countries) and the abolition of VAT and other national and local taxes (>20% of the final consumer price) for essential medicines, HIV-related medicines for example. In Bangladesh there is still a 15% VAT on pharmaceuticals (only pharmaceuticals produced exclusively for export are exempt) despite large numbers of people having access problems. This needs to be reduced or eliminated to increase affordability of medicines; most people bear the cost of their healthcare from their own pockets.

- Sustainable healthcare financing. Access to medicines must be viewed in the context of overall funding for healthcare, including financing for prevention and treatment of priority infectious diseases with a high public health impact. For decades, the public health sector in developing countries and the LDCs was mainly financed by the government, and it commonly provided medicines free of charge. Over the years, diminishing budgets have increasingly led to drug shortages in national health systems, particularly in rural areas, and to a widespread collapse of the free drug supply. In this regard, national health insurance schemes may be an option, though it may also be difficult to implement them in LDCs such as Bangladesh. Whereas social insurance schemes are common in Europe and are on the increase in Latin America and Asia, they are still quite uncommon in Bangladesh and need the attention of policymakers. Sustainable financing can also be achieved by a combination of several viable financing mechanisms, such as making provision for mandatory health insurance by public and private employers, reallocation of public funds, better use of out-of-pocket spending and international financing through grants, donations and loans in appropriate circumstances.[112]

- It may also be necessary to apply export restrictions to the local pharmaceutical company to prioritise supply in the local market. One interviewee argued that the local pharmaceutical market is dominated by 20 leading pharmaceutical companies, most of which are now more interested in exporting to make quick cash profits than in adequately supplying the local market.[113] He further suggested that in future this may create a shortage of supply in the

---

112 See WHO, 'Health Reform and Drug Financing, Selected Topics, Health Economics and Drugs', DAP series no. 6, WHO/DAP/98.3 (Geneva, 1998).

113 Interview with a public health activist working in a local public health NGO, in Dhaka, Bangladesh, 11 March 2009.

local market, or an artificial supply crisis.[114] Considering this, one participant suggested that the DDA, when giving drug registration and marketing approval, may include a condition that an "adequate supply to the local market needs to be ensured". If it is not, upon the application of any person, the DDA would have the option of cancelling marketing approval and imposing export restrictions on the drugs concerned.[115]

- Improved regulation, including improved enforcement and monitoring. It is important to ensure that the decisions adopted under an NDP are properly guided and supported by required national regulations, and are properly monitored and enforced.

It is suggested that Bangladesh could establish a national IP Institute to implement IP policy, and reorganise its existing National Public Health Institute to implement an NHS. As part of a pro-development IP policy and NHS, the Government of Bangladesh should establish cooperation between industries, universities and government institutions, as well as public-private partnerships.

5.7 Collaboration between Univeristies, Industry and Government and Public-private Partnerships

Universities in LDCs often face a host of problems: for example lack of funds, weak infrastructure, outdated reading and research materials, overcrowded classrooms, and overburdened and underpaid staff.[116] Students in the basic and health sciences often graduate without being equipped to address critical tasks pertinent to the burden of disease and epidemiologic scenarios for which their service is needed. Both researchers and faculty struggle to find resources for substantive research projects. The overall lack of opportunity and career advancement results in low morale and provides little incentive to work in academia or the public sector, or even remain in the country.[117] Therefore, strengthening universities, research centres and government institutes could have

---

114 Ibid.

115 Interview with a policy analyst working in a local public health NGO, in Dhaka, Bangladesh, 8 March 2009.

116 See John Ssebuwufu et al., *Strengthening University-industry Linkages in Africa* (2012).

117 Ibid.

a direct effect on the ability of Bangladesh to muster the internal resources needed to boost local research and innovation with respect to country-specific diseases, and thereby the possibility to address its own public health problems. In particular, cooperation between industry, government and universities would help to develop an environment of self-reliance, confidence, entrepreneurship and experimentation that brings together researchers, practitioners and policymakers across disciplines to solve some of the pressing health problems facing Bangladesh.[118]

Despite a lack of investment in basic R&D by the government and pharmaceutical companies in Bangladesh, one positive aspect is that there is a continuous supply of fresh graduates in relevant fields from local universities. Six public and 16 private universities in Bangladesh offer Bachelor of Science and Masters of Science courses relevant to the pharmaceutical sector. The total number of graduates each year is 860 in pharmacy, 1660 in chemistry, 650 in microbiology, 350 in applied chemistry and 250 in chemical engineering.[119] The job opportunities for graduates are ever increasing, so more and more universities are offering relevant degrees.

Although there are more graduates, necessary steps should be taken to ensure that those graduates are recruited, deployed, trained and retained in the pharmaceutical sector. If graduates are given proper training and the opportunity to undertake research under the supervision of qualified and experienced experts, it would be an important step in the right direction for the transition of the pharmaceutical industry in Bangladesh beyond 2021. Bangladesh has great potential in this regard because infrastructure and labour costs are substantially lower than those for its competitors, such as China and India.

However, to date there has been little cooperation between government, industry and universities for R&D, and universities have little participation in national policymaking, resulting in fragmented, meaningless and bureaucratic national plans of action with no positive outcomes. On the other hand, the absence of national and university

---

118 For details on positive outcomes of this type of cooperation, see Henry Etzkowitz, 'The Triple Helix-University-Industry-Government Innovation in Action' (2008).

119 See for details, http://www.boi.gov.bd/ and the report of the University Grants Commission of Bangladesh, 2009–12.

IP policies results in a lack of confidence and cooperation between industry and local universities. There is no evidence of public-private partnerships for R&D on country-specific technological needs and commercialisation.

Therefore, it is vital for Bangladesh to adopt IP policies at the national and university levels that will generate confidence and interest among faculty members, universities and industry partners for engaging in collaborative R&D. Such policies should indicate how to share the outcome of research or make it available to industry partners for the equitable sharing of royalties. An ideal policy would satisfy the faculty and student need for prompt publication to advance their research careers, and also satisfy the industry in the sense that firms will not have to pay royalties or unreasonable fees, nor risk infringement lawsuits to exploit the results of joint work. Finally, the government should address local problems such as the development and production of pharmaceuticals for some country-specific diseases.

It was suggested that the IP Institute and National Public Health Institute could identify priority areas for R&D in Bangladesh and then engage potential industry and university partners in generating local innovation in each particular sector. In this regard, Bangladesh could follow the U.S. model of the National Science Foundation[120] and the *Bayh–Dole Act, 1980*.[121] Local universities in Bangladesh need

---

120 "The National Science Foundation (NSF), which was established in 1973 encouraged the creation of university-industry cooperative programs nationwide in a variety of technical fields. Again, the *Bayh–Dole Act* of 1980 removed a major impediment for cooperation in fields such as pharmaceuticals and biotechnology, in which exclusive licensing of intellectual property is necessary. It transferred to universities rights, which reserved to Federal government agencies earlier. NSF expanded its commitment to cooperative research in 1985 with establishment of the Engineering Research Centers program. That program provides up to 11 years of NSF funding in partnership with industry". See for details, 'Working Together, Creating Knowledge: The University-industry Research Collaboration Initiative', Business-Higher Education Forum of the American Council on Education and the National Alliance of Business (2001), http://www.bhef.com/sites/g/files/g829556/f/201604/BHEF_2001_working_together.pdf

121 The *Patent and Trademark Law Amendments Act* (Pub. L. 96–517, 12 December 1980), or *Bayh–Dole Act*, is the key piece of U.S. legislation dealing with IP arising from federal government-funded research. The *Bayh–Dole Act* was designed to promote technology transfer by allowing universities, small business and research institutions to retain ownership of the patent rights resulting from federally-funded research, subject to an obligation to share royalties with the actual inventor.

to establish innovation promotion and technology commercialisation centres to facilitate the establishment of start-up companies by students and faculty members, ensuring that advanced technologies are created to bring benefits to industry partners, and to facilitate the economic and technological development of society at large.[122]

Despite the lack of R&D in most of the local research institutions, the International Centre for Diarrhoeal Disease Research, Bangladesh (ICDDR-B) has made a remarkable contribution to improving public health in Bangladesh. This international health research organisation located in Bangladesh involves cooperation among research institutions around the world, and operates through the translation of research into treatment, training and policy advocacy. It addresses some of the most critical health concerns facing Bangladesh and the developing world.[123] It has already made a considerable contribution in reducing the death rate due to diarrhoea and cholera, and has improved maternal health in Bangladesh. Bangladesh should perhaps consider engaging the international community and funding agencies and, through public-private partnerships, establishing additional research organisations to focus on the other most prevalent diseases in Bangladesh. This would have a real positive effect not only in terms of R&D but also in terms of improving public health in Bangladesh.

5.8 Limitations and Further Research

How the TRIPS Agreement will be implemented in Bangladesh is yet to be finalised, but this study has presented a number of options for consideration. What is certain is that there will be a need for regulatory agencies and the pharmaceutical industry in Bangladesh to be ready, willing and able to deal with pharmaceutical patents. At the moment there is concern that the current regulatory agencies—the DPDT and the DDA—and the local pharmaceutical industry lack such capacity.

---

122 Presently, the idea of university technology transfer and start-up companies is completely non-existent in Bangladesh. For details on successful university start-ups and venture capital, see David A. Hodges, 'Industry-University Cooperation, and the Emergence of Start-up Companies', http://andros.eecs.berkeley.edu/~hodges/UIC&ESUC.pdf

123 See for details, the website of the International Center for Diarrhoeal Disease Research, Bangladesh (ICCDDR, B), http://www.icddrb.org

This study has identified policy options and institutional and infrastructural issues that should be considered by Bangladesh and other LDCs in balancing pharmaceutical innovation and access to medicines, and also in progressing towards TRIPS compliance. However, the links between TRIPS, legislative changes and their effect on various stakeholders require further consideration, given their complex histories and relationships. This necessarily gives rise to a study focused not only on doctrinal legal issues but also on the social and regulatory effects of those issues.

It would be a misjudgement to say that TRIPS is an exogenous imposition to be implemented by Bangladesh while ignoring the socioeconomic conditions in the country. The TRIPS Agreement itself states that "the protection and enforcement of intellectual property rights should contribute to the mutual advantage of producers and users of technological knowledge and in a manner conducive to social and economic welfare, and to a balance of rights and obligations".[124] Therefore, future study in this field must explore the TRIPS compliance process not only in the context of legal norms, but also while giving consideration to the consequences of those legal norms on the various stakeholders involved. Issues with respect to change and transition also then need to be considered. Therefore, further empirical socio-legal study may investigate these issues in the context of the TRIPS Agreement.

Another area of further research is the effect of TRIPS on traditional medicines in the LDCs and what policy options may be taken to protect and enhance traditional medicine use in a post-TRIPS setting.[125]

5.9 Concluding Remarks

Since the ratification of the TRIPS Agreement, its effects in developing countries and the LDCs have been relentlessly examined. The situation

---

124 Article 7 of the TRIPS Agreement.

125 A study by the WHO mentions that 80% of the global population uses traditional medicines at some point in their lives. It also claims that the protection of traditional knowledge can include IP-related measures as well as non-IP-related mechanisms. This study added that diverse objectives need to be considered for the promotion of public health goals by facilitating the use of and access to traditional medicines. However, the study did not examine the effects of TRIPS on traditional medicines. See for details, 'Intellectual Property Rights and Access to Medicines'.

of LDCs has received special attention, and they have been granted extensions to the transition period for TRIPS compliance, up to 1 July 2021 and until January 1, 2033 for the introduction of pharmaceutical patents. Despite having a waiver for pharmaceuticals since the establishment of the WTO, little progress has been made by most LDCs in terms of both affordability and innovative capacity in the pharmaceutical sector. Therefore, simply blaming the patent system will not deliver meaningful suggestions for the LDCs to improve their fragile healthcare sectors and low technological capabilities. It is undeniable that the pharmaceutical industry has an important role to play in the future development of new pharmaceuticals, and a patent system provides a mechanism through which to encourage R&D. All agree that a patent system must not become overprotective and so create a barrier for access to pharmaceuticals. Therefore the use of TRIPS flexibilities and government intervention options as indicated in this study may help to improve the affordability of medicines and encourage the local generic sector, but over-use of those safeguards could affect the funding of future R&D.

The Government of Bangladesh will need to promote R&D in its universities and research institutions and provide technical and financial assistance to support local pharmaceutical companies to develop innovative capacities that enable them not only to make pharmaceuticals relevant to country-specific diseases in Bangladesh, but also to export them to gain economies of scale and to continue further investment in R&D. Initially, LDCs such as Bangladesh could introduce process patent and utility model law along with institutional facilities (e.g. research incentives, technology transfer offices, patent fee waiver and patent application support, venture capital or start-up support) to encourage innovation by local companies. This in turn could help them to improve their innovative capabilities and increase competition among local companies, which might further generate research in sectors of vital importance in the country by way of cooperation between government, industry and universities, and public-private partnerships.

Therefore, further study is needed to explore the ways and means to encourage pharmaceutical companies in Bangladesh and in other LDCs to invest in R&D so as to develop new drugs for country-specific diseases (currently neglected by the developed countries' pharmaceutical industries) and make them available for poor people at an affordable price. However, it is difficult to resolve the conflicts between the two competing objectives—covering R&D costs and minimising consumer costs.

Within the present technological capabilities of the LDCs, it is difficult to predict more generally whether the IP system could play a role in stimulating the capacity of developing countries themselves to develop and produce drugs for neglected diseases. The R&D financing issue has a long history at the WHO, where it has been the subject of tough negotiations. Members generally agree that there is a market failure in which the financial incentive for companies to invest in research on neglected diseases is lacking, although members have spent years in disagreement over how to solve it. The WHO Commission on Macroeconomics and Health (CMH)[126] stated that a large injection of additional public funds into health services, infrastructure and research was required to address the health needs of developing countries. It took the view that patent protection offered little incentive for research on developing country diseases, in the absence of a significant market.[127] WHA 2012 welcomed a report from the CEWG to adopt a possible R&D treaty and sustainable financing for negligent diseases. However, disagreement between the parties on issues around adopting an R&D treaty meant that it slipped from the list of possible approaches. The CEWG resolution contains three areas of action: establishing a global health R&D observatory, setting up demonstration projects, and developing norms and standards to better collect data on health R&D.[128]

Regarding access to medicines, a CMH–WHO study favoured coordinated action to establish a system of differential pricing in favour of developing countries, backed up if necessary by the more extensive use of compulsory licensing.[129] However, extensive compulsory licensing may be counterproductive for encouraging investment and technology transfer in the pharmaceutical sector, and lack of innovative technological capabilities in most LDCs will prevent local pharmaceutical companies

---

126 See WHO, *Macroeconomics and Health: Investing in Health for Economic Development* (Geneva: Commission on Macroeconomics and Health, 2001), http://www.who.int/pmnch/knowledge/topics/2001_who_cmh/en/

127 Ibid.

128 See 'WHO Experts to Narrow R&D Projects for Developing Countries at December Meeting', *Intellectual Property Watch* (6 November 2013).

129 *Macroeconomics and Health.*

from utilising compulsory licenses to produce cheaper medicines. Thus, the creation of sound competitive market structures through competition law and enforcement could be more effective in both enhancing access to medical technology and fostering innovation in the pharmaceutical sector.[130] It can serve as a corrective tool if IP rights hinder competition, and thus constitute a potential barrier to innovation and access.[131] While adopting TRIPS-compliant patent law, LDCs need to ensure that their IP protection regimes do not run counter to their public health policies, and that they are consistent with and supportive of such policies.

Apart from establishing mutually supportive IP and health rules, Bangladesh may need to use public awareness campaigns for improving drug quality and explaining the rational use of medicines. There is also a need to integrate pharmacies (retail suppliers of medicines at the grass-roots level) and health professionals to ensure rational use and ethical prescription practices—as consumers in Bangladesh have a tendency towards self-medication—and to prevent unethical prescription practices by doctors. Bangladesh could also investigate the possibility of a campaign combined with a toll-free number for consumers to report bad quality and unauthorised drugs. These initiatives would also have a positive effect on the health sector in Bangladesh.

This study has analysed the pharmaceutical industry and the status of relevant laws and regulatory bodies in Brazil, China, India, South Africa and Bangladesh. Policy options explored in this study are expected to guide future capacity building in developing countries and the LDCs, in terms of legislative, institutional, infrastructural and broader policy goals to preserve local pharmaceutical industries and accomplish the twin aims of promoting local innovation and ensuring access to medicines. The outcomes of the this research may also be helpful in addressing the competitiveness of the pharmaceutical sector and, with some modifications to other sectors of vital importance in the LDCs, in establishing a plan of action for progression towards innovation and TRIPS compliance.

---

130 WIPO, WHO and WTO, *Trilateral Study, Promoting Access to Medical Technologies and Innovation—Intersections between Public Health, Intellectual Property and Trade* (2013).
131 Ibid.

Bibliography

About the MPP, Medicines Patent Pool, http://www.medicinespatentpool.org/about

About PMPRB, Patented Medicine Prices Review Board, http://pmprb-cepmb.gc.ca/home

'Domestic Legislation and Court Decisions on Intellectual Property and Public Health in South Africa', http://www.localpharmaproduction.net/fileadmin/dateien/Country_studies/Country_analysis_-_South_Africa.pdf [accessed 12 December 2013].

'Draft National Policy on Intellectual Property 2013' (South Africa), http://ipasa.co.za/wp-content/uploads/2013/07/IPASA-Extracts-from-Submission-made-on-the-DRAFT-NATIONAL-POLICY-ON-IP....pdf

Global Communication on HIV and the Law, Regional Issues Brief: Intellectual Property Rights and Access to Medicines' (17 February 2011), http://www.hivlawcommission.org/resources/aprd/IssuesBrief_IPR.pdf

Human Development Index (HDI), Human Development Reports, UNDP, http://hdr.undp.org/en/statistics/hdi

Abbott, F., 'The Doha Declaration on the TRIPS Agreement and Public Health: Lighting a Dark Corner at the WTO', *Journal of International Economic Law*, 5 (2002), 469–505, http://dx.doi.org/10.1093/jiel/5.2.469

—, 'Seizure of Generic Pharmaceuticals in Transit Based on Allegations of Patent Infringement: A Threat to International Trade, Development and Public Welfare', *WIPO Journal*, 1 (2009), 43–50, http://dx.doi.org/10.4337/9781849804929.00012

Abbot, Ryan, 'Potential Elements of the WHO Global R&D Treaty: Tailoring Solutions for Disparate Contexts', *Intellectual Property Watch* (29 January 2013), http://www.ip-watch.org/2013/01/29/potential-elements-of-the-who-global-rd-treaty-tailoring-solutions-for-disparate-contexts

Abhiyan, Jan Swasthya, National Coordination Committee, 'Access to Essential Medicines' 37 (February 2007), http://www.healthpolicy.cn/rdfx/jbywzd/gjjy2/yd/yjwx/201002/P020100227572014659949.pdf

Abramowicz, Michael, 'Perfecting Patent Prizes,' *Vanderbilt Law Review*, 56 (2003), 115–21, http://dx.doi.org/10.2139/ssrn.292079

Addor, Felix, 'Switzerland's Proposal for Disclosure of the Source of Genetic Resources and Traditional Knowledge in Patent Applications', in *Disclosure Requirements: Ensuring Mutual Supportiveness between the WTO TRIPS Agreement and the CBD*, ed. by Martha Chouchena-Rojas, Manuel Ruiz Muller, David Vivas, and Sebastian Winkler (Geneva: International Centre for Trade and Sustainable Development, 2005), pp. 35–40.

Afrin, Rafia, and Daniel Sabet, 'Will Bangladesh's New Competition Law Prove Effective?' (1 July 2012), http://ces.ulab.edu.bd/wp-content/uploads/sites/18/2015/07/Competition_law_07-12.pdf

Agutu, Omolo Joseph, 'Least Developed Countries and the TRIPS Agreement: Arguments for a Shift to Voluntary Compliance', *African Journal of International and Comparative Law*, 20.3 (2012), 423–47, http://dx.doi.org/10.3366/ajicl.2012.0044

Agarwala, Aditi, and Akhil Prasad, 'Patent versus Patients: Reflections on Blatant Patent Regime', *International Journal of Liability and Scientific Enquiry*, 2.2 (2009), 147–61, http://dx.doi.org/10.1504/ijlse.2009.023984

Ahmad, A.K. *Monaw-war Uddin, Competition, Regulation and the Role of the State: The Case of Bangladesh* (10 July 2011).

Ahammad, H., 'Foreign Exchange and Trade Policy Issues in a Developing Country: The Case of Bangladesh' (Working Paper No. 95/1, Canberra Research School of Pacific and Asian Studies, Australian National University, 1995).

Amran, Md Shah, *TRIPS*, 'Impacts of TRIPS on local Pharma sector' (27 January 2005), http://www.pharmabiz.com/article/detnews.asp?articleid=25958&sectionid=50

Anand, Grover, 'Anti-competitive Practices in Patent Licensing Arrangements and the Scope of Competition Law/Policy in Dealing with Them' (AMTC, National Workshop on Patent and Public Health, Ministry of Health, India, 11 April 2005).

Anderson, R.D., and H. Wager, 'Human Rights, Development and the WTO: The Cases of Intellectual Property and Competition Policy', *Journal of International Economic Law*, 9.3 (2006), 707–47, http://dx.doi.org/10.1093/jiel/jgl022

Anwar, Syed Farhat, 'Pharmaceutical Sector of Bangladesh: Trade Prospects with Nepal and the Impact of TRIPS', in *Towards Greater Sub Regional Economic Cooperation: Limitation, Obstacles and Benefits*, ed. by Forrest E. Cookson and A.K.M. Shamsul Alam (Dhaka: University Press Limited, 2002), pp. 217–58.

Armstrong, Chris, Jeremy de Beer, Dick Kawooya, Achal Prabhala, and Tobias Schonwetter, *Copyright and Access to Knowledge in Eight African Countries* (Claremont: UCT Press, 2010).

Arthurs, H.W., *Law and Learning: Report to the Social Sciences and Humanities Research Council of Canada by the Consultative Group on Research and Education in Law* (Ottawa: Social Sciences and Humanities Research Council of Canada, 1983).

Arundel, A., and G. van de Paal, *Innovation Strategies of Europe's Largest Industrial Firms* (unpublished manuscript, Maastricht Economic and Social Research and Training Centre, 1995).

Arvind, S., 'Putting Some Numbers on the TRIPS Pharmaceutical Debate', *International Journal of Technology Management*, 10 (1995), 252–68.

Ayres, Ian, and John Braithwaite, *Responsive Regulation: Transcending the Deregulation Debate* (Oxford: Oxford University Press, 1992).

Avafia, Tenu, Jonathan Berger, and Trudy Hartzenberg, 'The Ability of Select Sub-Saharan Africa Countries to Utilize TRIPS Flexibilities and Competition Law to Ensure a Sustainable Supply of Essential Medicines: A Study of Producing and Importing Countries' (tralac Working Paper No. 12/2006, August 2006), http://www.section27.org.za/wp-content/uploads/2010/10/Avafia-Berger-and-Hartzenberg.pdf

Azam, Mohammad Monirul, and Morshed Mahmud Khan, 'TRIPS Agreement and Protection of National Interest: Contention between Developed and Developing Countries', *The Chittagong University Journal of Law*, 5 (2000), 1–34.

—, 'Establishment of the WTO and Impacts on the Legal System of Bangladesh', *Macquarie Journal of Business Law*, 3 (2006), 23–45.

—, *Effectiveness of the Intellectual Property Enforcement Mechanisms under the TRIPS Agreement: The Context of Bangladesh* (Geneva: World Intellectual Property Organization Academy—Turin Research Paper Series, 2007), 102–57.

—, *Intellectual Property, WTO and Bangladesh* (Dhaka: New Warsi Book Co., 2008).

—, 'Revisiting the Climate Change Negotiation under the UNFCCC: In Search of Effective Framework for Negotiation and Technology Transfer' (2009), http://www.conference.unitar.org/yale/sites/conference.unitar.org.yale/files/Paper_Azam.pdf

—, 'Journey towards WTO Legal System and the Experience of Bangladesh: The Context of Intellectual Property' (The Society of International Economic Law 2010 Conference, International Economic Law and Policy [IELPO], University of Barcelona, 2010).

—, and Kristy Richardson, 'Access to Medicines and Pharmaceutical Patent Protection under the TRIPS Agreement: A Review of Literature on the Challenges for Least Developed Countries,' *Intellectual Property Forum Journal*, 84 (2011), 59–67.

—, 'Climate Change Resilience and Technology Transfer: The Role of Intellectual Property', *Nordic Journal of International Law*, 80.4 (2011), 485–505, http://dx.doi.org/10.1163/157181011x598445

—, 'Globalising Standard of Patent Protection in WTO Law and Policy Options for the LDCs', *Chicago-Kent Journal of Intellectual Property*, 13.2 (2014), 402–88.

—, 'The Experiences of Patent Law Reforms in Brazil, India and South Africa and Lessons for Bangladesh, *Akron Intellectual Property Journal*, 7.2 (2014), 61–100.

—, and Kristy Richardson, 'Pharmaceutical Patent Protection and TRIPS Challenges for Bangladesh: An Appraisal of Bangladesh's Patent Office and Department of Drug Administration', *Bond Law Review*, 22.2 (2010a), 1–15.

—, and Kristy Richardson, 'TRIPS Compliant Patent Law and the Pharmaceutical Industry in Bangladesh: Challenges and Opportunities', *LAWASIA Journal* (2010b), 141–54.

—, and Yacouba Sabere Mounkoro, 'Intellectual Property Protection for the Pharmaceuticals: An Economic and Legal Impacts Study with Special Reference to Bangladesh and Mali', *Le Griot Du Développement*, § 7.1.2 (June 1, 2012), http://legriotdudeveloppement.blogspot.co.uk/2012/06/intellectual-property-protection-for.html

—, and Mahesti Okitasari, 'Environmental Governance and National Preparedness towards 2030 Agenda for Sustainable Development: A Tale of Two Countries', *Global Environmental Research* 19.2 (2015), 217–25.

Baker, Dean, and Noriko Chatani, 'Promoting Good Ideas on Drugs: Are Patents the Best Way? The Relative Efficiency of Patent and Public Support for Bio-Medical Research' (briefing Paper, 2002), http://cepr.net/publications/reports/promoting-good-ideas-on-drugs-are-patents-the-best-way

Balat, Mohamed Abu El Farag, and Mohamad Hossam Loutfi, 'The TRIPS Agreement and Developing Countries: A Legal Analysis of the Impacts of the New IPR's Law on the Pharmaceutical Industry in Egypt', *2 Web JCILI* (2004).

Banta, D.H., 'Worldwide Interest in Global Access to Drugs', *The Journal of the American Medical Association*, 285.22 (2001), 2844–46, http://dx.doi.org/10.1001/jama.285.22.2844

Barai, Munim Kumar, 'Economic Liberalization and Macro Economic Stability in Bangladesh: An Overview' (Paper presented at the National Workshop of the Bangladesh Institute of International and Strategic Studies [BIISS], Dhaka, 29 February to 1 March 2000).

Barbosa, D.B., M. Chon, and A.M. von Hase, 'Slouching Towards Development in International Intellectual Property', *Michigan State Law Review*, 1 (2007), 114–23.

Barnes, Stephen, 'Note: Pharmaceutical Patents and TRIPS: A Comparison of India and South Africa', *Kentucky Law Journal*, 91 (2003), 911–34.

Basheer, Shamnad, and Mrinalini Kochupillai, 'TRIPS, Patents and Parallel Imports: A Proposal for Amendment', *Indian Journal of Intellectual Property Law*, 2 (2009), 63–86.

—, 'Indian Government Committee Says "No" to Data Exclusivity' (6 June 2007), http://spicyip.com/2007/06/indian-government-committee-says-no-to.html

—, 'India's Tryst with TRIPS: *The Patents (Amendment) Act, 2005*', *Indian Journal of Law and Technology*, 1 (2005), 15–30.

Bass, Naomi A., 'Implications of the TRIPS Agreement for Developing Countries: Pharmaceutical Patent Laws in Brazil and South Africa in the 21st Century', *George Washington International Law Review 34* (2002), 191–222.

Basso, Maristela, 'Intervention of Health Authorities in Patent Examination: The Brazilian Approach of the Prior Consent', *International Journal of Intellectual Property Management*, 1 (2006), 54–74, http://dx.doi.org/10.1504/ijipm.2006.011022

Bermudez, Jorge A. Z., and Oliveira, Maria Auxiliadora (eds.) *Intellectual Property in the Context of the WTO TRIPS Agreement: Challenges for Public Health* (Rio de Janeiro: Centre for Pharmaceutical Policies and WHO, 2004).

Bhatt, Shiv Raj, 'Nepal: Public Health under WTO', *South Asian Journal*, 11 (2006), 29–40.

Bhattacharya, Debapriya, and Lisa Borgatti, 'An Atypical Approach to Graduation from LDC Category: The Case of Bangladesh', *South Asia Economic Journal*, 13.1 (2012), 1–25, http://dx.doi.org/10.1177/139156141101300101

Biadgleng, Ermias, and Viviana Tellez, The Changing Structure and Governance of Intellectual Property Enforcement' (South Centre Research Paper No. 15, January 2008), http://papers.ssrn.com/sol3/papers.cfm?abstract_id=1210622

Blakeney, Michael, *Trade Related Aspects of Intellectual Property Rights: A Concise Guide to the TRIPS Agreement* (London: Sweet & Maxwell, 1996).

Blake, R., 'Integrating Quantitative and Qualitative Methods in Family Research', *Families Systems and Health*, 7.4 (1989), 411–27, http://dx.doi.org/10.1037/h0089788

Blanche, Martin Terre, and Kevin Durrheim, *Research in Practice: Applied Methods for the Social Sciences* (Cape Town: University of Cape Town Press, 1999).

Blismas, Nick G., and Andrew R.J. Dainty, 'Computer-aided Qualitative Data Analysis: Panacea or Paradox?', *Building Research and Information*, 31.6 (2003), 455–63, http://dx.doi.org/10.1080/0961321031000108816

Board of Investment, Bangladesh, *Market Overview: Bangladesh is Poised for Major Growth in its Pharmaceutical Industry*, http://www.boi.gov.bd/site/page/7b31d826-368c-4ed9-8077-d16310433060/Life-Science

Boldrin, Michele, and David K. Levine, *Against Intellectual Monopoly* (Cambridge: Cambridge University Press, 2008), http://dx.doi.org/10.1017/cbo9780511510854

Bond, Patrick, 'Globalization, Pharmaceutical Pricing, and South African Health Policy: Managing Confrontation with U.S. Firms and Politicians', *International Journal of Health Services*, 29 (1999), 765–92, http://dx.doi.org/10.2190/4ma6-53e3-le1x-c1yy

Boonfueng, Krithpaka, 'Parallel Imports in Pharmaceuticals: Increase Access to HIV Drugs', *Thailand Law Forum* (2010), http://www.thailawforum.com/articles/hivdrugs1.html

Braithwaite, John and Ian Ayres, *Responsive Regulation: Transcending the Deregulation Debate* (Oxford: Oxford University Press, 1992).

Branstetter, Lee G., R. Fisman, and C.F. Foley, 'Do Stronger Intellectual Property Rights Increase International Technology Transfer? Empirical Evidence from U.S. Firm-level Panel Data' (Working Paper No. 3305, World Bank Policy Research, 2004).

Brant, Jennifer and Malpani, Rohit, 'Eye on the Ball Medicine Regulation—Not IP Enforcement—Can Best Deliver Quality Medicines' (2 February 2011), http://www.oxfam.org/sites/www.oxfam.org/files/eye-on-the-ball-medicine-regulation-020211-en.pdf

Brezis, Mayer, 'Big Pharma and Health Care: Unsolvable Conflict of Interests Between Private Enterprise and Public Health', *Israel Journal of Psychiatry and Related Sciences*, 45 (2008), 83–94.

Bronckers, Marco C.E.J., 'The Exhaustion of Patent Rights under World Trade Organization Law', *Journal of World Trade Law*, 32.5 (1998), 137–59.

Browne, Dennis, 'Dispute Settlement in the WTO: How Friendly Is It for the LDCs?' (Paper No. 45, Centre for Policy Dialogue [CPD], January 2005).

Business Wire Pharmaceutical, 'Research and Markets: Pharmaceutical Pricing and Reimbursement in Brazil: Population and Demand for Pharmaceuticals is Forecast to Increase in the Next 12 Years' (Press Release, 5 January 2010), http://www.reuters.com/article/2010/01/25/idUS147453+25-Jan-2010+BW20100125

Cahoy, Daniel R., 'An Incrementalist Approach to Patent Reform Policy', *Journal of Legislation and Public Policy*, 9 (2006), 589–618.

Calvani, Terry and Alderman, Karen, 'BRIC in the International Merger Review Edifice', *Cornell International Law Journal*, 43 (2010), 73–145.

Cameron, Edwin, and Jonathan Berger, 'Patents and Public Health: Principle, Politics and Paradox', *SCRIPT-ed*, 1.4 (2004), 517–44, http://www2.law.ed.ac.uk/ahrc/script-ed/docs/cameron.asp

Caracelli, V.J., and J.C. Greene, 'Data Analysis Strategies for Mixed-method Evaluation Designs', *Educational Evaluation and Policy Analysis*, 15.2 (1993), 195–207, http://dx.doi.org/10.3102/01623737015002195

Carlson, Steven C., 'Note, Patent Pools and the Antitrust Dilemma', *Yale Journal on Regulation*, 16 (1999), 352–59.

Cassier, Maurice, and Marilena Correa, 'Intellectual Property and Public Health: Copying of HIV/AIDS Drugs by Brazilian Public and Private Pharmaceutical Laboratories,' *RECIIS Electronic Journal of Communication, Information and Innovation in Health*, 1.1 (2007), 83–90, http://dx.doi.org/10.3395/reciis.v1i1.38en

Chandra, Rajshree, 'The Role of National Laws in Reconciling Constitutional Right to Health with TRIPS Obligations: An Examination of the Glivec Patent Case in India', in *Incentives for Global Public Health—Patent Law and Access to Essential Medicines*, ed. by Thomas Pogge, Mathew Rimmer, and Kim Rubenstein (Cambridge: Cambridge University Press, 2010), pp. 381–405, http://dx.doi.org/10.1017/cbo9780511750786.018

Charmaz, Kathy, 'The Grounded Theory Method: An Explication and Interpretation', in *Contemporary Field Research: A Collection of Readings*, ed. by Robert M. Emerson (Beverly Hills, CA: Sage Publications, 1983), pp. 109–26.

Chaudhary, Abhilash, 'Compulsory Licensing of IPRS and Its Effect on Competition', http://cci.gov.in/images/media/ResearchReports/Compulsory Licensing of IPRs and Its Effect on Competition.pdf [accessed 8 September 2014].

Chaudhuri, Sudip, 'Indian Generic Companies, Affordability of Drugs and Local Production in Africa with Special Reference to Tanzania, IKD' (Working Paper No. 37, September 2008), http://oro.open.ac.uk/26384/2/

Chaudhuri, Sudip, *The Indian Pharmaceutical Industry—Post TRIPS* (Indian Institute of Management, 2009).

Chen, S. Wu, S. Hang, J. and Shi, L., 'Impact of Medical Data Protection on Drug Expenditure and Accessibility in China', *Chinese Journal of New Drugs*, 21.20 (2012), 2353–5.

Choudhuri, Subham, Pinelopi K. Goldberg, and Panle Jia, 'Estimating the Effects of Global Patent Protection in Pharmaceuticals: A Case Study of Quinolones in India' (Yale University, 2004), http://www.nber.org/papers/w10159

Chowdhury, Samson H., 'Progress in Pharmaceutical Industries in Bangladesh', *Korea Times* (27 March 2009), http://www.koreatimes.co.kr/www/news/include/print.asp?newsIdx=21326

Chowdhury, Zafarullah, *The Politics of Essential Drugs—The Makings of a Successful Health Strategy: Lessons from Bangladesh* (London: Zed Books, 1995).

Cohen, W.M., R.R. Nelson, and J. Walsh, 'Appropriability Conditions and Why Firms Patent and Why They Do Not in the U.S. Manufacturing Sector' (Working Paper, Carnegie Mellon University, 1997).

Cohen, Dani and Jennifer Cohen, 'Competition Commission Finds Pharmaceutical Firms in Contravention of the Competition Act' (Competition Commission, 2003), http://www.cptech.org/ip/health/sa/cc10162003.html

Commission on Intellectual Property Rights (CIPRS), *Integrating Intellectual Property Rights and Development—Final Report* (2002).

Commonwealth Tertiary Education Commission, *Report of the Working Party on Post-secondary Rural Education* (AGPS, November 1987).

Conconi, Paola, and Carlo Perroni, 'Self-enforcing International Agreements and Domestic Policy Credibility' (Working Paper No. 114/03, CSGR, July 2003).

Converse, J.M., and S. Presser, *Survey Questions: Handcrafting the Standardized Questionnaire* (Beverley Hills, CA: Sage, 1986).

Cooper, Helene, Rachel Zimmerman, and Laurie Mcginley, 'AIDS Epidemic Puts Drug Firms in a Vise: Treatment vs. Profits', *Wall Street Journal* (March 2, 2001).

Correa, Carlos, 'Integrating Public Health Concerns into Patent Legislations in Developing Countries' (Geneva: South Centre, Chernin du Charnpd' Anier 17, 1211, 2000), http://apps.who.int/medicinedocs/pdf/h2963e/h2963e.pdf

—, *Intellectual Property Rights, The WTO and Developing Countries: The TRIPS Agreement and Policy Options* (London: Zed Books, 2000).

—, *Protection of Data Submitted for the Registration of Pharmaceuticals: Implementing the Standards of the Trips Agreement* (Geneva: South Centre, 2002)

—, 'The WTO Dispute Settlement Mechanism TRIPS Rulings and the Developing Countries', *The Journal of World Intellectual Property*, 4 (2001), 239–54, http://dx.doi.org/10.1111/j.1747-1796.2001.tb00088.x

—, 'Protecting Test Data for Pharmaceutical and Agrochemical Products under Free Trade Agreements, UNCTAD–ICTSD Dialogue on Moving the Pro-development IP Agenda Forward: Preserving Public Goods in Health, Education and Learning' (United Nations Conference on Trade and Development, 29 November to 3 December 2004), http://www.iprsonline.org/unctadictsd/bellagio/docs/Correa_Bellagio4.pdf

—, 'Guidelines for the Examination of Pharmaceutical Patents: Developing a Public Health Perspective: A Working Paper' (WHO ICTSD UNCTAD (January, 2007) http://ictsd.net/downloads/2008/04/correa_pharmaceutical-patents-guidelines.pdf

—, 'Intellectual Property in LDCs: Strategies for Enhancing Technology Transfer and Dissemination', 3, 18 (UNCTAD The Least Developed Countries Report 2007, Background Paper No. 4, 2007), http://unctad.org/Sections/ldc_dir/docs/ldcr2007_Correa_en.pdf

—, 'Intellectual Property and Competition Law: Exploration of Some Issues of Relevance to Developing Countries' (Geneva: International Centre for Trade and Sustainable Development, 2007), http://www.iprsonline.org/resources/docs/corea_Oct07.pdf

—, 'TRIPS and R&D Incentives in the Pharmaceutical Sector' (Communication on Macroeconomics and Health, Working Paper No. WG2:11, November 2011), http://library.cphs.chula.ac.th/Ebooks/HealthCareFinancing/Working Paper_WG2/WG2_11.pdf

—, and Yusuf Abdulqawi A. (eds.) *Intellectual Property and international Trade: TRIPs Agreement* (London: Kluwer Law International, 1998).

Cotterrell, Roger, 'Why Must Legal Ideas Be Interpreted Sociologically?', *Journal of Law and Society*, 25.2 (1998), 171–92, http://dx.doi.org/10.1111/1467-6478.00086

Cottier, Thomas, and Ingo Meitinger, 'The TRIPS Agreement without a Competition Agreement' (Paper presented at the Trade and Competition in the World Trade Organization and Beyond, Venice, 4–5 December 1998).

—, 'From Progressive Liberalization to Progressive Regulation in WTO Law', *Journal of International Economic Law*, 9.4 (2006), 779–821, http://dx.doi.org/10.1093/jiel/jgl029

—, 'The Exhaustion of Intellectual Property Rights—A Fresh Look', *IIC International Review of Intellectual Property and Competition*, 39 (2008), 755–57.

—, Lalani Shaheeza, and Michelangelo Temmerman, 'Use It or Lose It? Assessing the Compatibility of the Paris Convention and TRIPS with Respect to Local Working Requirements' (Working Paper, World Trade Institute, University of Bern, 18 February 2013), http://dx.doi.org/10.1093/jiel/jgu026

Cotula, Lorenzo, 'Property Rights, Negotiating Power and Foreign Investment: An International and Comparative law Study on Africa' (Unpublished doctoral thesis, University of Edinburgh School of Law, 2009).

Cownie, F., *Legal Academics: Culture and Identities* (Oxford and Portland, Oregon: Hart Publishing, 2004).

Cox, Krista L., 'The Medicines Patent Pool: Promoting Access and Innovation for Life-saving Medicines through Voluntary Licenses,' *Hastings Science and Technology Law Journal*, 4 (2012), 292–325.

Creswell, John W., and Vicki L. Plano Clark, *Designing and Conducting Mixed Methods Research* (London and Washington, DC: Sage Publications, 2007).

Creswell, John W., *Research Design: Qualitative, Quantitative, and Mixed Methods Approaches* (London and Washington, DC: Sage Publications, 2009).

Crosland, Maurice, and Antonio Galvez, 'The Emergence of Research Grants Within the Prize System of the French Academy of Sciences', *Social Studies of Science*, 19 (1989), 71–100, http://dx.doi.org/10.1177/030631289019001002

Cullet, Philippe, 'Patent Bill, TRIPS and Right to Health', *Economic and Political Weekly*, 36.43 (27 October 2001), http://www.ielrc.org/content/a0108.pdf

Danzon, Patricia and Michael Furakawa, 'Prices and Availability of Pharmaceuticals', *Health Affairs*, 27 (2008), 221–25, http://dx.doi.org/10.1377/hlthaff.27.1.221

Davis, Lee N., 'Should We Consider Alternative Incentives for Basic Research? Patents vs. Prizes' (Paper presented at the DRUID Summer Conference, 6–8 June 2002).

Dent, Chris, 'An Exploration of the Principles, Precepts and Purposes that Provide Structure to the Patent System', *Intellectual Property Quarterly*, 4 (2008), 456–77, http://dx.doi.org/10.2139/ssrn.1371925

Descombe, M., *The Good Research Guide: For Small-scale Social Research Projects* (Berkshire and New York: Open University Press, 1998).

Dorji, Tandi, 'Effect of TRIPS on Pricing, Affordability and Access to Essential Medicines in Bhutan', *Journal of Bhutan Studies*, 16 (2007), 128–41.

Drahos, Peter, 'BITS and BIPS: Bilateralism in Intellectual Property', *Journal of World Intellectual Property*, 4 (2001), 791–801, http://dx.doi.org/10.1111/j.1747-1796.2001.tb00138.x

—, and John Braithwaite, 'Intellectual Property, Corporate Strategy, Globalisation: TRIPs in Context', *Wisconsin International Law Journal*, 20.3 (2002), 451–80.

—, 'Developing Countries and International Intellectual Property Standard Setting' (Study Paper No. 8, CIPRS).

Dreyfuss, Rochelle Cooper, 'The Role of India, China, Brazil and Other Emerging Economies in Establishing Access Norms and Intellectual Property and Intellectual Property Law Making' (IICJ Working Paper, 2009), http://papers.ssrn.com/sol3/papers.cfm?abstract_id=1442785

Driscoll, David L., Afua Appiah-Yeboah, Philip Salib, and Douglas J. Rupert, 'Merging Qualitative and Quantitative Data in Mixed Methods Research: How To and Why Not', *Ecological and Environmental Anthropology*, 3.1 (2007), 19–28.

Duke, Lynne, 'Nkosazana Zuma—Activist Health Minister Draws Foes in S. Africa', *Washington Post* (11 December 1998).

Dutfield, Graham, 'Delivering Drugs to the Poor: Will the TRIPS Amendment Help?', *Journal of Law and Medicine*, 34.2 (2008), 107–24.

Edwards, Monica, Luis M. Sánchez-Ruiz, and Enrique Ballester-Sarrias, 'Analyzing the Obstacles for the Academic and Organizational Change in Universities' (Paper presented at the International Conference on Engineering Education—ICEE 2007, Coimbra, 3–7 September 2007).

Elbeshbishi, Amal Nagah, 'TRIPS and Public Health—What Should African Countries Do?' (Work in Progress No. 49, African Trade Policy Centre, January 2007).

Ellis, Karen, Rohit Singh, Shaikh Eskander, and Iftekharul Huq, *Assessing the Economic Impact of Competition: Findings from Bangladesh* (ODI, 2010).

El-Said, Mohammed, 'The Road from TRIPS-Minus, to TRIPS, to TRIPS-Plus Implications of IPRs for the Arab World', *The Journal of World Intellectual Property*, 4 (2001), 53–79, http://dx.doi.org/10.1111/j.1747-1796.2005.tb00237.x

—, *Public Health Related TRIPS-Plus Provisions in Bilateral Trade Agreements: A Policy Guide for Negotiators and Implementers in the Eastern Mediterranean Region* (WHO and ICTSD, 2010).

Faiz, Kermani, 'Brazil—Not a Market for Faint Hearted' (Contract Pharma, October, 2005).

Farlow, Andrew, 'A Global Medical Research and Development Treaty: An Answer to Global Health Needs?' (IPN Working Paper on Intellectual Property, Innovation and Health, 2007), http://www.andrewfarlow.com/global_medical_research_treaty.pdf

Fasan, Olu, 'Commitment and Compliance in International Law: A Study of the Implementation of the WTO TRIPS Agreement in Nigeria and South Africa', *African Journal of International and Comparative Law*, 20.2 (2012), 191–228, http://dx.doi.org/10.3366/ajicl.2012.0031

Ferranti, David de, 'Can Patent Pools Get More AIDS Drugs to Patients?', *Huffington Post* (9 April 2012), http://www.huffingtonpost.com/david-de-ferranti/aids-drugs_b_1404218.html

Ferreira, L., 'Access to Affordable HIV/AIDS Drugs: The Human Rights Obligations of Multinational Pharmaceutical Corporations', *Fordham Law Review*, 71.3 (2002), 1133–79.

Fink, C., 'How Stronger Patent Protection in India Might Affect the Behavior of Transnational Pharmaceutical Industries' (Working Paper No. 2352, World Bank, 2000), http://elibrary.worldbank.org/doi/abs/10.1596/1813-9450-2352

Finston, Susan, 'India: A Cautionary Tale on the Critical Importance of Intellectual Property Protection', *Fordham Intellectual Property, Media and Entertainment Law Journal*, 12 (2002), 887–95.

Fisher, William W., and Talha Syed, 'A Prize System as a Partial Solution to the Health Crisis in the Developing World' (Discussion Paper No. 5, Petrie-Flom Center for Health Law Policy, Biotechnology and Bioethics at Harvard Law School, 2009), https://www.law.berkeley.edu/files/Fisher_Prizes12.pdf

—, and Cyrill P. Rigamonti, 'The South Africa AIDS Controversy: A Case Study in Patent Law and Policy, Harvard Law School' (10 February 2005), http://cyber.law.harvard.edu/people/tfisher/South Africa.pdf

Flynn, Mathew, 'Corporate Power and State Resistance: Brazil's Use of TRIPS Flexibilities for Its National AIDS Program', in *Intellectual Property, Pharmaceuticals and Public Health*, ed. by Kenneth C. Shadlen, Samira Guennif, Alenka Guzman, and N. Lalitha (Cheltenham: Edward Elgar, 2011), pp. 149–77, http://dx.doi.org/10.4337/9780857938619.00011

Ford, Matthew W., and Bertie M. Greer, 'Profiling Change: An Empirical Study of Change Process Patterns', *Journal of Applied Behavioural Science*, 42.4 (2006), 445–67, http://dx.doi.org/10.1177/0021886306293437

Fukuda-Parr, Sakiko, 'The Human Development Paradigm: Operationalizing Sen's Ideas on Capabilities', *Feminist Economics*, 9 (2003), 301–03, http://dx.doi.org/10.1080/1354570022000077980

Gao, Yafei, *The Conflict and Coordination between Biological Pharmacy's Intellectual Property Protection and Public Health* (Peking: Peking University Press, October 2011).

Garrison, Christopher, 'Exception to Patent Rights in Developing Countries' (Issue Paper No. 17, UNCTAD–ICTSD Project on IPR and Sustainable Development, 2006), http://www.unctad.org/en/docs/iteipc200612_en.pdf

GATT, Negotiating Group on TRIPs, 'Including Trade in Counterfeit Goods', *Meeting of Negotiating Group of 11–13 September 1989*, GATT Doc. MTN.GNG/ NG11/15, p. 20 (26 October 1989), https://www.wto.org/gatt_docs/English/ SULPDF/92080131.pdf

Gerhardsen, Tove Iren S., 'Developing Countries Propose TRIPS Amendment on Disclosure', *Intellectual Property Watch* (1 June 2006, 1344), http://www. ip-watch.org/2006/06/01/developing-countries-propose-trips-amendment- on-disclosure

Ghosh, Goutam, 'Patent Pool: A Technology Management Option for Developing New Therapeutics' (12 November 2010), http://www.btc.iitkgp. ernet.in/dey/abstracts/14.pdf

Goswami, Rajdeep, 'Compliance of TRIPS in Indian Patent Law' (29 April 2012), http://www.legalservicesindia.com/article/article/compliance-of-trips-in- indian-patent-law-1103-1.html

Giust, John E., 'Non-compliance with TRIPs by Developed and Developing Countries: Is TRIPs Working?', *Indiana International and Comparative Law Review*, 69.95 (1997), 69–97.

Gonzalez, Javier Lopez, Maximillano Mendez Parra, and Anirudh Shingal, 'TRIPS and Special and Differential Treatment—Revisiting the Case for Derogations in Applying Patent Protection for Pharmaceuticals in Developing Countries' (Draft Working Paper No. 2011–37, NCCR Trade Regulation, 2011).

Gopakumar, K.M., 'TRIPS Implementation and Public Health Safeguards' in *South Asian Year Book of Trade and Development*, ed. by B.S. Chimni, Mustafizur Rahman, and Linu Mathew Philip (New Delhi: Academic Foundation, 2005), pp. 233–59.

—, 'Product Patents and Access to Medicines in India: A Critical Review of the Implementation of TRIPS Patent Regime' *The Law and Development Review*, 3.2 (2010), 324–68.

Government of India, Directorate General of Foreign Trade, 'India—The Generics Pharma Capital of the World' (Pharmaceutical Exports Report, IDMA, Mumbai, India, 2010), http://dgftcom.nic.in

Grace, C., 'Update on China and India and Access to Medicines' (Briefing Paper, DFID/HSRC, November 2005), 1–42.

Greene, J., V. Caracelli, and W. Graham, 'Toward a Conceptual Framework for Mixed-methods Evaluation Designs', *Educational Evaluation and Policy Analysis*, 11 (1989), 255–74, http://dx.doi.org/10.3102/01623737011003255

Grover, Anand, *Anti-competitive Practices in Patent Licensing Arrangements and the Scope of Competition Law/Policy in Dealing with them* (AMTC, National Workshop on Patent and Public Health, Ministry of Health, India, 11 April 2005).

Guell, Robert C., and Marvin Fischbaum, 'Toward Allocative Efficiency in the Prescription Drug Industry', *Milbank Quarterly*, 73.2 (1995), 213–30, http://dx.doi.org/10.2307/3350257

Gupta, Amit Sen, 'Should Drug Prices be Controlled?', *Economic Times* (6 August 2002), http://articles.economictimes.indiatimes.com/2002-08-06/news/27340990_1_drug-prices-price-controls-drug-companie

Gupta, V.K., 'Traditional Knowledge Documentation and Defensive Protection: An Example from India' (June 2011), http://www.wipo.int/edocs/mdocs/tk/en/wipo_tk_mct_11/wipo_tk_mct_11_ref_t_5_1.pdf

—, *Intellectual Property and Sustainable Development: Documentation and Registration of TK and Traditional Cultural Expressions* (12 December 2011), http://www.wipo.int/edocs/mdocs/tk/en/wipo_tk_mct_11/wipo_tk_mct_11_ref_t_5_1.pdf

Haider, Shawkat, 'Access to Medicines for All', *Dhaka Tribune* (20 November 2015), http://www.dhakatribune.com/op-ed/2015/nov/20/access-medicine-all

Hansen, Emily, and Clarissa Hughes, *Interviews in Qualitative Research*, The Primary Health Care Research, Evaluation and Development Strategy, University of Tasmania (11 September 2009).

Hart, H.L.A., *The Concept of Law* (Oxford: Oxford University Press, 1961).

Hasan, Nazmul, 'National Case Studies on the Institutional Framework and Procedures Regulating Access to Pharmaceutical Products Needed to Address Public Health Problems' (Dhaka, Bangladesh, 2000).

—, 'Post 2005: Great Time ahead for Exports', *Pharmabiz* (27 January 2005), http://www.pharmabiz.com/article/detnews.asp?articleid=25953&sectionid=50&z=y

—, 'Bangladesh—An Emerging Country for Generics' (12 June 2010), http://www.jacobfleming.com/buxus/docs/downloads/case-study-smgenerics-nazmul-hassan-finalapproed.pdf

—, 'Future Prospects of Pharmaceutical Industry in Bangladesh' (2010), http://documents.mx/documents/future-prospects.html

Hasina, Sheikh, Prime Minister of Bangladesh, 'Speech to the Sixty-fourth World Health Assembly' (May 17 2011), http://www.who.int/mediacentre/events/2011/wha64/sheikh_hasina_speech_20110517/en/index.html

Hassett, Kevin A., *Price Controls and the Evolution of Pharmaceutical Markets* (American Enterprise Institute, 2004), http://www.who.int/intellectual property/news/en/Submission-Hassett.pdf

Hawkins, Loraine, 'WHO/HAI Project on Medicine Prices and Availability Review Series on Pharmaceutical Pricing Policies and Interventions' (Working Paper No. 4, Competition Policy, May 2011).

Helfer, L.R., 'Towards a Human Rights Framework for Intellectual Property', *UC Davis Law Review*, 40.3 (2007), 971–1020.

Heller, M.A., and R.S. Eisenberg, 'Can Patents Deter Innovation? The Anti-commons in Biomedical Research', *Science*, 280 (1998), 698–701, http://dx.doi.org/10.1126/science.280.5364.698

Hepburn, Jonathan, 'A TRIPS Agenda for Development: Meeting Food, Health and Biodiversity Needs' (a report of the conference organized by The Netherlands Ministry of Foreign Affairs and The Quaker United Nations Office [QUNO], 2001).

Hestermeyer, Holger, *Human Rights and the WTO: The Case of Patents and Access to Medicines* (Oxford: Oxford University Press, 2007), http://dx.doi.org/10.1093/acprof:oso/9780199552177.003.0001

Hodges, David A., 'Industry-University Cooperation, and the Emergence of Start-up Companies' (Public Symposium at Research Institute of Economy, Trade, and Industry, Tokyo, December 2011), http://www.rieti.go.jp/en/events/01121101/Hodges_final.pdf

Hoekman, Bernard, and Michel Kosteki, *The Political Economy of the World Trading System* (Oxford: Oxford University Press, 1995), http://dx.doi.org/10.1093/019829431x.001.0001

Hoen, Ellen T., *The Global Politics of Pharmaceutical Monopoly Power* (Diemen: AMB Publishers, 2009).

Hold, Arno, and Mercurio, Bryan Christopher, 'Transitioning to Intellectual Property: How Can the WTO Integrate Least Developed Countries into TRIPS?' (Working Paper No. 2012/37, World Trade Institute [WTI], October 2012).

Hollis, Aidan, 'An Efficient Reward System for Pharmaceutical Innovation' 6 (10 June 2004) (unpublished manuscript), http://www.who.int/intellectual property/news/Submission-Hollis6-Oct.pdf

Hossain, Shakhawat, 'No Enforcement of Laws on Food Adulteration, Children, Fair Trade', *The New Age* (19 May 2014), http://newagebd.net/12634/no-enforcement-of-laws-on-food-adulteration-children-fair-trade/#sthash.IMYI3DvK.dpuf

Huberman, Michael, and Matthew B. Miles (eds.), *The Qualitative Researcher's Companion* (London: Sage, 2002), http://dx.doi.org/10.4135/9781412986274

Hutchinson, Terry, and Nigel Duncan, 'Defining What We Do—Doctrinal Legal Research' (Australian Law Teachers Conference, 2010).

Imam, K.H., 'Some Aspects of the Foreign Trade Policies of Bangladesh', in *The Economic Development of Bangladesh Within a Socialist Framework*, ed. by E.A.G. Robinson and Keith Griffin (New York: Halsted Press, 1974), pp. 289–308, http://dx.doi.org/10.1007/978-1-349-02363-9_11

Islam, Mohammad Towhidul, 'TRIPS Agreement and Public Health: Implications and Challenges for Bangladesh', *International Trade Law and Regulation*, 17.1 (2011), 10–39.

Islam, Muinul, *Prantio Punjibadi Rashtro O Onunnayan Proshongo* (Dhaka: Pa[yrus Publishers, 2003).

Jackson, John H., *The Jurisprudence of GATT and the WTO* (Cambridge: Cambridge University Press, 2000).

Jain, Dipika, 'Access to Drugs in India: Exploration of Compulsory Licensing as an Effective Tool' (LLM Paper, Harvard Law School, 2009).

Jayashree, Watal, *Intellectual Property Rights in the WTO and Developing Countries* (Oxford: Oxford University Press, 2001).

Johnson, R. Burke, and Anthony J. Onwuegbuzie, 'Mixed Methods Research: A Research Paradigm Whose Time Has Come', *Educational Researcher*, 33.7 (2004), 14–26, http://dx.doi.org/10.3102/0013189x033007014

Jones, Emily, 'Signing Away the Future: How Trade and Investment Agreements Between Rich and Poor Countries Undermine Development' (Oxfam Briefing Paper No. 101, March 2007), http://www.oxfam.org/sites/www.oxfam.org/files/Signing Away the Future.pdf

Jones, M.L., 'Using Software to Analyse Qualitative Data', *Malaysian Journal of Qualitative Research*, 1.1 (2007), 64–76.

Joseph, Reji K., 'India's Trade in Drugs and Pharmaceuticals: Emerging Trends, Opportunities and Challenges' (Discussion Paper No. 159, Research Information System for Developing Countries, 2009).

Kalam, Abul, 'Challenges of the Age of Globalization', *Regional Studies*, 19.4 (2001), 35–51.

Kalam, Abul, *Globalisation and Bangladesh, Dhaka* (Dhaka: Palok, 2002).

Kapczynski, Amy, Samantha Chaifetz, Zachary Katz, and Yochai Benkler, 'Addressing Global Health Inequities: An Open Licensing Approach for University Innovations', *Berkeley Technology Law Journal*, 20 (2005), 1032–113.

Kathuria, Sanjay and Mariem Mezghenni Malouche, 'Toward New Sources of Competitiveness in Bangladesh: Key Insights of the Diagnostic Trade Integration Study' (2016), https://openknowledge.worldbank.org/handle/10986/22712

Khan, Jashim Uddin, 'New Patent Rights of Drug Suspended', *The Daily Star* (14 March 2008), http://www.thedailystar.net/news-detail-27621

Khan, Md Farhad Hossain, 'IP Administration and Enforcement System: Towards Modernisation of IP Protection in Bangladesh and A Comparative Analysis of IP Administration between Japan and Bangladesh' (a fellowship report, Tokyo Institute of Technology, 1 April to 30 September 2004).

—, and Yoshitoshi Tanaka, 'IP Administration and Enforcement System towards Modernization of IP Protection in Bangladesh and a Comparison of IP Situation between Japan and Bangladesh', *IP Management Review*, 2 (2004), 1–15.

Khan, Zorina, 'Premium Inventions: Patents and Prizes as Incentive Mechanisms in Britain and the United States, 1750–1930' (24 November 2010), http://people.hss.caltech.edu/~jlr/courses/questions/khan.pdf

Khor, Martin, 'Rethinking Intellectual Property Rights and TRIPS', in *Global Intellectual Property Rights—Knowledge, Access and Development*, ed. by Peter Drahos and Ruth Mayne (New York: Palgrave Macmillan, 2002), pp. 201–13.

Klug, Heinz, 'Pharmaceutical Production and Access to Essential Medicines in South Africa', in *Intellectual Property, Pharmaceuticals and Public Health— Access to Drugs in Developing Countries*, ed. by Kenneth C. Shadlen, Samira Guennif, Alenka Guzman and N. Lalitha (Cheltenham: Edward Elgar, 2011), pp. 29–55.

Kongolo, T., 'Public Interest versus the Pharmaceutical Industry's Monopoly in South Africa' *Journal of World Intellectual Property*, 4 (2001), 605–16, http://dx.doi.org/10.1111/j.1747-1796.2001.tb00130.x

Kontic, Sasha, 'An Analysis of the Generic Pharmaceutical Industries in Brazil and China in the Context of TRIPS and HIV/AIDS', https://www.law.utoronto.ca/documents/ihrp/HIV_kontic.doc

Krikorian, Gaelle P. and Szymkowiak, Dorota M., 'Intellectual Property Rights in the Making: The Evolution of Intellectual Property Provisions in US Free Trade Agreements and Access to Medicine', *Journal of Intellectual Property Law*, 10 (2007), 388–418.

Kuanpoth, Jakkrit, 'Intellectual Property Rights and Pharmaceuticals: A Thai Perspective on Prices and Technological Capability', *Thailand Law Journal*, 11.2 (2008), 55–84.

—, *Patent Rights in Pharmaceuticals in Developing Countries: Major Challenges for the Future* (Cheltenham: Edward Elgar, 2010), http://dx.doi.org/10.4337/9781849808958

Kumar, K. Suresh, 'Patent Laws and Research Exemption Imperative—Do Scientists Have Enough Freedom to Operate?', *Current Science*, 99 (2010), 1488–524.

Kumar, Swarup, 'Compulsory Licensing Provision under TRIPS: A Study of Roche vs Natco Case in India vis-à-vis the Applicability of the Principle of *Audi Alteram Partem*', *SCRIPT-ed*, 7.1 (2010), 135–54.

Lahouel, Mohamed, and Keith E. Maskus, 'Competition Policy and Intellectual Property Rights in Developing Countries: Interests in Unilateral Initiatives and a WTO Agreement' (Paper presented at the WTO/World Bank Conference on Developing Countries in a Millennium Round, 20–21 September 1999).

Lalitha, N., 'Doha Declaration and Public Health Issues', *Journal of Intellectual Property Rights*, 13 (2008), 401–13.

—, 'TRIPS and Pharmaceutical Industry: Issues and Prospects' (12 December 2009), http://www.iprsonline.org/ictsd/docs/ResourcesHealthArticleLalitha.doc

—, 'Access to Indian Generic Drugs: Emerging Issues', in *Intellectual Property, Pharmaceuticals and Public Health*, ed. by Kenneth C. Shadlen, Samira Guennif, Alenka Guzman and N. Lalitha (Cheltenham: Edward Elgar, 2011), pp. 225–52, http://dx.doi.org/10.4337/9780857938619.00014

Lall, Sanjaya, 'Indicators of the Relative Importance of IPRs in Developing Countries' (UNCTAD-ICTSD Project on IPRs and Sustainable Development, 1 June 2003), http://dx.doi.org/10.7215/ip_ip_20030601b

Lanjouw, Jane O., 'The Introduction of Pharmaceutical Product Patents in India: "Heartless Exploitation of the Poor and Suffering"?' (Working Paper No. 6366, Yale University and the NBER, 26 August 1997), http://dx.doi.org/10.3386/w6366

Lee, Thomas H., '"Me-too" Products: Friend or Foe?', *New England Journal of Medicine*, 350.3 (2004), 211–12, http://dx.doi.org/10.1056/nejm200405133502019

Lee, Ting-Ting, 'Adopting a Personal Digital Assistant System: Application of Lewin's Change Theory', *Journal of Advanced Nursing* 55.4 (2006), 487–96, http://dx.doi.org/10.1111/j.1365-2648.2006.03935.x

Leesti M. and Pengelly, T., 'Assessing Technical Assistance Needs for Implementing the TRIPS Agreement in LDCs' (ICTSD Programme on Intellectual Property Rights and Sustainable Development, International Centre for Trade and Sustainable Development, Geneva, Switzerland 2007).

Lewin, K., 'Frontiers in Group Dynamics II. Channels of Group Life; Social Planning and Action Research', *Human Relations*, 1.1 (1947), 5–40.

Li, Xuan, 'The Impact of Higher Standards in Patent Protection for Pharmaceutical Industries under the TRIPS Agreement—A Comparative Study of China and India', *The World Economy*, 31.10 (2008), 1367–92, http://dx.doi.org/10.1111/j.1467-9701.2008.01133.x

Lorenzi, N.M., R.T. Riley, A.J.C. Blyth, G. Southon, and B.J. Dixon, 'Antecedents of the People and Organizational Aspects of Medical Informatics: Review of the Literature', *Journal of American Medical Informatics Association*, 4.2 (1997), 79–93, http://dx.doi.org/10.1136/jamia.1997.0040079

Love, James, 'Remuneration Guidelines for Non-voluntary Use of a Patent on Medical Technologies' (Health Economics and Drugs, TCM series no. 18, 2005), http://www.who.int/medicines/areas/technical_cooperation/WHO TCM2005.1_OMS.pdf

—, 'WHO Negotiators Propose Putting off R&D Treaty Discussions until 2016' (Knowledge Ecology International, 28 November 2012), http://keionline.org/node/1612

Lu, Bingbin, 'Best Mode Disclosure for Patent Applications: An International and Comparative Perspective', *Journal of Intellectual Property Rights*, 16 (2011), 409–17.

Madely, John, *Hungry for Trade* (London: Zed Books, 2000).

Maggi, Giovanni, and Andres Rodriguez-Clare, 'The Value of Trade Agreements in the Presence of Political Pressures', *Journal of Political Economy*, 106.3 (1998), 574–601, http://dx.doi.org/10.1086/250022

Malpani, Rohit, 'All Costs, No Benefits: How TRIPS-plus Intellectual Property Rules in the US–Jordan FTA Affect Access to Medicines', 11 (Oxfam Briefing Paper No. 102, 21 March 2007), http://www.oxfam.org/sites/www.oxfam.org/files/all costs, no benefits.pdf

Mahmud, Wahiduddin, 'Has Bangladesh Gained from its LDC status?' *The Daily Star* (28 May 2010).

Mansfield, Edwin, 'Patents and Innovation: An Empirical Study', *Management Science*, 32.2 (1986), 173–81, http://dx.doi.org/10.1287/mnsc.32.2.173

—, 'Intellectual Property Protection, Direct Investment and Technology Transfer: Germany, Japan and the United States' (Discussion Paper No. 27, World Bank and International Finance Corporation, 1995).

Martinez, Ana Paula, 'Abuse of Dominance: The Third Wave of Brazil's Antitrust Enforcement?', *Competition Law International*, 9 (2013), 168–81.

Maskus Keith E. and Denise Eby-Konan, 'Trade-related Intellectual Property Rights: Issues and Exploratory Results', in *Analytical and Negotiating Issues in the Global Trading System*, ed. by Alan V. Deardorff and Robert M. Stern (Ann Arbor, MI: University of Michigan Press 1994), pp. 401–54.

—, S.M. Dougherty, and A. Mertha, 'Intellectual Property Rights and Economic Development in China', in *Intellectual Property and Development: Lessons from Recent Economic Research*, ed. by C. Fink and K.E. Maskus (Washington, DC: World Bank and Oxford University Press, 2005), http://dx.doi.org/10.1596/0-8213-5772-7

Masum, H., and R. Harris, *Open Source for Neglected Diseases: Magic Bullet or Mirage?* (Washington, DC: Results for Development Institute, 2011).

Maurer S.M., A. Rai, and A. Sali, 'Finding Cures for Tropical Diseases: Is Open Source an Answer?', *PLoS Med*, 1.3 (2004), e56, http://dx.doi.org/10.1371/journal.pmed.0010056

May, Christopher and Susan K. Sell, *Intellectual Property Rights: A Critical History* (Boulder, CO: Lynne Rienner Pub. 2005).

Maynard, Alan, and Karen Bloor, 'Dilemmas in Regulation of the Market for Pharmaceuticals', *Health Affairs*, 22.3 (2003), 31–41, http://dx.doi.org/10.1377/hlthaff.22.3.31

Mazumdar, Satyajeet, 'Bolar Provisions (Patents): Position in Different Countries and Case Laws' (24 December 2009), http://knol.google.com/k/satyajeet-mazumdar/bolar-provisions-patents/3cc0jmgzt3vqu/6 [accessed on December 2015].

McConville, Mike, and Hong Chui Wing (eds.), *Research Methods for Law* (Edinburgh: Edinburgh University Press, 2007).

McKinsey and Company, 'Bangladesh's Ready-made Garments Landscape: The Challenge of Growth' (2011) http://www.mckinsey.de/sites/mck_files/files/2011_McKinsey_Bangladesh.pdf

Mercurio, Bryan, 'Resolving the Public Health Crisis in the Developing World: Problems and Barriers of Access to Essential Medicines', *Northwestern University Journal of International Human Rights*, 5 (2006), 1–40, http://dx.doi.org/10.2139/ssrn.980175

Mittal, Anshull, 'Patent Linkage in India: Current Scenario and Need for Deliberation', *Journal of Intellectual Property Rights*, 15 (2010), 187–96.

Moon S., J. Bermudez, E. 't Hoen, 'Innovation and Access to Medicines for Neglected Populations: Could a Treaty Address a Broken Pharmaceutical R&D System?' *PLoS Med* 9.5 (2012), e1001218 http://dx.doi.org/10.1371/journal.pmed.1001218

Moon, Suerie, 'Does Article 66.2 Encourage Technology Transfer to LDCs? An Analysis of Country Submissions to the TRIPS Council (1999–2007)' (UNCTAD/ICTSD Project on IPRs, and Policy Brief Number 2 2008).

Morton, Fiona M. Scott 'The Problems of Price Controls', Regulation 50 (2001), http://object.cato.org/sites/cato.org/files/serials/files/regulation/2001/4/morton.pdf

Mueller, Janice, 'The Tiger Awakens: The Tumultuous Transformation of India's Patent System and The Rise of Indian Pharmaceutical Innovation', *University of Pittsburgh Law Review*, 68.49 (2007), 491–641, http://dx.doi.org/10.5195/lawreview.2007.79

Mugambe, Lydia, 'The Exception to Patent Rights under the WTO-TRIPS Agreement: Where is the Right to Health Guaranteed?' (unpublished LLM thesis, University of Western Cape, South Africa, 2002).

Murshed, Md Mahboob, 'Trips Agreement and Patenting of Pharmaceutical Products', *The Daily Star* (3 August 2006), http://archive.thedailystar.net/law/2006/08/03/index.htm (accessed by searching the Internet Archive index).

Musungu, Sislu F., Susan Villanueva, and Roxana Blasetti, *Utilizing TRIPS Flexibilities for Public Health Protection through South-South Regional Framework* (South Centre, 2004).

Nair, Manisha Singh, 'Rationality of a Patent Pool' (12 December 2009), http://www.ipfrontline.com/depts/article.asp?id=22735&deptid=6

Nard, Craig Allen, 'American Patent Law: With European and TRIPS Comparative Perspectives, Materials' (prepared for WIPO-Turin LLM Program Intellectual Property Law, 18–22 September 2006).

Narayan, S.,'Some Approaches to Pricing Controls for Patented Drugs in India', *ISAS Insights*, 41 (1 December 2008), http://mercury.ethz.ch/serviceengine/Files/ISN/94707/ipublicationdocument_singledocument/f8515305-e6a3-4b13-9ba4-27d9ba38b937/en/42.pdf

Nwokike, Jude., and H.L. Choi, 'Assessment of the Regulatory Systems and Capacity of the Directorate General for Drug Administration in Bangladesh' (submitted to the US Agency for International Development by the Systems for Improved Access to Pharmaceuticals and Services Program, Arlington, VA: Management Sciences for Health, 2012).

Oh, Cecilia, and Sisule Musungu, 'The Use of Flexibilities in TRIPS by Developing Countries: Can They Promote Access to Medicines?' (Commission on Intellectual Property Rights, Innovation and Public Health, Study 4C, 12 October 2010), http://www.who.int/intellectualproperty/studies/TRIPSFLEXI.pdf

Oliveira, Bermudez, and Egleubia Oliveira, 'Expanding Access to Essential Medicines in Brazil: Recent Regulation and Public Policies', in *Intellectual Property in the Context of the WTO TRIPS Agreement: Challenges for Public Health*, ed. by Jorge A.Z. Bermudez and Maria Auxiliadora Oliveira (Rio de Janeiro, Center for Pharmaceutical Policies, 2004), pp. 129–52.

Oliveira, Maria Auxiliadora, 'Brazilian Intellectual Property Legislation', in *Intellectual Property in the Context of the WTO TRIPS Agreement: Challenges for Public Health*, ed. by Jorge A.Z. Bermudez and Maria Auxiliadora Oliveira (Rio de Janeiro, Center for Pharmaceutical Policies, 2004) (2005), 153–62.

Ostry, Sylvia, 'Intellectual Property Protection in the WTO: Misuses in the Millennium Round' (Fraser Institute Conference, Santiago, 19 April 1999).

Oxfam, 'Cut the Cost–Patent Injustice: How World Trade Rules Threaten the Health of Poor People' (8 October 2001), http://www.iatp.org/documents/cut-the-cost-patent-injustice-how-world-trade-rules-threaten-the-health-of-poor-people

—, *Make Vital Medicine Available for People—Bangladesh* (25 July 2010), http://policy-practice.oxfam.org.uk/publications/make-vital-medicines-available-for-poor-people-bangladesh-112437

Palmer, V.V., 'From Lerotholi to Lando: Some Examples of Comparative Law Methodology', *American Journal of Comparative Law*, 53 (2005), 1–29, http://dx.doi.org/10.2202/1535-1653.1126

Planning Commission of India, *Report of the Working Group on Drugs and Pharmaceuticals for the Eleventh Five Year Plan, 2007–2012* (2006), http://planningcommission.nic.in/aboutus/committee/wrkgrp11/wg11_pharma.pdf

Plessis, Esmé du Report Q.202 (South Africa), AIPPI, https://www.aippi.org/download/commitees/202/GR202south_africa.pdf

Pokorski da Cunha, Ulrike, 'Study on the Viability of High Quality Drugs Manufacturing in Bangladesh' (commissioned by Deutsche Gesellschaft für Technische Zusammenarbeitm, 2007), https://www.unido.org/fileadmin/user_media/Services/PSD/BEP/en-high-quality-drugs-bangladesh-2007.pdf

Polanvyi, Michael, 'Patent Reform', *Review of Economic Studies*, 11 (1944), 61–76, http://dx.doi.org/10.2307/2295967

Polit, D.F., and B.P. Hungler, *Nursing Research—Principles and Methods*, 6th edn. (Philadelphia: Lippincott Williams & Wilkins, 1999).

Primo-Braga, C.A., and C. Fink, 'The Relationship between Intellectual Property Rights and Foreign Direct Investment', *Duke Journal of Comparative and International Law*, 9 (1998), 163–87.

Quat, Pham Hong, 'How to Comply with the TRIPS and WTO Law—The New Challenges to Vietnam's Patent Legislation from WTO Dispute Settlement Practice' (Nagoya University, Japan, 2007).

Rai, Rajnish Kumar, 'Patentable Subject Matter Requirements: An Evaluation of Proposed Exclusions to India's Patent Law in Light of India's Obligations under the TRIPS Agreement and Options for India', *Chicago-Kent Journal of Intellectual Property*, 8 (2008), 41–84.

Raghavan, Chakravarthi, 'US to Withdraw TRIPS Dispute against Brazil', http://www.twn.my/title/withdraw.htm

Ram, Prabhu, 'India's New "Trips-compliant" Patent Regime between Drug Patents and the Right to Health', *Chicago-Kent Journal of Intellectual Property*, 5 (2006), 195–206.

Reddy, K.C. (ed.), *WTO and Implications for South Asia* (New Delhi: Serials Publications, 2006).

Reichman, J.H., 'From Free Riders to Fair Followers: Global Competition under the TRIPS Agreement', *New York University Journal of International Law and Politics*, 29 (1997), 11–93.

—, 'Universal Minimum Standards of Intellectual Property Protection under the TRIPs Component of the WTO Agreement', in *Intellectual Property and international Trade: TRIPs Agreement*, ed. by Abdulqawi A. Yusuf, Carlos M. Correa (Kluwer Law International, 1998).

Robson, Colin, *Real World Research: A Resource for Social Scientists and Practitioner Researchers* (Oxford: Blackwell, 1993).

Rossman, G., and B. Wilson, 'Numbers and Words Revisited: Being "Shamelessly Eclectic"', *Evaluation Review*, 9.5 (1991), 627–43, http://dx.doi.org/10.1007/bf01098947

Roumet, Rachel, 'Access to Patented Anti-HIV/AIDS Medicine: The South African Experience', *European Intellectual Property Review*, 3 (2010), 137–41.

Ruse-Khan, Henning Grosse and Thomas Jaeger, 'Policing Patents Worldwide? EC Border Measures Against Transiting Generic Drugs Under EC and WTO Intellectual Property Regimes', *International Review of Intellectual Property and Competition Law*, 40.5 (2009), 502–38.

Russell, Sabin, 'New Crusade to Lower AIDS Drug Costs', *The San Francisco Chronicle* (24 May 1999).

Saad, K., and Safwan, 'An Overview of the Pharmaceutical Sector in Bangladesh' (Brac EPL Study, Dhaka, Bangladesh, May 2012).

Sampath, Padmashree Gehl, 'Economic Aspects of Access to Medicines Post-2005: Product Patent Protection and Emerging Firm Strategies in the Indian Industry' (background study of the Commission on Intellectual Property Rights, Innovation and Public Health, WHO, 2005).

—, *Economic Aspects of Access to Medicine after 2005* (UNU-MERIT, 2005, 22), http://www.who.int/intellectualproperty/studies/PadmashreeSampathFinal.pdf

—, 'India's Product Patent Protection Regime: Less or More of "Pills for the Poor"?', *The Journal of World Intellectual Property*, 9.6 (2006), 694–702, http://dx.doi.org/10.1111/j.1422-2213.2006.00308.x

—, 'Intellectual Property in Least Developed Countries: Pharmaceutical, Agro-processing, and Textiles and RMG in Bangladesh' (study prepared for UNCTAD as a background Paper for *The Least Developed Countries Report*, Geneva: UNCTAD, 2007a).

—, 'Innovation and Competitive Capacity in Bangladesh's Pharmaceutical Sector' (Working Paper Series, Paper No. 2007–031, United Nations University, Maastricht Economic and Social Research and Training Centre [UNU-MERIT], September 2007b).

Scherer, F.M., and Jayashree Watal, 'Post-TRIPS Options for Access to Patented Medicines in Developing Countries' (Working Paper Series, Paper No. WG4:1, Commission on Macroeconomics and Health [CMH]), http://library.cphs.chula.ac.th/Ebooks/HealthCareFinancing/WorkingPaper_WG4/WG4_1.pdf

Scherer, F.M., S.E. Herzstein, A.W. Dreyfoos, W.G. Whitney, O.J. Bachman, C.P. Pesek, C.J. Scott, T.G. Kelly, and J.J. Galvin, *Patents and the Corporation: A Report on Industrial Technology under Changing Public Policy* (Cambridge, MA: Harvard University Press, 1959).

Sell, Susan, 'The Global IP Upward Ratchet, Anti-counterfeiting and Piracy Enforcement Efforts: The State of Play' (PIJIP Research Paper Series. No. 15, American University Washington College of Law, 2010), http://digitalcommons.wcl.american.edu/research/15

—, 'TRIPS Was Never Enough: Vertical Forum Shifting, FTAS, ACTA and TPP', *Journal of Intellectual Property Law*, 18 (2011), 447–78, http://infojustice.org/download/tpp/tpp-academic/Sell - TRIPS Was Never Enough - June 2011. pdf

Sen, Pronob, 'Taskforce to Explore Options other than Price Control for Achieving the Objective of Making Available Life-saving Drugs at Reasonable Prices' (Department of Chemicals and Petrochemicals, India, 2005).

Sengupta, Arghya, 'Parallel Imports in the Pharmaceutical Sector: Must India be More Liberal', *Journal of Intellectual Property Rights*, 12 (2007), 400–09.

Shadlen, Kenneth C., 'The Politics of Patents and Drugs in Brazil and Mexico: The Industrial Bases of Health Policies', *Comparative Politics*, 42.1 (2009), 41–58, http://dx.doi.org/10.4337/9780857938619.00012

Shanker, Archana, and Neeti Wilson, 'The Patent Opposition System in India', *IAM Magazine* (8 July 2010), http://www.iam-media.com/Intelligence/IP-Value-in-the-Life-Sciences/2008/Articles/The-patent-opposition-system-in-India

Shanker, Daya, 'Fault Lines in the World Trade Organization: An Analysis of the TRIPS Agreement and Developing Countries' (unpublished doctoral thesis, University of Wollongong, 2005).

Shanker, Daya, 'India, the Pharmaceutical Industry and the Validity of TRIPS', *The Journal of World Intellectual Property*, 5.3 (2002), 351–70, http://dx.doi.org/10.1111/j.1747-1796.2002.tb00162.x

—, 'Brazil, Pharmaceutical Industry and the WTO', *Journal of World Intellectual Property*, 5 (2002), 53–70, http://dx.doi.org/10.1111/j.1747-1796.2002.tb00148.x

Sharma, Animesh, 'Data Exclusivity with Regard to Clinical Data', *The Indian Journal of Law and Technology*, 3 (2007), 82–104.

Shiva, Vandana, *Protect or Plunder* (London: Zed Books, 2001).

Siddiqui, Hafiz G.A., 'WTO and Economic Security: Bangladesh Perspectives' (Paper presented at the BIISS Workshop, 29 February 2000).

Simons, J.J., 'Cooperation and Coercion: The Protection of Intellectual Property in Developing Countries', *Bond Law Review*, 11.1 (1999), 59–97.

Smarzynska, B., 'The Composition of Foreign Direct Investment and Protection of Intellectual Property Rights: Evidence from Transition Economies', *European Economic Review*, 48 (2004), 39–62, http://dx.doi.org/10.1016/s0014-2921(02)00257-x

South Centre and CIEL, 'Extension of the Transition Period for LDCs: Flexibility to Create a Viable Technological Base or Simply (A Little) More Time?', *Intellectual Property Quarterly Update* (2006), 1–15.

Sparrow, M. *The Regulatory Craft: Controlling Risks, Managing Problems and Managing Compliance* (Washington, DC: The Brookings Institution, 2000).

Srinivasan, S., 'How TRIPS Benefits Indian Industry and How It May Not Benefit the Indian People', *Indian Journal of Medical Ethics*, 5.2 (2008), 66–69.

St Martin, Anne, 'The Impact of Trade Related Aspects of Intellectual Property Rights (TRIPS) on Access to Essential Medicines in the Developing World' (a research report submitted to Worcester Polytechnic Institute, 1 May 2006).

Staiger, Robert W., and Guido Tabellini, 'Do GATT Rules Help Governments Make Domestic Commitments?', *Economics and Politics*, 11.2 (1999), 109–44, http://dx.doi.org/10.1111/1468-0343.00055

Staiger, Robert W., 'The World Trade Organization', in *The New Palgrave Dictionary of Economics*, ed. by Steven N. Durlauf and Lawrence E. Blume, 2nd edn. (London: Palgrave, 2006), pp. 777–80, http://dx.doi.org/10.1057/9780230226203.1843

State Intellectual property Office (SIPO) of the Peoples Republic of China (PRC), 'Patent Law of the Peoples Republic of China', http://english.sipo.gov.cn/laws/lawsregulations/201101/t20110119_566244.html

Stiglitz, Joseph E. 'Scrooge and Intellectual Property Rights', *British Medical Journal* 333 (2006), 1279–80, http://dx.doi.org/10.1136/bmj.39048.428380.80

—, *The Price of Inequality: How Today's Divided Society Endangers our Future* (New York: Norton, 2012).

Subramanian, A., 'Putting Some Number on the TRIPS Pharmaceutical Debate', *International Journal of Technology Management*, 10 (1995), 252–68.

Sussex, Jon, Koonal K. Shah, and Jim Butler, 'The Publicly Funded Vaccines Market in Australia' (Consulting Report No. 10/02, Office of Health Economics [OHE], 25 October 2010).

Suthersanen, Uma, 'Utility Models and Innovation in Developing Countries' (5–7 February 2006), http://unctad.org/en/Docs/iteipc20066_en.pdf

Swarns, Rachel L. 'Drug Makers Drop South Africa Suit over AIDS Medicine', *The New York Times* (20 April 2001).

Taylor, C.T., and Z.A. Silberston, *The Economic Impact of the Patent System* (Cambridge: Cambridge University Press, 1973).

Teljeur, Ethel, *Intellectual Property Rights in South Africa: An Economic Review of Policy and Impact* (Braamfontein: The Edge Institute, South Africa, 2003).

Third World Network Brief, 'WHO: WHA strengthens WHO's mandate on IP and Health' (27 May 2008), http://www.twn.my/title2/health.info/2008/twnhealthinfo20080602.htm

Tomar, David K., 'A Look into the WTO Pharmaceutical Patent Dispute between the United States and India', *Wisconsin International Law Journal*, 17 (1999), 579–603.

Tomlinson, Catherine and Lotti Rutter, '*The Economic and Social Case for Patent Law Reform in South Africa*' (2014), http://www.tac.org.za/sites/default/files/ The Economic and Social Case for Patent Law Reform in South Africa.pdf

Trebilcock, Michael J., and Robert Howse, *The Regulation of International Trade*, 2nd edn (Abingdon and New York: Routledge, 1999).

Trouiller, Patrice, P. Olliaro, E. Torreele, J. Orbinski, R. Laing, and N. Ford, 'Drug Development for Neglected Diseases: A Deficient Market and a Public-health Policy Failure', *Lancet*, 359 (2002), 2188–94, http://dx.doi. org/10.1016/s0140-6736(02)09096-7

Uddin, Khawaza Main, 'Govt Inching Closer Towards Signing TIFA with US', *Business Info Bangladesh* (7 November 2009), https://web.archive.org/ web/20101120054050/http://bizbangladesh.com/business-news-2758.php (accessed by searching the Internet Archive index).

Uddin, S., M. Anowar, 'TRIPS Waiver but Why the Pharmaceutical Medicines Hard to Get in Bangladesh' (project report submitted to Roskilde University, 2008), http://rudar.ruc.dk/bitstream/1800/4060/3/Project_WTO.pdf

United Nations Conference on Trade and Development (UNCTAD)/World Trade Organization (WTO), *Bangladesh: Supply and Demand Survey on Pharmaceuticals and Natural Products, International Trade Centre* (September 2005).

UN, *Report of the Open Working Group of the General Assembly on Sustainable Development Goals*, Resolution 68/970 (2014).

United States Trade Representative (USTR), *Special 301 Report, 2009* (10 July 2010), https://ustr.gov/about-us/policy-offices/press-office/reports-and-publications/2009/2009-special-301-report

UNCTAD-ICTSD, *Resource Book on TRIPS and Development* (Cambridge: Cambridge University Press, 2005), http://dx.doi.org/10.1017/ cbo9780511511363

UNCTAD-ICTSD, WTO Public Symposium, 'Disclosure Requirements: Incorporating the CBD Principles in the TRIPS Agreement on the Road to Hong Kong', p. 1 (21 April 2005), http://ictsd.org/downloads/2008/12/ meeting-report.pdf

Yamin, Farhana, 'Globalisation and the International Governance of Modern Biotechnology: IPRs, Biotechnology and FoodSecurity', Foundation for International Environmental Law and Development, http://www.sristi.org/ mdpipr2004/other_readings/OR 42.pdf

VanDuzer, Tony, 'TRIPS and Pharmaceutical Industry in Bangladesh: Towards a National Strategy' (Paper No. 24, CPD, April 2003), http://www.bdresearch. org/home/attachments/article/nArt/TRIPS_and_the_Pharmaceutical_ Industry_in_Bangladesh.pdf

Vaver, David, 'Intellectual Property Today: Of Myths and Paradoxes', *Canadian Bar Review*, 69 (1990), 98–126.

Volansky, M., 'Achieving Global Health: A Review of the World Health Organization's Response', *Tulsa Journal of Comparative International Law*, 10 (2002), 223–59.

Watal, J., 'Introducing Product Patents in the Indian Pharmaceutical Sector: Implications for Prices and Welfare', *World Competition*, 20 (1999), 5–21.

—, 'Pharmaceutical Patents, Prices and Welfare Losses: Policy Options for India under the WTO TRIPS Agreement', *The World Economy*, 23 (2000), 733–52.

Wei, Marlynn, 'Should Prizes Replace Patents? A Critique of the Medical Innovation Prize Act of 2005', *Boston University Journal of Science and Technology Law*, 13.1 (2007), 3–21.

Werner, Wendy J., 'Micro-insurance in Bangladesh: Risk Protection for the Poor?', *Journal of Health, Population and Nutrition*, 27 (2009), 563–73.

Wendt, Rasmus Alex, 'TRIPs in India' (unpublished doctoral thesis, Roskilde University, 2007).

World Bank, 'World Development Report: Building Institutions for Markets' 147 (2002), https://openknowledge.worldbank.org/handle/10986/5984

—, 'Public and Private Sector Approaches to Improving Pharmaceutical Quality in Bangladesh', 15 (March 2008), http://www-wds.worldbank.org/external/default/WDSContentServer/WDSP/IB/2008/09/01/000334955_20080901071115/Rendered/PDF/451900NWP0Box31uality0no2301PUBLIC1.pdf

World Health Organization (WHO), *Macroeconomics and Health: Investing in Health for Economic Development* (Commission on Macroeconomics and Health, 2001), http://www.who.int/pmnch/knowledge/topics/2001_who_cmh/en/

—, *Globalization and Access to Drugs: Implications of the WTO/TRIPS Agreement*, Health Economic and Drugs Series, No. 007 (1998), http://apps.who.int/medicinedocs/en/d/Jwhozip35e/3.5.html

—, 'Counterfeit Drugs. Guidelines for the Development of Measures to Combat Counterfeit Drugs' (1999), http://apps.who.int/medicinedocs/en/d/Jh1456e/

—, *Public–Private Roles in the Pharmaceutical Sector: Implications of Equitable Access and Rational Drug Use* (2002), http://apps.who.int/medicinedocs/en/d/Jwhozip27e/

—, *Drugs and Money Prices, Affordability and Cost Containment*, ed. by M.N.G. Dukes, C.P. de Joncheere et al. (2003), http://www.euro.who.int/__data/assets/pdf_file/0011/96446/e79122.pdf

—, *Resolution of the World Health Assembly: Intellectual Property Rights, Innovation and Public Health*, WHA56.27 (Geneva: WHO, 2003), http://www.who.int/intellectualproperty/documents/en/

—, 'Intellectual Property Protection: Impact on Public Health', *WHO Drug Information*, 19 (2005), 236, 240, http://apps.who.int/medicinedocs/pdf/s7918e/s7918e.pdf

—, 'Public Health, Innovation, and Intellectual Property Rights: Report of the Commission on Intellectual Property Rights, Innovation and Public Health', 133 (2006) (the "CIPIH Report"), http://www.who.int/intellectualproperty/documents/thereport/ENPublicHealthReport.pdf

—, *Public Health, Innovation, Essential Health Research and Intellectual Property Rights: Towards a Global Strategy and Plan of Action A59/55* (Geneva: WHO, 2006), http://apps.who.int/gb/archive/pdf_files/WHA59/A59_55-en.pdf

—, '[Global Framework on] Essential Health Research and Development', in *Executive Board, 117th Session, Resolutions, Decisions, and Annexes* 20 (27 January 2006), http://apps.who.int/gb/ebwha/pdf_files/EB117-REC1/B117_REC1-en.pdf

—, 'Intellectual Property Rights and Access to Medicines: A South-East Asia Perspective on Global Issues' (2008), http://apps.searo.who.int/pds_docs/B3468.pdf

—, 'Proposal by Bolivia, Suriname and Bangladesh: Prizes as a Reward Mechanism for New Cancer Treatments and Vaccines in Developing Countries' 1 (15 April 2009), http://www.who.int/phi/Bangladesh_Bolivia_Suriname_CancerPrize.pdf

—, 'Promoting Access to Medical Technologies and Innovation: Intersections between Public Health, Intellectual Property and Trade', 53 (2012), http://www.wto.org/english/res_e/booksp_e/pamtiwhowipowtoweb13_e.pdf

WHO, KEI, Intergovernmental Working Group Submission on Collective Management of Intellectual Property, 'The Use of Patent Pools to Expand Access to Needed Medical Technologies', 3 (30 September 2007), http://www.who.int/phi/public_hearings/second/contributions_section2/Section2_ManonRess-PatentPool.pdf

WHO, WHA Executive Board Res., 'Revised Drug Strategy' (EB 101/R.24), 2 (27 January 1998), http://apps.who.int/gb/archive/pdf_files/EB101/pdfangl/angr24.pdf

WHO and WTO, Joint study by the WHO and the WTO Secretariats on 'WTO Agreements and Public Health' (2002), p. 106, https://www.wto.org/english/res_e/booksp_e/who_wto_e.pdf

World Intellectual Property Organization (WIPO), 'Paris Convention for Protection of Industrial Property of 20 March 1883, as revised in Brussels on 14 December 1900, in Washington on 2 June 1911, at The Hague on 6 November 1925, in London on 2 June 1934, in Lisbon on 31 October 1958 and in Stockholm on 14 July 1967', http://www.wipo.int/treaties/en/text.jsp?file_id=288514

—, *Standing Committee on the Law of Patents, Exclusions from Patentable Subject Matter and Exceptions and Limitations to the Rights* (2009).

—, Lei No. 9.279 art. 24, de 14 de maio de 1996, Diario Oficial Da Uniao [DOU] de 15.05.1996. (Braz.), translated in Brazil: *IndustrialProperty Law*, 14/05/1996, No. 9.279, http://www.wipo.int/wipolex/en/details.jsp?id=515

—, *Study on Patent Related Flexibilities in the Multilateral Legal Framework and Their Legislative Implementation at the National and Regional Levels* (WIPO Committee on Development and Intellectual Property, Fifth Session, WIPO Secretariat, Geneva, 26–30 April, 2010).

WIPO, WHO and World Trade Organisation (WTO), *Trilateral Study, Promoting Access to Medical Technologies and Innovation—Intersections between Public Health, Intellectual Property and Trade* (2013).

WTO, 'Agreement on Trade-related Aspects of Intellectual Property Rights, Apr. 15, 1994, Marrakesh Agreement Establishing the World Trade Organization, Annex 1C, 1869 U.N.T.S. 299, 33 I.L.M. 1197, art. 65 (1994), http://www.wto.org/english/docs_e/legal_e/27-trips.pdf

—, document WT/TPR/M/75 (6 December 2000).

—, 'Responding to Least Developed Countries' Special Needs in Intellectual Property' (updated in 2012), http://www.wto.org/english/tratop_e/trips_e/ldc_e.htm

—, 'Panel Report, Canada—Term of Patent Protection' (WT/DS170/R, 5 May 2000).

—, 'Panel Report, Canada—Patent, Complaint by US, at 6.56; Appellate Report, Canada—Term of Patent Protection' (WT/DS170/AB/R, 11 August 2000).

—, 'Implementation of paragraph 6 of the Doha Declaration on the TRIPS agreement and public health. Decision of 30 August 2003' (WT/L/540, 2 September 2003).

—, 'WTO and the Least Developed Countries' http://www.wto.org/english/thewto_e/whatis_e/tif_e/org7_e.htm

—, 'Decision of the Council for TRIPS on the Extension of the Transition Period under Article 66.1 of the TRIPS Agreement for Least-developed Country Members for Certain Obligations with Respect to Pharmaceutical Products' (27 June 2002, Document IP/C/25).

—, 'Brazil: Measures Affecting Patent Protection' (Dispute Settlement: Dispute DS199, WTO), http://www.wto.org/english/tratop_e/dispu_e/cases_e/ds199_e.htm

—, 'Decision of The Council for TRIPS of 11 June 2013' (Document IP/C/64).

—, 'Communication from Bangladesh on behalf of the LDC Group' (23 February 2015, document IP/C/W/605).

—, 'Decision of the Council for TRIPS' (6 November 2015, document IP/C/73).

—, 'Notification of Rwanda' (July 2007, document IP/N/9/RWA/1).

—, 'Notification of Canada' (October 2007, document IP/N/10/CAN/1).

—, 'Communication from Haiti on Behalf of the LDC Group: Request for an Extension of the Transitional Period under Article 66.1 of the TRIPS Agreement' (5 November 2012, IP/C/W/583).

—, 'Developing Countries' Transition Periods', *Fact Sheet: TRIPS and Pharmaceutical Patents*, http://www.wto.org/english/tratop_e/trips_e/factsheet_pharm04_e.htm

—, Intellectual Property: Least Developed Countries, https://www.wto.org/english/tratop_e/trips_e/ldc_e.htm

WTO Council for TRIPS, 'Relationship Between the TRIPS Agreement and the CBD, and the Protection of Traditional Knowledge' (18 June 2003, IP/C/W/400/Rev.1), http://docsonline.wto.org/imrd/directdoc.asp?DDFDocuments/t/IP/C/W400R1.doc

—, 'Priority Needs for Technical and Financial Co-operation: Communication from Bangladesh' (23 March 2010, IP/C/W/546).

—, 'Elements of the Obligation to Disclose the Source and Country of Origin of Biological Resource and/or Traditional Knowledge Used in an Invention' 2 (21 September 2004 (IP/C/W/429), http://docsonline.wto.org/imrd/directdoc.asp?DDFDocuments/t/IP/C/W429.doc

Yunus, Muhammad, *Creating a World without Poverty: Social Business and the Future of Capitalism* (Philadelphia: Public Affairs, 2008).

—, and Qamrul Alam, 'WTO TRIPS Agreement—Current State of Pharmaceutical Industry and Policy Options for Bangladesh', *International Business Research*, 1.1 (2008), http://dx.doi.org/10.5539/ibr.v1n1p135

—, *Building Social Business: The New Kind of Capitalism That Serves Humanity's Most Pressing Needs* (Philadelphia, PA: Public Affairs, 2010).

Zainal, Zaidah, *Case Study As a Research Method*, http://psyking.net/htmlobj-3837/case_study_as_a_research_method.pdf

Zhang, Haiyang, 'Rethinking the Patent System from the Perspective of Economies', in *Emerging Markets and the World Patent Order*, ed. by Federick M. Abbott, Carlos M. Correa and Peter Drahos (Cheltenham: Edward Elgar, 2013), pp. 61–77, http://dx.doi.org/10.4337/9781783471256.00011

Appendices

Appendix 1: Status of Patents in Bangladesh (1972–2012)

Year	Patent Applied			Patent Granted		
	Local	Foreign	Total	Local	Foreign	Total
1972	51	158	209	9	3	12
1973	76	277	353	6	30	36
1974	74	171	245	10	265	275
1975	35	110	145	25	312	337
1976	35	119	154	10	119	129
1977	33	86	119	11	93	104
1978	36	113	149	13	1o8	121
1979	31	100	131	20	83	103
1980	34	102	136	19	92	111
1981	39	133	172	17	85	102
1982	40	104	144	13	105	118
1983	40	123	163	11	115	126
1984	62	108	170	17	94	111
1985	40	96	136	13	105	118
1986	16	77	93	26	81	107
1987	23	98	121	10	79	89

1988	24	109	133	8	67	75
1989	32	76	108	3	88	91
1990	32	76	108	8	86	94
1991	36	77	113	10	68	78
1992	72	89	161	6	55	61
1993	36	71	107	10	66	76
1994	39	99	138	29	69	98
1995	70	156	226	6	74	80
1996	22	131	153	18	52	70
1997	46	119	165	15	61	76
1998	32	184	216	14	126	140
1999	49	200	249	26	122	148
2000	70	248	318	4	138	142
2001	59	236	295	21	185	206
2002	43	246	289	24	233	257
2003	58	260	318	14	208	222
2004	48	268	316	28	202	230
2005	50	294	344	21	161	182
2006	22	288	310	16	146	162
2007	29	270	299	27	269	296
2008	60	278	338	01	36	37
2009	55	275	330	28	103	131
2010	55	287	342	20	71	91
2011	32	274	306	06	79	85
2012	65	289	354	14	139	153

Source: Department of Patents, Designs and Trademarks, Dhaka, Bangladesh, 2013.

Appendix 2: Relevant Provisions of the TRIPS Agreement

Article 1
Nature and Scope of Obligations

  1) Members shall give effect to the provisions of this Agreement. Members may, but shall not be obliged to, implement in their law more extensive protection than is required by this Agreement, provided that such protection does not contravene the provisions of this Agreement. Members shall be free to determine the appropriate method of implementing the provisions of this Agreement within their own legal system and practice.

Article 6
Exhaustion

For the purposes of dispute settlement under this Agreement, subject to the provisions of Articles 3 and 4 nothing in this Agreement shall be used to address the issue of the exhaustion of intellectual property rights.

Article 7
Objectives

The protection and enforcement of intellectual property rights should contribute to the promotion of technological innovation and to the transfer and dissemination of technology, to the mutual advantage of producers and users of technological knowledge and in a manner conducive to social and economic welfare, and to a balance of rights and obligations.

Article 8
Principles

  1) Members may, in formulating or amending their laws and regulations, adopt measures necessary to protect public health and nutrition, and to promote the public interest in sectors of vital importance to their socioeconomicand technological development, provided that such measures are consistent with the provisions of this Agreement.

  2) Appropriate measures, provided that they are consistent with the provisions of this Agreement, may be needed to prevent the abuse

of intellectual property rights by right holders or the resort to practices which unreasonably restrain trade or adversely affect the international transfer of technology.

SECTION 5: PATENTS

Article 27
Patentable Subject Matter

1) Subject to the provisions of paragraphs 2 and 3, patents shall be available for any inventions, whether products or processes, in all fields of technology, provided that they are new, involve an inventive step and are capable of industrial application.5 Subject to paragraph 4 of Article 65, paragraph 8 of

Article 70 and paragraph 3 of this Article, patents shall be available and patent rights enjoyable without discrimination as to the place of invention, the field of technology and whether products are imported or locally produced.

2) Members may exclude from patentability inventions, the prevention within their territory of the commercial exploitation of which is necessary to protect *ordre public* or morality, including to protect human, animal or plant life or health or to avoid serious prejudice to the environment, provided that such exclusion is not made merely because the exploitation is prohibited by their law.

3) Members may also exclude from patentability:

   a) diagnostic, therapeutic and surgical methods for the treatment of humans or animals;

   b) plants and animals other than micro-organisms, and essentially biological processes for the production of plants or animals other than non-biological and microbiological processes. However, members shall provide for the protection of plant varieties either by patents or by an effective *sui generis* system or by any combination thereof. The provisions of this subparagraph shall be reviewed four years after the date of entry into force of the WTO Agreement.

Article 29
Conditions on Patent Applicants

1) Members shall require that an applicant for a patent shall disclose the invention in a manner sufficiently clear and complete for the invention to be carried out by a person skilled in the art and may

require the applicant to indicate the best mode for carrying out the invention known to the inventor at the filing date or, where priority is claimed, at the priority date of the application.

2)   Members may require an applicant for a patent to provide information concerning the applicant's corresponding foreign applications and grants.

Article 30
Exceptions to Rights Conferred

Members may provide limited exceptions to the exclusive rights conferred by a patent, provided that such exceptions do not unreasonably conflict with a normal exploitation of the patent and do not unreasonably prejudice the legitimate interests of the patent owner, taking account of the legitimate interests of third parties.

Article 31
Other Use Without Authorization of the Right Holder

Where the law of a member allows for other use7 of the subject matter of a patent without the authorization of the right holder, including use by the government or third parties authorized by the government, the following provisions shall be respected:

a)   authorization of such use shall be considered on its individual merits;

b)   such use may only be permitted if, prior to such use, the proposed user has made efforts to obtain authorization from the right holder on reasonable commercial terms and conditions and that such efforts have not been successful within a reasonable period of time. This requirement may be waived by a member in the case of national emergency or other circumstances of extreme urgency or in cases of public non-commercial use. In situations of national emergency or other circumstances of extreme urgency, the right holder shall, nevertheless, be notified as soon as reasonably practicable.

In the case of public non-commercial use, where the government or contractor, without making a patent search, knows or has demonstrable grounds to know that a valid patent is or will be used by or for the government, the right holder shall be informed promptly;

c) the scope and duration of such use shall be limited to the purpose for which it was authorized, and in the case of semi-conductor technology shall only be for public non-commercial use or to remedy a practice determined after judicial or administrative process to be anti-competitive;

d) such use shall be non-exclusive;

e) such use shall be non-assignable, except with that part of the enterprise or goodwill which enjoys such use;

f) any such use shall be authorized predominantly for the supply of the domestic market of the member authorizing such use;

g) authorization for such use shall be liable, subject to adequate protection of the legitimate interests of the persons so authorized, to be terminated if and when the circumstances which led to it cease to exist and are unlikely to recur. The competent authority shall have the authority to review, upon motivated request, the continued existence of these circumstances;

h) the right holder shall be paid adequate remuneration in the circumstances of each case, taking into account the economic value of the authorization;

i) the legal validity of any decision relating to the authorization of such use shall be subject to judicial review or other independent review by a distinct higher authority in that member;

j) any decision relating to the remuneration provided in respect of such use shall be subject to judicial review or other independent review by a distinct higher authority in that member;

Article 33
Term of Protection

The term of protection available shall not end before the expiration of a period of twenty years counted from the filing date.

Article 34
Process Patents: Burden of Proof

1) For the purposes of civil proceedings in respect of the infringement of the rights of the owner referred to in paragraph 1(b) of Article 28, if the subject matter of a patent is a process for obtaining a product, the judicial authorities shall have the authority to order the defendant to prove that the process to obtain an identical product is different from the patented process. Therefore, members shall provide, in at

least one of the following circumstances, that any identical product when produced without the consent of the patent owner shall, in the absence of proof to the contrary, be deemed to have been obtained by the patented process:

Article 66
LDC Members

   1)   In view of the special needs and requirements of LDC members, their economic, financial and administrative constraints, and their need for flexibility to create a viable technological base, such Members shall not be required to apply the provisions of this Agreement, other than Articles 3, 4 and 5, for a period of 10 years from the date of application as defined under paragraph 1 of Article 65. The Council for TRIPS shall, upon duly motivated request by an LDC member, accord extensions of this period.

Developed country members shall provide incentives to enterprises and institutions in their territories for the purpose of promoting and encouraging technology transfer to LDC members in order to enable them to create a sound and viable technological base.

Article 67
Technical Cooperation

In order to facilitate the implementation of this Agreement, developed country Members shall provide, on request and on mutually agreed terms and conditions, technical and financial cooperation in favour of developing and least-developed country Members. Such cooperation shall include assistance in the preparation of laws and regulations on the protection and enforcement of intellectual property rights as well as on the prevention of their abuse, and shall include support regarding the establishment or reinforcement of domestic offices and agencies relevant to these matters, including the training of personnel.

Index

This book need not end here...

At Open Book Publishers, we are changing the nature of the traditional academic book. The title you have just read will not be left on a library shelf, but will be accessed online by hundreds of readers each month across the globe. OBP publishes only the best academic work: each title passes through a rigorous peer-review process. We make all our books free to read online so that students, researchers and members of the public who can't afford a printed edition will have access to the same ideas.

This book and additional content is available at:
http://www.openbookpublishers.com/9781783742288

Customise

Personalise your copy of this book or design new books using OBP and third-party material. Take chapters or whole books from our published list and make a special edition, a new anthology or an illuminating coursepack. Each customised edition will be produced as a paperback and a downloadable PDF. Find out more at:

http://www.openbookpublishers.com/section/59/1

Donate

If you enjoyed this book, and feel that research like this should be available to all readers, regardless of their income, please think about donating to us. We do not operate for profit and all donations, as with all other revenue we generate, will be used to finance new Open Access publications.

http://www.openbookpublishers.com/section/13/1

You may also be interested in:

The Universal Declaration of Human Rights in the 21st Century
Edited by Gordon Brown

https://www.openbookpublishers.com/product/467

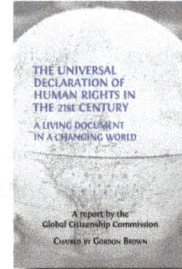

Animals and Medicine: The Contribution of Animal Experiments to the Control of Disease
By Jack Botting

https://www.openbookpublishers.com/product/327

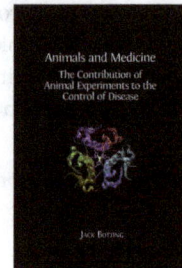

Peace and Democratic Society
Edited by Amartya Sen

https://www.openbookpublishers.com/product/78

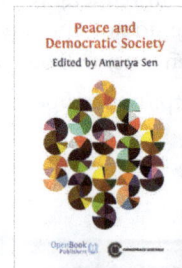